COMPUTATIONAL SEMANTIC FUNCTIONAL PROGRAMMING

Computational semantics is the art and science of computing meaning in natural language. The meaning of a sentence is derived from the meanings of the individual words in it, and this process can be made so precise that it can be implemented on a computer. Designed for students of linguistics, computer science, logic and philosophy, this comprehensive text shows how to compute meaning using the functional programming language Haskell. It deals with both denotational meaning (where meaning comes from knowing the conditions of truth in situations), and operational meaning (where meaning is an instruction for performing cognitive action). Including a discussion of recent developments in logic, it will be invaluable to linguistics students wanting to apply logic to their studies, logic students wishing to learn how their subject can be applied to linguistics, and functional programmers interested in natural language processing as a new application area.

JAN VAN EIJCK is a Senior Researcher at CWI, the Centre for Mathematics and Computer Science in Amsterdam, and Professor of Computational Linguistics at Uil-OTS, the Research Institute for Language and Speech, Utrecht University.

CHRISTINA UNGER is based in the Semantic Computing Group in the Cognitive Interaction Technology Center of Excellence at the University of Bielefeld.

COMPUTATIONAL SEMANTICS WITH FUNCTIONAL PROGRAMMING

JAN VAN EIJCK AND CHRISTINA UNGER

CAMBRIDGE
UNIVERSITY PRESS

CAMBRIDGE UNIVERSITY PRESS
Cambridge, New York, Melbourne, Madrid, Cape Town, Singapore,
São Paulo, Delhi, Dubai, Tokyo

Cambridge University Press
The Edinburgh Building, Cambridge CB2 8RU, UK

Published in the United States of America by Cambridge University Press, New York

www.cambridge.org
Information on this title: www.cambridge.org/9780521757607

First published 2010

Printed in the United Kingdom at the University Press, Cambridge

A catalogue record for this publication is available from the British Library

ISBN 978-0-521-76030-0 Hardback
ISBN 978-0-521-75760-7 Paperback

Contents

Foreword

The view of computational semantics that informs and drives this book is one that sees the computation of linguistic meaning as that of computing logically transparent representations of meaning from "raw linguistic data", linguistic input as it reaches a recipient when he hears something or reads it, and to which he has to attach a sense. The book abstracts away from the differences between hearing and reading in that it assumes that the "raw data" have already been preprocessed as strings of words. Such computations of meaning are generally assumed to involve the computation of structure at several levels, minimally at a level of syntactic form and then, via the syntactic structure obtained at that level, of the semantic representation. This implies that in order to do computational semantics properly you need proficiency in at least three things: (i) proficiency in computation (you need to be proficient in the use of at least one suitable programming language), (ii) proficiency in syntax, and (iii) proficiency in semantics, in the more narrow sense in which semantics is understood by many linguists, but also in a broader sense.

The message this book drives home is that computing semantic representations from "raw data" isn't all there is to computational semantics. Computing semantic representations wouldn't be of much use to us if, once we have constructed them, there wouldn't be anything we could do with them. But of course there is. One thing we do with the semantic representations we construct from linguistic input is to employ them as premises, usually in conjunction with representations we already have, and that often come from other sources (e.g. from what we have seen with our own eyes). In this way the new representation may yield additional information, information that follows neither from the information we already had, nor from the new representation when taken by itself. Or the new representation may be instrumental in practical reasoning, help us to develop a better idea of how we should proceed in order to get what we want. It is because we use semantic representations in these inferential ways that they must be "logically transparent":

they must be in a form on which the inference mechanisms of formal logic must have a purchase.

There is also something else that we can do with the semantic representations we get from what we hear or read: we evaluate them against models of the world. These can be models that we have put together on the basis of, say, what we learn by seeing, hearing, or touching. "Model checking", i.e., checking whether what a semantic representation says about a given model or data structure obtained in some such way is true or false, is no less important than drawing inferences from it. Model checking is implicit in what speakers do when they choose sentences to describe the models or data structures about which they want to say something, and it is what the recipient of an utterance does when he has independent access to the model or data structure that he assumes the speaker is talking about, for instance in situations where the speaker is making a comment on something which they are both looking at.

The importance of model checking and of the inferential uses we make of language may be plain enough in any case. But how important they really are comes even more dramatically into focus in connection with developing language skills for robots, which can tell us about things that they can see but we cannot, or that must be able to communicate with us when we are jointly working on a common task. Such uses of semantic representations are what makes them worth having in the first place. A computational semantics that tells us how representations get built, but has nothing to say about what is done with them would hardly be worth having.

This book adds accounting for the uses of semantic representations to the Computational Semantics task list, thus making the agenda more ambitious than it would have been in any case by a good stretch. As far as I know no one has so far made an attempt to address this amplified agenda within the scope of a single text. This is one respect in which the present book breaks new ground, both conceptually, as a presentation of what computational semantics, defined by this agenda, is actually like, and pedagogically, by introducing the readers to the various different items on this agenda and showing them how each of those items can be tackled and what is needed for that.

The book's third novelty is that it starts without any presuppositions. Nothing is assumed beyond common sense: no programming skills, no knowledge of syntax, no knowledge of semantics, no knowledge of natural language processing of any sort. The book begins by introducing the basics of Haskell, the programming language that is used throughout. Haskell is a member of the family of functional programming languages and suitable for the theoretical purposes of this book because of its exceptional transparency. The use of Haskell in an introduction to computational semantics is a departure from the widespread use of Prolog in introductions to symbolic natural language processing. The authors motivate this choice by pointing out that much of symbolic computational linguistics consists, like so many other types of computational problems, in defining the right data structures and the right functions that map one data structure (the one that presents the problem) into another (the one that presents its solution).

Indeed, the first applications that are shown in the book are non-linguistic, and chosen solely for the purpose of giving the reader a good grasp of how Haskell works and what can be done with it. From these first applications there is a gradual progress, via applications that involve elementary forms of language processing (such as word counts in texts), to applications that belong to computational semantics proper. One important benefit of this way of easing into the subject is that it makes the reader aware of how much language processing has in common with problem solving and data processing tasks that do not involve language. On the face of it such an awareness might sit awkwardly with the cherished view of many linguists that our ability to acquire and use language is unique among the cognitive capacities we have; but I do not think that there is likely to be any real conflict here. As demonstrated amply by the diversities of the actual algorithms and programs presented in this book, what similarities between linguistic and non-linguistic processing there are still leaves plenty of room for the cognitive distinctness and uniqueness of those algorithms that characterise the computational aspects of the human language capacity.

Although the book starts from scratch, and presupposes nothing beyond common sense, it nevertheless manages to penetrate into some of the more advanced areas of computational semantics: the final chapters present continuation semantics, discourse representation theory, and a system of dynamic epistemic logic that serves as a first step in the direction of a full-fledged computational theory of verbal communication. And yet, this wide span notwithstanding, the book complies with current demands on texts in computational linguistics in that it presents for every bit of theory that it introduces a Haskell implementation, which the reader can run herself and play with, if she downloads the relevant, freely available supporting software. The same goes for the numerous implementation-related exercises. This means that the diligent student of this book will, by the time she gets to the end of it, have not only learned a good deal about syntax and semantics, but have also acquired much of that which distinguishes the computational from the theoretical linguist.

All this goes to make this book into the important and innovative contribution to the field of computational semantics that I think it is. Most important of all is the influence that I believe and hope it will have on coming generations of computational linguists, by instilling in them the elements of sophisticated programming expertise at the same time as introducing them to many aspects of theoretical linguistics, and conveying some of that passion for the structural aspects of language that makes theoretical linguistics a must and (sometimes) a source of satisfaction for the true linguist. It has been pointed out again and again that the practical potential of computational linguistics, and of computational semantics as an essential part of it, is immense. Still, it is fair to say that the practical achievements of computational semantics have so far been quite limited. The reasons for that, I think, are two-fold. Automated symbolic processing of natural language is notoriously brittle: even where it is clear what the system should compute, it often lacks the necessary resources, in particular wide coverage lexicons with substantive semantic information and world knowledge in accessible form. But in many cases the problem goes deeper. We still haven't even properly understood yet what it is that should be computed. These are hard problems, which will be solved – to the extent that they can be solved at all – only by people who have the combination of skills that are presented and taught here as parts that naturally fit into a coherent whole.

HANS KAMP

Professor of Formal Logic
and Philosophy of Language,
University of Stuttgart

Preface

This book on applications of logic in the semantic analysis of language pays the reader the compliment of not assuming anything about what he or she knows (in particular, no specific logical knowledge or experience with programming is presupposed), while making very flattering assumptions about his or her intelligence and interest in the subject matter.

The method used throughout in the book is the pursuit of logical questions and implementation issues occasioned by concrete examples of formally defined language fragments. At first, no distinction is made between formal and natural language; in the first chapter it is explained why. At the end of the text the reader should have acquired enough knowledge and skills for the development of (at least the semantic part of) fairly serious Natural Language Processing applications. The reader who makes it to the end of the book will also find that he or she has acquired considerable programming skills, and will have learned how to put a wide variety of logical systems to use for natural language analysis.

Throughout the text, abstract concepts are linked to concrete representations in the functional programming language Haskell. Haskell is a language that is well suited for our purposes because it comes with a variety of very easy to use interpreters: Hugs, GHCi, and Helium. Haskell interpreters, compilers, and documentation are freely available from the Internet.† Everything one has to know about programming in Haskell to understand the programs in the book is explained as we go along, but we do not cover every aspect of the language. Further on we will mention various good introductions to Haskell. The only thing we do assume is that the reader is able to retrieve the appropriate software from the Internet, and that he or she is acquainted with the use of a text editor for the creation and modification of programming code.

The book is intended for linguists who want to know more about logic, including

---

† See http://www.haskell.org

recent developments in dynamic logic and epistemic logic, and its applicability to their subject matter, for logicians with a curiosity about applications of their subject to linguistics, and for functional programmers who are interested in a new application domain for their programming skills.

This text has quite a long prehistory. The prefinal version of this book grew out of a series of lectures the first author gave at UiL OTS in the fall of 2000, for a mixed audience of linguists and formal semanticists. This was extended with material from a tutorial at the LOLA7 Pecs Summer School of 2002, with the results of an implementation project for Theta Theory at UiL OTS, Utrecht, in the fall of 2002 (follow-up to a course on Theta Theory that the first author co-taught with Tanya Reinhart), and with examples from a natural language technology course developed in collaboration with Michael Moortgat.

This manuscript would have remained only an Internet resource if Helen Barton, CUP editor in charge of linguistics and humanities, had not made a Spring visit to UiL OTS in 2008, in enthousiastic pursuit of suitable textbook manuscripts. And it would not have turned into the book you are now reading if it weren't for an intellectual support group, the *reading group*, which met up with the authors once every two weeks, September through December 2008, for feedback. We really owe its members a lot. The rock solid core of the group consisted of Arno Bastenhof, Gianluca Giorgolo, Jeroen Goudsmit and Andres Löh, who were always there. They kept us on track with their support and with their keen eye for failings of the draft chapters under discussion. The members of the outer shell of the group, who also made important contributions, were Marta Castella, Anna Chernilovskaya, Stefan Holdermans, Matthijs Melissen, and Hanna de Vries. An early version of the manuscript also had two anonymous Cambridge University Press readers, who encouraged us to carry on with the project and gave valuable feedback.

There is a web page devoted to this book, at address

http://www.computational-semantics.eu,

where the full code given in the various chapters can be found. Suggestions and comments on the text can be sent to the first author, at email address jve@cwi.nl, and will be very much appreciated.

Acknowledgements Many thanks to the reading group; the names of the members were mentioned above. Helen Barton, commissioning editor at CUP, was supportive and encouraging throughout, and CUP production editor Rosina Di Marzo gave us generous help in the final stage of production. Thanks also to Herman Hendriks for acting as an oracle on references, to Michael Moortgat for pleasant cooperation with the first author in teaching various natural language technology courses, to Rick Nouwen for joint work with the first author on implementations of pronominal reference algorithms, to Albert Visser for illuminating discussions on dynamic semantics, life and everything, to Krzysztof Apt and Willemijn Vermaat for advice on LaTeX matters, to the course participants of the first author's UiL OTS courses, to the participants in the 2002 Pecs Summer School Tutorial, and to Nicole Gregoire and Rianne Schippers, members of the 2002 Theta Theory implementation group for pleasant discussions. Theo Janssen made a number of useful suggestions concerning presentation. Aarne Ranta gave valuable advice, as did Doaitse Swierstra. Harm Brouwer, Matteo Capelletti, Daniël de Kok, Nickolay Kolev, Greg Matheson, Stefan Minica, Patrick O'Neill, Jim Royer, and Ken Shirriff sent us corrections via email. Yoad Winter, Makoto Kanazawa, and Reinhard Muskens corresponded with us about issues of intensionalization. Shalom Lappin tried out a version of the book in a course, which resulted in numerous update requests, inspiring editorial suggestions and bug reports. Finally, we thank Hans Kamp for having graced the book with a foreword.

JAN VAN EIJCK, Amsterdam
CHRISTINA UNGER, Bielefeld

1

Formal Study of Natural Language

Summary

This chapter introduces computational semantics as the art and science of computing meanings for the expressions of a language. The chapter starts with a general overview of the formal study of language. The broad areas of syntax, semantics and pragmatics are distinguished, and the concept of meaning is discussed. Since the book will focus on language as a tool for describing states of affairs and for conveying information, and since logicians have designed special purpose tools for just these tasks, logic will be important to us. The chapter emphasizes the similarities between natural languages and the formal languages that have been designed by logicians and computer scientists. The chapter ends with a discussion of the usefulness of (functional) programming for computational semantics, and with an overview of the rest of the book.

1.1 The Study of Natural Language

Language is one of the most remarkable capacities of human beings and one of the distinctive features that set us apart from other inhabitants of this planet. Human languages are sophisticated systems for manipulating information-encoding symbols, and for composing sounds into structured expressions such as words, phrases, and sentences. These expressions can then serve in numerous ways for communicative actions like information exchange, persuading and deceiving, expressing thoughts, reasoning, and much more.

Linguistics is the scientific study of human language. To make linguistics into a science it is necessary to specify the object of study. In his book *Syntactic Structures* (1957) the linguist Noam Chomsky made the influential proposal to identify a human language with the set of all correct (or: grammatical) sentences of that language. This idealization abstracts from cognitive limitations of language users. Chomsky called the ability of language users to recognize the members of this set, at least in principle, *competence*, and he distinguished this from *performance*, the actual abilities of language users, affected by conditions like memory limitations, distraction, and errors. In this book we will make the same distinction. We will focus on studying competence and therefore assume that a particular language is given to us as a set of sentences.

What exactly makes us competent speakers of our language? What is linguistic knowledge? It is certainly something we have only limited access to. For most speakers of a language the rules and regularities of their native tongue are implicit. They know how to apply them correctly, but when asked to state them, they usually are at a loss. Explicit descriptions of the rules and regularities of a language are called *grammars*. Grammars can be viewed as models of our language competence.

How grammars are represented as a cognitive device in the brain of the language user, we have no way of knowing. As a matter of fact, grammars can be represented in very different ways. In everyday life we encounter them, for example in dictionaries, in online language references, and in textbooks for learning foreign languages. Their design differs with their purpose. Grammars for language learners usually follow pedagogical guidelines and may oversimplify rules. Grammars used in linguistics usually aim to be as explicit and complete as possible. They may start with specifying basic elements such as sounds, words, and meanings. They then state rules for how to combine these into more complex structured expressions. Usually there are various representation levels, in accordance with the subdisciplines of grammar theory:

- *Phonology* explores what the smallest meaning-distinguishing units (sounds) are and how they are combined into the smallest meaning-carrying units (morphemes).
- *Morphology* is concerned with how morphemes are combined into words.
- *Syntax* studies how words are combined into phrases and sentences.
- *Semantics* investigates meanings of basic expressions and how meaning is assigned to complex expressions based on the meaning of simpler expressions and syntactic structure.

In this book, we will not be concerned at all with phonology, and we will also ignore most aspects of morphology. We will concentrate on linguistic form at the level of phrases and sentences. That means we will start with words as basic building blocks. The main task then will be to develop a grammar that provides us with notions of syntactic well-formedness and syntactic structure, and allows us to develop the notion of meaning for well-formed structures. Thus, our grammars

- should be capable of building exactly those expressions that are well-formed in the language of our choice,

- should determine the constituents of complex linguistics expressions, as well as their internal structure,
- and should allow us to assign appropriate meanings to syntactically well-formed expressions, on the basis of their structure.

In other words, the notion of syntactic well-formedness allows us to determine whether a particular expression is indeed a well-formed expression of a given category, and to determine its internal structure. The structure in turn will help us to relate the linguistic forms to the extralinguistic world (what they are about).

1.2 Syntax, Semantics, and Pragmatics

A basic trichotomy in the study of language is that between syntax, semantics, and pragmatics. Roughly speaking, syntax concerns the form aspect of language, semantics its meaning aspect, and pragmatics its use. Developing insight about the semantics of a language presupposes knowledge of the syntax of that language; study of language use presupposes knowledge about both syntax and semantics. It is not surprising, then, that for lots of languages we know more about their syntax and semantics than about pragmatic aspects of their use. Here are approximate definitions of the three notions:

Syntax is the study of strings and the structure imposed on them by grammars generating them.

Semantics is the study of the relation between strings and their meanings, i.e. their relation with the extralinguistic structure they are about.

Pragmatics is the study of the use of meaningful strings to communicate about extralinguistic structure in an interaction process between users of the language.

In a slogan: syntax studies Form, semantics studies Form + Content, and pragmatics studies Form + Content + Use. In this chapter we will examine what can be said about this trichotomy in concrete cases.

It is a matter of stipulation what is to be taken as 'form' in natural language. In the following we will concentrate on written language, more specifically on well-formed sentences. Thus, we will look at languages as sets of strings of symbols taken from some alphabet.

This choice makes it particularly easy to bridge the gap between formal and natural languages, for formal languages can also be viewed as sets of strings. The difference between natural and formal languages lies in the manner in which the sets of strings are given. In the case of formal languages, the language is given by stipulative definition: a string belongs to the language if it is produced by a grammar for that language, or recognized by a parsing algorithm for that language. A parsing algorithm for C, say, can be wrong in the sense that it does not comply with the International Standard for the C programming language, but ultimately there is no right or wrong here: the way in which formal languages are given is a matter of definition.

In the case of natural languages, the situation is quite different. A proposed grammar formalism for a natural language (or for a fragment of a natural language) can be wrong in the sense that it does not agree with the intuitions of the native speakers of the language. Whether a given string is a well-formed sentence of some language is a matter to be decided on the basis of the linguistic intuitions of the native speakers of that language.

Once a grammar for a language is given, we can associate structures with sentences. For natural languages, native speakers have intuitions about which constituents of a sentence belong together, and a natural language grammar will have to comply with these judgements. This might constitute an argument for considering constituent trees rather than strings as the forms that are given.

Still other choices are possible, depending on one's aim. If one considers the problem of natural language recognition, one might consider strings of phonemes (smallest distinctive units of sound of a language) as the basic forms. If one wants to allow for uncertainty in language recognition, the basic forms become lists of words with the possibility of choice, so-called word lattices (with *full proof* and *fool proof* listed on a par as alternatives), or phoneme lattices (strings of phonemes involving the possibility of choice). Maybe we can attach probabilities to the choices. And so on. And so on.

An alternative road to meaning is pointing, or direct demonstration, arguably the starting point of basic concept learning. One's views of the principles of concept learning tend to be coloured by philosophical bias, so let us not get carried away by speculation. Instead, here is an account of first-hand experience. This is how Helen Keller, born deaf-mute and blind, learnt the meaning of the word *water* from her teacher, Miss Sullivan:

We walked down the path to the well-house, attracted by the fragrance of the honeysuckle with which it was covered. Some one was drawing water and my teacher placed my hand under the spout. As the cool stream gushed over one hand she spelled into the other the word *water*, first slowly, then rapidly. I stood still, my whole attention fixed upon the motions of her fingers. Suddenly I felt a misty consciousness as of something forgotten – a thrill of returning thought; and somehow the mystery of language was revealed to me. I knew then that "w-a-t-e-r" meant the wonderful cool something that was flowing over my hand. That living word awakened my soul, gave it light, hope, joy, set it free!

[Kel02, p. 34]

Explanations of meaning fall in two broad classes: meaning as *knowing how* and meaning as *knowing that*. If we say that Johnny doesn't know the meaning of a good spanking, we refer to operational meaning. If Helen Keller writes that *water* means the wonderful cool something that was flowing over her hand, then she refers to meaning as reference, or denotational meaning.

Usually the two are intertwined. Suppose we ask you directions to the Opera House. You might say something like: 'Turn right at the next traffic light and you will see it in front of you.' Understanding the meaning of this involves being able to follow the directions (being able to work out which traffic light counts as the 'next' one, which direction is 'right', and being able to recognize the building in front). Phrased in terms of 'being able to work out ... ', 'being able to recognize ... ', this is meaning as knowing how. Being able to understand the meaning of the directions also involves being able to distinguish correct directions from wrong directions. In other words, the directions classify situations, with me being positioned at some location in some town, facing in a particular direction: in some situations the directions provide a description which is true, in other situations a description which is false. This is denotational meaning.

Denotational meaning can be formalized as knowledge of the conditions for truth in situations. Operational meaning can be formalized as algorithms for performing (cognitive) actions. The operational semantics of *plus* in the expression *seven plus five* is the operation of adding two natural numbers; this operation can be given as a set of calculating instructions, or as a description of the workings of a calculating machine. The distinction between denotational and operational semantics is basic in computer science, and often a lot of work is involved in showing that the two kinds match.

Often operational meaning is more fine-grained than denotational meaning. For instance, the expressions *seven plus five* and *two times six* both refer to the natural number twelve, so their denotational meaning is the same. But they have different operational meaning, for the recipe for adding seven and five is different from the recipe for multiplying two and six.

1.3 The Purposes of Communication

The most lofty aim of communication is to use language as a tool for collective truth finding. But language is also a tool for making your fellow citizens believe things, or for confusing your enemies. Even if two language users agree on non-deception, this does not exclude the use of irony.

A very important use of language, and one that we will be concerned with a lot in the following pages, is as a tool for describing states of affairs and as a reasoning tool. This is a use which formal languages and natural language have in common.

Formal languages are often designed as query tools or reasoning tools, or at least as tools for formal reconstructions of reasoning processes. Therefore, they are a natural focus point for the formal study of language.

One can look at it like this. Suppose we want to use language to communicate basic facts, like 'the sun is shining', 'it is cold', 'it is raining', and so on. If you want to deny such a fact, you need to be able to say a thing like 'it is not cold'. You might also wish to express your uncertainty about which of two facts is the case, so you might like to say 'either it is cold or it is raining'. Similarly, you might like to say 'it is cold and it rains', or: 'if it rains, then it is cold.' So the ingredients of just about the simplest kind of communication are: basic facts, negations, conjunctions, disjunctions, and implications. A fragment of natural language that has only these is already quite useful. In fact, the usefulness of this simple fragment has been evident to logicians for a long time. The study of what can be expressed in this fragment is called *propositional logic* or *Boolean logic*, after the British mathematician George Boole (1815–1864).

To see how propositional logic can be used to express what goes in simple communicative discourses, suppose we want to talk about basic facts a, b. Suppose you know nothing about whether these facts are true or not. Then for you there are four possibilities: both facts are true, both facts are false, the first fact is true and the second one is false, or the first fact is false and the second one is true. Now we tell you 'a or b'. If you believe us, this will allow you to rule out one of the four possibilities, the possibility where both a and b are false. Or if you take our statement in the exclusive sense, it will even allow you to rule out two of the four possibilities. Your knowledge has grown by elimination of possibilities.

Exercise 1.1 We have seen that (complete) ignorance about the truth or falsity of two facts can be modelled as uncertainty between four possibilities. Now suppose there are ten basic facts. How many possibilities would that give? How about the general case of n basic facts?

If you just want to study simple factual information exchange, it makes sense to focus on the fragment of natural language that can be translated into propositional logic. But suppose you want to be more explicit about expressing relations between things. If you wish to declare your love to someone, say, then stating a basic proposition like 'there is love' is maybe not articulate enough. You might wish to say something more daring, like 'I love you.' Talk like this expresses relations between subjects and objects. You can use pronouns like 'I' and 'you', but also proper names. You can still do the propositional stuff, like disjunctions, negations, but you can also express quantificational facts. You can use the power of quantification to add to your romantic declaration, strengthening it to 'I love no-one but you'. You are now in the realm that is called *predicate logic*.

You can say interesting things with predicate logic, at least if you know how to use it, for predicate logic is very expressive. We will see below that predicate logic gets us a long way in expressing the meanings of natural language statements. Still more expressive is *typed higher-order logic*, which will also be used extensively in this book. In typed logic you can say more abstract (but still romantic) things like 'To love someone like you makes me very happy.' Finally, at the end of the book, we will have a look at the logic of knowledge, or *epistemic logic*. This will shed light on the meaning of statements like 'I am not completely sure whether I still love you.' It will also allow us to give an abstract picture of how communication by means of declarative statements leads to growth of knowledge, in subtle ways. We will study growth of audience knowledge about what the speaker knows, but also growth of speaker knowledge about audience knowledge about speaker knowledge, and so on.

Logic is a field that has made tremendous progress by focussing on well-defined formal languages, such as the example languages above, and studying their properties in depth. It is possible to view logical languages like the language of propositional logic or the language of predicate logic as fragments of natural language, by focussing at the specific set of sentences of natural language that can be translated into the logical language. This is going to be an important method in this book. This method of fragments, of taking things step by step, was first proposed for natural language analysis by logician and philosopher Richard Montague (1930–1971) in the 1970s, when he made the following famous statement:

There is in my opinion no important theoretical difference between natural languages and the artificial languages of logicians; indeed, I consider it possible to comprehend the syntax and semantics of both kinds of languages within a single natural and mathematically precise theory.

[Mon74b, p. 222]

Montague's pioneering work has shown how natural languages can be formally described using techniques borrowed from logic. It introduced tools to compute meanings in a systematic way and gave rise to a whole tradition of *formal semantics*, a very general term covering logical approaches to natural language semantics.

Our ultimate goal is to form an adequate model of parts of our language competence. Adequate means that the model has to be realistic in terms of complexity and learnability. We will not be so ambitious as to claim that our account mirrors real cognitive processes, but what we do claim is that our account imposes constraints on what the real cognitive processes can look like. In the rest of this chapter, we are going to explore the means that will help us fulfilling this goal.

1.4 Natural Languages and Formal Languages

English, Swedish, Russian, and Hindi are natural languages. The language of primary school arithmetic, the language of propositional logic, and the programming language Haskell are formal languages. But the distinction is not absolute, since we can find cases in between, like Esperanto. In order to see whether we can draw a dividing line, let us look at some crucial design features of human languages.

- *Duality of patterning* (or *double articulation*): The construction of linguistic content can be analyzed on two structural levels. One is the level containing the smallest meaningful units of language: morphemes or words, like *cat*. However, they are not minimal but on another level are made of a small set of speech sounds, the so-called phonemes. These do not carry a meaning themselves but only differentiate meaningful units, e.g. /k/ and /m/, that distinguish between *cat* and *mat*.
- *Recursion*: Structural patterns in sentences or phrases can repeat themselves. A common noun *bird* can be modified to a complex common noun *green bird*, this can be modified again, to form *small green bird*, and again, to form *beautiful small green bird*.
- *Contextuality*: What a phrase or sentence means is determined in part by the context in which the phrase is used.

Exercise 1.2 Pollard and Sag, in their textbook [PS94], give the following example of the use of recursion to extend sentences:

- Sentences can go on.
- Sentences can go on and on.
- Sentences can go on and on and on.
- Sentences can go on and on and on and on.
- ...

Can you give a concise description of this recursion pattern?

Exercise 1.3 Does it follow from the example in Exercise 1.2 that there are infinitely many English sentences? Or does it follow that English sentences can have infinite length? Or both?

The properties of duality of patterning, recursion, and contextuality set human languages apart from communicative systems of animals, such as bee dancing. They are responsible for the creative economy of language, because they allow us to build and understand infinitely many sentences using only finitely many sounds and rules – a precondition for enabling children to learn language as quickly and easily as they do.

Another key notion when talking about properties of human languages is *compositionality*. The so-called principle of compositionality will concern us a lot in what follows. This principle is usually attributed to the German mathematician Gottlob Frege (1848–1925). What it says is that the meaning of a complex expression depends on the meanings of its parts and the way they are combined syntactically. This formulation is quite vague, however, because nothing is said yet about what meanings are, what counts as a part of an expression, and what kind of dependence we are talking about. In order to make sense, the principle has to be specified with respect to these matters. Moreover, it is meaningful only when understood against the background of further requirements on a semantic theory, for example the requirement that meaning assignment is systematic. Such a systematic account will capture the fact that once we know the meaning of *white unicorn* and *brown elk*, we also know what *brown unicorn* and *white elk* mean.

Compositionality does not occur in our list of the crucial properties of human languages listed above, because we assume that it is primarily a matter of methodology. The question is not whether natural languages satisfy the principle of compositionality, but rather whether we can and want to design meaning assembly in a way that this principle is respected. Setting up the representation of meaning in a compositional way has the merit of elegance, but it is not always straightforward. A recurring difficulty is the context-dependence of natural language meaning. To state the meaning of a pronoun, information is needed about the context in which the pronoun occurs. Something similar holds for presuppositions. In such cases, there are in general two kinds of reactions. The easy way out is to give up on compositionality. The other kind of reaction is to enrich and extend our semantic theory in ways that allow us to capture seemingly non-compositional phenomena in a compositional way. We will return to these matters in due time, when we take a closer look at pronoun resolution, in Chapter 12, and at presupposition, in Chapter 13.

Besides natural languages, there are other symbol-manipulating systems that also show some of the properties listed above, for example the language of predicate logic and high-level programming languages like C, LISP, and Haskell. But these apparently lack other properties of human languages. For example, they lack the whole pragmatic dimension that human languages employ: deception, irony, conveying information without explicitly stating it, and capabilities like creating and understanding metaphors. Formal languages also lack the flexibility of human languages induced by vagueness together with heavy use of context and background knowledge. These differences, in fact, are the reason why natural languages are well-suited for efficient inter-human communication, whereas formal languages excel for doing mathematics and for interacting with computers.

These important differences become visible if we focus on the way natural languages and formal languages are used. The differences disappear from view if we look at languages as sets of sentences. When we focus on fragments of natural languages and describe their grammar in a formal way, we are, in fact, doing just the same as when describing formal languages.

1.5 What Formal Semantics is Not

A widespread prejudice against formal semantics for natural language is that it is just an exercise in typesetting. You explain the meaning of *and* in natural language by saying that the meaning of *Toto barked and Dorothy smiled* equals A **and** B, where A is the meaning of *Toto barked* and B is the meaning of *Dorothy smiled*. It looks like nothing is gained by explaining *and* as **and**.

The answer to this is that **and** refers to an operation one is assumed to have grasped already, namely the operation of taking a Boolean meet of two objects in a Boolean structure. Assuming that we know what a Boolean structure is, this is a real explanation, and not just a typesetting trick. On the other hand, if one is just learning about Boolean structures by being exposed to an account of the semantics of propositional logic, it may well seem that nothing happens in the semantic explanation of propositional conjunction.

A well known story about the linguist Barbara Partee has it that she once ended a course on Montague semantics with the invitation to her students to ask questions. As this was the end of the course, they could ask any question, however vaguely related to the subject matter. So a student asked: 'What is the meaning of life?' And Partee said: 'To answer that question we just have to see how Montague would treat the word *life*. He would translate it into his intensional logic as the constant *life'*, and he would use a cup operator to indicate that he was referring to the meaning, i.e. the extension in all possible worlds. So the answer to your question is: the meaning of *life* is ^*life'*. Any other questions?'

The core of the problem is that it is hard to avoid reference to meaning by means of symbols anyway. Compare the process of explaining the meaning of the word *bicycle* to someone who doesn't speak English. One way to explain the meaning of the word is by drawing a picture of a bicycle. If your pupil is familiar with bicycles, the meaning will get across once he or she grasps that the drawing is just another way to refer to the actual meaning. The drawing itself is just another symbol, for 🚲 is just another way to refer to bicycles. In the same way **and** is just another symbol for Boolean meet.

One of the things that make the study of language from a formal point of view so fascinating is that we can borrow insights from the formal sciences – mathematics, logic, and theoretical computer science – just like linguistics also borrows insights from psychology, philosophy, and so on. Formal insights and tools can be used for modelling language competence in a clear and precise framework, that finally allows us to implement natural language in a machine. Whether this is helpful depends on one's aims. When we decide to concern ourselves with the processing of language by means of computers, formal methods are indispensable, because we cannot rely on informal insights of the language user, for computers do not learn languages the way humans do. To put meanings into a computer, we have to represent meanings exactly and compactly. To this end we are going to use meaning representations in a formal language, which has the advantages of being unambiguous and precise, and which also gives us the possibility to prove our claims and supplies us with a tool for reasoning.

In contrast with the situation with informal studies, we will forge the conceptual tools for our study ourselves, by means of formal definitions. These definitions are meant to be taken very literally. Time and again it will prove necessary to remind oneself of the definitions to understand the analysis. In this respect formal study is quite different from reading novels. The formal approach to language invites you to chew, and chew, and chew again, to arrive at proper digestion. If you are not yet used to reading things written in formal style, you might have the feeling that the explanations go too fast for you. This is not your fault, and besides, the remedy is easy: simply remind yourself to proceed more slowly.

1.6 Computational Semantics and Functional Programming

The approach to natural language semantics that was propagated by Richard Montague – sometimes called the Montagovian program – has proved very fruitful in the past three decades. More recently, in the last decade and a half, a discipline of so-called functional programming has developed that is a natural fit for the approach of Montague. Like Montague grammar, functional programming is based on the so-called typed lambda calculus.

Now, why, indeed, should linguists have to acquire programming skills at all? Functional programming is a useful skill for linguists not only because of the dovetail fit with Montague grammar, but also because it allows illuminating experiments with linguistic rule formats. Implementing a rule system forces the linguist to be fully precise about the rules he or she proposes. You will find that once you are well-versed in functional programming, your programming efforts will give you immediate feedback on your linguistic theories.

There are basically two things that machines are used for in computational semantics. One is automatizing the construction of meaning representations. The other one is operating on the results. Possible operations are model checking (or model building) and performing inference tasks. Such operations are essential for Natural Language Processing applications, e.g. for searching for information within documents or databases (*information retrieval*), as implemented in web search engines, for developing and implementing dialogue systems or question-

answering systems, and in the long run also for having machines performing artificial intelligence tasks.

But besides these practical applications, there are also benefits that arise from
the process of automatizing the construction of meaning representations. In this
context, the choice of functional programming is not accidental. With Haskell,
the step from formal definition to program is particularly easy. This presupposes,
of course, that you are at ease with formal definitions. Our reason for combining
training in reasoning and computational linguistics with an introduction to functional programming is that they can mutually be fruitful for each other. On the one
hand, the Haskell programs will serve as concrete illustrations of the things that
computational semantics allows you to compute. And on the other hand, being
forced to be fully explicit about the semantic theory you want to implement can
give you insights in how to refine and improve your theory. Also, since programming languages like Haskell rest on a solid formal basis, implementing a semantic
theory offers an easy way to check that it is correct and that it does what it is supposed to do (or what you expect it to do). We hope to show you in the course of the
book how Haskell can help in reflecting on the formal semantics you want to use.
After all, computational semantics is to a large extent not only the science but also
the art of processing meaning by computer.

Most current work on computational semantics uses Prolog, a language based on
predicate logic and designed for knowledge engineering. We have decided to steer
away from this tradition. Prolog programs are meant to be implementations of logical predicates, but there is a snag. To make Prolog into a full-fledged programming
language, control operators had to be added, such as 'assert', 'retract', and 'cut'.
Without the power of this control the language is simply not expressive enough, but
the control effects make Prolog programs often hard to understand and debug, and
they spoil the logical purity. Unlike the logic programming paradigm, the functional programming paradigm allows for logical purity. Functional programming
can yield implementations that are remarkably faithful to formal definitions. At
this stage this is just a statement of a claim, of course, but the rest of the book
can be viewed as an illustration of this claim. Our use of Haskell imposes no limitations on us, by the way. If one needs Prolog-like features, Haskell can easily
provide them, as is demonstrated by the embedding of Prolog in Haskell in [SS99].

1.7 Overview of the Book

Although this book focuses on semantics, we cannot avoid saying a thing or two
about syntax. We will be agnostic about the general format of natural language
syntax, and try to get by with the simplest formalisms that allow us to make our
points about semantics. This means that we will rely on context-free rewriting

rules wherever possible. In the spirit of the method of fragments, we believe that syntactic formalisms should not be complicated without necessity.

Many of our fragments will in fact be fragments of formal languages, but as our fragments grow larger, the dividing line between the formal languages and the mini-fragments of natural language will get blurred. Formal languages are indispensable in computational semantics anyway, as representation languages for meaning. In the choice of meaning representation languages we will also try to work with the simplest possible candidate that will allow us to illustrate what we have to say about natural language meaning. In the course of the book, we will discuss the syntax and semantics of simple games, the syntax and semantics of propositional logic and predicate logic, the syntax and semantics of various typed logics, and the syntax and semantics of propositional epistemic logic, i.e. the logic of propositional knowledge.

Chapter 2 gives an overview of the computational formalisms that we are going to use: set notation, lambda calculus, types, and functional programming. Next, in Chapter 3, the reader will get a crash course in functional programming. Chapter 4 presents a number of syntactic fragments, and Chapter 5 treats the semantics of those fragments in a precise way, including implementations, except for the semantics of predicate logic. Chapter 6 treats the important topic of model checking for predicate logic. This will introduce the reader to what it means to relate expressions of a language fragment to appropriate structures in the outside world. It will also give a first example of systematic translation from syntactic form into logical form, where logical form appears in the shape of the syntax of predicate logic. In Chapter 7 we take a more systematic look at the process of meaning composition, and at the typed logical tools needed for this. Chapter 8 treats the important distinction between extension and intension of expressions, allowing us to construct plausible meanings for intensional constructs like 'fake princess' and 'wanting to catch a dwarf.' Chapter 9 covers the whole road from syntactic analysis (*natural language parsing*) to translation into logical form. The next Chapter, 10, develops the theme of relational interpretation; this leads to a type-theoretic account of the process of operator scoping. The Chapter ends with the development of a framework for underspecified logical form. Chapter 11 gives an introduction to an alternative perspective on the process of constructing natural language meaning representations, by means of so-called continuation passing style processing. A more specific example of this is given in Chapter 12, where pronoun linking and reference resolution are analysed in the context of a general theory of discourse representation and context. The final Chapter, 13, broadens the scope still further, and sketches the outlines of a general theory of communication as informative action, thus linking the area of natural language semantics to that of pragmatics. It will turn out that presupposition and the notion of the appropriateness of answers to questions can be analysed in the context of the communicative uses of natural language. In this connection we will discuss concepts such as common knowledge between speaker and audience, to analyse what happens when declarative statements of natural language are made in front of an audience, and we will look at declarations and questions as communicative actions of different kinds.

1.8 Further Reading

The important distinction between competence and performance is from Chomsky [Cho57]. A classic textbook on the application of logical methods to the study of language is Reichenbach [Rei47]. A beautiful book on historical and philological aspects of the evolution of word meaning is C.S. Lewis [Lew60]. The viewpoint that the real mystery in the understanding of natural language lies in the way human beings grasp meanings of single words can be found in Plato's dialogue *Cratylus*. Percy's [Per83] has a particularly amusing version of this. Helen Keller [Kel02] gives a moving account of the process of awakening by grasping the concept of language.

An excellent introduction to what the principle of compositionality involves is in [Gam91a]. See [Jan97] for further information, and [BJ07] for recent discussion.

An accessible introduction to Montague grammar is [DWP81]. Many of the key papers in formal semantics are collected in [PP02]. Foundations of computational semantics are discussed in [FL05]. Broad coverage of topics in logic and language can be found in [BtM97]. An overview of developments in semantics of natural language is given in [Lap97].

2

Lambda Calculus, Types, and Functional Programming

Summary

This chapter explains the basics of formal notation, lambda calculus, type theory, and functional programming.

2.1 Sets and Set Notation

All mathematical and logical concepts we will come across in the course of the book can be defined in terms of the fundamental concept of a set. We will thus start by introducing some basic set theory.

A set is a collection of definite, distinct objects. This is too vague for a definition, but unfortunately we cannot do better, and fortunately that does not matter. Let us give some examples of sets instead. Our first example is the set of words in the third edition of the *Oxford Advanced Learner's Dictionary of Current English*. Other examples are the set of colours of the Dutch flag, or the set of letters of the Greek alphabet. Yet another example is the set of even natural numbers greater than seven. And so on.

The elements of a set are also called its *members*. To indicate that a is an element of a set A we write $a \in A$. To deny that a is an element of a set A we write $a \notin A$. The symbol $\in$ is the symbol for membership. The elements of a set can be anything: words, colours, people, numbers. The elements of a set can also themselves be sets. The set consisting of the set of even natural numbers and the set of odd natural numbers is an example. This set has two members; each of these members has an infinite number of members.

To check whether two sets are the same one has to check that they have the same members. The fact that membership is all there is to set identity, or that sets are fully determined by their members, is called the principle of extensionality. It follows that to check that two sets A and B are identical, one has to check two

15

things: (i) does it hold that every element a of A is also an element of B, and (ii) does it hold that every element b of B is also an element of A?

To specify a set, there are several methods: give a list of its members, as in 'the set having the numbers 1, 2, and 3 as its only members', give some kind of semantic description, as in 'the set of colours of the Dutch flag', or separate out a set from a larger set by means of a suitable restriction. This last method is called the method of *set comprehension*. Here is an example: the even natural numbers are the natural numbers with the property that division by 2 leaves no remainder. We can express this by means of the multiplication operator, as follows:

$$E = \{2n \mid n \in \mathbb{N}\}.$$

The braces are also used to list the members of a finite set:

$$D = \{\text{red}, \text{white}, \text{blue}\}.$$

Mentioning a set element more than once does not make a difference. The set

$$\{\text{white}, \text{blue}, \text{white}, \text{red}\}$$

is identical to the set D, for it has the same members.

Another way of specifying sets is by means of operations on other sets. An example is the following definition of the odd natural numbers:

$$O = \mathbb{N} - E.$$

Here $\mathbb{N} - E$ is the set of all elements of $\mathbb{N}$ that are not members of E. Equivalent definitions are the following:

$$O = \{n \in \mathbb{N} \mid n \notin E\}$$

or

$$O = \{n \mid n \in \mathbb{N}, n \notin E\}$$

or

$$O = \{2n + 1 \mid n \in \mathbb{N}\}.$$

Some important sets have special names. $\mathbb{N}$ is an example. Another example is $\mathbb{Z}$, for the set of integer numbers. Yet another example is the set without any members. Because of the principle of extensionality there can be only one such set. It is called $\emptyset$, or the empty set.

If every member of a set A is also a member of set B we say that A is a subset of B, written as $A \subseteq B$. If $A \subseteq B$ and $B \subseteq A$ then it follows by the principle of extensionality that A and B are the same set. Conversely, if $A = B$ then it follows that $A \subseteq B$ and $B \subseteq A$.

Exercise 2.1 Explain why $\emptyset \subseteq A$ holds for every set A.

Exercise 2.2 Explain the difference between $\emptyset$ and $\{\emptyset\}$.

The *complement* of a set A, with respect to some fixed universe U with $A \subseteq U$, is the set consisting of all objects in U that are not elements of A. A universe set U is also called a domain. The complement set $U - A$ is written as $\overline{A}$. It is defined as the set $\{x \mid x \in U, x \notin A\}$. For example, if we take U to be the set $\mathbb{N}$ of natural numbers, then the set of even numbers is the complement of the set of odd numbers and vice versa.

Exercise 2.3 Check that $\overline{\overline{A}} = A$.

2.2 Relations

Usually, we are not only interested in meaningful collections of objects but also in the ways in which objects are related to each other. Examples of how objects can be related are numerous, ranging from family relations between people, like motherhood, being married, or being the brother of someone's sister-in-law, to mathematical relations between numbers, like divisibility or being twin primes.

Formally, we can describe a *relation* between two sets A and B as a collection of ordered pairs (a, b) such that $a \in A$ and $b \in B$. An ordered pair is, as the name already gives away, a collection of two distinguishable objects, in which the order plays a role. E.g. we use $(Bonnie, Clyde)$ to indicate the ordered pair that has *Bonnie* as its first element and *Clyde* as its second element.

The notation for the set of all ordered pairs with their first element taken from A and their second element taken from B is $A \times B$. This is called the *Cartesian product* of A and B. A relation between A and B is a subset of $A \times B$.

The Cartesian product of the sets $A = \{a, b, \ldots, h\}$ and $B = \{1, 2, \ldots, 8\}$, for example, is the set

$$A \times B = \{(a, 1), (a, 2), \ldots, (b, 1), (b, 2), \ldots, (h, 1), (h, 2), \ldots, (h, 8)\}.$$

This is the set of positions on a chess board. And if we multiply the set of chess colours $C = \{\text{White}, \text{Black}\}$ with the set of chess figures,

$$F = \{\text{King}, \text{Queen}, \text{Knight}, \text{Rook}, \text{Bishop}, \text{Pawn}\},$$

we get the set of chess pieces $C \times F$. If we multiply this set with the set of chess positions, we get the set of piece positions on the board, with $((\text{White}, \text{King}), (e, 1))$ indicating that the white king occupies square $e1$. To get the set of moves on a chess board, take $((C \times F) \times ((A \times B) \times (A \times B)))$, and read $((\text{White}, \text{King}), ((e, 1), (f, 2)))$

as 'white king moves from $e1$ to $f2$', but bear in mind that not all moves in $((C \times F) \times ((A \times B) \times (A \times B)))$ are legal in the game.

Exercise 2.4 Take A to be the set {Kasparov, Karpov, Anand}. Find $A \times A$. This is sometimes also denoted by A^2.

As an example of a relation as a set of ordered pairs consider the relation of authorship between a set A of authors and a set B of books. This relation associates with every author the book(s) he or she wrote. It can be represented as a set, e.g. {(*L. Frank Baum, The Wonderful Wizard of Oz*), (*Jan Weirich, Fimfarum*), (*Michael Ende, The Neverending Story*), (*Michael Ende, Momo*), . . .}.

Sets of ordered pairs are called binary relations. We can easily generalize this to sets of triples, to get so-called ternary relations, to sets of quadruples, and so on. An example of a ternary relation is that of borrowing something from someone. This relation consists of triples, or: 3-tuples, (a, b, c), where a is the borrower, b is the owner, and c is the thing borrowed. In general, an n-ary relation is a set of n-tuples (ordered sequences of n objects). We use A^n for the set of all n-tuples with all elements taken from A.

Unary relations are called *properties*. A property can be represented as a set, namely the set that contains all entities having the property. For example, the property of being divisible by 3, considered as a property of integer numbers, corresponds to the set $\{\ldots, -9, -6, -3, 0, 3, 6, 9, \ldots\}$.

An important operation on binary relations is composition. If R and S are binary relations on a set U, i.e. $R \subseteq U^2$ and $S \subseteq U^2$, then the composition of R and S, notation $R \circ S$, is the set of pairs (x, y) such that there is some z with $(x, z) \in R$ and $(z, y) \in S$. E.g. the composition of $\{(1, 2), (2, 3)\}$ and $\{(2, 4), (2, 5)\}$ is $\{(1, 4), (1, 5)\}$.

Exercise 2.5 What is the composition of $\{(n, n + 2) \mid n \in \mathbb{N}\}$ with itself?

Another operation on binary relations is converse. If R is a binary relation, then its converse (or: inverse) is the relation given by $R^{\smallsmile} = \{(y, x) \mid (x, y) \in R\}$. The converse of the relation 'greater than' on the natural numbers is the relation 'smaller than' on the natural numbers. If a binary relation has the property that $R^{\smallsmile} \subseteq R$, then R is called *symmetric*.

Exercise 2.6 Show that it follows from $R^{\smallsmile} \subseteq R$ that $R = R^{\smallsmile}$.

If U is a set, then the relation $I = \{(x, x) \mid x \in U\}$ is called the identity relation on U. If a relation R on U has the property that $I \subseteq R$, i.e. if every element of U stands in relation R to itself, then R is called *reflexive*. The relation $\leq$ ('less than or equal') on the natural numbers is reflexive, the relation $<$ ('less than') is not.

The relation $A^2 - I$ is the set of all pairs $(x, y) \in A^2$ with $x \neq y$. If A is the set of chess players {Kasparov, Karpov, Anand}, then $A^2 - I$ gives the relation where each player plays against each of the other players (once with white, once with black – assuming that the order indicates that the first player plays with white).

A relation R is called *transitive* if it holds for all x, y, z that if $(x, y) \in R$ and $(y, z) \in R$, then also $(x, z) \in R$. To say that the relation of friendship is transitive boils down to saying that it holds for anyone that the friends of their friends are their friends.

Exercise 2.7 Which of the following relations are transitive?

(1) $\{(1, 2), (2, 3), (3, 4)\}$
(2) $\{(1, 2), (2, 3), (3, 4), (1, 3), (2, 4)\}$
(3) $\{(1, 2), (2, 3), (3, 4), (1, 3), (2, 4), (1, 4)\}$
(4) $\{(1, 2), (2, 1)\}$
(5) $\{(1, 1), (2, 2)\}$

The next exercise shows that transitivity can be expressed in terms of relational composition.

Exercise 2.8 Check that a relation R is transitive if and only if it holds that $R \circ R \subseteq R$.

Exercise 2.9 Can you give an example of a transitive relation R for which $R \circ R = R$ does not hold?

2.3 Functions

Functions are relations with the following special property: for any (a, b) and (a, c) in the relation it has to hold that b and c are equal. Thus a *function* from a set A (called *domain*) to a set B (called *range*) is a relation between A and B such that for each $a \in A$ there is one and only one associated $b \in B$. In other words, a function is a mechanism that maps an input value to a uniquely determined output value. Looking at the relation *author of* from above, it is immediately clear that it is not a function, because the input *Michael Ende* is not mapped to a unique output but is related to more than one element from the set B of books.

Functions are an important kind of relation, because they allow us to express the concept of *dependence*. For example, we know that the gravitational potential energy of a wrecking ball depends on its mass and the height we elevate it to, and this dependence is most easily expressed in a functional relation.

Functions can be viewed from different angles. On the one hand, they can be seen as sets of data, represented as a collection of pairs of input and output values. This tells us something about the behaviour of a function, i.e. what input is mapped to which output. As an example, consider the following conversions between temperature scales.

Kelvin	Celsius	Fahrenheit	
0	−273.15	−459.67	(absolute zero)
273.15	0	32	(freezing point of water)
310.15	37	98.6	(human body temperature)
373.13	99.98	211.96	(boiling point of water)
505.9	232.8	451	(paper auto-ignites)

The function converting temperatures from Kelvin to Celsius can be seen as a set of pairs $\{(0, -273.15), \ldots\}$, and the function converting temperatures from Celsius to Fahrenheit as a set $\{(-273.15, -459.67), \ldots\}$. Determining the output of the function, given some input, simply corresponds to a table lookup. Any function can be viewed as a – possibly infinite – database table. This is called the extensional view of functions. Another way to look at functions is as *instructions for computation*. This is called the intensional view of functions. In the case of temperature conversion the intensional view is more convenient than the extensional view, for the function mapping Kelvin to Celsius can easily be specified as a simple subtraction:

$$x \mapsto x - 273.15.$$

This is read as 'an input x is mapped to x minus 273.15'. Similarly, the function from Celsius to Fahrenheit can be given by

$$x \mapsto x \times \frac{9}{5} + 32.$$

For example, if we have a temperature of 37 degrees Celsius and want to convert it to Fahrenheit, we replace x by 37 and compute the outcome by multiplying it with $\frac{9}{5}$ and then adding 32:

$$37 \times \frac{9}{5} + 32 \rightarrow 66.6 + 32 \rightarrow 98.6.$$

The example shows that the intensional view of functions can be made precise by representing the function as an expression, and specifying the principles for simplifying (or: rewriting) such functional expressions. Rewriting functional expressions is a form of simplification where part of an expression is replaced by something simpler, until we arrive at an expression that cannot be simplified (or: reduced) any further. This rewriting corresponds to the computation of a function. For example, the function converting Celsius to Fahrenheit applied to the input 37 is the expression $37 \times \frac{9}{5} + 32$. This expression denotes the output, and at the same time it shows how to arrive at this output: First, $37 \times \frac{9}{5}$ is rewritten to 66.6, according to the rewriting rules for multiplication. The result of this simplification is $66.6 + 32$, which is then rewritten to 98.6, in accordance with the rewriting rules for addition.

Functions can be composed, as follows. Let g be the function that converts from Kelvin to Celsius, and let f be the function that converts from Celsius to Fahrenheit. Then $f \cdot g$ is the function that converts from Kelvin to Fahrenheit, and that works as follows. First convert from Kelvin to Celsius, then take the result and convert this to Fahrenheit. It should be clear from this explanation that $f \cdot g$ is defined by

$$x \mapsto f(g(x)),$$

which corresponds to

$$x \mapsto (x - 273.15) \times \frac{9}{5} + 32.$$

Exercise 2.10 The successor function $s \colon \mathbb{N} \to \mathbb{N}$ on the natural numbers is given by $n \mapsto n + 1$. What is the composition of s with itself?

A special function which is simple yet very useful is the *characteristic function* of a set. The characteristic function of subset A of some universe (or: domain) U is a function that maps all members of A to the truth-value **True** and all elements of U that are not members of A to **False**. E.g. the function representing the property of being divisible by 3, on the domain of integers, would map the numbers

$$\dots, -9, -6, -3, 0, 3, 6, 9, \dots$$

to **True**, and all other integers to **False**. Characteristic functions characterize membership of a set. Since we specified relations as sets, this means we can represent every relation as a characteristic function.

Exercise 2.11 $\leq$ is a binary relation on the natural numbers. What is the corresponding characteristic function?

Exercise 2.12 Let $f \colon A \to B$ be a function. Show that the relation $R \subseteq A^2$ given by $(x, y) \in R$ if and only if $f(x) = f(y)$ is an equivalence relation (reflexive, transitive, and symmetric) on A.

In natural language semantics, relations are pervasive, because a lot of lexical items express relations: transitive verbs like *love* express binary relations, ditransitive verbs like *give* express ternary relations, adjectives like *nice* express properties, and so on. However, what we are mainly interested in is not how to exactly capture all the meaning components of these lexical items. Instead we want to concentrate on how the meanings of expressions are combined, so as to compose the meaning of bigger expressions. For capturing meaning assembly in natural languages, we will consider meanings of expressions not as relations but as their characteristic functions. Until now we have considered mostly extensional properties of functions, i.e. which objects they map to which other objects. To consider intensional properties of functions, i.e. the way functions are built up and how they combine, mathematical logic knows a simple and powerful tool: the lambda calculus. In the next section, we are going to give you an overview of what it is and how it works. It will be one of the main tools in the remainder of the book, because it provides us with a means to inspect the structure of functions.

2.4 Lambda calculus

We already talked about functions informally. Now we want to take up a more formal stance, by means of a short introduction to the so-called lambda calculus or λ-calculus. The lambda calculus was developed by the mathematician and logician Alonzo Church in the 1930s as a proposal for a precise definition of the notion of mechanical computation, more in particular of the notion of a computable function. Around the same time, Alan Turing, mathematician and founder of computer science, developed a different notion of computable function in terms of computation on an abstract machine (later called a Turing machine). These notions turned out to be equivalent: both kinds of computations define the same class of functions, now called the *recursive functions*. See [Chu36, Tur36, BB00].

Church intended the lambda calculus as a foundation of constructive mathematics. As such his proposal was not entirely successful, but the notion of functional computation turned out to be extremely useful in theoretical computer science. Later, in the 1960s, the seminal work of Richard Montague showed the way towards beautiful applications of lambda calculus in linguistics. The linguist Barbara Partee testified to this when she once remarked: 'Lambdas have changed my life.'

To motivate the notation of the lambda calculus, consider a mathematical expression like $x^2 + y$. This can be thought of as a function on x (considering y as fixed) or as a function on y (considering x as fixed), or perhaps as a function on x and y together. The lambda calculus provides a notation for distinguishing between these possibilities.

In the lambda calculus functions are represented by means of so-called function abstraction. To see how this works, first consider the notation $x \mapsto x^2 + y$. This can be thought of as the function mapping x to $x^2 + y$, for some fixed y. To make a clear distinction between the *bound* variable x and the *unbound* variable y we introduce an explicit variable binder, and we write:

$$\lambda x \mapsto x^2 + y.$$

This is sometimes written with a dot instead of the arrow, as $\lambda x.x^2 + y$. Clearly, the name of the variable is not important: $\lambda z \mapsto z^2 + y$ would indicate the same function. The lambda operator indicates that $\lambda x \mapsto x^2 + y$ is a function that depends on one parameter, x, and given some instantiation of x as input, it will return the result of doing the calculation $x^2 + y$ for that input. The variable x that represents the input is bound by the lambda operator λ.

As it turns out, this representation by means of lambda binding offers a general way to write functions. In case a function takes several arguments, such as the function for adding a number to the square of another number, we can use two bound variables, and represent the function as $\lambda x \lambda y \mapsto x^2 + y$. Now look at what happens when we apply this function to an argument, say the argument 3.

$$(\lambda x \lambda y \mapsto x^2 + y)\, 3 \;\rightarrow\; \lambda y \mapsto 3^2 + y$$

We start with a function of two arguments, feed it its first argument, and end up with a function of one argument, namely the function for incrementing with 3^2.

For applying a function to its argument we use juxtaposition: if F is a function expression and A is an argument expression, then $(F\ A)$ denotes the application of F to A.

The actual computation that takes place when the application of F to A is computed depends on the form of F. If F is an abstraction it will have the form $\lambda x \mapsto E$, and E will contain occurrences of the variable x that are bound by the lambda operator. The application of $\lambda x \mapsto E$ to A can now be computed by replacing these occurrences of x in E by occurrences of A. Look at the example $(\lambda x \mapsto x^2 + 1)\, 3$. This simplifies to $3^2 + 1$, which is the result of replacing x in $x^2 + 1$ by 3.

So these are the things we want to talk about in our calculus. Formally, we will build the set of expressions in the calculus from an infinite set of variables using application and abstraction. Our definition of the language of the lambda calculus will be our first example of a definition using abstract grammar notation for defining formal languages. The grammar defines expressions E by indicating how E can be rewritten. The notation for 'can be rewritten as' is ::=.

$$
\begin{array}{rcl}
E & ::= & v \\
E & ::= & (E\ E) \\
E & ::= & (\lambda v \mapsto E)
\end{array}
$$

This can be abbreviated by means of the symbol | for 'or':

$$E \quad ::= \quad v \mid (E\ E) \mid (\lambda v \mapsto E).$$

This notation is called Backus-Naur Form, or BNF, and a grammar written in BNF is called a BNF grammar or context-free grammar. ('Context-free' expresses the fact that expressions can be rewritten without regard to the context in which they occur.) What the grammar for lambda calculus says is that you can build expressions, denoted by E, in three ways:

- First, you can take any variable and this itself will be an expression. For this to make sense we will also have to specify what variables can look like, of course. Here is one possible way to do this:

$$v \quad ::= \quad x \mid v'.$$

  This states that a variable is either the character x, or an already built variable suffixed by $'$. This generates the variables $x, x', x'', x''', \ldots$, which serve as the basic building blocks of expressions. Starting from them, we can build more complex expressions in the following two ways.
- If you already have built two expressions, their juxtaposition is also an expression. This is called function application.
- If you have built an expression, then prefixing a λ and a variable also yields an expression. This is called function abstraction.
- Finally, nothing else is an expression.

Here is an example. We can start with the variable x and abstract over it to get the expression $(\lambda x \mapsto x)$. Next, we can take another variable x' and apply the function $(\lambda x \mapsto x)$ to it. This gives the expression $((\lambda x \mapsto x)\ x')$. By contrast, the string $(f \lambda\ x)$ is not a well-formed expression of our lambda calculus.

For convenience, we will not only use variables as basic building blocks but also constants for natural numbers, arithmetic operators like $+, \times$, strings like *Dorothy*, and so on, without specifying them further at this point. We will also often write x, y, z for variables, instead of x, x', x'', and so on. Finally, we will omit parentheses when there is no danger of confusion.

So we will usually write expressions like $\lambda x \mapsto x + 42$ and $\lambda y \mapsto$ *Dorothy likes y*. And note that we are actually cheating in doing so. Officially, the expressions in our language are defined in prefix form: write the function first, followed by the arguments it is applied to. So we should have written $((+\ x)\ 42)$ instead of $x + 42$. Having said this, we will continue to be sloppy with notation in the interest of readability. Instead of $\lambda x \mapsto \lambda y \mapsto x + y$ we will write $\lambda x \lambda y \mapsto x + y$, or even $\lambda xy \mapsto x + y$. But you should keep in mind that all this is only syntactic sugar.

Now that we have defined our language, we also want to make precise how the outcome of function application is arrived at, i.e. what happens with an expression of form $(F\ A)$. For that, we define a reduction rule, which we actually already saw at work a bit earlier. Remember that we said that application of a function to an argument means that we substitute the parameter the function depends on by the argument. So for computing $(\lambda x.x + 42)\ 5$, we would replace x by 5 and get $5 + 42$. This is stated for the general case by the following reduction rule:

$$(\lambda x \mapsto E)\ A \to E[x := A],$$

where $E[x := A]$ means that every occurence of x in the expression E is replaced by A.

Let us walk through an example to see how to build and use functions in the lambda calculus. Consider the string *things* as being composed of the stem and the suffix: *thing*++*s*. Here ++ is string concatenation. We will see it again later, in Chapter 3. By means of abstraction we can get a function for pluralization:

$$\lambda x \mapsto x + s.$$

Applying this function to nouns gives their plural forms, as in (2.1) and (2.2).

$$(\lambda x \mapsto x + s)\ ship \quad \to \quad ships \qquad (2.1)$$
$$(\lambda x \mapsto x + s)\ dragon \quad \to \quad dragons \qquad (2.2)$$

Now we can also abstract over the plural suffix and produce a general suffixation function:

$$\lambda y \lambda x \mapsto x + y.$$

We can use this, for example, to create a function for building the past form of verb stems:

$$(\lambda y \lambda x \mapsto x + y)\ ed = \lambda x \mapsto x + ed.$$

This is way too naive, of course, but it illustrates how we can use functions. Two examples are given in (2.3) and (2.4).

$$(\lambda x \mapsto x + ed)\ walk \quad \to \quad walked \qquad (2.3)$$
$$(\lambda x \mapsto x + ed)\ laugh \quad \to \quad laughed \qquad (2.4)$$

If we are not careful, simplifying lambda expressions by means of substitution can easily produce errors. Consider, e.g., what happens when we want to simplify the following expression:

$$(\lambda y \lambda x \mapsto x + y)\ x. \qquad (2.5)$$

Note the difference between $+\!\!+$ and $+$: $+\!\!+$ expresses concatenation of strings; $+$ expresses addition of numbers.

Following the instructions given above, reduction of (2.5) will yield $\lambda x \mapsto x + x$, the function for adding a number to itself. To see why this is strange, observe that

$$(\lambda y \lambda z \mapsto z + y)\, x,$$

where the same function is applied to x, yields $\lambda z \mapsto z + x$, the function for adding x to a given number. This is what the result of application should be; the problem with $\lambda x \mapsto x + x$ is that the argument x gets *accidentally captured* by the lambda operator λx.

There are several ways to prevent accidental capture of variables. One way is to insist that bound variables are always distinct from free variables in an expression (this forbids $(\lambda y \lambda x \mapsto x + y)\, x$, for x occurs both bound and free), and that binders always bind variables that do not yet have bound occurrences (this forbids $\lambda x \mapsto ((\lambda x \mapsto x^2)\, x)$, for not all bound occurrences of x are bound by the same lambda operator). We will choose to rename variables in case they would be accidentally captured by some operation (cf. Section 4.7 for some further discussion in the context of predicate logic, and Section 7.4 for renaming variables in lambda calculus).

Up to now we applied functions only to basic objects and also abstracted only over basic objects. But function abstraction and application as defined are completely general. This means that functions can also take functions as arguments. They can even be applied to themselves. This might seem a bit arcane at first sight, but it is not. Our calculus is a purely syntactic device for building and manipulating expressions. There is no strict distinction between data – i.e. objects like numbers and strings – and functions. They all are expressions, so they can all be used to build other expressions. Hence a function like our pluralization function can also be the input to another function. Imagine we have a function $\lambda f \mapsto (f\ dragon)$. As input it takes a function and then it applies that function to the string *dragon*. To this function, we can feed the pluralization function as an argument:

$$(\lambda f \mapsto f\ dragon)\,(\lambda x \mapsto x +\!\!+ s)$$
$$\rightarrow (\lambda x \mapsto x +\!\!+ s)\ dragon$$
$$\rightarrow dragons$$

Exercise 2.13 Another example for a higher-order function is $\lambda f \lambda x \mapsto f\,(f\,x)$, which applies some function twice to some given input. Put it to work by reducing the following expression:

$$(\lambda f \lambda x \mapsto f\,(f\,x))\,(\lambda y \mapsto 1 + y).$$

Exercise 2.14 One aspect of the lambda calculus we have seen is that reductions need not come to an end but can go on infinitely. To see this, observe the reduction behaviour of the expression $(\lambda x \mapsto x\, x)\, (\lambda x \mapsto x\, x)$. And if you want things to get wilder, also look at the reduction behaviour of $(\lambda x \mapsto x\, x\, x)\, (\lambda x \mapsto x\, x\, x)$.

Let us briefly turn to natural language semantics. We can now represent the meaning of a transitive verb such as *likes* as a two-place function

$$\lambda x \lambda y \mapsto y \text{ likes } x,$$

with *likes* being the characteristic function for the relation of liking. I.e., *x likes y* would return **True** if *x* indeed likes *y*, and **False** otherwise. This is what makes formal semantics look like an exercise in typesetting. Therefore keep in mind that we do not specify the lexical meaning of a word or phrase but only with what other expressions it can combine and the role it plays in a bigger expression. This is what makes lambda calculus a suitable tool for compositional semantics: it allows us to illustrate how the semantic derivation of a sentence proceeds in accordance with the sentence's syntactic structure, as is sketched very roughly in the following tree.

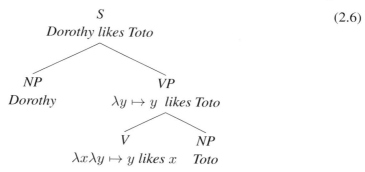

(2.6)

This way of thinking about semantic composition is pervasive in formal semantics nowadays. It goes back to the work of Richard Montague in a time when it was commonly believed to be impossible to capture the meaning of natural languages in a formal way. We will come back to this in much more detail later in the book.

2.5 Types in Grammar and Computation

With the lambda calculus above, every expression may be applied to every other expression. This way we can build a lot of terms that are not sensible at all, such as $4\,(\lambda f \mapsto f\, dragons)$, i.e. the number 4 applied to the function that maps some function *f* to its application to *dragons*. Or assume that we have an English-to-Swedish dictionary. It can be viewed as a function from English words to Swedish words. Then we might want to classify words according to the language they belong to, in order to express that it is a function that takes English words as input (which implies that you cannot look up Italian or Czech words), and that the output will be a Swedish word (which implies that you will not get a Japanese or Arabic translation).

For allowing only sensible expressions and applications, we will introduce types. Types play the role of classifying our expressions, such that we can label the expression $\lambda x \mapsto x+42$ as being a function that takes a number as input and produces a number as output.

We specify types by the following BNF rule:

$$\tau ::= b \mid (\tau \to \tau).$$

Here b is a placeholder for whatever basic types we assume, e.g. $\mathbb{Z}$ for integers. We will return to what basic types we assume a bit later in this section. The BNF specification tells us that these basic types are types, and that from them, we can build more complex types of form $\tau \to \tau$. These will be types for functions. For example, $\mathbb{Z} \to \mathbb{Z}$ would be the function type that is appropriate for the function $\lambda x \mapsto x + 42$.

Now, each lambda expression is assigned a type. This is written as $E: \tau$, standing for 'E is an expression of type τ.' The types for lambda expressions are specified as follows:

Variables: For each type τ we have variables for that type, e.g. $x: \tau$, $x': \tau$, and so on.

Abstraction: If $x: \delta$ and $E: \tau$, then $(\lambda x \mapsto E): \delta \to \tau$.

Application: If $E_1: \delta \to \tau$ and $E_2: \delta$, then $(E_1\ E_2): \tau$.

The first clause ensures that we have variables at our disposal for all types. Basic types could be e for entities and t for truth values. It is customary to use different fonts for variables of different types, e.g. $x: e$, $p: t$, $Y: e \to t$, and so on.

The second clause tells us how to type an abstraction. We would, for example, express the property of being happy as a function $\lambda x \mapsto (happy\ x)$, with x being a variable of type e. Once applied to an argument of type e, this function should return a truth-value, telling us whether the entity is happy or not. So the body of the function is of type t. According to the rule in in the second clause, the function expression is of type $e \to t$ – a function that takes an argument of type e and then returns a value of type t.

The clause for application is equally straightforward. If we apply the function $\lambda x \mapsto (happy\ x)$ of type $e \to t$ to *peter*, an object of type e, this application will have type t.

Exercise 2.15 Assign types to the lambda expressions in example (2.6) on page 27.

Exercise 2.16 What about the term $(\lambda x \mapsto x\ x)\ (\lambda x \mapsto x\ x)$ from exercise 2.14 above? Can you find a type for it?

In programming, types are a way of grouping similar values, like numbers, strings, etc. The general typing scheme for a function is

$$f \ :: \ a \ -> \ b$$

Here, a -> b is the type of f, where f is a program (or: instruction) that defines the function. The types we will encounter in Haskell are basic types denoted by the type constants Int (the type of integers), Bool (the type of truth-values), Char (the type of characters), as well as type variables a,b, ..., which stand for arbitrary types, list types [a], and function types a -> b. For example, f :: a -> Bool reads as 'for all types a, f is an instruction for a function that takes a value of type a and returns a Boolean value'. We will get to know them better as we move along. Moreover, Haskell allows user-defined data types, which are very useful and which we will look at in more detail in section 3.13.

Types in the lambda calculus and in programming actually have a lot in common with syntactic categories in grammars. For example, basic types can be thought of as corresponding to terminal categories in phrase-structure grammars, like NP for noun phrases. They categorize expressions that are, in some sense, complete, and that constitute the primary bearers of meaning. Function types, on the other hand, categorize incomplete expressions like verb phrases. Their meaning is derivative in the sense that it consists in their contribution to the meaning of the expressions they appear in.

Consider the following very simple phrase-structure rule.

$$\mathbf{S} \longrightarrow \mathbf{NP \ VP}$$

Reading it from right to left, it says that given an expression of category NP and an expression of category VP, we can form an expression of category S. If we think of the categories as types, we can read the rule as follows: If a: NP and b: VP, then $a \mathbin{+\!\!\!+} b$: S. That is, if we have an expression a of type NP and an expression b of type VP, then their concatenation $a \mathbin{+\!\!\!+} b$ is of type S.

An approach to grammars from this point of view is categorial grammar, which, in its simplest form, goes back to the Polish logician Kazimierz Ajdukiewicz. It captures the same information as phrase-structure rules by assigning function types to grammatical expressions. For example, a VP would be of type NP $\rightarrow$ S, i.e. the type of a function that takes something of type NP as input and gives something of type S as output. In other words, a VP is an expression that combines with an expression of type NP and then yields and expression of type S. Accordingly, the type of a transitive verb would be NP $\rightarrow$ (NP $\rightarrow$ S), i.e. a transitive verb is an expression that combines with two expressions of type NP and produces an expression of type S.

For combining expressions, we have the general rule that an expression of category A can combine with an expression of category $A \to B$ into an expression of category B. Thus, a simple derivation of the sentence in (2.6) looks as follows.

$$Dorothy_{\text{NP}} + (likes_{\text{NP} \to (\text{NP} \to \text{S})} + Toto_{\text{NP}})$$
$$= Dorothy_{\text{NP}} + (\ likes\ Toto)_{\text{NP} \to \text{S}}$$
$$= (\ Dorothy\ likes\ Toto)_{\text{S}}$$

Exercise 2.17 Adjectives are words that combine with nouns to form complex nouns. For example, *friendly* combines with the noun *wizard* to form the noun *friendly wizard*. So, adjectives are of type $N \to N$.

$$friendly_{\text{N} \to \text{N}} + wizard_{\text{N}} = (\ friendly\ wizard)_{\text{N}}$$

Find a type for the adverbial *very*, such that we can build expressions like *very friendly wizard* and *very very friendly wizard*. (Hint: assume these expressions are structured as *(very friendly) wizard* and *(very (very friendly)) wizard*.)

2.6 Functional Programming

Programs and subroutines within programs are actually very similar to functions. They take parameters as arguments and return a result. For example, a program for calculating the prime factors of some number takes an integer as input and returns a list of integers. The difference to functions, however, is that programs can have side effects. Side effects are changes in the state of the system besides the output that the function returns and that remain after the procedure has returned. They can consist in a change of variable names, in writing some intermediate result to a database, and so on. For example, the Ruby program

```
x = 4 ; x += 2
```

first assigns the value 4 to the variable x, then changes this assignment to $x + 2$. So after execution of the program the variable x evaluates to 6.

There are basically two things about computation: the evaluation of an expression and the change of state that this evaluation brings about. Imperative programming focuses on the state and how to modify it with a sequence of commands. In contrast to this, declarative programming focuses on the evaluation itself. In the case of functional programming, computation corresponds to the evaluation of functions. This becomes clear already by looking at the basic syntax of Haskell:

$$E ::= x \mid E\ E \mid \lambda x \to E \mid \texttt{let}\ x = E\ \texttt{in}\ E.$$

It is not by accident that it looks a lot like the syntax of lambda calculus. Indeed, functional programming languages actually are lambda calculi, though usually more sophisticated than the one we saw earlier.

Now, what does all this have to do with natural language analysis? There are at least two ways to answer this. The very straightforward answer is that we want to automatize the association of natural language expressions with semantic representations, and that lambda calculus happens to be a suitable tool for combining semantic representations. Since Haskell basically is an executable lambda calculus, functional programming is a very useful tool to implement formal semantics. The way from theory to implementation is short and easy. Usually it is quite straightforward to translate a piece of natural language analysis into Haskell code. This is not only of great use for writing an implementation but also for reflecting on the analysis itself.

Another way of connecting functional programming and linguistic theory goes far beyond practical reasons. It claims that once we formalized natural languages, they can actually be seen as programming languages themselves: they form a collection of instructions on how to build complex expressions from simple ones along with their meaning. And just as side effects in programming are state changes that reach beyond the functional core, linguistic phenomena defying compositionality can be seen as side effects of the computation of meaning. This analogy opens the door for using insights from programming language theory for handling non-compositional phenomena in natural language semantics; it is executed by Chung-chieh Shan in his dissertation [Sha05]. We will see more on this perspective in Chapter 11.

The best way of learning is still by doing, for as the common saying goes: semantics is not a spectator sport. That's why we will give you an introduction to Haskell and then right away dive into implementing fragments. But before doing so, let us again emphasize the gist of this chapter and the reason for doing computational semantics with Haskell: reducing expressions in lambda calculus, evaluating a program (i.e. function) in Haskell, and composing the meaning of a natural language sentence are, in a way, all the same thing.

2.7 Further reading

An illuminating introduction to the lambda calculus is [BB00]. The standard reference is [Bar84]. [Han04] is a textbook that stresses the practical applications of lambda calculus. Earlier work in computational semantics for natural language typically uses Prolog as a computational tool. See [Als92] for a description of an influential full-fledged computational engine written in Prolog. The standard – and truly excellent – textbook for Prolog-based computational semantics is [BB05]. An early plea for functional programming as a tool for natural language interpretation is [FL89], and a recent survey of natural language processing with lazy functional programming is [Fro06].

3

Functional Programming with Haskell

Summary

In this chapter we introduce the computational toolset that we are going to use throughout the book: the programming language Haskell. No prior knowledge of programming is assumed; you will learn everything you need to know about Haskell and (functional) programming as we go along.

3.1 The Programming Language Haskell

As a functional programming language, Haskell is a member of the Lisp family, as are Scheme, ML, Occam, Clean, and Erlang. It was designed to form a standard for functional programming languages and was named after the mathematician and logician Haskell B. Curry. We already mentioned that it is based on the lambda calculus, just like the other family members. In fact, Haskell is so faithful to its origins that it is purely functional, i.e. functions in Haskell do not have any side effects. (However, there is a way to perform computations with side effects, like change of state, in a purely functional fashion. We will come across this later on in the book, but it will not be of concern for us now.)

Three very important characteristic features of Haskell are the following. First, functions are first-class citizens. This means that functions may be passed as arguments to other functions and also can be returned as the result of some function. Second, functions are permitted to be recursive. The significance of this we will see in Section 3.5. And third, arguments of functions are only evaluated when needed, if at all. This is called *lazy evaluation* and it allows the use of infinite and partially-defined data structures. We will see some examples of infinite lists in Section 3.6.

33

3.2 Using the Book Code

In order to run the programs in this book, you need a so-called *interpreter* or *compiler*. An interpreter is a system that allows you to execute function definitions interactively. The two most widely used for Haskell are *Hugs* and *GHCi*. The former can be downloaded from `http://haskell.org/hugs/`, and the latter comes with the *Glasgow Haskell Compiler* (GHC), which can be found at `http://haskell.org/ghc/` and at `http://hackage.haskell.org/platform/`. Both Hugs and GHCi will cater for your needs. GHCi is slowly but surely becoming the standard, but it may be a good idea to install both, for the two interpreters give slightly different error messages, and if the feedback of one interpreter baffles you, the other one may give you a better hint. If the error messages of both Hugs or GHCi confuse you, you might want to try *Helium*, a Haskell interpreter designed for learning Haskell, with better error messages than either Hugs or GHCi. See `http://www.cs.uu.nl/helium/`. (But be aware that it does not yet support all Haskell features that we will use in this book.)

Haskell code will be typeset in frames, in `dark grey typewriter` font. It constitutes the chapter modules, with exception of code that defines functions that are already predefined by the Haskell system or somewhere else in the chapter. This code defined elsewhere is shaded `light grey`. Typewriter font is also used for pieces of interaction with the Haskell interpreter, but these illustrations are not framed.

Subparts of bigger programs are usually collected in modules, each of which sits in an own file. This way you can easily use old code when writing new programs. The following lines declare the Haskell module for the code of this chapter. This module is called FPH.

```
module FPH

where

import Data.List
import Data.Char
```

We import the predefined modules `List` and `Char`, which provide useful functions for handling lists and characters as well as strings. The `Data` in front of the module names serves to indicate the place of these modules in Haskell's module hierarchy. The effect of the imports is that the functions defined in the imported modules become available for use as ingredients in the functions that we want to define ourselves. All the book source and chapter modules can be found at the book website: `http://www.computational-semantics.eu`.

3.3 First Experiments

We assume that you succeeded in retrieving a Haskell interpreter and that you managed to install it on your computer. When you start it, you will get a prompt that looks as follows in the case of Hugs:

```
Prelude>
```

or

```
Hugs.Base>
```

And like this in the case of GHCi and Helium:

```
Prelude>
```

This string is the prompt when no user-defined files are loaded. If this prompt is shown, only the predefined functions from the Haskell Prelude are available; these definitions are given in the online Haskell report.† If you want to quickly learn a lot about how to program in Haskell, you should get into the habit of consulting this file regularly. The definitions of all the standard operations are open source code, and are there for you to learn from. The Haskell Prelude may be a bit difficult to read at first, but you will soon get used to the syntax.

Online user manuals for Hugs and GHCi can be found on the Internet.‡ The most important commands to know in the beginning are:

- `:l` ⟨ *file name* ⟩ for loading a file or module
- `:r` for reloading the currently loaded file
- `:t` ⟨ *expression* ⟩ for displaying the type of an expression
- `:q` for quitting the interpreter.

You can use the interpreter as a calculator. Let's calculate the number of seconds in a leap year. A leap year has 366 days, each day has 24 hours, each hour has 60 minutes, and each minute has 60 seconds, so this is what we get:

```
Prelude> 366 * 24 * 60 * 60
31622400
```

† `http://www.haskell.org/onlinereport/standard-Prelude.html`
‡ At `http://cvs.haskell.org/Hugs/pages/hugsman/index.html` for Hugs, and at `http://www.haskell.org/ghc/docs/latest/html/users_guide/ghci.html` for GHCi.

Exercise 3.1 Try out a few calculations using ∗ for multiplication, + for addition, − for subtraction, ^ for exponentiation, / for division. By playing with the system, find out what the precedence order is among these operators.

Parentheses can be used to override the built-in operator precedences:

```
Prelude> (2 + 3)^4
625
```

Exercise 3.2 How much is 2^3^4? Does the interpreter read this as (2^3)^4 or as 2^(3^4)?

We can also define our own functions. We use a function `square`, after having told the interpreter what we mean by it, using the reserved keywords `let` and `in`:

```
Prelude> let square x = x * x in square 3
9
```

We could also write the square function by means of lambda abstraction and simply apply this lambda expression to the desired argument.

```
Prelude> (\ x -> x * x) 4
16
```

Usually, however, we define functions not in a single line at the prompt but in a module in a text file, and we give them names and proper type declarations. The definition of the square function could be the following piece of text in a file (in fact, the following lines are part of the code of the Chapter module, which you can find as `FPH.hs` on the book website):

```
square :: Int -> Int
square x = x * x
```

The intention is that variable x stands proxy for a number of type `Int`. The result, the squared number, also has type `Int`. The function `square` is a function that, when combined with an argument of type `Int`, yields a value of type `Int`. This is precisely what the type indication `Int -> Int` expresses.

In Haskell it is not strictly necessary to always give explicit type declarations. For instance, the definition of `square` would also work without the type declaration, since the system can infer the type from the definition. However, it is good programming practice to give explicit type declarations even when this is not strictly necessary. These type declarations are an aid to understanding, and they greatly improve the digestibility of functional programs for human readers. Moreover, by writing down the intended type of a function you constrain what you can implement, for you rule out all definitions that take arguments or yield values that do not agree with the type declaration. If you try to write a definition with such a type conflict, the interpreter will immediately reject it.

To load and use the chapter code, simply start up the interpreter with hugs FPH or ghci FPH, or explicitly load the module with :1 FPH.

```
Prelude> :1 FPH
FPH> square 7
49
FPH> square (-3)
9
FPH> square (square 7)
2401
FPH> square (square (square 7))
5764801
```

Let us briefly look at three other types that we are going to use quite often: types for characters and strings, and the so-called Boolean type. The Haskell type of characters is Char. Strings of characters have type String, which is an abbreviation for [Char], a list of characters. Similarly, lists of integers have type [Int]. The empty string (or the empty list) is []. Examples of characters are 'a', 'b' (note the single quotes) and an example of a string is "Hello World!" (note the double quotes). In fact, "Hello World!" can be seen as an abbreviation of the following character list:

```
['H','e','l','l','o',' ','W','o','r','l','d','!']
```

This in turn can be seen as shorthand for the result of putting 'H' in front of the list that results from putting 'e' in front of the list ... in front of the list that results from putting '!' in front of the empty list, as follows:

```
'H':'e':'l':'l':'o':' ':'w':'o':'r':'l':'d':'!':[]
```

Exercise 3.3 The colon : in the last example is an operator. Can you see what its type is?

Since strings have type String, properties of strings have type String -> Bool. (Recall that properties are unary relations, which can be seen as characteristic functions of sets, i.e. functions from elements of the set to truth values.) ' Here is a simple property, the property of being a word that contains an 'h':

```
hword :: String -> Bool
hword []    = False
hword (x:xs) = (x == 'h') || (hword xs)
```

This definition uses *pattern matching*: (x:xs) is the prototypical non-empty list. More on this in Sections 3.6 and 3.13 below.

What the definition of hword says is that the empty string is not an hword, and a non-empty string is an hword if either the head of the string is the character h, or the tail of the string is an hword. Note that the function hword is called again from the body of its own definition. We will encounter such *recursive* function definitions again and again in the course of this book.

As you can see, characters are indicated in Haskell with single quotes. The following calls to the definition show that strings are indicated with double quotes:

```
FPH> hword "shrimptoast"
True
FPH> hword "antiquing"
False
```

The type Bool of Booleans (so-called after George Boole) consists of the two truth-values True and False. If we say that an expression is of type Boolean, we mean that the expression is either true or false, i.e. that it denotes a truth value. Boolean expressions can be combined with the logical operators for negation, conjunction, and disjunction. Here are the Haskell versions:

- Conjunction is &&.
- Disjunction is ||.
- Negation is not.

The type of negation is Bool -> Bool. The types of the prefix versions of conjunction and disjunction are given by:

- (&&) :: Bool -> Bool -> Bool.
- (||) :: Bool -> Bool -> Bool.

Note that the parentheses ( ) change an infix operator into a prefix operator. To express 'bright and beautiful' in Haskell, we can either say bright && beautiful or (&&) bright beautiful. In general, if op is an infix operator, (op) is the prefix version of the operator. Thus, 2^10 can also be written as (^) 2 10. In general, if op is an infix operator, (op x) is the operation resulting from applying op to its right hand side argument, (x op) is the operation resulting from applying op to its left hand side argument, and (op) is the prefix version of the operator (this is like the abstraction of the operator from both arguments). Thus (^2) is the squaring operation, (2^) is the operation that computes powers of 2, and (^) is exponentiation. Functions like these are called *sections*.

Exercise 3.4 Which property does (>3) denote? And which property does (3>) denote?

We can also change a prefix operator into an infix operator by using backticks. As an example, assume we define a function `plus x y = x + y`. Instead of calling it with `plus 2 3`, we can also call it with `2 ʻplusʻ 3`. We will use backticks very often with the function `elem`, introduced in Section 3.9 below.

3.4 Type Polymorphism

One of Haskell's characteristics is a polymorphic type system. For example, the Haskell Prelude contains the following definition of the identity function:

```
id :: a -> a
id x = x
```

This function can be applied to objects of any type. Applied to an argument, it just returns that argument. Since the type of the argument does not matter, we say that the `id` function is *polymorphic*. In the type declaration of `id`, a is a type variable. The use of a indicates that any type will fit. So, instances of `id`'s type are `Bool -> Bool, Int -> Int, String -> String`, but also

`(String -> Bool) -> (String -> Bool)`

and so on.

```
FPH> id 42
42
FPH> id "Jabberwocky"
"Jabberwocky"
FPH> (id hword) "Jabberwocky"
False
```

Type polymorphism, and the use of a, b as type variables, allow us to define polymorphic types for properties and relations. The polymorphic type of a property is `a -> Bool`. The polymorphic type of a relation is `a -> b -> Bool`. The polymorphic type of a relation over a single type is `a -> a -> Bool`.

If a is a type, `[a]` is the type of lists over a. Since it does not matter which type a is, `[a]` is a polymorphic type. The type of the concatenation function `(++)` illustrates this:

```
FPH> :t (++)
(++) :: [a] -> [a] -> [a]
```

The type indicates that `(++)` not only concatenates strings. It works for lists in general.

```
FPH> [2,3] ++ [4,7]
[2,3,4,7]
FPH> "Hello " ++ "world!"
"Hello world!"
```

3.5 Recursion

Point your webcam at your computer screen. What do you see? A computer screen, with on it a picture of a computer screen, with on it .... This is an example of *recursion*.

A recursive definition is a definition that refers to itself, while avoiding an infinite regress. Let us make this precise for the case of the recursive screen picture. A screen picture is either (i) a tiny blob showing nothing, or (ii) a screen showing a screen picture. The case of the tiny blob showing nothing is the base case. The case of the screen showing a screen picture is the recursive case.

Definition by recursion is important in mathematics, programming, and linguistics. A recursive function is a function that calls itself, but without infinite regress. To ensure that the recursion will eventually stop, we have to give a base case, a case that can be computed without calling the function. Keep in mind that recursive definitions always have a base case. As an example for recursion, recall Exercise 1.2. Here is a Haskell version.

```
gen :: Int -> String
gen 0 = "Sentences can go on"
gen n = gen (n-1) ++ " and on"

genS :: Int -> String
genS n = gen n ++ "."
```

The following storytelling function gives another example of recursion.

```
story :: Int -> String
story 0 =
 "Let's cook and eat that final missionary, and off to bed."
story k =
 "The night was pitch dark, mysterious and deep.\n"
 ++ "Ten cannibals were seated around a boiling cauldron.\n"
 ++ "Their leader got up and addressed them like this:\n'"
 ++ story (k-1) ++ "'"
```

Line ends are encoded as \n. This is the linefeed control character. To display the story on the screen we will use an output function that executes the linefeeds: putStrLn. To loop the function story five times, we say

```
FPH> putStrLn (story 5)
```

Exercise 3.5 What happens if you ask for putStrLn (story (-1))? Why?

Exercise 3.6 Why is the definition of 'GNU' as 'GNU's Not Unix' not a recursive definition?

3.6 List Types and List Comprehension

An important operation is :, which prepends an element to a list.

```
FPH> :t (:)
(:) :: a -> [a] -> [a]
```

Note that the type of (:) is more general than you probably guessed when you answered Exercise 3.3. There, we talked about combining a character with a string to produce a new string. Here, we talk about combining an element of any type whatsoever (call it a) with a list of elements of that same type into a new list of elements of that type.

The expression (x:xs) is used to denote the prototypical non-empty list. The *head* of (x:xs) is the element x of type a, the *tail* is the list xs of type [a]. According functions are defined in the Haskell Prelude as follows:

```
head :: [a] -> a
head (x:_) = x

tail :: [a] -> [a]
tail (_:xs) = xs
```

The underscores _ indicate anonymous variables that can be matched by anything of the right type. Thus, in (x:_), the underscore _ matches any list, and in (_:xs), the underscore _ matches any object. The important list patterns for pattern matching are:

- the list pattern [] matches only the empty list,
- the list pattern [x] matches any singleton list,
- the list pattern (x:xs) matches any non-empty list.

These patterns are used again and again in recursive definitions over list types.

It is common Haskell practice to refer to non-empty lists as x:xs, y:ys, and so on, as a useful reminder of the facts that x is an element of a list of x's and that xs is a list.

Lists in computer science are an approximation of the mathematical notion of a set. The important differences are that multiplicity (whether a certain element occurs once or more than once) matters for lists but not for sets, and that order of occurrence matters for lists but not for sets. Two sets that contain the same elements are the same, but not so for lists. The sets $\{1, 2\}$, $\{2, 1\}$, and $\{1, 1, 2\}$ are all identical, but the lists [1,2], [2,1], and [1,1,2] are all different.

Lists can also be given by not enumerating all their elements but by indicating the range of elements: [n..m] is the list bounded below by n and above by m. For example, the list [1..423] are all numbers from 1 to 423, and the list ['g'..'s'] are all characters from g to s. Of course, it only works for objects that are ordered in a way that Haskell knows. In general, the ordered types are the types in class Ord. The data types in this class are the types on which functions <= (less than or equal), >= (greater than or equal), < (less than), and > (greater than) are defined.

Predefined instances of class Ord are numerical types and characters. (For more on type classes, see Section 3.9.)

By use of .., we can also work with infinite lists, e.g. [0..] denotes the list of all positive natural numbers. When keying in [0..] at the interpreter system prompt, the interpreter will start printing the list of all natural numbers starting from 0. This display will go on until you abort it with *Ctrl-c* or your computer runs out of memory, for Haskell knows arbitrary size integers.

Infinite lists are where lazy evaluation matters. Since Haskell does not evaluate an argument unless it needs it, it can handle infinite lists as long as it has to compute only a finite amount of its elements. If you, for example, ask for take 5 [0..], the interpreter will only consider the first five elements of the infinite list of natural numbers and give you [0,1,2,3,4].

And there is yet another way to form lists, which is analogous to set comprehension. The latter says that if A is a set and P is a property, then $\{x \mid x \in A,\ P(x)\}$ is the set of all objects from A that satisfy P. *List comprehension* is the list counterpart of that; it is written as [x | x <- A, P x]. Here are some examples:

```
FPH> [ n | n <- [0..10], odd n ]
[1,3,5,7,9]
FPH> [ odd n | n <- [0..10] ]
[False,True,False,True,False,True,False,True,False,True,False]
FPH> [ square n | n <- [0..10] ]
[0,1,4,9,16,25,36,49,64,81,100]
```

```
FPH> [ x ++ y | x <- ["use","faith"], y <- ["ful","less"] ]
["useful","useless","faithful","faithless"]
```

3.7 List processing with map and filter

The function map takes a function and a list and returns a list containing the results of applying the function to the individual list members. Thus, if f is a function of type a -> b and xs is a list of type [a], then map f xs will return a list of type [b].

```
map :: (a -> b) -> [a] -> [b]
map f [] = []
map f (x:xs) = (f x) : map f xs
```

For example, map (+ 1) [0..9] will add 1 to each number in [0..9], so it will give the list of numbers from 1 to 10. Another example is the following one:

```
FPH> map ("un" ++) ["friendly","believable"]
["unfriendly","unbelievable"]
```

Accordingly, map hword will produce a list of truth values.

```
FPH> map hword ["fish","and","chips"]
[True,False,True]
```

The filter function takes a property and a list, and returns the sublist of all list elements satisfying the property. It has the type (a -> Bool) -> [a] -> [a]. Here a again denotes an arbitrary type. Indeed, one can filtrate strings, or lists of integers, or lists of whatever, given a property of the right type: String -> Bool for strings, Int -> Bool for integers, and so on. Here is the definition of the filter function:

```
filter :: (a -> Bool) -> [a] -> [a]
filter p [] = []
filter p (x:xs) | p x       = x : filter p xs
                | otherwise = filter p xs
```

A new programming element is the use of *guarded equations* by means of the Haskell condition operator |. A definition with a list of guarded equations such as

```
foo t | condition_1 = body_1
      | condition_2 = body_2
      | otherwise   = body_3
```

is read as follows:

- in case `condition_1` holds, `foo t` is by definition equal to `body_1`,
- in case `condition_1` does not hold but `condition_2` holds, `foo t` is by definition equal to `body_2`,
- and in case none of `condition_1` and `condition_2` hold, `foo t` is by definition equal to `body_3`.

Of course, you can specify as many conditions as you want to.

The first line of the definition of `filter p (x:xs)` handles the case where the head of the list `(x:xs)` satisfies property p. The second line applies otherwise, i.e. it covers the case where the head of the list `(x:xs)` does not satisfy property p.

The `filter` function can be applied as follows:

```
FPH> filter even [1..10]
[2,4,6,8,10]
FPH> filter hword ["fish","and","chips"]
["fish","chips"]
```

3.8 Function Composition, Conjunction, Disjunction, Quantification

In Section 2.3 of the previous chapter, we introduced function composition. We wrote $f \cdot g$ for the composition of the two functions f and g, i.e. for applying f after g. To illustrate this again, assume that we have a Dutch-to-English dictionary and an English-to-French dictionary. These can be viewed as a function g for translating Dutch words into English words, and a function f for translating English words into French words. E.g. $g(haas)$ will give *hare*, and $f(ant)$ will give *fourmi*. Now we can simply combine the two dictionaries into a Dutch-to-French dictionary by first looking up the meaning of a Dutch word in English, and then look up the French meaning of the result. Thus, if we want to know the French word for Dutch *haas*, we first find $g(haas) = hare$, and next, $f(hare) = lièvre$.

Composing two functions f and g means that f is applied to the result of g: $(f \cdot g)(x) = f(g(x))$. In Haskell, we use the operator `(.)` instead of $\cdot$ and write `f . g`. For that to make sense, the result type of g should equal the argument type of f, i.e. if `f :: b -> c`, then `g :: a -> b`. Under this typing, the type of `f . g` is `a -> c`. This is used, for example, in the Haskell Prelude to define odd as `not . even`.

Thus, the operator `(.)` that composes two functions has the following type and definition:

```
(.) :: (b -> c) -> (a -> b) -> a -> c
(f . g) x = f (g x)
```

In Section 3.3 we saw the Haskell versions of && and || of the logical operators conjunction and disjunction. The conjunction operator && is generalized to lists of Booleans by the predefined function and.

```
and ::  [Bool] -> Bool
and []      = True
and (x:xs) = x && (and xs)
```

And the disjunction operator || is generalized to lists of Booleans by the prede-fined function or.

```
or ::  [Bool] -> Bool
or []      = False
or (x:xs) = x || (or xs)
```

These generalized Boolean operations are used for stating the definitions of the list quantification operators any and all (these are also predefined in the Haskell Prelude):

```
any, all  :: (a -> Bool) -> [a] -> Bool
any p = or  . map p
all p = and . map p
```

They can be used for checking whether all elements of a list satisfy a property, or any elements of the list, respectively.

```
FPH> all hword ["fish","and","chips"]
False
FPH> any hword ["fish","and","chips"]
True
```

3.9 Type Classes

Consider the function (\ x y -> x /= y). At first sight, this is just a check for inequality. Let us check its type.

Exercise 3.7 Check the type of the function (\ x y -> x /= y) in Haskell. What do you expect? What do you get? Can you explain what you get?

Exercise 3.8 Is there a difference between (\ x y -> x /= y) and (/=)?

Exercise 3.9 Check the type of the function composition all . (/=). If you were to give this function a name, what name would be appropriate?

Exercise 3.10 Check the type of the function composition any . (==). If you were to give this function a name, what name would be appropriate?

The exercises show that the Haskell interpreter puts a constraint on the types of all functions that somehow involve equality or inequality. Why is this? Because not all types of things are testable for equality. Numbers and strings are examples of types that can be tested for equality, but functions generally are not.

Exercise 3.11 How would you go about testing two infinite strings for equality?

The predefined Haskell functions elem and notElem that check whether an object is an element of a list are only defined for types that allow for equality tests. They have type Eq a => a -> [a] -> Bool. In this type specification, Eq a => specifies a as a type in the Eq class, i.e. as a type for which equality (==) and inequality (/=) are defined. Here is what happens if you try to use elem with a function:

```
FPH> elem not [not]
ERROR - Cannot infer instance
*** Instance    : Eq (Bool -> Bool)
*** Expression  : not 'elem' [not]
```

Let us look at another type constraint. The predefined Haskell function min computes the minimum of two objects. If we check its type, we find that it is min :: Ord a => a -> a -> a. It indicates that a is constrained to be a type for which 'less than' and 'less than or equal' are defined (Haskell (<) and (<=)).

We can also have types that have more than one constraint. Constraints are combined by means of parentheses: (Eq a,Ord a) => a is the class of types for which equality and an ordering are defined, and so on.

Exercise 3.12 Use min to define a function minList :: Ord a => [a] -> a for computing the minimum of a non-empty list.

Exercise 3.13 Define a function delete that removes an occurrence of an object x from a list of objects in class Eq. If x does not occur in the list, the list remains unchanged. If x occurs more than once, only the first occurrence is deleted.

How would you need to change delete in order to delete every occurence of x?

Now we can define a function `srt` that sorts a list of objects (in class `Ord`, i.e., in a class for which (<) and (<=) are defined) in order of increasing size, by means of the following algorithm:

- An empty list is already sorted.
- If a list is non-empty, we put its minimum in front of the result of sorting the list that results from removing its minimum.

Note that this sorting procedure can be viewed as a kind of dual to insertion sort (where you sort by going through a list and construct a new, sorted list by inserting each item from the old list at the correct position in the new list). The implementation is an exercise for you.

Exercise 3.14 Define a function `srt :: Ord a => [a] -> [a]` that implements the above. Use the function `minList` from Exercise 3.12.

Another type class, that we will use very often throughout the book, is `Show`. It contains all types that can be printed on the screen. We will see some usage of it in Section 3.13.

3.10 Strings and Texts

Consider the following differences:

```
Prelude> "Hello World!"
"Hello World!"
Prelude> putStr "Hello World!"
Hello World!
Prelude> show "Hello World!"
"\"Hello World!\""
```

The double quotes " and " serve to indicate that what is between them is a string. The command `putStr` displays its string argument, but without the enclosing double quotes. The command `show` quotes its argument, by putting double quotes around it, and treating the inner quotes as part of the string. These inner quotes have changed function from string markers to characters. The double quote character is a so-called escaped "; it is rendered in Haskell as \".

In Section 3.5 we saw Haskell's linefeed character \n. The following example shows how `putStr` executes linefeeds:

```
FPH> putStr "Hello\nWorld!"
Hello
World!
```

Exercise 3.15 Try to figure out what the following Haskell program does, without actually running it. Next, save the program in a file xxx.hs, and run it as a script, by means of the command runhugs xxx.hs or runghc xxx.hs, from the command prompt, to check your guess. If you run a Haskell program as a script, its main function will get executed.

```
main = putStrLn (s ++ show s)
  where s = "main = putStrLn (s ++ show s) \n  where s = "
```

Our next example for manipulating strings is a program reversal for the reversal of a string, which is of type String -> String. The instruction for reversal explains how lists of characters are reversed. A useful description is the following:

- For reversing the empty string, you have to do nothing (the reversal of the empty string is the empty string).

- For reversing a string consisting of a first element x followed by a tail, first reverse the tail, and next put x at the end of the result of that.

We can render this string reversal instruction in Haskell as the following function (not the most efficient implementation, but effiency does not concern us here):

```
reversal :: String -> String
reversal []    = []
reversal (x:t) = reversal t ++ [x]
```

You can try this out, as follows:

```
FPH> reversal "Chomsky"
"yksmohC"
FPH> reversal (reversal "Chomsky")
"Chomsky"
```

Next, we want to consider some examples of shallow text processing, using two of Shakespeare's sonnets as text material.

```
sonnet18 =
  "Shall I compare thee to a summer's day? \n"
  ++ "Thou art more lovely and more temperate: \n"
  ++ "Rough winds do shake the darling buds of May, \n"
  ++ "And summer's lease hath all too short a date: \n"
  ++ "Sometime too hot the eye of heaven shines, \n"
  ++ "And often is his gold complexion dimm'd; \n"
  ++ "And every fair from fair sometime declines, \n"
  ++ "By chance or nature's changing course untrimm'd; \n"
  ++ "But thy eternal summer shall not fade \n"
  ++ "Nor lose possession of that fair thou owest; \n"
  ++ "Nor shall Death brag thou wander'st in his shade, \n"
  ++ "When in eternal lines to time thou growest: \n"
  ++ "  So long as men can breathe or eyes can see, \n"
  ++ "  So long lives this and this gives life to thee."
```

```
sonnet73 =
  "That time of year thou mayst in me behold\n"
  ++ "When yellow leaves, or none, or few, do hang\n"
  ++ "Upon those boughs which shake against the cold,\n"
  ++ "Bare ruin'd choirs, where late the sweet birds sang.\n"
  ++ "In me thou seest the twilight of such day\n"
  ++ "As after sunset fadeth in the west,\n"
  ++ "Which by and by black night doth take away,\n"
  ++ "Death's second self, that seals up all in rest.\n"
  ++ "In me thou see'st the glowing of such fire\n"
  ++ "That on the ashes of his youth doth lie,\n"
  ++ "As the death-bed whereon it must expire\n"
  ++ "Consumed with that which it was nourish'd by.\n"
  ++ "This thou perceivest, which makes thy love more strong,\n"
  ++ "To love that well which thou must leave ere long."
```

To split a string consisting of several lines separated by linefeed characters, use
`lines sonnet73`. This function creates a list of strings.

We will now develop a simple counting tool, for counting characters and words
in a piece of text. Instead of defining two different counting functions, one for
words and one for text, it is more convenient to define a single polymorphic func-

tion that can count any data type for which equality tests are possible, i.e. which
are in class Eq.

The counting function we are after has type Eq a => a -> [a] -> Int. What
this means is that for any type a that is an instance of the Eq class, the function has
type a -> [a] -> Int.

We should be able to use count for counting the number of 'e' characters in the
string "temperate", for counting the number of "thou" occurrences in Sonnet
18, and so on.

We define count as the following straightforward function.

```
count :: Eq a => a -> [a] -> Int
count x []                     = 0
count x (y:ys) | x == y    = succ (count x ys)
               | otherwise = count x ys
```

Here are examples of using the count function, employing the predefined functions toLower for converting characters to lowercase, and words for splitting lines
into words. You should check out their definitions in the Haskell Prelude.

```
FPH> count 'e' sonnet18
63
FPH> [ count x (map toLower sonnet18) | x <- ['a'..'w'] ]
[40,5,9,20,63,10,10,31,27,0,1,23,23,33,44,4,0,29,42,40,13,5,5]
FPH> count "thou" (words sonnet18)
3
FPH> count "thou" (words (map toLower sonnet18))
4
```

Here is a function that calculates the average of a list of integers: the average of
m and n is given by $\frac{m+n}{2}$; the average of a list of k integers $n_1, \ldots, n_k$ is given by
$\frac{n_1 + \cdots + n_k}{k}$. In general, averages are fractions, so the result type of average should
not be Int but the Haskell data type for fractional numbers, which is Rational.
There are predefined functions sum for the sum of a list of integers, and length
for the length of a list. The Haskell operation for division / expects arguments
of type Rational (or, more precisely, of a type in the class Fractional, and
Rational is in that class), so we need a conversion function for converting Ints
into Rationals. This is done by toRational. The function average can now be
written as:

```
average :: [Int] -> Rational
average [] = error "empty list"
average xs = toRational (sum xs) / toRational (length xs)
```

Haskell allows a call to the `error` operation in any definition. This is used to break off operation and issue an appropriate message when `average` is applied to an empty list. Note that `error` has a parameter of type `String`.

Exercise 3.16 Write a function to compute the average word length in Shakespeare's sonnets 18 and 73. You can use `filter (`notElem` "?;:,.")` to get rid of the interpunction signs. The predefined function `length` (from the `List` module) gives the length of a list.

Suppose we want to check whether a list `xs1` is a prefix of a list `xs2`. Then the answer to the question `prefix xs1 xs2` should be either yes (true) or no (false), i.e. the type declaration for `prefix` should be:

$$\text{prefix} :: \text{Eq a} => [a] ->[a] -> \text{Bool}.$$

Prefixes of a list `ys` are defined as follows:

- $[\,]$ is a prefix of `ys`.
- If `xs` is a prefix of `ys`, then `x:xs` is a prefix of `x:ys`.
- Nothing else is a prefix of `ys`.

Here is the code for `prefix` that implements this definition:

```
prefix :: Eq a => [a] -> [a] -> Bool
prefix []      ys       = True
prefix (x:xs) []       = False
prefix (x:xs) (y:ys) = (x==y) && prefix xs ys
```

Exercise 3.17 Write a function `sublist` that checks whether `xs1` is a sublist of `xs2`. The type declaration should be:

$$\text{sublist} :: \text{Eq a} => [a] -> [a] -> \text{Bool}.$$

The sublists of an arbitrary list `ys` are given by:

(1) If `xs` is a prefix of `ys`, `xs` is a sublist of `ys`.
(2) If `ys` equals `y:ys'` and `xs` is a sublist of `ys'`, `xs` is a sublist of `ys`.
(3) Nothing else is a sublist of `ys`.

In order to remove duplicates from a list, the items in the list have to belong to a type in the Eq class, the class of data types for which (==) is defined. It is standard to call the function for duplicate removal nub:

```
nub :: Eq a => [a] -> [a]
nub []     = []
nub (x:xs) = x : nub (filter (\ y -> (y /= x)) xs)
```

The code below uses the built-in Haskell function sort (from the List module); sort xs sorts the list xs in increasing order. The code provides utilities for analysing Shakespeare's sonnets. cnt sonnet18 will give a word count for the words occurring more than once in the sonnet.

```
preprocess :: String -> String
preprocess = (map toLower) . filter ('notElem' "?;:,.")

process :: String -> [String]
process = sort . nub . words
```

```
cnt :: String -> [(String,Int)]
cnt sonnet = [ (x,n)| x <- (process.preprocess) sonnet,
               n <- [count x (words (preprocess sonnet))],
               n > 1                                    ]
```

3.11 Finnish Vowel Harmony

Vowel harmony is a phonological process by which vowels come to share certain features. Consider the case of Finnish, which has the back vowels *a,o,u*, the front vowels *ä*, *ö*, *y*, and the neutral vowels *i, e*. A Finnish word may contain only back (and neutral) vowels or contain only front (and neutral) vowels.†

pouta	'fine weather'
koti	'home'
pöytä	'table'

Back and front vowels are furthermore vowel harmony inducing. That is, if a stem contains only back vowels, then the suffix also contains only back vowels; if the

† Data are taken from Ringen and Heinämäki [RH99].

stem consists of front vowels, the suffix vowels assimilate to being front. Here are some examples, taken from essive case formation.

$$pouta \mathbin{+\mkern-8mu+} na \rightarrow poutana$$
$$koti \mathbin{+\mkern-8mu+} na \rightarrow kotina$$
$$pöytä \mathbin{+\mkern-8mu+} na \rightarrow pöytänä$$

This can be captured in a simple way by a function inspired by Forsberg [For07, p. 13], that changes the vowels of the suffix according to whether the stem vowels are front or back vowels. One small detail: the character '*ä*' is not standard ASCII, but is part of the Latin 1 supplement of the ASCII character set. It has decimal code 228. The character '*ö*' has decimal code 246. These characters can be referred to in Haskell as '\228' and '\246', or chr(228) and chr(246), respectively.

```haskell
aUml,oUml :: Char
aUml = chr(228)
oUml = chr(246)
```

```haskell
appendSuffixF :: String -> String -> String
appendSuffixF stem suffix = stem ++ map vh suffix
 where vh | or [elem c "aou"           | c <- stem] = back
          | or [elem c [aUml,oUml,'y'] | c <- stem] = front
          | otherwise                              = id

front :: Char -> Char
front s | s == 'a'  = aUml
        | s == 'o'  = oUml
        | s == 'u'  = 'y'
        | otherwise = s

back :: Char -> Char
back s | s == aUml = 'a'
       | s == oUml = 'o'
       | s == 'y'  = 'u'
       | otherwise = s
```

Haskell has two ways to locally define auxiliary functions, the `where` and `let` constructions. The `where` construction is illustrated in the definition given above of `appendSuffixF`. This can also be expressed with `let`, as in the following alternative version of that definition:

```
appendSuffixF stem suffix =
  let vh | or [elem c "aou"                  | c <- stem] = back
         | or [elem c [aUml,oUml,'y']  | c <- stem] = front
         | otherwise                                = id
  in stem ++ map vh suffix
```

The `let` construction uses the reserved keywords `let` and `in`.

Exercise 3.18 What type does the function vh have?

Next consider Swedish.† Swedish nouns form the plural according to one of five declination classes.

- Nouns of the first class end in *a* and their plural is formed by appending the suffix *-or*. When this suffix is appended to the stem, the last vowel of the stem is deleted. Examples for this are:

$$flicka + or \rightarrow flickor \qquad \text{'girls'}$$
$$blomma + or \rightarrow blommor \qquad \text{'flowers'}$$

- Nouns of the second class end in *e* and the plural suffix is *-ar*. Again, when appending it, the last vowel of the stem is deleted.

$$pojke + ar \rightarrow pojkar \qquad \text{'boys'}$$

- Ignoring the possible suffix *-ar*, nouns of the third class form the plural with the suffix *-er* if the stem ends in a consonant, and with *-r* if the stem ends in a vowel.

$$rad + er \rightarrow rader \qquad \text{'rows'}$$
$$ko + r \rightarrow kor \qquad \text{'cows'}$$

- Nouns of the fourth class form the plural simply by appending *-n*.

$$äpple + n \rightarrow äpplen \qquad \text{'apples'}$$

- Nouns of the fifth class remain unchanged.

$$hus \rightarrow hus \qquad \text{'houses'}$$

† For a comprehensive book about Swedish morphology, see, e.g., [Hel78].

Here is a data type `DeclClass` for the declination classes (this uses a facility of Haskell to define your own data types, more about which in Section 3.13).

```
data DeclClass = One | Two | Three | Four | Five
```

We will use this to write a function

```
swedishPlural :: String -> DeclClass -> String
```

for plural declination of Swedish nouns. We will assume the following set of Swedish vowels:

```
oSlash,aRing :: Char
oSlash = chr(248)
aRing  = chr(229)

swedishVowels = ['a','i','o','u','e','y',aUml,aRing,oUml,oSlash]
```

The solution uses a `case` construction and pattern matching on the shape of `DeclClass`. It also uses the function `init` that removes the last element from a list.

```
swedishPlural :: String -> DeclClass -> String
swedishPlural noun d = case d of
  One   -> init noun ++ "or"
  Two   -> init noun ++ "ar"
  Three -> if  (last noun) `elem` swedishVowels
             then noun ++ "r"
             else noun ++ "er"
  Four  -> noun ++ "n"
  Five  -> noun
```

3.12 Identifiers in Haskell

As the reader may have noticed already from the code examples in this chapter, Haskell uses the distinction between upper and lower case to tell two kinds of identifiers apart:

- Variable identifiers are used to name functions. They have to start with a lower-case letter. Examples are `map, swedishVowels, list2OnePlacePred, foo_bar.`

- Constructor identifiers are used to name types and their inhabitants. Constructor identifiers have to start with an upper-case letter. An example of a type constructor is `Bool`, and examples of data constructors are `True`, `False`, the two constructors that make up the type `Bool`.

Functions are operations on data structures; constructors are the building blocks of the data structures themselves (trees, lists, Booleans, and so on).

Names of functions always start with lower-case letters, and may contain both upper- and lower-case letters, but also digits, underscores, and the prime symbol '. The following *reserved keywords* have special meanings and cannot be used to name functions.

case	class	data	default	deriving	do	else
if	import	in	infix	infixl	infixr	instance
let	module	newtype	of	then	type	where
_						

The character _ at the beginning of a word is treated as a lower-case character; _ all by itself is a reserved word for the wild card pattern that matches anything.

And there is one more reserved keyword that is particular to Hugs: `forall`, for the definition of functions that take polymorphic arguments. See the Hugs documentation for further particulars.

3.13 User-defined Data Types and Pattern Matching

Besides the predefined data types like `Int`, `Char`, and `Bool`, you can define data types yourself. Imagine, for example, we want to implement our own data structure for subjects and predicates as sentence ingredients.

```
data Subject   = Chomsky | Montague deriving Show
data Predicate = Wrote String       deriving Show
```

The data type `Predicate` is built from another data type; in fact, the data type declaration specifies `Wrote` as a function from strings to predicates:

```
FPH> :t Wrote
Wrote :: String -> Predicate
```

Note that we added `deriving Show` to the specification of our data types. This puts these data types in the `Show` class and tells Haskell to print its instances exactly like they are given. Another way would be to tell Haskell that these data types are instances of the Show class and then define a show function for them ourselves. This is useful if we want a data type to be displayed in a certain way. We will do that below for the data type Sentence.

We would like to use these data types to construct a more complex data type, say a Sentence. For this we use a data constructor S, as follows:

```
data Sentence  = S Subject Predicate

type Sentences = [Sentence]
```

The last line defines a type synonym. We added it simply to illustrate this abbreviated way of talking about types. This is exactly like String was defined as [Char].

The specification of Sentence says that the data type has the form of a tree. Such trees are familiar in linguistics. Linguists would display a sentence tree as:

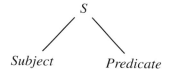

But maybe we do not want it to get displayed like a tree. In order to display instances of the Sentence type in a natural way, we can tell Haskell explicitly how to display a value of the type.

```
instance Show Sentence where
    show (S subj pred) = show subj ++ " " ++ show pred
```

We can specify functions for constructing predicates and sentences:

```
makeP :: String -> Predicate
makeP title = Wrote title

makeS :: Subject -> Predicate -> Sentence
makeS subj pred = S subj pred
```

Here they are in action:

```
FPH> makeS Chomsky (makeP "Syntactic Structures")
Chomsky Wrote "Syntactic Structures"
```

The Booleans True and False are an example of a so-called enumerated datatype in Haskell. The two items True and False are called data constructors. The following standard definition of not uses pattern matching on these data to define negation.

```haskell
not :: Bool -> Bool
not True  = False
not False = True
```

Another kind of pattern matching on data occurs with the structured datatype of lists:

```haskell
null :: [a] -> Bool
null []    = True
null (_:_) = False
```

The pattern [] is matched by the empty list, and the pattern (_:_) is matched by any non-empty list. The underscore _ is called a *wild card pattern*. It matches anything. So (_:_) stands for anything that can be constructed with :, and it follows that (_:_) matches any non-empty list.

Here is another example from the Haskell Prelude:

```haskell
last         :: [a] -> a
last [x]     = x
last (_:xs)  = last xs
last []      = error "Prelude.last: empty list"
```

Pattern matching in Haskell takes place top to bottom. The top equation is tried first. When there is a match, this equation is applied, otherwise the next equation is tried for a match, and so on. The following alternative way to write the last function illustrates this:

```haskell
myLast         :: [a] -> a
myLast [x]     = x
myLast (_:xs)  = myLast xs
myLast _       = error "myLast: empty list"
```

The pattern used in myLast _ always matches, but because it is at the bottom of the list of patterns, it will only be selected in case the list is empty.

Data constructors may have arguments, as in the following example of a datatype for colours:

```
data Colour = RGB Int Int Int deriving Show
```

The `deriving Show` guarantees that we can display colour values on screen, by means of `show`, which converts colour values to strings. But a string like `"RGB 0 0 0"` is not very informative. Pattern matching on the data allows us to get a more illuminating string description of colours. The following `showColour` function converts certain 'special' colour values to informative names, while relying on the ordinary show function for the other cases:

```
showColour :: Colour -> String
showColour (RGB 0 0 0)       = "black"
showColour (RGB 255 255 255) = "white"
showColour (RGB 255 0 0)     = "red"
showColour (RGB 0 255 0)     = "green"
showColour (RGB 0 0 255)     = "blue"
```

```
showColour (RGB 255 255 0)   = "yellow"
showColour (RGB 0 255 255)   = "cyan"
showColour (RGB 255 0 255)   = "magenta"
showColour c                 = show c
```

There is a close connection between constructing a value, e.g., constructing the value `RGB 0 0 0`, by applying a constructor to a number of arguments, and pattern matching on a value. `RGB 0 _ _` matches all colours that have no red in them, `RGB _ _ 0` matches all colours that have no blue in them, and so on. Pattern matching can be viewed as kind of reversal of the construction process. It is because we know how particular values are constructed that we can pattern match on them. Here is another example:

```
redAlert   :: Colour -> String
redAlert c@(RGB r _ _) = case r of
   0 -> show c ++ " has no red"
   _ -> show c ++ " has red"
```

The pattern c@(RGB r _ _) in this definition is called an *as-pattern*. What it means is: bind the value of *c* to whatever matches what comes after the @.

3.14 Application: Representing Phonemes

Now, let us turn to a more serious example. We saw a simple implementation of Finnish vowel harmony with string manipulation. This is not satisfying from a linguistic point of view, because phonological processes like vowel harmony don't seem to be simple string replacement rules, but instead are driven by phonological features. Thus, an implementation of vowel harmony would be more adequate if phonemes are represented as feature bundles, especially when vowel harmony shows more complex patterns. We can do this by defining data structures like the following.

```haskell
data Feature = F Attr Value deriving (Eq,Show)

data Attr    = Back | High | Round | Cons deriving (Eq,Show)
data Value   = Plus | Minus                deriving (Eq,Show)

type Phoneme = [Feature]
```

Representing phonemes with features proves helpful when considering more complex vowel harmony systems, like the one in Yawelmani, an extinct variety of the Yokuts language of California. Yawelmani has the surface vowels *i u e o a* (ignoring the distinction between short and long vowels). They can be represented as being of type phoneme, i.e., as lists of features:

```haskell
yawelmaniVowels = [i,a,o,u,e]

i = [F Cons Minus,  F High Plus,
     F Round Minus, F Back Minus]
a = [F Cons Minus,  F High Minus,
     F Round Minus, F Back Plus ]
o = [F Cons Minus,  F High Minus,
     F Round Plus,  F Back Plus ]
u = [F Cons Minus,  F High Plus ,
     F Round Plus,  F Back Plus ]
e = [F Cons Minus,  F High Minus,
     F Round Minus, F Back Minus]
```

Since we are concerned with vowels only, we will represent consonants simply as:

```
c = [F Cons Plus]
```

The surface form of these phonemes can be generated by a function `realize` of type `Phoneme -> Char`.

```
realize :: Phoneme -> Char
realize x | x == i = 'i'
          | x == a = 'a'
          | x == o = 'o'
          | x == u = 'u'
          | x == e = 'e'
          | x == c = 'c'
```

The vowel harmony in Yawelmani has the following shape: suffix vowels agree in backness and roundedness with the stem vowel. However, trigger and target of this harmony have to be of the same height. Thus, high stem vowels condition harmony on high suffix vowels but not on low ones, and low stem vowels condition harmony only on low suffix vowels, cf. the following examples taken from [CK97]:

$$xil + hin \rightarrow xilhin \qquad \text{'tangles'}$$
$$dub + hin \rightarrow dubhun \qquad \text{'leads by the hand'}$$
$$xat + al \rightarrow xatal \qquad \text{'might eat'}$$
$$bok' + al \rightarrow bok'ol \qquad \text{'might find'}$$

$$xat + hin \rightarrow xathin \qquad \text{'eats'}$$
$$bok' + hin \rightarrow bok'hin \qquad \text{'finds'}$$
$$xil + al \rightarrow xilal \qquad \text{'might tangle'}$$
$$dub + al \rightarrow dubal \qquad \text{'might lead by the hand'}$$

Exercise 3.19 Write a function

```
appendSuffixY :: [Phoneme] -> [Phoneme] -> [Phoneme]
```

that captures the vowel harmony in Yawelmani. You can use the following auxiliary functions for extracting the value of a certain feature in a phoneme, and for matching a certain feature in a phoneme with a certain value.

```
fValue :: Attr -> Phoneme -> Value
fValue attr [] = error "feature not found"
fValue attr ((F a v):fs) | attr == a = v
                         | otherwise = fValue attr fs

fMatch :: Attr -> Value -> Phoneme -> Phoneme
fMatch attr value fs = map (match attr value) fs
   where match a v f@(F a' v') | a == a'   = F a' v
                               | otherwise = f
```

3.15 Further Reading

The Haskell homepage http://www.haskell.org provides links to everything about Haskell that you might want to know, including information on how to download the latest version and the online tutorial. Among the tutorials on Haskell that can be found on the Internet, [DI07] and [HFP96] are recommended. The definitive reference for the language is [PJ03]. Recommended textbooks on functional programming in Haskell are [Bir98], [Tho99], and [Hut07], and the more recent [OSG08]. A textbook that bridges the gap between reasoning and functional programming is [DE04].

Stringology is a nickname for *string algorithms*; a nice book devoted to this subject is [CR02]. Lists are the fundamental data type of the programming language Lisp. An illuminating textbook on Lisp is [Gra93], and a splendid book on programming concepts in general, using the Lisp dialect Scheme, is [AS96].

4

Formal Syntax for Fragments

Summary

In this chapter we present definitions of some example languages: languages for playing simple games, logical languages, fragments of programming languages, and fragments of natural language. When we turn to the semantics of natural language fragments in the following chapters, we will use predicate logic as a basic tool. As a preparation for this, we introduce propositional and predicate logic, look at how they can be used to represent the meaning of natural language sentences, and show how to implement their syntax in Haskell.

4.1 Grammars for Games

Certain games can be played with a very limited linguistic repertoire. An example is *Sea Battle* (or: *Battleship*), which is played by two people on two pads of paper, each containing two square grids. The grids each contain 10×10 squares, identified by letter and number.

	A	B	C	D	E	F	G	H	I	J
10										
9										
8										
7										
6										
5										
4										
3										
2										
1										

The grids of each player are made invisible to the opposite player. The game begins by each player distributing his fleet over one of his grids. Each player disposes of a float of ships, each ship occupying a number of adjacent squares on the grid, either horizontally or vertically: a battleship (5 squares), a frigate (4 squares), two submarines (3 squares each), and a destroyer (2 squares). Before the game starts, the ships are positioned on a grid by each player, without overlap (two ships cannot occupy the same square). This grid is also used for recording enemy shots. The other grid is for recording shots fired at the enemy.

Here is a typical start situation for one half of the battlefield: the battleship occupies squares D4, E4, F4, G4, H4, the frigate squares B4, B5, B6, B7, the first submarine G7, G8, G9, the second submarine A9, B9, C9, and the destroyer squares H1 and I1.

	A	B	C	D	E	F	G	H	I	J
10										
9	○	○	○				○			
8							○			
7		○					○			
6		○								
5		○								
4		○		○	○	○	○	○		
3										
2										
1								○	○	

A grammar for the language of the game is given below. We state it in BNF notation, with rewriting (or: nonterminal) symbols written in **boldface** and terminal symbols or strings written in *italics*. The grammar rules consist of a rewrite symbol followed by $\longrightarrow$ followed by a number of alternatives separated by |. Recall that this means that the rewrite symbol can *produce* any of the alternatives listed in the right-hand side of the rule.

column	$\longrightarrow$	*A* | *B* | *C* | *D* | *E* | *F* | *G* | *H* | *I* | *J*
row	$\longrightarrow$	*1* | *2* | *3* | *4* | *5* | *6* | *7* | *8* | *9* | *10*
attack	$\longrightarrow$	**column row**
ship	$\longrightarrow$	*battleship* | *frigate* | *submarine* | *destroyer*
reaction	$\longrightarrow$	*missed* | *hit* **ship** | *sunk* **ship** | *lost_battle*
turn	$\longrightarrow$	**attack reaction**

To be fully precise we have to say that the language defined by Sea Battle consists of all strings one can get by rewriting the *start symbol* **turn**, and repeating the rewrite process until only *terminal symbols* are left. An example should make this clear:

turn ⇒ **attack reaction** ⇒ **attack** *missed* ⇒ **column row** *missed* ⇒

⇒ *B* **row** *missed* ⇒ *B* 2 *missed*.

Here ⇒ is short for 'rewrites in one step to'. Another example:

turn ⇒ **attack reaction** ⇒ **attack** *hit* **ship** ⇒ **column row** *hit* **ship** ⇒

⇒ *B* **row** *hit* **ship** ⇒ *B* 3 *hit* **ship** ⇒ *B* 3 *hit battleship*.

The 'rewrites in one step' relation is formally defined as the smallest relation satisfying the following. If $A \longrightarrow \alpha$ is a production of the grammar (i.e. α is one of the alternatives listed at the right-hand side of the rule with A at the left-hand side), and $\beta A \gamma$ is a list of symbols, with β, γ both consisting of zero or more terminals and rewrite symbols, then $\beta A \gamma \Rightarrow \beta \alpha \gamma$.

The symbol for 'rewrites in zero or more steps to' is $\Rightarrow^*$. We call this the *reflexive transitive closure* of ⇒. In the example we have: **turn** $\Rightarrow^*$ *B* 2 *missed*.

The expression *B 2 missed* does happen to fit the situation of the figure above, but this has nothing to do with the syntax of the language. It is a matter of semantics, and we will turn to that in the next chapter.

A possible extension of the grammar is a rule for a complete game between two players:

game $\longrightarrow$ **turn** | **turn game**.

Exercise 4.1 Revise the grammar in such a way that it is made explicit in the grammar rules that the game is over once one of the players is defeated.

The exercise illustrates the fact that semantic desiderata may influence the syntactic design. And this is not all. The rule 'do not attack the same position twice', for instance, is not a part of syntax or semantics, but of pragmatics: whoever plays the game in order to win will comply with it.

For the Haskell implementation, first declare the module:

```
module FSynF where

import Data.List
```

Here is one possible way of rendering the Battleship language in Haskell. We declare a type synonym `Column` for columns, and use the Haskell data type `Int` for rows. An attack is a pair consisting of a column and a row. The data type `Ship` enumerates the war vessel types, the data type `Reaction` lists the possible reactions, and the type for `Turn` gives pairs consisting of an attack and a reaction.

```
data Column = A' | B' | C' | D' | E'
            | F' | G' | H' | I' | J'
              deriving (Eq,Ord,Show,Enum)

type Row    = Int
type Attack = (Column,Row)

data Ship = Battleship | Frigate | Submarine | Destroyer
            deriving Show

data Reaction = Missed | Hit Ship | Sunk Ship | LostBattle
                deriving Show

type Turn = (Attack,Reaction)
```

We use `A'` for *A*, and so on, because we will need `A` for other purposes (see below, on page 133).

The `deriving` phrase at the end of each data declaration is there to ensure that the data type gets some appropriate properties. The phrase `deriving Show` guarantees that the datatype can be displayed on screen exactly as it was defined. The phrase `deriving Eq` ensures that equality is defined for a datatype. The phrase `deriving (Eq,Ord,Show)` ensures that equality, ordering, and display are defined for it.

Note that declaring the data types for playing the game does not say anything at all about how the game is to be played.

Another very simple language is the language of *Mastermind*. Mastermind is a code-breaking game for two players. One of them (the code maker) decides on a row of four coloured pegs, with the colours picked from a fixed range. The other player (the codebreaker) tries to guess the colour pattern. After each guess that is made the code maker gives feedback as to its correctness. A feedback reaction consists of a sequence of black and white pegs: a black one for each peg of the right colour in the right place, and a white one for each additional peg of the right colour, but in a wrong place. If the secret code is red, blue, green, yellow, and the guess is green, blue, red, orange, then the feedback consists of one black, for blue occurs in the right place, and two whites, for both green and red occur in the guess, but in the wrong positions. Next, guesses and feedback alternate until the pattern is discovered. The challenge is to guess the pattern in the least number of tries.

A grammar for Mastermind looks as follows. We use an extended BNF notation (called EBNF) with curly brackets enclosing items that are repeated zero or more times.

$$
\begin{array}{rcl}
\textbf{colour} & \longrightarrow & \textit{red} \mid \textit{yellow} \mid \textit{blue} \mid \textit{green} \mid \textit{orange} \\
\textbf{answer} & \longrightarrow & \textit{black} \mid \textit{white} \\
\textbf{guess} & \longrightarrow & \textbf{colour colour colour colour} \\
\textbf{reaction} & \longrightarrow & \{\textbf{answer}\} \\
\textbf{turn} & \longrightarrow & \textbf{guess reaction} \\
\textbf{game} & \longrightarrow & \textbf{turn} \mid \textbf{turn game}
\end{array}
$$

Exercise 4.2 Revise the grammar in order to guarantee that a game has at most four turns.

Exercise 4.3 Write your own grammars for chess and bingo.

All these example grammars have the property that they generate infinite languages.

Exercise 4.4 Check this. Next, change the definition of **reaction** in the grammar of Exercise 4.2 to ensure that the revised grammar generates a finite language.

A possible Haskell representation for the language of Mastermind is given below. In the interest of flexibility we implement colour patterns and answer sequences as lists.

```
data Colour   = Red | Yellow | Blue | Green | Orange
                deriving (Eq,Show,Bounded,Enum)

data Answer   = Black | White deriving (Eq,Show)

type Pattern  = [Colour]
type Feedback = [Answer]
```

Again, the implementation of the data type for Mastermind games tells us nothing about how these games are to be played. We will say more about this in the next chapter, when we discuss the semantics of these fragments.

If one is lenient enough one might consider these example languages as fragments of English. Conversely, it is also very simple to write a grammar for a language which has English contained in it as a fragment:

$$\textbf{character} \longrightarrow A \mid \cdots \mid Z \mid a \mid \cdots \mid z \mid \_ \mid , \mid . \mid ? \mid ! \mid ; \mid :$$

$$\textbf{string} \longrightarrow \textbf{character} \mid \textbf{character string}$$

The set of all strings, according to this definition, contains the set of sentences of written English.

Note, by the way, that we have tacitly introduced $\cdots$ as a new abbreviation. This is strictly for human consumption: if a computer is supposed to read this, we have to explain how. But we all have learnt the alphabet at primary school, and the abbreviation relies on this common knowledge. It is extremely tedious to write prose meant for human consumption without tacitly relying on such background knowledge. In computer programming, one has to make all these shortcuts explicit, of course. This may be why people with a talent for human relationships – and a skill for seeking common ground – find it often difficult to relate to computers, and vice versa. It should be noted, by the way, that Haskell is rather smart at guessing what ellipsis means:

```
FSynF>  ['A'..'Z']
"ABCDEFGHIJKLMNOPQRSTUVWXYZ"
```

If we want to be on good terms with computers, functional programming is a handy tool for communication.

Exercise 4.5 Give a grammar for strings which also generates the empty string. Use ϵ as a symbol for the empty string. (In Haskell, the empty string is given by "" or [].)

In the next section we will turn to a more serious fragment of English.

4.2 A Fragment of English

Suppose we wish to write grammar rules for sentences of English like the following:

The girl laughed.	(4.1)
No dwarf admired some princess that shuddered.	(4.2)
Every girl that some boy loved cheered.	(4.3)
The wizard that helped Snow White defeated the giant.	(4.4)

What we need is a rule for the subject–predicate structure of sentences, a rule for the internal structure of noun phrases, a rule for common nouns with or without relative clauses, and that is just about it. The following grammar copes with the examples:

S	$\longrightarrow$	**NP VP**
NP	$\longrightarrow$	*Snow White* | *Alice* | *Dorothy* | *Goldilocks* | *Little Mook* | *Atreyu*
		| **DET CN** | **DET RCN**
DET	$\longrightarrow$	*the* | *every* | *some* | *no*
CN	$\longrightarrow$	*girl* | *boy* | *princess* | *dwarf* | *giant* | *wizard* | *sword* | *dagger*
RCN	$\longrightarrow$	**CN** *that* **VP** | **CN** *that* **NP TV**
VP	$\longrightarrow$	*laughed* | *cheered* | *shuddered*
		| **TV NP** | **DV NP NP**
TV	$\longrightarrow$	*loved* | *admired* | *helped* | *defeated* | *caught*
DV	$\longrightarrow$	*gave*

This is very basic and much too crude, of course, but it should give an idea of what a grammar for a fragment of English might look like.

Exercise 4.6 Extend this fragment with adjectives *happy* and *evil*.

Exercise 4.7 Extend the fragment with preposition phrases, in such a way that the sentence *A dwarf defeated a giant with a sword* is generated in two structurally different ways, while there is only one way to generate *A dwarf defeated Little Mook with a sword*.

Exercise 4.8 Extend the fragment with complex relative clauses, where the relative clause can be a sentence conjunction. The fragment should generate, among other things, the sentence: *The dwarf that Snow White helped and Goldilocks admired cheered.* What problems do you encounter?

For the record, here is one way to define (a slight extension of) this language fragment in Haskell. Some of the stuff, such as the adjective Fake and the attitude verbs Wanted and Hoped, is thrown in for purposes of illustrating intensionality. See below, Section 8.3.

```
data Sent = Sent NP VP deriving Show
data NP   = SnowWhite  | Alice  | Dorothy | Goldilocks
            | LittleMook | Atreyu | Everyone | Someone
            | NP1 DET CN | NP2 DET RCN
            deriving Show
```

Fig. 4.1. Example structure tree

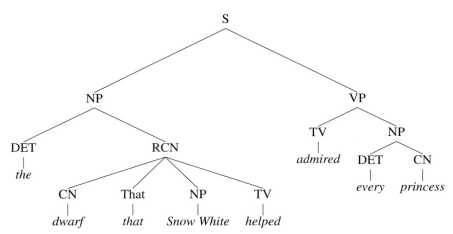

```
data DET  = The | Every | Some | No | Most
            deriving Show
data CN   = Girl   | Boy    | Princess | Dwarf | Giant
          | Wizard | Sword | Dagger
            deriving Show
data ADJ  = Fake deriving Show
data RCN  = RCN1 CN That VP | RCN2 CN That NP TV
          | RCN3 ADJ CN
            deriving Show
data That = That deriving Show
data VP   = Laughed | Cheered | Shuddered
          | VP1 TV NP | VP2 DV NP NP
          | VP3 AV To INF
            deriving Show
data TV   = Loved   | Admired | Helped
          | Defeated | Caught
            deriving Show
data DV   = Gave deriving Show
data AV   = Hoped | Wanted deriving Show
```

```
data INF  = Laugh | Cheer | Shudder | INF TINF NP deriving Show
data TINF = Love | Admire | Help | Defeat | Catch
            deriving Show
data To   = To deriving Show
```

The way to look at this is as a definition of syntactic structures. The structure for *The dwarf that Snow White helped admired every princess* is given in Figure 4.1.

The problem of using the grammar for mapping the string *The dwarf that Snow White helped admired every princess* to this syntactic structure is an instance of the *parse problem* for this grammar. We will say more about this in Chapter 9.

4.3 A Language for Talking about Classes

To see that even very simple fragments of English can be useful, consider the following interaction language for a so-called inference engine. An interactive inference engine is a program that handles interaction with a knowledge base (a kind of smart database). The interaction language in our case is a tiny fragment of English that allows questions and statements about classes.

Questions (or: queries) are of the form

$$
\begin{aligned}
Q \quad ::= \quad & \text{Are all PN PN?} \\
| \quad & \text{Are no PN PN?} \\
| \quad & \text{Are any PN PN?} \\
| \quad & \text{Are any PN not PN?} \\
| \quad & \text{What about PN?}
\end{aligned}
$$

Statements are of the form

$$
\begin{aligned}
S \quad ::= \quad & \text{All PN are PN.} \\
| \quad & \text{No PN are PN.} \\
| \quad & \text{Some PN are PN.} \\
| \quad & \text{Some PN are not PN.}
\end{aligned}
$$

That's all. The intention is that the knowledge base can be extended by means of statements, and queried by means of questions. We will not attempt to constrain the shape of the plural nouns PN. In Section 5.7 a semantics for this fragment will be given, which puts it to use.

4.4 Propositional Logic

Our next example is a grammar for *propositional logic*, where we use

$$p, q, r, p', q', r', p'', q'', r'', \ldots$$

to indicate atomic propositions.

$$\mathbf{atom} \longrightarrow p \mid q \mid r \mid \mathbf{atom'}$$
$$\mathbf{F} \longrightarrow \mathbf{atom} \mid \neg\mathbf{F} \mid (\mathbf{F} \wedge \mathbf{F}) \mid (\mathbf{F} \vee \mathbf{F}).$$

Here $\neg$ is the symbol for *not*, $\wedge$ the symbol for *and*, and $\vee$ the symbol for *or*.

Some formulas generated by this grammar are $\neg\neg\neg p'''$, $((p \vee p') \wedge p'')$, and $(p \wedge (p' \wedge p'''))$. The brackets force unique readability. Without those brackets, one wouldn't know whether to read $p \wedge p' \vee p''$ as

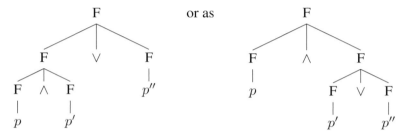

This structural ambiguity does affect the meaning, just as for the English sentence *She was young and beautiful or depraved*.

The formal definition of the language of propositional logic makes it possible to reason about the properties of the language in a formal way. For this we use the following principle:

Theorem 4.1 (Principle of Structural Induction) Every formula of propositional logic has property P provided

Basic step: Every atom has property P.
Induction step: If F has property P, then so does $\neg F$; if F_1 and F_2 have property P, then so do $(F_1 \wedge F_2)$ and $(F_1 \vee F_2)$.

To see this, let P' be the set of all propositional formulas with property P. Then the basic step and the induction step together ensure that all propositional formulas are members of P'. But this just means that every propositional formula has property P.

This can be used as follows:

Proposition 4.2 Every propositional formula has equal numbers of left and right parentheses.

Proof Basic step: atoms do not have parentheses at all, so it holds vacuously that they have the same numbers of left and right parentheses.

Induction step: If F has the same numbers of left and right parentheses, then so does $\neg F$, for no parentheses are added. If F_1 and F_2 both have equal numbers of left and right parentheses, then so do $(F_1 \wedge F_2)$ and $(F_1 \vee F_2)$, for both numbers are increased by one. □

Of course, as a proposition this is not very interesting. The interest is in the proof method. The same holds for the next result.

Proposition 4.3 Propositional formulas are uniquely readable (have only one parse tree).

Proof Basic step: If F is an atom, then F has only one parse tree.

Induction step: If F has only one parse tree, then $\neg F$ has only one parse tree too. If F_1 and F_2 have only one parse tree each, then the same holds for $(F_1 \wedge F_2)$ and $(F_1 \vee F_2)$. □

Note the use of so-called *metasymbols* F_1 and F_2 in the reasoning above. Metasymbols come in handy whenever one wants to talk about the general form of a formula. A formula of the form $(F_1 \wedge F_2)$ is called a *conjunction*, a formula of the form $(F_1 \vee F2)$ a *disjunction*, and a formula of the form $\neg F$ a *negated formula*.

Sometimes the 'official' way of writing formulas is a bit clumsy. We will usually write p_2 for p'', q_3 for q''', and so on. Also, we will often omit parentheses when this does not result in ambiguity. Furthermore, propositional conjunction is associative, so $(p \wedge (q \wedge r))$ means the same as $((p \wedge q) \wedge r)$. Therefore, there is no harm in writing $(p \wedge q \wedge r)$ or even $p \wedge q \wedge r$ for both. Disjunction is also associative, so we will also write $(p \vee (q \vee r))$ and $((p \vee q) \vee r)$ as $p \vee q \vee r$. And so on, for longer conjunctions and disjunctions.

While we are at it, it is useful to introduce the following abbreviations. We will write $F_1 \rightarrow F_2$ for $\neg(F_1 \wedge \neg F_2)$. A formula of the form $F_1 \rightarrow F_2$ is called an *implication* and read as 'F_1 implies F_2' or 'if F_1, then F_2'. Also, we write $F_1 \leftrightarrow F_2$ for $(F_1 \rightarrow F_2) \wedge (F_2 \rightarrow F_1)$. A formula of the form $F_1 \leftrightarrow F_2$ is called an *equivalence*.

The logical connectives $\neg, \wedge, \vee, \rightarrow, \leftrightarrow$ were designed to correspond to the natural language connectives *not, and, or, if... then*, and *if and only if*. For example, the sentence

If it rains and the sun is shining, then there will be a rainbow. (4.5)

can be represented as the propositional formula $(p \wedge q) \rightarrow r$, with p, q, and r being the atomic propositions *It rains*, *The sun is shining*, and *There will be a rainbow*, respectively.

Exercise 4.9 Translate the following sentences into propositional logic, making sure that their truth conditions are captured. What shortcomings do you encounter?

> *The wizard polishes his wand and learns a new spell, or he is lazy.*   (4.6)
>
> *The peasant will deal with the devil only if he has a plan to outwit him.*   (4.7)
>
> *If neither unicorns nor dragons exist, then neither do goblins.*   (4.8)

Exercise 4.10 The logical connective $\vee$ is inclusive, i.e. $p \vee q$ is true also if both p and q are true. In natural language, however, *or* is usually used exclusively, as in

> *You can either have ice cream or candy floss, but not both.*   (4.9)

Define a connective $\oplus$ for exclusive *or*, using the already defined connectives.

It is possible to write formulas for propositional logic which are uniquely readable, but without using parentheses. The solution is to use prefix or postfix notation. Prefix notation is sometimes called Polish notation. Here is a grammar for prefix formulas of propositional logic:

$$\mathbf{P} \longrightarrow \mathbf{atom} \mid \neg \, \mathbf{P} \mid \wedge \, \mathbf{P} \, \mathbf{P} \mid \vee \, \mathbf{P} \, \mathbf{P}.$$

This definition generates, for example, $\neg\neg\neg p$, $\wedge \vee pqr$, $\wedge p \vee qr$.

Exercise 4.11 Use the principle of structural induction to prove that the formulas of propositional logic in prefix notation are uniquely readable.

It is also possible to put the operators after their operands; this gets us reverse Polish notation or postfix notation:

$$\mathbf{R} \longrightarrow \mathbf{atom} \mid \mathbf{R} \, \neg \mid \mathbf{R} \, \mathbf{R} \, \wedge \mid \mathbf{R} \, \mathbf{R} \, \vee.$$

When implementing the syntax of propositional logic in Haskell, it is possible to make use of the predefined list syntax. We can promote the conjunction and disjunction operators to functions that create formulas from formula lists, as follows:

```
data Form =  P String | Ng Form | Cnj [Form] | Dsj [Form]
             deriving Eq

instance Show Form where
 show (P name) = name
 show (Ng   f) = '-': show f
 show (Cnj fs) = '&': show fs
 show (Dsj fs) = 'v': show fs
```

Note that this is Polish notation, and that the types of `Ng`, `Cnj`, and `Dsj` are as follows:

```
FSynF> :t Ng
Ng :: Form -> Form
FSynF> :t Cnj
Cnj :: [Form] -> Form
FSynF> :t Dsj
Dsj :: [Form] -> Form
```

Here are some example formulas:

```
form1, form2 :: Form
form1 = Cnj [P "p", Ng (P "p")]
form2 = Dsj [P "p1", P "p2", P "p3", P "p4"]
```

And this is how they get displayed:

```
FSynF> form1
&[p,-p]
FSynF> form2
v[p1,p2,p3,p4]
```

Exercise 4.12 Implement a function `opsNr` for computing the number of operators in a formula. The type is `opsNr :: Form -> Int`. The call `opsNr form1` should yield 2.

Exercise 4.13 Implement a function `depth` for computing the depth of the parse tree of a formula. The type is `depth :: Form -> Int`. The call `depth form1` should yield 2.

Exercise 4.14 Implement `propNames :: Form -> [String]` for collecting the list of names of propositional atoms that occur in a formula. Make sure the resulting list is sorted and without duplicates.

4.5 Predicate Logic

There are many aspects of natural language that propositional logic cannot express. For example, when translating the sentences (4.10) and (4.11) into propositional logic, the connection between their meanings is lost because they would have to be represented as completely different proposition constants p and q.

Every prince saw a lady.	(4.10)
Some prince saw a beautiful lady.	(4.11)

To capture some of the internal structure of sentences like this, in particular the role of predication and quantifiers, we now turn to predicate logic. Predicate logic is an extension of propositional logic with *structured basic propositions* and *quantifications*.

- A structured basic proposition consists of an n-ary predicate followed by n variables.
- A universally quantified formula consists of the symbol $\forall$ followed by a variable followed by a formula.
- An existentially quantified formula consists of the symbol $\exists$ followed by a variable followed by a formula.
- Other ingredients are as in propositional logic.

Other names for predicate logic are first-order logic or first-order predicate logic. 'First-order' indicates that the quantification is over entities (objects of the first order).

We will now give a formal definition of the language of predicate logic, on the assumption that predicates combine with at most three variables. More formally, we assume that the predicates have arity less or equal to 3. What this means is that we can refer to one-place relations or properties (such as the property of being happy, or being an even number), to two-place relations (such as the relation 'greater than' between numbers, or the relation 'older than' between people), and to three-place relations (such as the relation of giving, which has a subject, an object and a recipient or indirect object), but not to relations with more than three arguments. Relations with more than three arguments are hardly ever needed, anyway.

Here is the definition of the language of predicate logic with infinitely many one-placed predicates, infinitely many two-placed predicates, and infinitely many three-placed predicates:

$$
\begin{aligned}
\mathbf{v} &\longrightarrow x \mid y \mid z \mid \mathbf{v'} \\
\mathbf{P} &\longrightarrow P \mid \mathbf{P'} \\
\mathbf{R} &\longrightarrow R \mid \mathbf{R'} \\
\mathbf{S} &\longrightarrow S \mid \mathbf{S'} \\
\mathbf{atom} &\longrightarrow \mathbf{P\,v} \mid \mathbf{R\,v\,v} \mid \mathbf{S\,v\,v\,v} \\
\mathbf{F} &\longrightarrow \mathbf{atom} \mid (\mathbf{v} = \mathbf{v}) \mid \neg\mathbf{F} \mid (\mathbf{F} \wedge \mathbf{F}) \mid (\mathbf{F} \vee \mathbf{F}) \mid \forall\,\mathbf{v}\,\mathbf{F} \mid \exists\,\mathbf{v}\,\mathbf{F}.
\end{aligned}
$$

The following strings are examples of formulas of this predicate logical language:

- $\neg P'x$
- $(Px \wedge P'x'')$

- $((Px \wedge P'x'') \vee Rxx'')$
- $\forall x\, Rxx$
- $\exists x (Rxx' \wedge Sxyx)$
- $\forall x \forall x' \neg ((x = x') \wedge \neg (x' = x))$

Exercise 4.15 Prove that the formulas of this language have the property of unique readability.

The symbol $\forall$ is the symbol for universal quantification; it means 'for all'. The symbol $\exists$ expresses existential quantification; it means 'there exists'. Thus, $\forall x\, Rxx$ means that everything bears the R relation to itself, and $\forall x \exists x'\, Rxx'$ means that for everything there is something which is R-ed by that first thing. Incidentally, this paraphrase shows that the variable notation is quite handy. More information about the semantics of first-order predicate logic will be given in Chapters 5 and 6.

Exercise 4.16 Give a BNF grammar for a predicate logical language with infinitely many predicate letters for every finite arity. (Hint: use $'''P, '''P', '''P'', \ldots$ for the set of three-place predicate letters, and so on.)

Again, it is convenient to be lenient about notation. We will use

$$x, y, z, x_1, y_1, z_1, x_2, y_2, z_2, \ldots$$

for individual variables, and

$$P, R, S, P_1, R_1, S_1, P_2, R_2, S_2, \ldots$$

for predicate symbols, plus the conventions for omitting parentheses when they are not essential for disambiguation. We will also use the abbreviations $F_1 \rightarrow F_2$ for formulas of the form $\neg (F_1 \wedge \neg F_2)$, and $F_1 \leftrightarrow F_2$ for formulas of the form $(F_1 \rightarrow F_2) \wedge (F_2 \rightarrow F_1)$.

In talking about predicate logical formulas we want to be able to distinguish between the variable occurrences that are *bound* by a quantifier in that formula and the occurrences that are not. Binding is a syntactic notion, and it can simply be stated as follows: in a formula $\forall x\, F$ (or $\exists x\, F$), the quantifier occurrence binds all occurrences of x in F that are not bound by an occurrence of $\forall x$ or $\exists x$ inside F.

Alternatively, we can define it in terms of properties of syntax trees: an occurrence of $\forall x$ (or $\exists x$) in a formula F binds an occurrence of x in F if in the syntax tree for F the occurrence $\forall x$ (or $\exists x$) c-commands x, and inside F there are no other occurrences of $\forall x$ or $\exists x$ that c-command x. The notion of c-command is defined as follows: node a in a syntax tree c-commands (i.e. 'constituent'-commands) node b in that tree if the first branching node above a dominates b, where a node a dominates node b in a syntax tree if there is a downward path through the tree leading from a to b (with $a = b$ in the limit case). We will look at trees and relations between tree nodes in more detail in Chapter 9.

As an example, consider the formula $Px \land \forall x(Qx \to Rxy)$. Here is its syntax tree:

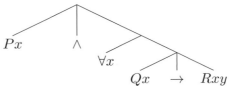

The first occurrence of x is free, because it is not c-commanded by a quantifier; the other occurrences of x are bound, because they are c-commanded by $\forall x$. In such a case we also say that that occurrence of x is *in the scope* of the quantifier occurrence $\forall x$ or $\exists x$.

An occurrence of x is *bound* in F if there is some quantifier occurrence that binds it, it is free otherwise.

Exercise 4.17 Give the bound occurrences of x in the following formula.

$$\exists x(Rxy \lor Sxyz) \land Px$$

A predicate logical formula is called *open* if it contains at least one variable occurrence which is free; it is called *closed* otherwise. A closed predicate logical formula is also called a predicate logical *sentence*. Thus, $(Px \land \exists x Rxx)$ is an open formula, but $\exists x(Px \land \exists x Rxx)$ is a sentence.

Now we can have a go at representing the sentences (4.10) and (4.11) from earlier, here repeated for convenience as (4.12) and (4.13):

> *Every prince saw a lady.* (4.12)
>
> *Some prince saw a beautiful lady.* (4.13)

The first sentence is ambiguous between two readings. Either it holds for every prince that he saw some lady, which corresponds to the formula

$$\forall x(\textit{Prince } x \to \exists y(\textit{Lady } y \land \textit{Saw } x\ y)),$$

or there is one specific lady that every prince saw. This reading corresponds to the formula

$$\exists y(\textit{Lady } y \land \forall x(\textit{Prince } x \to \textit{Saw } x\ y)).$$

The second sentence does not give rise to ambiguity but can straightforwardly be represented as

$$\exists x \exists y(\textit{Prince } x \land \textit{Lady } y \land \textit{Beautiful } y \land \textit{Saw } x\ y).$$

Note that universally quantified statements are translated with → as main connective, while in the existentially quantified statements we made use of ∧. Think about why this is so. We will come back to this issue in Section 5.5 (more specifically, in Exercise 5.17 on page 102).

4.6 Predicate Logical Formulas in Haskell

In this section we will give a formal definition of the language of predicate logic in Haskell. Once we have data types for terms and formulas, we can study the problem of specifying a semantic interpretation for them.

Haskell lists allow for an elegant solution to the arity problem. We simply combine predicates with lists of variables, letting the length of the list determine the arity of the predicate. This way, we allow the same relation symbol to occur with different arities, but there is no harm in this. (Indeed, it is common practice to do this in programming languages like Prolog and Erlang.)

As a first step towards a Haskell implementation of the data type of predicate logical formulas, we modify the syntax given in the previous section by giving basic predicates a list argument, and by defining conjunctions and disjunctions as operators on lists of formulas, as follows:

$$
\begin{aligned}
\mathbf{v} &\longrightarrow\ x \mid y \mid z \mid \mathbf{v}' \\
\mathbf{vlist} &\longrightarrow\ [\,]\mid \mathbf{v} : \mathbf{vlist} \\
\mathbf{P} &\longrightarrow\ P \mid \mathbf{P}' \\
\mathbf{atom} &\longrightarrow\ \mathbf{P}\ \mathbf{vlist} \\
\mathbf{F} &\longrightarrow\ \mathbf{atom} \mid \mathbf{v} = \mathbf{v} \mid \neg \mathbf{F} \mid \wedge \mathbf{Flist} \mid \vee \mathbf{Flist} \mid \forall \mathbf{v}\ \mathbf{F} \mid \exists \mathbf{v}\ \mathbf{F} \\
\mathbf{Flist} &\longrightarrow\ [\,]\mid \mathbf{F} : \mathbf{Flist}
\end{aligned}
$$

We start out with a data type for variables. It is convenient to give a variable both a name and an index. The indices will be needed for picking fresh variables in Chapter 6.

```
type Name     = String
type Index    = [Int]
data Variable = Variable Name Index deriving (Eq,Ord)
```

Variables are the type of object that can be shown on the screen. We therefore put them in the Show class, and define a function for showing them:

```
instance Show Variable where
  show (Variable name [])  = name
  show (Variable name [i]) = name ++ show i
  show (Variable name is ) = name ++ showInts is
    where showInts []      = ""
          showInts [i]      = show i
          showInts (i:is) = show i ++ "_" ++ showInts is
```

Some example variables, that we will use later on:

```
x, y, z :: Variable
x = Variable "x" []
y = Variable "y" []
z = Variable "z" []
```

In the definition of formulas we let conjunction and disjunction operate on lists of formulas, and we use prefix notation for implications and equivalences. To start with, we will assume that all terms are variables, but we will modify this in the next section. It therefore make sense to define a so-called parametrized data type or abstract data type, where we use a type variable for the terms occurring in formulas. This gives:

```
data Formula a = Atom String [a]
               | Eq a a
               | Neg  (Formula a)
               | Impl (Formula a) (Formula a)
               | Equi (Formula a) (Formula a)
               | Conj [Formula a]
               | Disj [Formula a]
               | Forall Variable (Formula a)
               | Exists Variable (Formula a)
               deriving Eq
```

The construct `Atom String [a]` corresponds to predicate constants named by `String`, with a list of terms (or more general values of type a) as arguments. For example, $R(x, y)$ would be represented as `Atom "R" [x,y]`.

The function for showing formulas assumes that we use terms that are themselves showable. This is indicated by means of a type class constraint `Show a`.

```
instance Show a => Show (Formula a) where
  show (Atom s [])    = s
  show (Atom s xs)    = s ++ show xs
  show (Eq t1 t2)     = show t1 ++ "==" ++ show t2
  show (Neg form)     = '~' : (show form)
  show (Impl f1 f2)   = "(" ++ show f1 ++ "==>"
                            ++ show f2 ++ ")"
  show (Equi f1 f2)   = "(" ++ show f1 ++ "<=>"
                            ++ show f2 ++ ")"
  show (Conj [])      = "true"
  show (Conj fs)      = "conj" ++ show fs
  show (Disj [])      = "false"
  show (Disj fs)      = "disj" ++ show fs
  show (Forall v f)   = "A " ++  show v ++ (' ' : show f)
  show (Exists v f)   = "E " ++  show v ++ (' ' : show f)
```

Why we chose to display `Conj []` as `"true"` and `Disj []` as `"false"` will become clear when we look at their semantics in the next chapter on page 94.

Here are some example formulas of type `Formula Variable`:

```
formula0 = Atom "R" [x,y]
formula1 = Forall x (Atom "R" [x,x])
formula2 = Forall x
              (Forall y
                (Impl (Atom "R" [x,y]) (Atom "R" [y,x])))
```

These get displayed as follows:

```
FSynF> formula0
R[x,y]
FSynF> formula1
Ax R[x,x]
FSynF> formula2
Ax Ay (R[x,y]==>R[y,x])
```

Formula `formula1` expresses that the R relation is reflexive, while `formula2` expresses that R is symmetric.

Exercise 4.18 Write a function `closedForm :: Formula Variable -> Bool` that checks whether a formula is closed. (Hint: first write a function that collects the list of free variables of a formula. The closed formulas are the ones with an empty free variable list.)

Exercise 4.19 Implications and equivalences can be considered as abbreviations, for they can be defined in terms of negation and conjunction. Write a function

```
withoutIDs :: Formula Variable -> Formula Variable
```

that replaces each formula by an equivalent one without occurrences of `Impl` or `Equi`.

Exercise 4.20 Each formula of predicate logic is equivalent to a formula in so-called negation normal form, where negations only occur in front of atoms. The recipe is to 'push' negations through quantifiers by means of $\neg \forall x F \equiv \exists x \neg F$ and $\neg \exists x F \equiv \forall x \neg F$, and through disjunctions and conjunctions by means of the so-called laws of De Morgan: $\neg(F_1 \wedge F_2) \equiv \neg F_1 \vee \neg F_2$ and $\neg(F_1 \vee F_2) \equiv \neg F_1 \wedge \neg F_2$. $\neg\neg F \equiv F$ can be used for getting rid of double negations. Write a function

```
nnf :: Formula Variable -> Formula Variable
```

for transforming a formula into negation normal form. (Hint: use the function from the previous exercise for getting rid of implication and equivalence operators.)

4.7 Adding Function Symbols

One would hope that predicate logic is powerful enough to express the equations of primary school arithmetic. The above definition does not quite give us that expressive power, however, for we have only allowed for simple terms (terms that are either constants or variables), while an arithmetical term like $((5 + 3) \times 4)$ is a complex expression. Just adding the term forming operators $+$ and $\times$ is not the best solution, for we want our predicate logical language to be general enough to also apply to other domains than the domain of natural numbers. So instead of introducing a name for the sum and product operations, we introduce names for arbitrary operations — just like we have introduced names for arbitrary two-place relations instead of introducing a name for the 'smaller than' relation. Names for arbitrary operations are called function constants and are intended to represent functions.

In the above data type for formulas it is assumed that all terms are variables. The following data type for terms caters for variables plus functional terms. Functional terms with an empty variable list are the individual constants of the language. We will later use them as denotations for proper names.

Again we start with a version of the syntax of terms that uses lists:

$$
\begin{aligned}
\mathbf{t} &\longrightarrow \mathbf{v} \mid \mathbf{f} \ \mathbf{tlist} \\
\mathbf{f} &\longrightarrow f \mid \mathbf{f'} \\
\mathbf{tlist} &\longrightarrow [\,] \mid \mathbf{t} : \mathbf{tlist}
\end{aligned}
$$

This allows for complex terms like $f[x]$ and $f''[f'[x], f'''[x, f[z]]]$.

Exercise 4.21 Give a parse tree for the term $f''[f'[x,y], f'''[z,z,f[x]]]$.

Again, we will write $f', f'', \ldots$ as f_1, f_2, and so on.
Here is an implementation of a data type for terms:

```
data Term = Var Variable | Struct String [Term]
            deriving (Eq,Ord)
```

Here is the declaration of `Term` as an instance of the `Show` class:

```
instance Show Term where
  show (Var v)       = show v
  show (Struct s []) = s
  show (Struct s ts) = s ++ show ts
```

Let us define some examples of variable terms:

```
tx, ty, tz :: Term
tx = Var x
ty = Var y
tz = Var z
```

A term t is *free for variable v in formula F* if every free occurrence of v in F can be replaced by t without any of the variables in t getting bound. For example, y is free for x in $(Px \to \forall x Px)$, but the same term is not free for x in $(\forall y Rxy \to \forall x Rxx)$. Similarly, $g(x,y)$ is not free for x in $(\forall y Rxy \to \forall x Rxx)$.

Being free for a variable v in a formula is an important notion, for a term with this property can be *substituted* for free occurrences of v without an unintended change of meaning. As an example for a substitution that changes the meaning, consider the open formula $(\forall y Rxy \to \forall x Rxx)$. If we replace the free occurrence of x in this formula by y we get a closed formula: $(\forall y Ryy \to \forall x Rxx)$. The result of the substitution is a sentence: a variable which originally was free has got captured. This kind of accident we would like to avoid.

If a term t is free for a variable v in a formula F we can substitute t for all free occurrences of v in F without worrying about variables in t getting bound by one of the quantifiers in F. If, on the other hand, t is not free for v in F, we can always rename the bound variables in F to ensure that substitution of t for v in F has the right meaning. Although $g(y,c)$ is not free for x in $(\forall y Rxy \to \forall x Rxx)$, the term is free for x in $(\forall z Rxz \to \forall x Rxx)$, which is a so-called *alphabetic variant* of the original formula. An alphabetic variant of a formula is a formula which only differs from the original in the fact that it uses different bound variables.

The function isVar checks whether a term is a variable:

```
isVar :: Term -> Bool
isVar (Var _) = True
isVar _       = False
```

The functions varsInTerm and varsInTerms give the variables that occur in a term or a term list. Variable lists should not contain duplicates; the function nub cleans up the variable lists.

```
varsInTerm :: Term -> [Variable]
varsInTerm (Var v)     = [v]
varsInTerm (Struct s ts) = varsInTerms ts

varsInTerms :: [Term] -> [Variable]
varsInTerms = nub . concat . map varsInTerm
```

Now that we have Term, we can use Formula Term for formulas with structured terms.

Exercise 4.22 Implement a function varsInForm :: Formula Term -> [Variable] that gives the list of variables occurring in a formula.

Exercise 4.23 Implement a function

```
freeVarsInForm :: Formula Term -> [Variable]
```

that gives the list of variables with free occurrences in a formula.

Exercise 4.24 Implement a function openForm :: Formula Term -> Bool that checks whether a formula is open (see Section 4.5).

4.8 Further Reading

Formal language theory is the theory behind syntactic fragments. See, e.g., [Révon]. Formal language theory started with [Cho59], where the so-called Chomsky hierarchy of formal languages is defined. Chomsky himself drew the conclusion that the formalism of context-free grammars (the key formalism underlying the fragments above) is inadequate for a full description of natural language, as natural languages exhibit phenomena that are provably beyond the generative capacity of context-free grammar rules. This motivated Chomsky's adoption of transformation rules. A formal study of generative grammar formalisms is taken up in [Rog98]. Somewhat surprisingly, many linguistics faculties do not offer any training in formal language theory. Linguistics students who are interested in it are advised to shop around for courses in the computing science departments of their universities, where the topic is in the core curriculum.

Formal Semantics for Fragments

Summary

The semantics of all the example languages from the previous chapter, except for the case of the natural language fragment, is given in formal detail, with a word or two about pragmatics thrown in here and there for good measure. Again we will use Haskell to make the step from formal definitions to working implementations.

5.1 Semantics of Sea Battle

To specify the semantics of Sea Battle, we should first know something about the extralinguistic reality that the game is about. And in the second place we should find out how to describe the way in which the expressions which are part of the game relate to that reality.

The reality of Sea Battle is made up of a set of *states* of the game board. In fact, there are two game boards, one for each player, but for simplicity we confine attention to one of these. A game state is a board with positions of ships indicated on it, and marks indicating the fields on the board that were under attack so far in the game. For example:

	A	B	C	D	E	F	G	H	I	J
10										
9	○	○	○			X	○			
8					X		○			
7		○		X			○			
6		○	X							
5		○								
4		○		○	○	○	○	○		
3										
2										
1								○	○	

The meaning of an attack is given by a state change. For example, the meaning of the attack $B5$ for the state just given can be specified as follows:

$$\xrightarrow{B5}$$

	A	B	C	D	E	F	G	H	I	J
10										
9	○	○	○			X	○			
8					X		○			
7		○		X			○			
6		○	X							
5		Ⓧ								
4		○		○	○	○	○	○		
3										
2										
1								○	○	

The complete meaning of the attack $B5$ can be given by a function from 'input' states to 'output' states that for every input state of the game board returns that state adorned with an extra X at position $B5$ as output state. The Haskell implementation will make this clear.

When declaring the module, we import the modules List and FSynF, as well as the function toUpper from the module Char.

```
module FSemF where

import Data.List
import Data.Char (toUpper)
import FSynF
```

A grid is simply a list of coordinates. The example grid with the ship positions from the picture above would be the following.

```
type Grid = [(Column,Row)]

exampleGrid :: Grid
exampleGrid = [(A',9),
              (B',4),(B',5),(B',6),(B',7),(B',9),
              (C',9),(D',4),(E',4),(F',4),
              (G',4),(G',7),(G',8),(G',9),
              (H',1),(H',4),(I',1)]
```

The example grid with the attacks so far is this:

```
attacks :: Grid
attacks = [(F',9),(E',8),(D',7),(C',6)]
```

A game state is represented as a number of grids, for the ship positions and for the attacks. It will be convenient to have a separate grid for each ship. Let us assume a battleship occupies five squares on the grid (adjacent, and either in the same row or on the same column), a frigate four, a submarine three, and a destroyer two. Here is how the ships are distributed in the example above:

```
battleship, frigate, sub1, sub2, destroyer :: Grid
battleship = [(D',4),(E',4),(F',4),(G',4),(H',4)]
frigate    = [(B',4),(B',5),(B',6),(B',7)]
sub1       = [(A',9),(B',9),(C',9)]
sub2       = [(G',7),(G',8),(G',9)]
destroyer  = [(H',1),(I',1)]
```

A state consists of a list of ship positions together with a grid with an account of the squares that have been under attack so far.

```
type State = ([Grid],Grid)
```

Our example state is:

```
shipsDistrib :: [Grid]
shipsDistrib = [battleship,frigate,sub1,sub2,destroyer]

exampleState = (shipsDistrib,attacks)
```

Of course, we have to check whether a state is legal. Two ships cannot be at the same place, and the ships all have to be at adjacent squares in a single row or column. Here is a check for the first part:

```
noClashes :: State -> Bool
noClashes (distrib,_) = nodups (concat distrib)
  where nodups []     = True
        nodups (x:xs) = notElem x xs && nodups xs
```

The next exercise invites you to write a check for the second part:

Exercise 5.1 Write a check `lineupOK :: State -> Bool` to make sure that all ships in a state are on adjacent squares in a single row or column.

The Sea Battle reactions *missed*, *hit*, *sunk*, and *defeated* are interpreted as follows. Given a state and the position of the last attack, any of these reactions gives the value 'true' ($= 1$) or 'false' ($= 0$). We can express this as a function F from $S \times P \times R$ to $\{0, 1\}$, where S is the set of states of the game, P the set of positions, and R the set of reactions (so $S \times P \times R$ is the set of triples consisting of a state, a position and a reaction).

$$F(s, p, \mathit{missed}) = \begin{cases} 1 & \text{if there is no ship at position } p \text{ in state } s, \\ 0 & \text{otherwise.} \end{cases}$$

$$F(s, p, \mathit{hit}) = \begin{cases} 1 & \text{if there is a ship at position } p \text{ in state } s, \\ 0 & \text{otherwise.} \end{cases}$$

$$F(s, p, \mathit{sunk}) = \begin{cases} 1 & \text{if there is a ship at position } p \text{ in state } s \\ & \text{which is covered by X's everywhere but at } p, \\ 0 & \text{otherwise.} \end{cases}$$

$$F(s, p, \mathit{defeated}) = \begin{cases} 1 & \text{if there is a ship at position } p \text{ in state } s \\ & \text{which is covered by X's everywhere but at } p, \\ & \text{while all other ships are covered everywhere,} \\ 0 & \text{otherwise.} \end{cases}$$

This can be implemented as follows:

```
hit :: Attack -> State -> Bool
hit pos (gs,_) = elem pos (concat gs)

missed :: Attack -> State -> Bool
missed pos = not . (hit pos)

defeated :: State -> Bool
defeated (gs,g) = all ('elem' g) (concat gs)
```

For example:

```
FSemF> defeated exampleState
False
FSemF> hit (B',5) exampleState
True
FSemF> hit (A',4) exampleState
False
```

Exercise 5.2 Implement a Boolean function sunk for indicating whether a particular attack sinks a ship of a particular type in a state. The type is

$$\text{sunk :: Attack -> Ship -> State -> Bool.}$$

The function that updates the state with a record of a new attack is given by:

```
updateBattle :: Attack -> State -> State
updateBattle p (gs,g) = (gs, insert p g)
```

Note that it follows from the semantic clauses for *defeated*, *hit*, and *sunk* that if a certain attack is a defeating attack, then it is also a sinking attack, and that if a certain attack is a sinking attack, it is also a hitting attack. It follows from this that the game rule 'Always react to an attack with a truthful statement' does not in all cases determine the appropriate reaction.

Game rules like this are within the province of pragmatics. The rudiments of a systematic treatment of this field were given by Paul Grice [Gri75], a philosopher of language, with his observation that language users should try to fit their own and their partners' contributions to spoken communication into a coherent whole by means of the following global principles (also called *Gricean Maxims*):

Cooperation Try to adjust every contribution to the spoken communication to what is perceived as the common goal of the communication at that point in the interaction.

Quality Aspire to truthfulness. Do not say anything that you do not believe to be true. Do not say anything for which you have inadequate support.

Quantity Be as explicit as the situation requires, no more, no less.

Mode of Expression Don't be obscure, don't be ambiguous, aspire to conciseness and clarity.

As you can see, this is prescriptive in the vague way that all exhortations to behave well tend to be. Also, there is some overlap between the principles. Finally, the principles employ notions like *truth* and *informativeness* which are key notions of semantics. In this sense, pragmatics does indeed presuppose semantics.

But however vague they are, Grice's maxims are applicable to the Sea Battle example. The semantics of Sea Battle gives a very precise measure for informativeness of reactions. For why is the reaction *sunk* (when it is true) more informative than the reaction *hit* (also true in that same situation)? Because the reaction *sunk* applies truthfully to a strictly smaller set of game states, in other words, because this reaction excludes a larger number of states. The same holds for the relation between *defeated* and *sunk*. It follows from the principle of cooperation, based on insight in the goal of the utterance of letting the other player know where he or she stands, that in a situation where *sunk* applies the reaction *hit* is inappropriate. This same conclusion can also be argued for on the basis of the maxim of quantity, which states that the game demands maximally informative reactions at every stage.

Exercise 5.3 What more can be said about the pragmatics of Sea Battle in terms of Grice's maxims?

5.2 Semantics of Propositional Logic

The first issue we must address for the semantics of propositional logic is: what are the extralinguistic structures that propositional logical formulas are about? Our answer to this is: pieces of information about the truth or falsity of atomic propositions. This answer is encoded in so-called *valuations*, functions from the set P of proposition letters to the set $\{0, 1\}$ of *truth values*. If V is such a valuation, then V can be extended to a function V^+ from the set of all propositional formulas to the set $\{0, 1\}$. In the following definition of V^+, and further on in the book, we use the abbreviation *iff* for *if and only if*.

$$
\begin{aligned}
V^+(p) &= V(p) && \text{for all } p \in P, \\
V^+(\neg F) &= 1 && \text{iff } V^+(F) = 0, \\
V^+(F_1 \wedge F_2) &= 1 && \text{iff } V^+(F_1) = V^+(F_2) = 1 \\
V^+(F_1 \vee F_2) &= 1 && \text{iff } V^+(F_1) = 1 \text{ or } V^+(F_2) = 1
\end{aligned}
$$

Exercise 5.4 Let V be given by $p \mapsto 0, q \mapsto 1, r \mapsto 1$. Give the V^+ values of the following formulas:

(1) $\neg p \vee p$
(2) $p \wedge \neg p$
(3) $\neg\neg(p \vee \neg r)$
(4) $\neg(p \wedge \neg r)$
(5) $p \vee (q \wedge r)$

Another way of presenting the semantics of the propositional connectives is by means of *truth tables*, which specify how the truth value of a complex formula is calculated from the truth values of its components.

F_1	F_2	$\neg F_1$	$F_1 \wedge F_2$	$F_1 \vee F_2$	$F_1 \rightarrow F_2$	$F_1 \leftrightarrow F2$
1	1	0	1	1	1	1
1	0	0	0	1	0	0
0	1	1	0	1	1	0
0	0	1	0	0	1	1

It is not difficult to see that there are formulas F for which the V^+ value does not depend on the V value of F. Formulas F with the property that $V^+(F) = 1$ for any V are called *tautologies*. The common notation for 'F is a tautology' is $\models F$. Formulas F with the property that $V^+(F) = 0$ for any V are called *contradictions*.

Exercise 5.5 Explain why the negation of a tautology is always a contradiction, and vice versa.

A formula F is *satisfiable* if there is at least one valuation V with $V^+(F) = 1$. A formula F is called *contingent* if it is satisfiable but not a tautology.

Exercise 5.6 Which of the following are satisfiable? If a formula is satisfiable, you should also give a valuation which satisfies it.

(1) $p \wedge \neg q$
(2) $p \wedge \neg p$
(3) $p \rightarrow \neg p$

Clearly, every tautology is satisfiable, but not every satisfiable formula is a tautology.

Two formulas F_1 and F_2 are called *logically equivalent* if $V^+(F_1) = V^+(F_2)$ for any V. Notation for 'F_1 and F_2 are logically equivalent' is $F_1 \equiv F_2$.

Further on, we will often ignore the distinction between a valuation V and its extension V^+, and we will refer to both as V.

Exercise 5.7 Which of the following are true?

(1) $\neg\neg p \equiv p$
(2) $p \rightarrow q \equiv \neg p \vee q$
(3) $\neg(p \leftrightarrow q) \equiv \neg p \wedge q$

Note that it follows from the definition of logical equivalence that all tautologies are logically equivalent to one another, and so are all contradictions.

Formulas $P_1, \ldots, P_n$ logically imply formula C (P for premise, C for conclusion) if every valuation which makes every member of $P_1, \ldots, P_n$ true also makes C true. Notation for '$P_1, \ldots, P_n$ logically implies C' is $P_1, \ldots, P_n \models C$.

Exercise 5.8 Which of the following are true?

(1) $p \models p \vee q$
(2) $p \rightarrow q \models \neg p \rightarrow \neg q$
(3) $\neg q \models p \rightarrow q$
(4) $\neg p, q \rightarrow p \models \neg q$

Exercise 5.9 Show that the following *principle of contraposition* is true:

$$F_1 \models F_2 \text{ iff } \neg F_2 \models \neg F_1.$$

5.3 Propositional Reasoning in Haskell

Exercise 4.14 asked you to collect the names of the proposition letters occurring in a propositional formula. Here is the solution:

```
propNames :: Form -> [String]
propNames (P name) = [name]
propNames (Ng f)   = propNames f
propNames (Cnj fs) = (sort.nub.concat) (map propNames fs)
propNames (Dsj fs) = (sort.nub.concat) (map propNames fs)
```

A valuation for a propositional formula is a map from its variable names to the Booleans. The following function generates the list of all valuations over a set of names:

```
genVals :: [String] -> [[(String,Bool)]]
genVals [] = [[]]
genVals (name:names) = map ((name,True) :) (genVals names)
                    ++ map ((name,False):) (genVals names)
```

The list of all valuations for a propositional formula is given by:

```
allVals :: Form -> [[(String,Bool)]]
allVals = genVals . propNames
```

For evaluation of propositional formulas in the implemented format, we should ask ourselves what is a reasonable convention for the truth of Cnj []. A conjunction is true if all its conjuncts are true. This requirement is trivially fulfilled in case there are no conjuncts. So Cnj [] is always true. Similarly, a disjunction is true if at least one disjunct is true. This requirement is never fulfilled in case there are no disjuncts. So Dsj [] is always false. In the implementation we can use all for conjunctions and any for disjunctions.

```
eval :: [(String,Bool)] -> Form -> Bool
eval [] (P c)    = error ("no info about " ++ show c)
eval ((i,b):xs) (P c)
     | c == i    = b
     | otherwise = eval xs (P c)
```

```
eval xs (Ng f)   = not (eval xs f)
eval xs (Cnj fs) = all (eval xs) fs
eval xs (Dsj fs) = any (eval xs) fs
```

Tautologies are formulas that evaluate to `True` for every valuation:

```
tautology :: Form -> Bool
tautology f = all (\ v -> eval v f) (allVals f)
```

A propositional formula was called satisfiable if there is a propositional valuation that makes the formula true.

```
satisfiable :: Form -> Bool
satisfiable f = any (\ v -> eval v f) (allVals f)
```

Contradictions are formulas that evaluate to `True` for no valuation. Clearly, a formula is contradiction if it is not satisfiable:

```
contradiction :: Form -> Bool
contradiction = not . satisfiable
```

We get:

```
FSemF> contradiction form1
True
FSemF> tautology (Ng form1)
True
FSemF> satisfiable form2
True
FSemF> satisfiable (Ng form2)
True
```

A propositional formula F_1 implies another formula F_1 if every valuation that satisfies F_1 also satisfies F_2. From this definition we get the following proposition.

Proposition 5.1 F_1 implies F_2 iff $F_1 \wedge \neg F_2$ is a contradiction.

The implementation is straightforward:

```
implies :: Form -> Form -> Bool
implies f1 f2 = contradiction (Cnj [f1,Ng f2])
```

Exercise 5.10 Extend the check for propositional implication to the case with a list of premisses. The type is `impliesL :: [Form] -> Form -> Bool`.

Exercise 5.11 Implement a check for logical equivalence between propositional formulas. The type is `propEquiv :: Form -> Form -> Bool`.

The semantics for propositional logic can also be given in update format. First fix a set of relevant valuations. This is the current state. Then define an update function that leaves only those valuations that satisfy a given formula.

```
update :: [[(String,Bool)]] -> Form -> [[(String,Bool)]]
update vals f = [ v | v <- vals, eval v f ]
```

Updating the state of all relevant valuations with a contradiction leaves nothing, updating with a tautology takes nothing away:

```
FSemF> allVals form1
[[("p",True)],[("p",False)]]
FSemF> update (allVals form1) form1
[]
FSemF> update (allVals form1) (Ng form1)
[[("p",True)],[("p",False)]]
```

Updating the state of all relevant valuations with a contingent formula takes something away, updating with its negation takes the complement away:

```
FSemF> length (allVals form2)
16
FSemF> length (update (allVals form2) form2)
15
FSemF> length (update (allVals form2) (Ng form2))
1
```

Exercise 5.12 Instead of the data type `[(String,Bool)]` for valuations, we might as well simply have used `[String]`, with presence or absence in the list indicating truth or falsity. Reimplement the semantics of propositional formulas using this data type.

5.4 Semantics of Mastermind

The semantics of Mastermind can be viewed as an example application of propositional logic. In the grammar for Mastermind of Section 4.1 it is assumed that there are five colours (red, yellow, blue, green, orange) and four positions. According to the language definition, colours may be repeated.

Exercise 5.13 How many possible settings are there for this game? And how many possible settings are there if colour repetition is forbidden?

For an analysis in terms of propositional logic, use propositional formulas for the encoding, with proposition letters r_1 for 'red occurs at position one', and so on.

Exercise 5.14 Find a formula of propositional logic that expresses that all positions have exactly one colour.

Assume the initial setting is *red, yellow, blue, blue*. The problem is solved as soon as the correct formula $r_1 \wedge y_2 \wedge b_3 \wedge b_4$ is logically implied by the formulas that encode the information about the rules of the game and the information provided by the answers to the guesses.

Note that again there is a role for pragmatics in this game. The pragmatic rule 'ask for relevant information' would forbid to make a guess that is already ruled out by answers to earlier guesses.

Let us turn to the implementation. The key element in the semantics of Mastermind is the computation that determines appropriate reactions to a guess. The guess is compared with the secret pattern, and the appropriate reaction is returned. To compute the reaction, first the elements that occur at the same position are counted, next the elements that occur somewhere are counted, and finally the counts are combined. Note that we do not forbid repetition of colours.

```
samepos :: Pattern -> Pattern -> Int
samepos _          []                  = 0
samepos []         _                   = 0
samepos (x:xs) (y:ys) | x == y         = samepos xs ys + 1
                      | otherwise      = samepos xs ys


occurscount ::  Pattern -> Pattern -> Int
occurscount xs []        = 0
occurscount xs (y:ys)
            | y 'elem' xs = occurscount (delete y xs) ys + 1
            | otherwise   = occurscount xs ys
```

```
reaction :: Pattern -> Pattern -> [Answer]
reaction secret guess = take n (repeat Black)
                        ++ take m (repeat White)
  where n = samepos secret guess
        m = occurscount secret guess - n
```

Let's fix a pattern:

```
secret = [Red,Blue,Green,Yellow]
```

Here is a check of the results:

```
FSemF> secret
[Red,Blue,Green,Yellow]
FSemF> reaction secret [Blue,Red,Yellow,Orange]
[White,White,White]
FSemF> reaction secret [Green,Blue,Red,Yellow]
[Black,Black,White,White]
FSemF> reaction secret secret
[Black,Black,Black,Black]
```

As in the case of propositional logic, we can now give a Mastermind update function that updates a current list of possible arrangements with the information conveyed in a reaction.

In updating the list of possible patterns, given a particular reaction, we have to keep all patterns that generate the same reaction and discard the rest.

```
updateMM :: [Pattern] -> Pattern -> Feedback -> [Pattern]
updateMM state guess answer =
  [ xs | xs <- state, reaction xs guess == answer ]
```

For playing an actual Mastermind game, we need a way to convert strings to colour sequences.

```
string2pattern :: String -> Pattern
string2pattern = convertP . (map toUpper)
```

```
convertP :: String -> Pattern
convertP []        = []
convertP (' ':xs) =              convertP xs
convertP ('R':xs) = Red     : convertP xs
convertP ('Y':xs) = Yellow : convertP xs
convertP ('B':xs) = Blue    : convertP xs
convertP ('G':xs) = Green   : convertP xs
convertP ('O':xs) = Orange : convertP xs
```

Finally, here is an implementation of a Mastermind game. For simplicity, we have assumed that `secret` contains the secret colour pattern. The function `playMM` uses some I/O-tricks that we are not going to explain at this point: see the Haskell documentation for further illumination.

```
playMM :: IO ()
playMM =
  do
    putStrLn "Give a sequence of four colours from RGBYO"
    s <- getLine
    if (string2pattern s) /= secret
      then
        let answer = reaction secret (string2pattern s) in
        do
          putStrLn (show answer)
          putStrLn "Please make another guess"
          playMM
      else putStrLn "correct"
```

You can try this out by loading the code from this chapter, and typing `playMM` at the system prompt. Here is a sample of what you will get:

```
FSemF> playMM
Give a sequence of four colours from RGBYO
rgyo
[Black,White,White]
Please make another guess
Give a sequence of four colours from RGBYO
gboy
[Black,Black,White]
Please make another guess
```

```
Give a sequence of four colours from RGBYO
rbgo
[Black,Black,Black]
Please make another guess
Give a sequence of four colours from RGBYO
rbgy
correct
```

Exercise 5.15 Find out from the Haskell documentation how to generate random colour patterns using the Random module. Modify the function playMM so that it generates a new secret colour pattern at the beginning of each game.

Hint: here is an auxiliary function you can use, provided the module System.Random is loaded:

```
getColours :: IO [Colour]
getColours = do
             i <- getStdRandom (randomR (0,4))
             j <- getStdRandom (randomR (0,4))
             k <- getStdRandom (randomR (0,4))
             l <- getStdRandom (randomR (0,4))
             return [toEnum i,toEnum j, toEnum k, toEnum l]
```

This will give you a list of four colours, but wrapped inside the I/O-monad. To get the list out, use a do construct with an action secret <- getColours inside, and use the secret inside the do construct.

Exercise 5.16 A guess that contradicts the information that was already supplied earlier on in the game is a stupid guess. Modify the game function so that it can recognize stupid guesses and let the user know about them, while taking care to keep the responses polite, of course.

5.5 Semantics of Predicate Logic

The semantics of predicate logic is static again. For convenience we limit ourselves to a language fragment with just three predicate letters P, R, S, where P is a one-place predicate, R is a two-place predicate, and S is a three-place predicate.

How should an extralinguistic structure for the constants P, R, S look? Such a structure should at least contain a domain of discourse D consisting of individual entities, with an interpretation for P, for R and for S. These interpretations are given by a function I. We need an I with $I(P) \subseteq D$, $I(R) \subseteq D \times D$, and $I(S) \subseteq D \times D \times D$. Here $D \times D$ (which is sometimes written as D^2) the set of all pairs of elements from D, and $D \times D \times D$ (also written as D^3 sometimes) the set of all ordered triples of elements from D. (Recall the definition of the

Cartesian product from Section 2.2.) Figure 5.5 gives an example of a domain with a possible $I(P)$ and $I(R)$. Shading marks objects with property P, $\rightarrow$ indicates that two objects are R-related, a $\longleftrightarrow$ link indicates that the R-relation runs in both directions, and loops indicate that an object is R-related to itself.

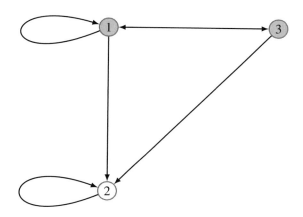

A set of relation symbols, with their arities given, specifies a predicate logical language L. A structure $M = (D, I)$ consisting of a non-empty domain D with an interpretation function for the relation symbols of L is called a *model for L*. We will always assume that the domain D of a model is non-empty. Looking at the example case above, the language is given by the relation symbols P and R. In Figure 5.5 we numbered the nodes, so we can say that the domain consists of the set $\{1, 2, 3\}$. The interpretation function I is given by $I(P) = \{1, 3\}$ and $I(R) = \{(1, 1), (1, 2), (2, 2), (3, 1), (3, 2)\}$.

Given a structure with interpretation function $M = (D, I)$, we can define a valuation for the predicate logical formulas, provided we know how to deal with the values of individual variables. Let V be the set of variables of the language. A function $g : V \rightarrow D$ is called a *variable assignment* or *valuation*.

We use $g[v := d]$ for the valuation that is like s except for the fact that v gets value d (where g might have assigned a different value). For example, let $D = \{1, 2, 3\}$, and let $V = \{v_1, v_2, v_3\}$. Let g be given by $g(v_1) = 1, g(v_2) = 2, g(v_3) = 3$. Then $g[v_1 := 2]$ is the valuation that is like g except for the fact that v_1 gets the value 2, i.e. the valuation that assigns 2 to v_1, 2 to v_2, and 3 to v_3.

Let M be a model for language L, let g be a variable assignment for L in M, let F be a formula of L. Now we are ready to define the notion $M \models_g F$, for F is true in M under assignment g, or: g satisfies F in model M.

$M \models_g Pv$	iff	$g(v) \in I(P)$
$M \models_g R(v_1, v_2)$	iff	$(g(v_1), g(v_2)) \in I(R)$
$M \models_g S(v_1, v_2, v_3)$	iff	$(g(v_1), g(v_2), g(v_3)) \in I(S)$
$M \models_g (v_1 = v_2)$	iff	$g(v_1) = g(v_2)$
$M \models_g \neg F$	iff	it is not the case that $M \models_g F$.
$M \models_g (F_1 \wedge F_2)$	iff	$M \models_g F_1$ and $M \models_g F_2$
$M \models_g (F_1 \vee F_2)$	iff	$M \models_g F_1$ or $M \models_g F_2$
$M \models_g \forall v F$	iff	for all $d \in D$ it holds that $M \models_{g[v:=d]} F$
$M \models_g \exists v F$	iff	for at least one $d \in D$ it holds that $M \models_{g[v:=d]} F$

What we have presented just now is a recursive definition of truth for predicate logical formulas.

If we evaluate closed formulas (formulas without free variables), the assignment g becomes irrelevant, so for a closed formula F we can simply put $M \models F$ iff there is some assignment g with $M \models_g F$.

Exercise 5.17

   (1) Show that $\forall x(Ax \wedge Bx)$ means something stronger than *All A are B*.
   (2) Show that $\exists x(Ax \rightarrow Bx)$ means something weaker than *Some A are B*.

Exercise 5.18 Translate the following sentences into predicate logic, making sure that their truth conditions are captured.

Someone walks and someone talks.	(5.1)
No wizard cast a spell or mixed a potion.	(5.2)
Every balad that is sung by a princess is beautiful.	(5.3)
If a knight finds a dragon, he fights it.	(5.4)

Exercise 5.19 Let M be the model pictured in Figure 5.5. Which of the following statements are true?

   (1) $M \models \exists x(Px \wedge Rxx)$
   (2) $M \models \forall x(Px \rightarrow \exists y Rxy)$
   (3) $M \models \forall x(\exists y Ryx \rightarrow Rxx)$

A predicate logical sentence F is called *logically valid* if F is true in every model. Notation for 'F is logically valid' is $\models F$. From the convention that the domains of our models are always non-empty it follows that $\models \forall x F \rightarrow \exists x F$, for all F with at most the variable x free.

Exercise 5.20 Which of the following statements are true?

(1) $\models \forall x Px \vee \exists x \neg Px$
(2) $\models \exists x \exists y Rxy \rightarrow \exists x \exists y Ryx$
(3) $\models \forall x Rxx \rightarrow \forall x \exists y Rxy$
(4) $\models \exists x Rxx \rightarrow \forall x \exists y Rxy$

The truth definition makes essential use of assignments, and still, in the exercises so far, where we have looked only at closed formulas, truth or falsity does not depend on which assignment we use. One might think, therefore, that we can do without assignments altogether if we confine ourselves to defining the truth values of the closed formulas of predicate logic.

The trouble is that when we apply the truth definition above to a sentence, e.g. to the sentence $\forall x(Px \rightarrow \exists y Rxy)$, then the clause for dealing with the universal quantifier makes reference to the notion of truth for the formula $(Px \rightarrow \exists y Rxy)$, which is an open formula. In order to determine whether this is true we have to be told which object x denotes. The situation is entirely analogous to the interpretation of natural language sentences:

$$\textit{Every master has an apprentice.} \tag{5.5}$$
$$\textit{He has an apprentice.} \tag{5.6}$$

To determine the truth of (5.6) we have to be told who is the referent of the pronoun *he*.

Exercise 5.21 Here is a function that substitutes a name a for a variable v in a term t, with notation t_a^v:

$$
\begin{aligned}
c_a^v &:= c \\
v_a^v &:= a \\
u_a^v &:= u \text{ for } u \text{ different from } v
\end{aligned}
$$

Use this to define a function that substitutes a name a for all free occurrences of a variable v in a formula F. Use F_a^v for the result.

Exercise 5.22 Assume that we can extend the language with a set A of proper names for objects, in such a way that every object in D is named by an element from A, by means of an extension I' of the interpretation function I of the model. In other words, we have for all $d \in D$ that there is some $\hat{d} \in A$ with $I'(\hat{d}) = d$. Give an alternative truth definition for predicate logic that does not use assignments, but these extra names, plus the notion of substituting names from A for variables. Use the function $F_{\hat{d}}^v$ that you defined in Exercise 5.21.

In order to extend the truth definition to structured terms (terms containing function symbols), we have to assume that the interpretation function I knows how to deal with a function symbol. If f is a one-place function symbol, then I should map f to a unary operation on the domain D, i.e. to a function $I(f) \colon D \to D$. In general it holds that if f is an n-place function symbol, then I should map f to an n-ary operation on the domain D, i.e. to a function $I(f) \colon D^n \to D$. We use C for the set of zero-place function symbols; these are the constants of the language, and we have that if $c \in C$ then $I(c) \in D$.

Instead of the assignment function g for variables we now need a value function **g** for functional terms, defined as follows (note the recursion in the definition):

$$\mathbf{g}_{I,g}(t) = \begin{cases} I(t) & \text{if} \quad t \in C, \\ g(t) & \text{if} \quad t \in V, \\ I(f)(\mathbf{g}_{I,g}(t_1), \ldots, \mathbf{g}_{I,g}(t_n)) & \text{if} \quad t \text{ has the form } f(t_1, \ldots, t_n). \end{cases}$$

This value function is used in the truth definition, but we leave the details to you:

Exercise 5.23 Write out the truth definition for predicate logical languages with function constants.

An important aim of any logic language is to study the process of valid reasoning in that language. Every logical language comes with an appropriate notion of 'valid consequence' for that language. Intuitively, when can we draw a conclusion C from premises $P_1, \ldots, P_n$? When it is inconceivable that the premises are true and the conclusion false, or in other words when the truth of the premises brings the truth of the conclusion in its wake.

Now that we have a fully precise notion of truth for predicate logic we can use this to make the intuitive notion of valid consequence fully precise too. We say that a predicate logical sentence C logically follows from a predicate logical sentence P (P for premise and C for conclusion; we also say that P logically implies C) if every model which makes P true also makes C true. Notation for 'P logically implies C' is $P \models C$.

How do we judge statements of the form $P \models C$ (where P, C are closed formulas of predicate logic)? It is clear how we can refute the statement $P \models C$, namely by finding a *counterexample*. A counterexample to $P \models C$ is a model M with $M \models P$ but not $M \models C$, or in abbreviated notation: $M \not\models C$. Here are some example questions about valid consequence in predicate logic.

Exercise 5.24 Which of the following statements hold? If a statement holds, then you should explain why. If it does not, then you should give a counterexample.

(1) $\forall x Px \models \exists x Px$
(2) $\exists x \exists y Rxy \models \exists x Rxx$
(3) $\exists y \forall x Rxy \models \forall x \exists y Rxy$

We can make this slightly more general by allowing sets of more than one premise.

Assume that $P_1, \ldots, P_n, C$ are closed formulas of predicate logic. We say that C logically follows from $P_1, \ldots, P_n$, or, formally, that $P_1, \ldots, P_n \models C$, if for every model M for the language with the property that $M \models P_1$ and ... and $M \models P_n$ it is the case that $M \models C$.

Exercise 5.25 Which of the following hold?

(1) $\forall x \forall y (Rxy \rightarrow Ryx), Rab \models Rba$
(2) $\forall x \forall y (Rxy \rightarrow Ryx), Rab \models Raa$

This was not too difficult, but still, models for predicate logical languages can be extremely complex, so the fact that in some particular case we cannot find a counterexample does not always tell us that the conclusion follows logically from the premises. The jump from premises to conclusion may be too dangerous. It is for this reason that logicians have proposed systems of reasoning where the jumps from premise to conclusion are decomposed into smaller jumps, until the jumps become so small that we can easily check their correctness. The implementation of the semantics of predicate logic will be taken up in Chapter 6.

5.6 Semantics of Natural Language Fragments

Now what about the meanings of the sentences in our simple fragment of English? Using what we know now about the meanings of predicate logical formulas, and assuming we have predicate letters available for the nouns and verbs of the fragment, we can easily translate the sentences generated by the example grammar into predicate logic. Assume the following translation key:

lexical item	translation	type of logical constant
girl	*Girl*	one-place predicate
boy	*Boy*	one-place predicate
princess	*Princess*	one-place predicate
dwarf	*Dwarf*	one-place predicate
giant	*Giant*	one-place predicate
wizard	*Wizard*	one-place predicate
sword	*Sword*	one-place predicate
dagger	*Dagger*	one-place predicate

laughed	*Laugh*	one-place predicate
cheered	*Cheer*	one-place predicate
shuddered	*Shudder*	two-place predicate
loved	*Love*	two-place predicate
admired	*Admire*	two-place predicate
helped	*Help*	two-place predicate
defeated	*Defeat*	two-place predicate
gave	*Give*	three-place predicate
Snow White	s	individual constant
Alice	a	individual constant
Dorothy	d	individual constant
Goldilocks	g	individual constant
Little Mook	m	individual constant
Atreyu	y	individual constant

Then the translation of *Every boy loved a girl* could become:

$$\forall x(Boy\ x \to \exists y(Girl\ y \land Love\ x\ y)).$$

Exercise 5.26 Check with the truth definition for predicate logic that this translation expresses the correct meaning (if we disregard the past tense, that is).

Exercise 5.27 Give predicate logical translations for the following sentences from the fragment:

Every girl that laughed helped a boy.	(5.7)
No giant that shuddered defeated every dwarf.	(5.8)
Every princess loved every dwarf that defeated a giant.	(5.9)
Every boy admired a girl that no wizard helped.	(5.10)

Still, there is a sense in which these predicate logical translations do not 'count' as a semantic account of the sentences in the example grammar. The trouble is that one has to understand English in order to check that the translations are correct. In other words, one has to know the meanings of the sentences already. In Section 6.2 an account of the semantics of this and similar fragments will be presented that 'counts'.

5.7 An Inference Engine with a Natural Language Interface

In this final section we turn to the task of building a natural language inference engine, using the fragment for talking about classes from Section 4.3. This fragment uses the so-called Aristotelean quantifiers, and it can be seen as an implementation of the theory of quantification originating with the Greek philosopher Aristotle

(384 BC–322 BC). In his theory of the syllogism Aristotle studied the following inferential pattern:

$$\frac{\text{Quantifier}_1 \ \text{CN}_1 \ \text{VP}_1}{\text{Quantifier}_2 \ \text{CN}_2 \ \text{VP}_2}$$
$$\text{Quantifier}_3 \ \text{CN}_3 \ \text{VP}_3$$

An example is the valid syllogism BARBARA:

$$\frac{\text{All A are B}}{\text{All B are C}}$$
$$\text{All A are C}$$

Syllogistic theory focusses on the quantifiers in the so called *Square of Opposition*; see Figure 5.1.

Fig. 5.1. The Square of Opposition

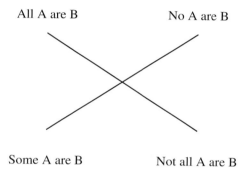

The quantifiers in the square express relations between a first and a second argument. Both arguments denote sets of entities taken from some domain of discourse. The quantified expressions in the square are related across the diagonals by external (sentential) negation, and across the horizontal edges by internal (or verb phrase) negation. It follows that the relation across the vertical edges of the square is that of internal plus external negation; this is the relation of so-called *quantifier duality*. Because Aristotle assumes that the domain of discourse is non-empty, the two quantified expressions on the top edge of the square cannot both be true; these expressions are called *contraries*. Similarly, the two quantified expressions on the bottom edge cannot both be false: they are so-called *subcontraries*. Next, Aristotle interprets his quantifiers with *existential import*: *All A are B* and *No A are B* are taken to imply that there are *A*. Under this assumption, the quantified expressions at the top edge of the square imply those immediately below them. The universal affirmative quantifier *all* implies the individual affirmative *some* and the universal negative *no* implies the individual negative *not all*. The universal and individual affirmative quantifiers are said to be of types **A** and **I**, respectively, from Latin A*ff***I***rmo*, the universal and individual negative quantifiers of type **E** and **O**, from Latin *N***E**g**O**. The Medieval mnemonics for the Aristotelean syllogisms derive from these abbreviations: *Barbara* is the name of the syllogism with two universal affirmative premisses and a universal affirmative conclusion, and so on.

Our application will be a slight extension of Aristotelian logic, for we consider the case where there is a whole knowledge base of possible premises, instead of just two. Our knowledge base will be as simple as it can get. The two relations we are going to model in the knowledge base are that of inclusion $\subseteq$ and that of non-inclusion $\not\subseteq$.

- *All A are B* is expressed by inclusion, as $A \subseteq B$.
- *No A are B* is expressed by inclusion in the complement, as $A \subseteq \overline{B}$.
- *Some A are not B* is expressed by non-inclusion, as $A \not\subseteq B$.
- *Some A are B* is expressed by non-inclusion in the complement, as $A \not\subseteq \overline{B}$. Note that this is equivalent to $A \cap B \neq \emptyset$.

A *knowledge base* is a list of triples

$$(\text{Class}_1, \text{Class}_2, \text{Boolean})$$

where $(A, B, \textbf{True})$ expresses that $A \subseteq B$, and $(A, B, \textbf{False})$ expresses that $A \not\subseteq B$.

The rules of the inference engine are the following. Let $\widetilde{A}$ be given by: if A is of the form $\overline{C}$, then $\widetilde{A} = C$, otherwise $\widetilde{A} = \overline{A}$. Let $A \Longrightarrow B$ express $A \subseteq B$. That is, $\Longrightarrow$ is a syntactic symbol that is semantically interpreted as the subset relation. In one of the rules below we will reverse the direction of the arrow and write $A \Longrightarrow B$ as $B \Longleftarrow A$. Let $A \not\Longrightarrow B$ express $A \not\subseteq B$.

Computing the subset relation from a knowledge base **K** is done with the following rules:

$$\frac{(A, B, \top) \in \mathbf{K}}{A \Longrightarrow B} \qquad \frac{A \Longrightarrow B}{\widetilde{B} \Longrightarrow \widetilde{A}} \qquad \frac{A \Longrightarrow B \quad B \Longrightarrow C}{A \Longrightarrow C}$$

Computing the non-subset relation from the knowledge base is done with:

$$\frac{(A, B, \bot) \in \mathbf{K}}{A \not\Longrightarrow B} \qquad \frac{A \not\Longrightarrow B}{\widetilde{B} \not\Longrightarrow \widetilde{A}} \qquad \frac{A \Longleftarrow B \quad B \not\Longrightarrow C \quad C \Longleftarrow D}{A \not\Longrightarrow D}$$

Next we need an axiom (a rule without a premise) to express reflexivity of $\subseteq$:

$$\frac{}{A \Longrightarrow A}$$

Finally, we will follow Aristotle in reading the classes with existential import, so we assume that classes are non-empty:

$$\frac{A \text{ not of the form } \overline{C}}{A \not\Longrightarrow \widetilde{A}}$$

The following two exercises are about checking soundness and completeness of our inference engine. They ensure that its syntax (i.e. the expressions of form $A \Longrightarrow B$ and $A \not\Longrightarrow B$ together with the above inference rules) and its semantics (i.e. subset relations between classes) correspond.

Exercise 5.28 An inference system is called *sound* if all conclusions that can be derived are valid, i.e. if all axioms are true and all inference rules preserve truth. Show that the inference system for Aristotelian syllogistics is sound.

Exercise 5.29 An inference system is called *complete* if it can derive all valid conclusions from a set of premises. In other words: if $A \Longrightarrow B$ does not follow from a knowledge base, then there is a class model for the knowledge base where $A \not\subseteq B$, and if $A \not\Longrightarrow B$ does not follow from a knowledge base, then there is a class model for the knowledge base where $A \subseteq B$. Show that the inference system for Aristotelian syllogistics is complete.

We now turn to the application. For convenience, we put the code in a separate module. We will need to read natural language sentences from a file and write them back, so we import the I/O-module `System.IO`.

```
module InfEngine where

import Data.List
import Data.Char
import System.IO
```

In our implementation we use `[(a,a)]` for relations. Here is a convenient type synonym:

```
type Rel a = [(a,a)]
```

If $R \subseteq A^2$ and $x \in A$, then $xR := \{y \in A \mid (x, y) \in R\}$. This is called a *right section* of a relation.

```
rSection :: Eq a => a -> Rel a -> [a]
rSection x r = [ y | (z,y) <- r, x == z ]
```

Eq a indicates that a is in the equality class. This is needed because of the equality test == inside the function definition.

The next concept we need is that of the composition of two relations R and S on A. Recall that the composition $R \circ S$ is defined as the set of pairs

$$\{(x, z) \mid \text{ there is some } y \in A \text{ with } (x, y) \in R \text{ and } (y, z) \in S\}.$$

Here is the Haskell implementation:

```
(@@) :: Eq a => Rel a -> Rel a -> Rel a
r @@ s = nub [ (x,z) | (x,y) <- r, (w,z) <- s, y == w ]
```

Also recall that a relation R is transitive if it holds for all x, y, z that if $(x, y) \in R$ and $(y, z) \in R$, then also $(x, z) \in R$. If a relation is not transitive, then it can always be made into a transitive relation by adding pairs. The *transitive closure* of a relation R is by definition the smallest transitive relation S with $R \subseteq S$.

Exercise 5.30 Find the transitive closures of the example relations in Exercise 2.7.

Recall that a relation R on A is reflexive if $I \subseteq R$, where I is the identity relation on R, i.e. $I = \{(x, x) \mid x \in A\}$. The *reflexive transitive closure* of a relation R is by definition the smallest reflexive and transitive relation S with $R \subseteq S$.

Exercise 5.31 Find the reflexive transitive closures of the example relations in Exercise 2.7 on page 19.

To compute the reflexive transitive closure of R, we proceed as follows. We start from I, and compute relations R', R'', and so on, by checking whether composing R with the present stage of the relation yields anything new. If this is the case, we add the new pairs and go on. If it is not the case, we know that the relation is reflexive and transitive, and we stop. This process of gradually adding new stuff until nothing changes is called a fixed point construction. A fixpoint of a function F is an argument S for which $F(S) = S$. The least fixpoint of F is the smallest S for which this happens. Think of S as the present state of the relation that extends R, and think of F as the result of adding the pairs in $R \circ S$ to S. The code is much shorter than the explanation.

```
rtc :: Ord a => [a] -> Rel a -> Rel a
rtc xs r = lfp (\ s -> (sort.nub) (s++(r@@s))) i
           where i = [ (x,x) | x <- xs ]

lfp :: Eq a => (a -> a) -> a -> a
lfp f x | x == f x   = x
        | otherwise = lfp f (f x)
```

Now we are ready to define a knowledge base of classes of things. We assume that each class has an opposite class. For example, the opposite class of the class of mammals is the class of non-mammals, and the opposite class of the class of non-mammals is the class of mammals.

```
data Class = Class String | OppClass String
             deriving (Eq,Ord)

instance Show Class where
  show (Class xs)    = xs
  show (OppClass xs) = "non-" ++ xs

opp :: Class -> Class
opp (Class name)    = OppClass name
opp (OppClass name) = Class name
```

The two relations we are going to model in the knowledge base are that of inclusion $\subseteq$ and that of non-inclusion $\not\subseteq$. In terms of these we can express 'all A are B' as $A \subseteq B$, 'no A are B' as $A \subseteq \overline{B}$, 'some A are not B' as $A \not\subseteq B$, and 'some A are B' as $A \not\subseteq \overline{B}$. Note that $A \not\subseteq \overline{B}$ is equivalent to $A \cap B \neq \emptyset$. Since everything we need can be expressed in terms of inclusion and non-inclusion, a knowledge base can look like this:

```
type KB = [(Class,Class,Bool)]
```

A triple (c,c',True) expresses that class c is included in class c', and likewise (c,c',False) expresses that c is not included in c'.

Next, we need data types for statements and queries, to interact with the knowledge base. We will put them in a single data type, and define a function for distinguishing the declarative statements from the queries below.

```
data Statement =
    All   Class   Class | No      Class Class
  | Some Class    Class | SomeNot Class Class
  | AreAll Class Class | AreNo   Class Class
  | AreAny Class Class | AnyNot  Class Class
  | What    Class
  deriving Eq
```

For ease of reading, we define a show function for statements:

```
instance Show Statement where
  show (All as bs)      =
    "All "  ++ show as ++ " are " ++ show bs ++ "."
  show (No as bs)       =
    "No "   ++ show as ++ " are " ++ show bs ++ "."
  show (Some as bs)     =
    "Some " ++ show as ++ " are " ++ show bs ++ "."
  show (SomeNot as bs) =
    "Some " ++ show as ++ " are not " ++ show bs ++ "."
  show (AreAll as bs)  =
    "Are all " ++ show as ++ show bs ++ "?"
  show (AreNo as bs)    =
    "Are no "  ++ show as ++ show bs ++ "?"
  show (AreAny as bs)  =
    "Are any " ++ show as ++ show bs ++ "?"
  show (AnyNot as bs)  =
    "Are any " ++ show as ++ " not " ++ show bs ++ "?"
  show (What as)        = "What about " ++ show as ++ "?"
```

Classification of statements into interrogative and declarative is done by:

```
isQuery :: Statement -> Bool
isQuery (AreAll _ _) = True
isQuery (AreNo _ _)  = True
isQuery (AreAny _ _) = True
isQuery (AnyNot _ _) = True
isQuery (What _)     = True
isQuery  _           = False
```

It will turn out useful to define the negation of a question:

```
neg :: Statement -> Statement
neg (AreAll as bs) = AnyNot as bs
neg (AreNo  as bs) = AreAny as bs
neg (AreAny as bs) = AreNo  as bs
neg (AnyNot as bs) = AreAll as bs
```

Now the real action starts. We use the reflexive transitive closure operation to compute the subset relation from the knowledge base.

```
subsetRel :: KB -> [(Class,Class)]
subsetRel kb = rtc
  (domain kb) ([(x,y)         | (x,y,True) <- kb ]
          ++  [(opp y,opp x) | (x,y,True) <- kb ])
```

This uses the following function for getting the domain of a knowledge base:

```
domain :: [(Class,Class,Bool)] -> [Class]
domain = nub . dom where
  dom [] = []
  dom ((xs,ys,_):facts) =
           xs : opp xs : ys : opp ys : dom facts
```

The supersets of a particular class are given by a right section of the subset relation. I.e. the supersets of a class are all classes of which it is a subset.

```
supersets :: Class -> KB -> [Class]
supersets cl kb = rSection cl (subsetRel kb)
```

Computing the non-subset relation from the knowledge base, i.e. the set of class pairs $\{(A, B) \mid A \not\subseteq B\}$, is a bit more involved, for we have to take care of existential import.

```
nsubsetRel :: KB -> [(Class,Class)]
nsubsetRel kb = s @@ r @@ s
  where
            r = nub ([(x,y) | (x,y,False) <- kb ]
                ++ [(opp y,opp x) | (x,y,False) <- kb ]
                ++ [(Class xs,OppClass xs) |
                                    (Class xs,_,_) <- kb ]
                ++ [(Class ys,OppClass ys) |
                                    (_,Class ys,_) <- kb ]
                ++ [(Class ys,OppClass ys) |
                                    (_,OppClass ys,_) <- kb ])
            s = [(y,x) | (x,y) <- subsetRel kb ]
```

The non-supersets of a class are given by a right section:

```
nsupersets :: Class -> KB -> [Class]
nsupersets cl kb = rSection cl (nsubsetRel kb)
```

By now we have all that we need to *query* a knowledge base. Query by means of yes/no questions is simple:

```
derive :: KB -> Statement -> Bool
derive kb (AreAll as bs) = bs 'elem' (supersets  as kb)
derive kb (AreNo  as bs) =
  (opp bs) 'elem' (supersets  as kb)
derive kb (AreAny as bs) =
  (opp bs) 'elem' (nsupersets as kb)
derive kb (AnyNot as bs) = bs 'elem' (nsupersets as kb)
```

Recall that the backticks turn the prefix operator `elem` into an infix operator (cf. p. 39).

Caution is needed with the use of this function. Note that there are three possibilities:

- `derive kb query` is true. This means that the statement corresponding to the query is derivable, hence true.
- `derive kb (neg query)` is true. This means that the negation of the statement corresponding to the `query` is derivable, hence true. So the answer to `query` is 'No'.

- neither `derive kb query` nor `derive kb (neg query)` is true. This means that the knowledge base does not have the answer to `query`.

Open queries ('How about A?') are slightly more complicated. We should take care to select the most natural statements to report on a class:

- $A \subseteq B$ is expressed with 'all',
- $A \subseteq \overline{B}$ is expressed with 'no',
- $A \not\subseteq B$ is expressed with 'some not',
- $A \not\subseteq \overline{B}$ is expressed with 'some'.

This defines a function from facts in the knowledge base to appropriate statements:

```
f2s :: (Class,Class,Bool) -> Statement
f2s (as, Class bs,    True)  = All     as (Class bs)
f2s (as, OppClass bs, True)  = No      as (Class bs)
f2s (as, OppClass bs, False) = Some    as (Class bs)
f2s (as, Class bs,    False) = SomeNot as (Class bs)
```

Exercise 5.32 Write a function that filters the facts from a knowledge base that mention a class A or its opposite. Next, use this to define a function

$$\text{report :: Class -> KB -> [Statement]}$$

that gives an exhaustive report of a particular class, as a list of statements.

Instead of just listing relevant facts from the knowledge base, we will give an exhaustive account of what is known about a class:

```
tellAbout :: KB -> Class -> [Statement]

tellAbout kb as =
  [All as (Class bs) | (Class bs) <- supersets as kb,
                       as /= (Class bs) ]
  ++
  [No  as (Class bs) | (OppClass bs) <- supersets as kb,
                       as /= (OppClass bs) ]
```

Next, a bit of pragmatics comes in: we will not tell *Some A are B* if the stronger statement *All A are B* also holds. Note that *All A are B* is stronger than *Some A are B* because of the assumption of existential import.

```
++
[Some as (Class bs) | (OppClass bs) <- nsupersets as kb,
                     as /= (OppClass bs),
                     notElem (as,Class bs) (subsetRel kb) ]
```

Similarly, we do not tell *Some A are not B* if *No A are B* also holds.

```
++
[SomeNot as (Class bs) | (Class bs) <- nsupersets as kb,
                        as /= (Class bs),
                        notElem (as,OppClass bs) (subsetRel kb) ]
```

To build a knowledge base we need a function for updating an existing knowledge base with a statement. But note that the result may be inconsistent. To cater for that possibility, we use the Haskell data type `Maybe`. This data type is useful in cases like this, where we are not sure whether a function is successful. If the function is successful, we want an updated knowledge base. If it is not, we want to get an indication of failure. The `Maybe` data type gives us just this. It is defined in the Standard Prelude as follows:

```
data Maybe a = Nothing | Just a
```

The following definition of the update function illustrates its use. The update function checks for possible inconsistencies. E.g. a request to add an $A \subseteq B$ fact to the knowledge base leads to an inconsistency if $A \not\subseteq B$ is already derivable.

```
update   :: Statement -> KB -> Maybe (KB,Bool)

update (All as bs) kb
  | bs 'elem' (nsupersets as kb) = Nothing
  | bs 'elem' (supersets  as kb) = Just (kb,False)
  | otherwise = Just (((as,bs,True):kb),True)
```

A request to add $A \subseteq \overline{B}$ leads to an inconsistency if $A \not\subseteq \overline{B}$ is already derivable.

```
update (No as bs) kb
  | bs' 'elem' (nsupersets as kb) = Nothing
  | bs' 'elem' (supersets  as kb) = Just (kb,False)
  | otherwise = Just (((as,bs',True):kb),True)
 where    bs' = opp bs
```

Similarly for the requests to update with $A \not\subseteq \overline{B}$ and with $A \not\subseteq B$:

```
update (Some as bs) kb
  | bs' 'elem' (supersets  as kb) = Nothing
  | bs' 'elem' (nsupersets as kb) = Just (kb,False)
  | otherwise = Just (((as,bs',False):kb),True)
 where    bs' = opp bs

update (SomeNot as bs) kb
  | bs 'elem' (supersets  as kb) = Nothing
  | bs 'elem' (nsupersets as kb) = Just (kb,False)
  | otherwise = Just (((as,bs,False):kb),True)
```

With the use of this function for updating a knowledge base with a statement, we can build a knowledge base from a list of statements. Again, this process can fail, and once more we indicate this by means of Maybe.

```
makeKB :: [Statement] -> Maybe KB
makeKB = makeKB' []
    where
        makeKB' kb []      = Just kb
        makeKB' kb (s:ss) = case update s kb of
            Just (kb',_) -> makeKB' kb' ss
            Nothing      -> Nothing
```

It is time we turn our attention to parsing the natural language expressions of our inference engine. Here is a preprocessing function for strings, to prepare them for parsing:

```
preprocess :: String -> [String]
preprocess = words . (map toLower) .
            (takeWhile (\ x -> isAlpha x || isSpace x))
```

The predicate `isAlpha` checks whether the character is an alphabetic character, and `isSpace` is true only for whitespace characters. The function `takeWhile` takes elements from an input list until the condition fails. The `preprocess` function will map a string to a list of words:

```
InfEngine> preprocess "Are any sailors drunk?"
["are","any","sailors","drunk"]
```

This function can be used in a simple parser for statements:

```
parse :: String -> Maybe Statement

parse = parse' . preprocess
  where
    parse' ["all",as,"are",bs] =
      Just (All (Class as) (Class bs))
    parse' ["no",as,"are",bs] =
      Just (No (Class as) (Class bs))
    parse' ["some",as,"are",bs] =
      Just (Some (Class as) (Class bs))
    parse' ["some",as,"are","not",bs] =
      Just (SomeNot (Class as) (Class bs))
```

And for queries:

```
    parse' ["are","all",as,bs] =
      Just (AreAll (Class as) (Class bs))
    parse' ["are","no",as,bs] =
      Just (AreNo (Class as) (Class bs))
    parse' ["are","any",as,bs] =
      Just (AreAny (Class as) (Class bs))
    parse' ["are","any",as,"not",bs] =
      Just (AnyNot (Class as) (Class bs))
    parse' ["what", "about", as] = Just (What (Class as))
    parse' ["how", "about", as]  = Just (What (Class as))
    parse' _ = Nothing
```

To illustrate the use of this, here is a function that parses a text and constructs a knowledge base from the resulting statements:

```
process :: String -> KB
process txt = maybe [] id (mapM parse (lines txt) >>= makeKB)
```

This uses the maybe function, for getting out of the Maybe type. Instead of returning Nothing in case the parse or the knowledge base construction process fails, this returns an empty knowledge base.

```
maybe :: b -> (a -> b) -> Maybe a -> b
maybe _ f (Just x) = f x
maybe z _ Nothing  = z
```

Here is an example piece of text:

```
mytxt = "all bears are mammals\n"
     ++ "no owls are mammals\n"
     ++ "some bears are stupids\n"
     ++ "all men are humans\n"
     ++ "no men are women\n"
     ++ "all women are humans\n"
     ++ "all humans are mammals\n"
     ++ "some men are stupids\n"
     ++ "some men are not stupids"
```

And a knowledge base that is constructed from this text:

```
InfEngine> process mytxt
[(men,stupids,False),(men,non-stupids,False),
 (humans,mammals,True),(women,humans,True),
 (men,non-women,True),(men,humans,True),
 (bears,non-stupids,False),(owls,non-mammals,True),
 (bears,mammals,True)]
```

Now suppose we have a text file of declarative natural language sentences about classes on disk, accessible under a particular name. Here is how to turn that into a knowledge base.

```
getKB :: FilePath -> IO KB
getKB p = do
          txt <- readFile p
          return (process txt)
```

Constructing a knowledge base from a text file involves reading from this file, so it involves an input/output action. IO is a type constructor that indicates this. So the type IO KB indicates that there is some I/O-action going on with knowledge bases. An easy way of listing I/O-actions is by using do, which is an expression that evaluates, in order, the I/O-computations it contains. Let us have a closer look at the I/O-computations in our example above. The function readFile is of type FilePath -> IO String, i.e. it returns the entire contents of a file as a single string, wrapped into an IO to indicate that we performed some I/O-action. The line txt <- readFile p binds the name txt to the value returned by the I/O-computation readFile p. It also removes the IO-wrapping, so xs is a value of type String and not IO String. The second line inside the do-expression constructs the knowledge base and wraps it inside an I/O-action.

And here is how to write a knowledge base to a text file on disk. This time the result is of type IO (), the type of I/O-action without result.

```
writeKB :: FilePath -> KB -> IO ()
writeKB p kb = writeFile p (unlines (map (show.f2s) kb))
```

We now have all the ingredients to put our inference engine in action. We define an input/output process that reads a knowledge base from disk – it is assumed that a file called kb.txt exists in the working directory – and start an interaction process. Interaction goes on until the user inputs an empty line (by just hitting the return key). The interaction is implemented as an infinite chat loop. Inside the loop, the keyboard input is parsed. If it is an empty line, the loop ends. If the input is not parsable as as statement, the user gets feedback to that effect. If the input parses as a statement which is a query, the query is answered with 'Yes', 'No', or 'I don't know', as the occasion demands. If the input parses as a declarative statement, the system checks for consistency with the knowledge base, acts accordingly, and gives appropriate feedback to the user.

```
chat :: IO ()
chat = do
 kb <- getKB "kb.txt"
 writeKB "kb.bak" kb
 putStrLn "Update or query the KB:"
 str <- getLine
 if str == "" then return ()
  else do
   case parse str of
     Nothing          -> putStrLn "Wrong input.\n"
     Just (What as) -> let
          info = (tellAbout kb as, tellAbout kb (opp as)) in
        case info of
         ([],[])        -> putStrLn "No info.\n"
         ([],negi)     -> putStrLn (unlines (map show negi))
         (posi,negi)   -> putStrLn (unlines (map show posi))
     Just stmt        ->
      if isQuery stmt then
        if derive kb stmt then putStrLn "Yes.\n"
          else if derive kb (neg stmt)
                  then putStrLn "No.\n"
                  else putStrLn "I don't know.\n"
        else case update stmt kb of
          Just (kb',True) -> do
                              writeKB "kb.txt" kb'
                              putStrLn "OK.\n"
          Just (_,False)  -> putStrLn
                              "I knew that already.\n"
          Nothing         -> putStrLn
                              "Inconsistent with my info.\n"
   chat
```

Finally, we wrap the whole thing into a main function inside a Main module:

```
module Main where
import InfEngine
main :: IO ()
main = do putStrLn "Welcome to the Knowledge Base."
          chat
```

This code can be used with an interpreter, but it can also be compiled into a separate program with a Haskell compiler. Assuming you have the GHC Haskell compiler installed and you have a Unix/Linux system, this works as follows.† The knowledge base in the coderun below was read from `kb.txt`, available from the book website.

```
$ ghc --make Main
[1 of 2] Compiling InfEngine ( InfEngine.hs, InfEngine.o )
[2 of 2] Compiling Main     ( Main.hs, Main.o )
Linking Main ...
$ ./Main
Welcome to the Knowledge Base.
Update or query the KB:
How about women?
All women are humans.
No women are men.

Update or query the KB:
All mammals are animals.
OK.

Update or query the KB:
No owls are mammals.
I knew that already.

Update or query the KB:
Are any owls stupids?
I don't know.

Update or query the KB:
Not all owls are stupids.
Wrong input.

Update or query the KB:
What about owls?
No owls are bears.
No owls are mammals.

Update or query the KB:
```

† For Windows systems the procedure is similar. See your GHC documentation.

```
All owls are mammals.
Inconsistent with my info.
```

```
Update or query the KB:
```

And so on.

5.8 Further Reading

Grice [Gri75] gives the classical account of pragmatics. An excellent textbook on pragmatics is Levinson [Lev83]. A good introduction to logic for linguists is Gamut [Gam91a]. More mathematically oriented introductions are Van Dalen [Dal83] and Enderton [End72]. Logic textbooks with good explanations of the many connections to applications in computer science are [Bur98] and [HR04]. The idea for the natural language inference engine in Section 5.7 is taken from `http://rubyquiz.com` (Quiz # 37). The Aristotelian class language is a simple example of a concept description language; see the first and second chapter [NB02, BN02] of the Description Logic Handbook [BCM+02] for more information. Connections between Aristotelian logic and predicate logic are discussed in [Łuk51]. Extensions of the Aristotelian fragment are given in [PH04] and [Mos08].

6

Model Checking with Predicate Logic

Summary

In this chapter, we show how predicate logic can be employed as a semantic representation language, or, in the idiom of linguists, as a language for logical form. Next, we demonstrate how models of predicate logic are defined as Haskell data types. Finally, we turn to the problem of interpreting predicate logical languages in appropriate models. In the end we will have an indirect interpretation procedure for our natural language fragment, which consists of two steps: first, we construct a logical form from a natural language expression, and second, we evaluate this logical form with respect to a model.

```
module MCWPL where

import Data.List
import FSynF
import Model
```

6.1 Linguistic Form and Translation Into Logic

> *'I see nobody on the road,' said Alice. 'I only wish I had such eyes,' the King remarked in a fretful tone. 'To be able to see Nobody! And at that distance too!'*
>
> Lewis Carroll, *Alice in Wonderland*

From the sentence *Alice walked on the road* it follows that someone walked on the road, but from *No one walked on the road* it does not follow that someone walked on the road. Therefore, logicians such as Gottlob Frege (1848–1925),

125

Bertrand Russell (1872–1970), Alfred Tarski (1902–1983), and Willard Van Orman Quine (1908–2000) have maintained that the structure of these two sentences must differ, and that it is not enough to say that they are both compositions of a subject and a predicate.

The logicians who used first-order predicate logic to analyse the logical structure of natural language were struck by the fact that the logical translations of natural language sentences with quantified expressions did not seem to follow the linguistic structure. In the logical translations, the quantified expressions seemed to have disappeared. The logical translation of (6.1) does not reveal a constituent corresponding to the quantified subject noun phrase.

$$\textit{Every dwarf loved Goldilocks.} \tag{6.1}$$

$$\forall x (\textit{Dwarf } x \rightarrow \textit{Love } x \; g) \tag{6.2}$$

In the translation (6.2) the constituent *every dwarf* has disappeared; it is contextually eliminated. Frege remarks that a quantified expression like *every dwarf* does not give rise to a concept by itself (*eine selbständige Vorstellung*), but can only be interpreted in the context of the translation of the whole sentence. Considering this particular example, the literal paraphrase of (6.2) is:

All objects in the domain of discourse have the property of either not being dwarves or being objects who loved Goldilocks.

In this restatement of sentence (6.1) the phrase *every dwarf* does not occur any more.

The logical properties of sentences involving quantified expressions (and descriptions, analysed in terms of quantifiers) suggested indeed that the way a simple noun phrase such as a proper name combines with a predicate is logically different from the way in which a quantified noun phrase or a definite description combines with a predicate. This led to the belief that the linguistic form of natural language expressions was misleading.

The application of the logical tools of abstraction and reduction of the lambda calculus allow us to see that this conclusion was unwarranted. Using translation of natural language in expressions of typed logic we will see that natural language constituents correspond to typed expressions that combine with one another as functions and arguments. After full reduction of the results, quantified expressions and other constituents may have been contextually eliminated, but this elimination is a result of the reduction process, not of the supposed misleading form of the original natural language sentence. Thus, while fully reduced logical translations of natural language sentences may be misleading in some sense, the fully unreduced original expressions are not.

As an example of the way in which the tools of lambda calculus smooth logical appearances, consider the logic of the combination of subjects and predicates. In the simplest cases (like *Goldilocks laughed*) one could say that the predicate takes the subject as an argument. But this does not work for quantified subjects (as in *no one laughed*). All is well, however, when we say that the subject always takes the predicate as its argument, and make this work for simple subjects by logically raising their status from argument to function. Using lambda expressions, this is easy enough: we translate *Goldilocks* not as the constant g, but as the expression $\lambda P \mapsto P\,g$. This expression denotes a function from properties to truth values, so it can take a predicate translation as its argument. The translation of *no one* is of the same type: $\lambda P \mapsto \neg\exists x(Person\ x \wedge P\,x)$. Before reduction, the translations of *Goldilocks laughed* and *no one laughed* look very similar. These similarities disappear only after both translations have been reduced to their simplest forms.

In the next section, we demonstrate this by constructing predicate logic formulas as translations of the natural language sentences produced by the fragment from Section 4.2. This translation is the first step for interpreting natural language expressions indirectly. The next step, taken up in the remaining sections, is to assign the formulas in predicate logic a model-theoretic object as denotation. This way, the represented natural language expression is given a model-theoretic interpretation. En route, we will see limitations of this procedure. Finally, the next chapter will show that the detour via translation into a logical language is not necessary, but that we can give a direct interpretation of natural language expressions. There we will also talk about quantifiers and noun phrase denotations in much more detail.

6.2 Predicate Logic as Representation Language

Predicate logic gives us representations for two types: the type of entities is represented by terms (recall the definition of the data type `Term` on page 83), and the type of truth values by formulas (recall the definition of the data type `Formula` on page 80). Let us call the type of predicate logical formulas LF.

```
type LF = Formula Term
```

Assuming that we deal with a fragment that generates declarative sentences with meanings that can be represented with predicate logic, it is reasonable to give the type LF to representations of sentences.

To translate the fragment from Section 4.2 into predicate logic, all we have to do is find appropriate translations for all the categories in the grammar of the fragment. But the first rule, **S $\longrightarrow$ NP VP**, already presents us with a difficulty. In looking for NP translations and VP translations, should we represent NP as a function that takes a VP representation as argument, or vice versa?

In any case, VP representations will have a functional type, for VPs denote properties. A reasonable type for the function that represents a VP is `Term -> LF`. If we feed it with a term, it will yield a logical form. Proper names now can get the type of terms. Take the example *Goldilocks laughed.* The verb *laughed* gets represented as the function that maps the term x to the formula `Atom "laugh" [x]`. Therefore, we get an appropriate logical form for the sentence if x is a term for *Goldilocks,*

A difficulty that we already mentioned at the end of the last section is that phrases like *no boy* and *every girl* do not fit into this pattern. But we also mentioned that we can solve this if we assume such phrases translate into functions that take VP representations as arguments. Let us first find a representation for *everyone.* Intuitively, this combines with a VP representation to yield a logical form expressing that every individual in the domain satisfies the property expressed by the VP. But we know how to express this in predicate logic, for we have the universal quantifier. An appropriate translation for *everyone* would be a function of type `(Term -> LF) -> LF`. If we feed it a VP representation (an expression of type `Term -> LF`), it yields a logical form. Presumably, the translation of *everyone* should run `Forall v (p v)`, where p is of type `Term -> LF`. The only remaining difficulty is finding an appropriate variable for v, but we will solve that problem when we come to it. For now, the upshot of the discussion is that in the LF representation of a [s NP VP] structure, the NP representation should be the function and the VP representation the argument. This gives us:

```
lfSent :: Sent -> LF
lfSent (Sent np vp) = (lfNP np) (lfVP vp)
```

Next, NP-representations are of type `(Term -> LF) -> LF`.

```
lfNP :: NP -> (Term -> LF) -> LF
lfNP SnowWhite    = \ p -> p (Struct "SnowWhite"  [])
lfNP Alice        = \ p -> p (Struct "Alice"      [])
lfNP Dorothy      = \ p -> p (Struct "Dorothy"    [])
lfNP Goldilocks   = \ p -> p (Struct "Goldilocks" [])
lfNP LittleMook   = \ p -> p (Struct "LittleMook" [])
lfNP Atreyu       = \ p -> p (Struct "Atreyu"     [])
lfNP (NP1 det cn)  = (lfDET det) (lfCN cn)
lfNP (NP2 det rcn) = (lfDET det) (lfRCN rcn)
```

Verb phrase representations are of type `Term -> LF`.

```
lfVP :: VP -> Term -> LF
lfVP Laughed   = \ t -> Atom "laugh"   [t]
lfVP Cheered   = \ t -> Atom "cheer"   [t]
lfVP Shuddered = \ t -> Atom "shudder" [t]
```

Assume that representations of transitive verbs have type (Term,Term) -> LF, where the first term slot is for the subject, and the second term slot for the object. Accordingly, the representations of ditransitive verbs have type

$$(Term,Term,Term) -> LF$$

where the first term slot is for the subject, the second one is for the indirect object, and the third one is for the direct object. The result should in both cases be a property for VP subjects. This gives us:

```
lfVP (VP1 tv np) =
    \ subj -> lfNP np (\ obj -> lfTV tv (subj,obj))
lfVP (VP2 dv np1 np2) =
    \ subj -> lfNP np1 (\ iobj -> lfNP np2 (\ dobj ->
                        lfDV dv (subj,iobj,dobj)))
```

Representations for transitive verbs are:

```
lfTV :: TV -> (Term,Term) -> LF
lfTV Loved    = \ (t1,t2) -> Atom "love"   [t1,t2]
lfTV Admired  = \ (t1,t2) -> Atom "admire" [t1,t2]
lfTV Helped   = \ (t1,t2) -> Atom "help"   [t1,t2]
lfTV Defeated = \ (t1,t2) -> Atom "defeat" [t1,t2]
```

The representation for the ditransitive verb *gave* is:

```
lfDV :: DV -> (Term,Term,Term) -> LF
lfDV Gave = \ (t1,t2,t3) -> Atom "give" [t1,t2,t3]
```

Representations for common nouns have the same type as those for VPs.

```
lfCN :: CN -> Term -> LF
lfCN Girl = \ t -> Atom "girl" [t]
lfCN Boy  = \ t -> Atom "boy"  [t]
```

```
lfCN Princess = \ t -> Atom "princess" [t]
lfCN Dwarf    = \ t -> Atom "dwarf"    [t]
lfCN Giant    = \ t -> Atom "giant"    [t]
lfCN Wizard   = \ t -> Atom "wizard"   [t]
lfCN Sword    = \ t -> Atom "sword"    [t]
lfCN Dagger   = \ t -> Atom "dagger"   [t]
```

The type of the logical form translation of determiners indicates that the translation takes a determiner phrase and two arguments for objects of type `Term -> LF` (logical forms with term holes in them), and produces a logical form. In the case of quantifiers, the first argument of type `Term -> LF` is the restriction, and the second one is the scope. We will talk about this in the next chapter.

```
lfDET :: DET -> (Term -> LF) -> (Term -> LF) -> LF
```

In the translation of determiners we hit on a limitation of the present approach. As we will see in Section 7.2, some determiners do not admit a translation into predicate logic. This holds for the determiner *most*, for example. Determiners such as *at least n* and *at most n* do have predicate logical translations, but the logical forms become very cumbersome. We will postpone the treatment of those determiners until the next chapter and for now concentrate on the ones in our fragment: *every*, *no*, *the*, *some*, and *a*. The translation of these determiners should be done with some care, for it involves the construction of a logical form where a variable gets bound. To ensure proper binding, we have to make sure that the newly introduced variable will not get accidentally bound by a quantifier already present in the logical form. But if we reflect on how variables get introduced, we see that variables will always appear together with their binders, and that no binding is vacuous. So we are done if we collect the binding occurrences of indices. For that we define functions `bInLF` and `bInLFs`.

```
bInLF :: LF -> [Int]
bInLF (Atom _ _)         = []
bInLF (Eq _ _)           = []
bInLF (Neg lf)           = bInLF lf
bInLF (Impl lf1 lf2)     = bInLFs [lf1,lf2]
bInLF (Equi lf1 lf2)     = bInLFs [lf1,lf2]
```

```
bInLF (Conj lfs)                       = bInLFs lfs
bInLF (Disj lfs)                       = bInLFs lfs
bInLF (Forall (Variable _ [i]) f) = i : bInLF f
bInLF (Exists (Variable _ [i]) f) = i : bInLF f


bInLFs :: [LF] -> [Int]
bInLFs = nub . concat . map bInLF
```

To compute a fresh variable index, we need to pick an index outside this list. All variables will get introduced by means of the same mechanism, so if we start out with variables of the form `Variable "x" [0]`, and only introduce new variables of the form `Variable "x" [i]` for non-negative integers i, we can assume that all variables occurring in our logical form will have the shape `Var "x" [i]` for some non-negative integer i. One final subtlety is that we add 0 to the list of indices to ensure that the list will be non-empty. This is needed because the list is fed to `maximum`, which expects a non-empty argument.

```
freshIndex   :: [LF] -> Int
freshIndex lfs = i+1
        where i = maximum (0:(bInLFs lfs))

fresh :: [Term -> LF] -> Int
fresh preds   = freshIndex (map ($ dummy) preds)
  where dummy = Struct "" []
```

Now, here is `lfDET` for the quantifiers *some*, *every*, and *no*:

```
lfDET Some  p q = Exists v (Conj [p (Var v), q (Var v)])
        where v = Variable "x" [fresh[p,q]]
lfDET Every p q = Forall v (Impl (p (Var v)) (q (Var v)))
        where v = Variable "x" [fresh[p,q]]
lfDET No    p q = Neg (Exists v (Conj [p (Var v),q (Var v)]))
        where v = Variable "x" [fresh[p,q]]
```

For the representation of the definite determiner, we will for now use the theory of definite descriptions proposed by Bertrand Russell [Rus05]. Russell proposed to translate *The king of France is bald* as the conjunction of *there is exactly one person who is king of France* and *that person is bald*. This can be expressed as follows in predicate logic, slightly compressed.

$$\exists x \forall y ((King\ y \leftrightarrow x = y) \wedge Bald\ x)$$

Using this for the fragment at hand gives:

```
lfDET The p q = Exists v1 (Conj
                   [Forall v2 (Equi (p (Var v2))
                                    (Eq (Var v1) (Var v2))),
                    q (Var v1)])
          where
                i  = fresh[p,q]
                v1 = Variable "x" [i]
                v2 = Variable "x" [i+1]
```

We use `Conj` to conjoin the logical form for a common noun and the logical form for a relative clause into a logical form for a complex common noun.

```
lfRCN :: RCN -> Term -> LF
lfRCN (RCN1 cn _ vp)    = \ t -> Conj [lfCN cn t, lfVP vp t]
lfRCN (RCN2 cn _ np tv) = \ t -> Conj [lfCN cn t,
                          lfNP np (\ subj -> lfTV tv (subj,t))]
```

Let us define some examples:

```
lf1 = lfSent (Sent (NP1 Some Dwarf)
                   (VP1 Defeated (NP1 Some Giant)))
lf2 = lfSent (Sent (NP2 The (RCN2 Wizard
                                 That Dorothy Admired))
                   Laughed)
lf3 = lfSent (Sent (NP2 The (RCN1 Princess
                                 That (VP1 Helped Alice)))
                   Shuddered)
```

This gives us:

```
MCWPL> lf1
E x1 conj[dwarf[x1],Ex2 conj[giant[x2],defeat[x1,x2]]]
MCWPL> lf2
E x1 conj[conj[wizard[x1],admire[Dorothy,x1]],laugh[x1]]
MCWPL> lf3
```

```
E x1 conj[Ax2 (conj[princess[x2],
                help[x2,Alice]]<=>x1==x2),shudder[x1]]
```

We now have representations of declarative natural language sentences as formulas of predicate logic. In the following sections, we will show how to check whether these formulas are true. For this, we first need to specify a model, i.e. a domain of entities and interpretations of proper names and predicates, and then describe how to evaluate formulas with respect to this model.

6.3 Representing a Model for Predicate Logic

```
module Model where


import Data.List
```

All we need to specify a first-order model in Haskell is a domain of entities and suitable interpretations of proper names and predicates. We start by constructing a small example domain of entities consisting of individuals $A, \ldots, Z$, by declaring a data type Entity.

```
data Entity = A | B | C | D | E | F | G
            | H | I | J | K | L | M | N
            | O | P | Q | R | S | T | U
            | V | W | X | Y | Z | Unspec
       deriving (Eq,Show,Bounded,Enum)
```

The special entity Unspec will play an important part in our account of underspecified relations. It will allow us to define relations with some argument places unspecified.

The clause deriving (Eq,Bounded,Enum,Show) is there to enable us to do equality tests on entities (Eq), to refer to A as the minimum element and Unspec as the maximum element (Bounded), and to enumerate the elements (Enum). Because Entity is a bounded and enumerable type, we can put all of its elements in a finite list:

```
entities :: [Entity]
entities =  [minBound..maxBound]
```

To display the entities on the screen, we also put the entities in the class Show.

Now, proper names will simply be interpreted as entities.

```
snowWhite, alice, dorothy, goldilocks, littleMook, atreyu
                                              :: Entity


snowWhite  = S
alice      = A
dorothy    = D
goldilocks = G
littleMook = M
atreyu     = Y
```

Common nouns such as *girl* and *dwarf* as well as intransitive verbs like *laugh* and *shudder* are interpreted as properties of entities. Transitive verbs like *love* are interpreted as relations between entities.

For properties and relations on the domain Entity, we could use a general type [Entity] -> Bool. Although this would allow us to talk about relations of all arities in a unified way, it would not be very useful for composition of meaning in the next chapter, because in syntax a transitive verb first combines with a direct object and then with a subject, and a ditransitive verb combines with an indirect and a direct object, and then with a subject. Thus we want verbs to denote functions from entities to Bool that take their arguments one by one. We thus define types for one-place, two-place, and three-place predicates as follows.

```
type OnePlacePred   = Entity -> Bool
type TwoPlacePred   = Entity -> Entity -> Bool
type ThreePlacePred = Entity -> Entity -> Entity -> Bool
```

Since it is very natural to think about one-place predicates as lists, namely the list of entities for which the predicate holds, we define a conversion function, that converts a list of entities into a one-place predicate, i.e. a function from entities to truth values.

```
list2OnePlacePred :: [Entity] -> OnePlacePred
list2OnePlacePred xs = \ x -> elem x xs
```

This function allows the specification of one-place predicates in terms of lists of entities.

```
girl, boy, princess, dwarf, giant, wizard, sword, dagger
                                           :: OnePlacePred

girl     = list2OnePlacePred [S,A,D,G]
boy      = list2OnePlacePred [M,Y]
princess = list2OnePlacePred [E]
dwarf    = list2OnePlacePred [B,R]
giant    = list2OnePlacePred [T]
wizard   = list2OnePlacePred [W,V]
sword    = list2OnePlacePred [F]
dagger   = list2OnePlacePred [X]
```

With the predicates defined so far, we can also define other predicates like being a person or a thing: a person is a boy, girl, princess, dwarf, giant, or wizard, and a thing is everything which is neither a person nor the special object Unspec. It is also convenient to have men and women: we assume that the women are the princesses and that the men are the dwarfs, giants, and wizards.

```
child, person, man, woman, male, female, thing :: OnePlacePred

child  = \ x -> (girl x  || boy x)
person = \ x -> (child x || princess x || dwarf x
                          || giant x    || wizard x)
man    = \ x -> (dwarf x || giant x || wizard x)
woman  = \ x -> princess x
male   = \ x -> (man x || boy x)
female = \ x -> (woman x || girl x)
thing  = \ x -> not (person x || x == Unspec)
```

Since intransitive verbs also denote properties, their meanings are represented as OnePlacePred as well.

```
laugh, cheer, shudder :: OnePlacePred

laugh   = list2OnePlacePred [A,G,E]
cheer   = list2OnePlacePred [M,D]
shudder = list2OnePlacePred [S]
```

Let us now turn to transitive verbs. We said that they denote relations between entities, so we want to represent them as two-place predicates. Analogous to one-place predicates, it is convenient to think of two-place predicates as lists of pairs, namely the pairs for which the predicate holds. In order to represent the meaning of transitive verbs using pairs, we will make use of the predefined function curry. *Currying* is the conversion of a function of type `((a,b) -> c)` to one of type `a -> b -> c`, i.e. it converts a function that takes a pair as argument into a function that takes the elements of the pair as separate arguments.

```
curry :: ((a,b) -> c) -> a -> b -> c
curry f x y = f (x,y)
```

The converse operation is called *uncurrying*. Just like the programming language Haskell, these operations are named after one of the inventors of lambda calculus, the logician Haskell B. Curry. Uncurrying is also predefined in the Haskell Prelude, like this:

```
uncurry :: (a -> b -> c) -> ((a, b) -> c)
uncurry f p =  f (fst p) (snd p)

fst :: (a,b) -> a
fst (x,y) = x

snd :: (a,b) -> b
snd (x,y) = y
```

We use currying in the definition of the following two-place predicates.

```
love, admire, help, defeat :: TwoPlacePred

love   = curry (`elem` [(Y,E),(B,S),(R,S)])
admire = curry (`elem` [(x,G) | x <- entities, person x])
help   = curry (`elem` [(W,W),(V,V),(S,B),(D,M)])
defeat = curry (`elem` [(x,y) | x <- entities,
                                y <- entities,
                                dwarf x && giant y]
            ++ [(A,W),(A,V)])
```

Meanings of ditransitive verbs can be represented as three-place predicates in the same way as transitive verbs were represented as two-place predicates. The only additional technical detail we have to take care of is that our currying function only works for pairs so far. It can be defined for triples straightforwardly.

```
curry3 :: ((a,b,c) -> d) -> a -> b -> c -> d
curry3 f x y z = f (x,y,z)
```

Now, the denotation of *give* can be given as follows.

```
give :: ThreePlacePred
give = curry3 ('elem' [(T,S,X),(A,E,S)])
```

Exercise 6.1 Consider the verbs *help* and *defeat*, and the noun phrases *Alice*, *Snow White*, *every wizard*, and *a dwarf*. Check for each sentence of the form [s NP (V NP)] using these verbs and noun phrases whether that sentence is true or false in this model.

The entity `Unspec` can be used for defining underspecified relations. For example, we can add a verb *kill* to our fragment and interpret it as a three-place relation, with the first argument giving the agent, the second argument the victim, and the third argument the instrument. In cases where there is no instrument or agent, we leave the argument unspecified. Now the meaning of *kill* can be given as:

```
kill :: ThreePlacePred
kill = curry3 ('elem' [(Y,T,F),(Unspec,D,X),
                       (Unspec,M,Unspec)])
```

What this entry says is that Atreyu killed the giant with the sword, Dorothy was stabbed (leaving unspecified who stabbed her), and Little Mook just died.

Using `Unspec` as a way of leaving arguments implicit can be exploited in a more general way than we did above. One example of this are passives. Passivization is a process of argument reduction: the agent of an action is dropped. Without going into detail of subtle properties of passive constructions, we can specify a semantic passivization function like this:

```
passivize :: TwoPlacePred -> OnePlacePred
passivize r = \ x -> r Unspec x
```

Exercise 6.2 Check how `passivize` works by applying it to the predicates `admire` and help. Also note that (passivize admire) G returns False, although we want it to return True. Why is that? And how can you fix it?

Exercise 6.3 As is already clear from the type, this function only works for two-place predicates. Define another passivization function that works for three-place predicates.

Passivization is not the only example for argument reduction in natural languages. Another case is an analysis of reflexive pronouns as it can be found, for example, in Daniel Büring's book on Binding Theory [Bür05, pp. 43–45]. Under this view, reflexive pronouns like *himself* and *herself* differ semantically from non-reflexive pronouns like *him* and *her* in that they are not interpreted as individual variables. Instead, they denote argument reducing functions. Consider, for example, the following sentence:

$$\text{\textit{Snow White admired herself.}} \qquad (6.3)$$

The reflexive *herself* is interpreted as a function that takes the two-place predicate *admired* as an argument and turns it into a one-place predicate, which takes the subject as an argument and expressing that this entity admires itself. This can be achieved by the following function self.

```
self ::  (a -> a -> b) -> a -> b
self p = \ x -> p x x
```

Note that applying self to a function of type TwoPlacePred will yield a function of type OnePlacePred. For example, applying self to the two-place predicate $\lambda y\, x \mapsto Admire\ x\ y$ yields the one-place predicate $\lambda x \mapsto Admire\ x\ x$. Applying this to *Snow White* will give $Admire\ s\ s$.

This approach to reflexives has two desirable consequences. The first one is that the locality of reflexives immediately falls out. Since self is applied to a predicate and unifies arguments of this predicate, it is not possible that an argument is unified with a non-clause mate. So in a sentence like (6.4), *herself* can only refer to *Alice* but not to *Snow White*.

$$\text{* \textit{Snow White thinks that Alice admired herself.}} \qquad (6.4)$$

The second one is that it also immediately follows that reflexives in subject position are out.

$$\text{* \textit{Herself admired Snow White.}} \qquad (6.5)$$

Given a compositional interpretation, we first apply the predicate *admired* to *Snow White*, which gives us the one-place predicate $\lambda x \mapsto Admire\ x\ s$. Then trying to apply the function `self` to this will fail, because it expects a two-place predicate. In other words, there are no two argument position left, which could be unified.

Exercise 6.4 When considering ditransitive verbs like *introduce* and *give*, we see that a reflexive can be both the direct and the indirect object.

$$\text{Alice introduced herself to the rabbit.} \tag{6.6}$$

$$\text{Little Mook gave the figs to himself.} \tag{6.7}$$

Define functions `self3DO` and `self3IO` of type `ThreePlacePred -> TwoPlacePred` that unify the subject with the direct and indirect object, respectively.

After this little digression, let us turn back to our task of giving an indirect interpretation for our natural language fragment. Up to now we specified how to represent models for predicate logic. The next thing to do is to evaluate formulas with respect to these models.

6.4 Evaluating Formulas in Models

We now turn to the problem of the evaluation of formulas of predicate logic with respect to a model. Two of the ingredients we need are interpretation functions and variable assignments. An interpretation function is a function from relation names to appropriate relations in the model. We will not distinguish according to the arity of the relation, but let an interpretation be a function of the type `String -> [a] -> Bool`. For this type it is convenient to have a type synonym:

```
type Interp a = String -> [a] -> Bool
```

In our specific case we will use interpretation functions of type `Interp Entity`, i.e. `String -> [Entity] -> Bool`.

Here is an example interpretation function for some one-place and two-place relation symbols:

```
int0 :: Interp Entity
int0 "Laugh"   = \ [x]     -> laugh x
int0 "Cheer"   = \ [x]     -> cheer x
int0 "Shudder" = \ [x]     -> shudder x
int0 "Love"    = \ [x,y]   -> love y x
int0 "Admire"  = \ [x,y]   -> admire y x
int0 "Help"    = \ [x,y]   -> help y x
int0 "Defeat"  = \ [x,y]   -> defeat y x
int0 "Give"    = \ [x,y,z] -> give z y x
```

Now, the evaluation of the formula `Forall x (Atom "Love" [x,x])` in the model specified in Section 6.3, with respect to interpretation function `int0`, should yield `False`, for in the example model it is not the case that the *love* relation is reflexive.

To bring this about, we have to implement the evaluation function given in Section 5.5. This uses variable assignments g. In the implementation, these have type `Variable -> Entity`, or more generally `Variable -> a`. It pays to declare a data type for variable assignments (or: variable lookup functions).

```
type Lookup a = Variable -> a
```

The crucial notion is $g[x := d]$, for the assignment that is like g, but with x interpreted as d. Here are its type and its definition:

```
change :: Lookup a -> Variable -> a -> Lookup a
change g x d = \ v -> if x == v then d else g v
```

As an example for a variable assignment, here is a definition of the assignment that maps every variable to object A.

```
ass0 :: Lookup Entity
ass0 = \ v -> A
```

The function that is like `ass0`, except for the fact that y gets mapped to B, is given by:

```
ass1 :: Lookup Entity
ass1 = change ass0 y B
```

Before we give an implementation of the evaluation function for predicate logic, we must emphasize the crucial difference between *defining* an evaluation function for predicate logic and *implementing* such a definition. Implementations allow us to check the value of a formula in a model. But it is unreasonable to expect to be able to check the evaluation of arbitrary formulas in arbitrary models. Take the famous Goldbach conjecture as an example. This conjecture – from a letter that Christian Goldbach wrote to Leonhard Euler in 1742 – says that every even natural number can be written as the sum of two primes. It can easily be stated in predicate logic as follows:

$$\forall x \exists y \exists z (2 * x = y + z \land Prime\ y \land Prime\ z). \tag{6.8}$$

This uses function symbols $*$ and $+$ for multiplication and addition, and a predicate symbol *Prime* for being a prime number. The predicate *Prime* can be defined in predicate logic using a binary relation symbol $<$ for 'smaller than' and a binary relation symbol *Div* for 'divisibility' (where *Div x y* expresses that x is a proper divisor of y):

$$\neg\exists d(1 < d \land d < y \land Div\ d\ y).$$

Exercise 6.5 Give an equivalent formula that just uses $0, s, *, +, <$, i.e. show how *Div d y* can be defined in predicate logic with $0, s, *, +, <$ (with s for the successor function).

Although the interpretations of $<$ and *Div* are easy to check for given natural numbers, it is unreasonable to expect an implementation of an evaluation function for predicate logic to check whether formula (6.8) is true. The Goldbach conjecture is one of the many open problems of the theory of natural numbers. At the moment of writing, nobody knows whether it is true or not, because nobody has been able to provide a proof or a counterexample, although the conjecture has been verified for numbers up to 4×10^{14}.

We will make two assumptions about the domain of evaluation. In the first place, we will assume that tests for equality are possible on the domain. In Haskell terminology: the type a of our domain should be in the class Eq. Secondly, we will assume that the domain can be enumerated, and we will use this domain as an argument to the evaluation function.

Note that our example domain of entities on page 133 satisfies these requirements. However, the domain of non-negative integers satisfies the requirements as well. Indeed, the requirements are not enough to guarantee termination of the evaluation function for all possible arguments.

Let us look at how to implement an evaluation function. It takes as its first argument a domain, as its second argument an interpretation function, as its third argument a variable assignment, as its fourth argument a formula, and it yields a truth value. It is defined by recursion on the structure of the formula. The type of the evaluation function eval reflects the above assumptions.

```
eval :: Eq a =>
    [a]                 ->
    Interp a            ->
    Lookup a            ->
    Formula Variable -> Bool
```

The evaluation function is defined for all types a that belong to the class Eq. The assumption that the type a of the domain of evaluation is in Eq is needed in the evaluation clause for equalities. The evaluation function takes a universe (represented as a list, [a]) as its first argument, an interpretation function for relation symbols (Interp a) as its second argument, a variable assignment (Lookup a) as its third argument, and a formula as its fourth argument. The definition is by structural recursion on the formula:

```
eval domain i = eval' where
  eval' g (Atom str vs) = i str (map g vs)
  eval' g (Eq    v1 v2) = (g v1) == (g v2)
  eval' g (Neg   f)     = not (eval' g f)
  eval' g (Impl f1 f2)  = not ((eval' g f1) &&
                                  not (eval' g f2))
  eval' g (Equi f1 f2)  = (eval' g f1) == (eval' g f2)
  eval' g (Conj fs)     = and (map (eval' g) fs)
  eval' g (Disj fs)     = or  (map (eval' g) fs)
  eval' g (Forall v f)  = and [ eval' (change g v d) f |
                                  d <- domain ]
  eval' g (Exists v f)  = or  [ eval' (change g v d) f |
                                  d <- domain ]
```

We can check the claim that the formula Forall x (Atom "Love" [x,x]) from above makes about the model from Section 6.3, as follows. (The interpretation function int0 was given on page 139, and the assignment ass0 was given on page 140.)

```
MCWPL> eval entities int0 ass0 (Forall x (Atom "Love" [x,x]))
False
```

For checking that the formula Atom "R" [x,y] holds for the interpretation of "R" as $<$ on the non-negative integers and for an assignment that maps x to 1 and y to 2, we need an interpretation in the type Int:

```
int1 :: String -> [Int] -> Bool
int1 "R" = rconvert (<)
    where
        rconvert :: (a -> a -> Bool) -> [a] -> Bool
        rconvert r [x,y] = r x y
```

Here is an appropriate assignment:

```
ass2 :: Variable -> Int
ass2 v = if v == x then 1 else if v == y then 2 else 0
```

Now suppose we want to evaluate the formula

$$\text{Forall x (Exists y (Atom "R" [x,y]))} \tag{6.9}$$

in the infinite domain of non-negative integers. This domain can be listed in Haskell as `[0..]`. Because Haskell is a lazy functional programming language, we can use infinite lists as arguments to functions. Recall from Chapter 3 that the laziness consists in the fact that arguments are only evaluated when needed, and as far as needed. The elements of `[0..]` will be accessed one at a time, and only at a point where they are actually needed. So we can check the open formula `Atom "R" [x,y]` in the domain `[0..]`, with respect to a fixed variable assignment:

```
MCWPL> eval [0..] int1 ass2 (Atom "R" [x,y])
True
```

However, checking the claim that the closed formula (6.9) makes about the non-negative integers, with R interpreted as the 'less than' relation, is not a feasible matter, for the evaluation procedure will keep on trying different numbers.

6.5 Evaluating Formulas with Structured Terms

The previous section dealt with evaluation for formulas of type `Formula Variable`. In this section we turn to the general case, and write an evaluation function for formulas of type `Formula Term`.

As in the case of the interpretation of relation symbols, it is useful to have a general type for the interpretation of function symbols. We will use the following abbreviation:

```
type FInterp a = String -> [a] -> a
```

Here is an example interpretation for function symbols, for the case where our domain of entities consists of integers. Let us define a constant term `zero` as a name for the integer 0.

```
zero = Struct "zero" []
```

The interpretation function has to ensure that the name points to the right entity. We also provide interpretations of the one-place successor function s, and of the two-place functions plus and times.

```
fint1 :: FInterp Int
fint1 "zero"  []    = 0
fint1 "s"     [i]   = succ i
fint1 "plus"  [i,j] = i + j
fint1 "times" [i,j] = i * j
```

In Haskell, the type Int is bounded by primMinInt (for the smallest integer that gets represented, which is -2147483648) and primMaxInt (for the greatest integer that gets represented, which is 2147483648).

For the case where the domain consists of objects of type Entity, we get FInterp Entity. Before we can turn to evaluation of formulas, we have to lift valuation functions from type Lookup a to type Term -> a, given appropriate interpretations for function symbols. Again, it is useful to have an abbreviation:

```
type TVal a = Term -> a
```

Lifting from Lookup a to TVal a is done with recursion on the structure of terms, as follows:

```
liftLookup :: FInterp a -> Lookup a -> TVal a
liftLookup fint g (Var v)        = g v
liftLookup fint g (Struct str ts) =
          fint str (map (liftLookup fint g) ts)
```

Finally, we are ready to extend the semantic evaluation function from the previous section to the present case. The evaluation function takes one extra argument, for the function symbol interpretation. Here is its type:

```
evl :: Eq a =>
  [a]            ->
  Interp   a     ->
  FInterp  a     ->
  Lookup   a     ->
  Formula Term -> Bool
```

And here is the definition:

```
evl domain i fint = evl' where
  lift = liftLookup fint
  evl' g (Atom str ts) = i str (map (lift g) ts)
  evl' g (Eq   t1 t2)  = lift g t1 == lift g t2
  evl' g (Neg  f)      = not (evl' g f)
  evl' g (Impl f1 f2)  = not ((evl' g f1) &&
                               not (evl' g f2))
  evl' g (Equi f1 f2)  = evl' g f1 == evl' g f2
  evl' g (Conj fs)     = and (map (evl' g) fs)
  evl' g (Disj fs)     = or  (map (evl' g) fs)
  evl' g (Forall v f)  = and [ evl' (change g v d) f |
                               d <- domain ]
  evl' g (Exists v f)  = or  [ evl' (change g v d) f |
                               d <- domain ]
```

As an example, we evaluate the formula Exists x (Atom "R" [zero,tx]) in the domain of the natural numbers, i.e., the non-negative integers. For this, we need a relation symbol interpretation, a function symbol interpretation, and a variable assignment. For the first, let us take int1, for the second fint1, and for the third the variable assignment that maps every variable to 0. Finally, we need to specify the domain as a list. Under this interpretation, the formula expresses that there is a number greater than 0. And surely, this evaluates as True:

```
MCWPL> evl [0..] int1 fint1 (\ (Variable _ _) -> 0)
       Exists x (Atom "R" [zero,tx])
True
```

The formula Exists x (Atom "R" [tx,zero]), on the other hand, should yield False under interpretation int1, but in fact the evaluation procedure will not terminate, because in order to check this formula, the evaluation procedure will keep on trying candidates from the infinite list [0..]. Even in cases where there are solutions, it may take a long time before the right candidate or the right tuple of candidates has been found. This suggests that it makes sense to perform model checking in an interactive fashion, so that the user can state that there are no solutions for certain queries, and influence the choice of suitable referents for free variables for certain other queries.

Here is an example of a formula with nested quantifiers:

```
formula3 = Forall x (Forall y (Impl (Atom "R" [tx,ty])
                      (Exists z
                         (Conj [Atom "R" [tx,tz],
                                Atom "R" [tz,ty]])))))
```

This gets displayed as follows:

```
MCWPL> formula3
Ax Ay (R[x,y]==>Ez conj[R[x,z],R[z,y]])
```

Exercise 6.6 What does `formula3` express, assuming that R is interpreted as $<$? Is this formula true on the natural numbers? Is it true on the rational numbers (the numbers that can be written as $\frac{n}{m}$, with n and m integers and $m \neq 0$)?

Again, we cannot expect to get an answer to the query

```
MCWPL> evl [0..] int1 fint1 (\ (Variable _ _) -> 1) formula4
```

in feasible time, if `formula4` is the following formula:

```
formula4 =  Impl (Atom "R" [tx,ty])
                 (Exists z
                    (Conj [Atom "R" [tx,tz],
                           Atom "R" [tz,ty]]))
```

The evaluation procedure will keep trying different values for z, and never find one that yields true.

Now let us try this on the model from Section 6.3, with R interpreted as the *defeat* relation. Here is an appropriate interpretation function.

```
int3 :: String -> [Entity] -> Bool
int3 "R" = \ [x,y] -> defeat y x
```

Since `formula4` does not contain function symbols, it does not matter which function symbol interpretation we use. Let us assume the following:

```
fint2 :: String -> [Entity] -> Entity
fint2 "zero" [] = A
```

```
MCWPL> evl entities int3 fint2 (\ (Variable _ _) -> A) formula4
True
```

Exercise 6.7 Implement an evaluation function for natural language sentences in our fragment in the example model of this chapter. The type should be
```
checkSentence :: Sent -> Bool.
```

6.6 Further Reading

In computer science, evaluation of formulas of suitable logical languages (predicate logic, but also temporal logics) in appropriate models is called model checking. This has developed into a discipline in its own right; see [HR04] for an introduction. The use of typed logic for semantics of natural language was pioneered by Richard Montague, who used typed logic as a stepping stone on the way to semantic specification in [Mon73] and [Mon74b]. Elsewhere, in [Mon74a], the meaning of a fragment of English is specified without a detour through logical form.

7

The Composition of Meaning in Natural Language

Summary

In the last chapter we gave an indirect interpretation for our natural language fragment. We translated natural language sentences into logical forms and then evaluated these logical forms with respect to a model. Logical forms were predicate logical formulas, which were constructed from type logical expressions. We used Haskell as a lambda calculus engine for this construction procedure. This worked very well, but it has the disadvantage that the Haskell interpreter hides the details of how expressions of typed logic get simplified. In this chapter, we will demonstrate that the composition of meaning can be carried out without a logical form language as intermediate representation level. We will give direct instructions for connecting natural language expressions to the "world" outside language (represented by an appropriate model). We will show how models of predicate logic can be extended to models of typed logic, and how typed logic yields appropriate meaning representations for the lexical items of natural language fragments and provides the means for building up meanings in a compositional way. But before we engage in this, we must focus on a key ingredient in natural language semantics: quantifiers.

7.1 Rules of the Game

An invitation to translate English sentences from an example fragment of natural language given by some set of grammar rules into some logic – predicate logic, or typed logic – presupposes two things: (i) that you grasp the meanings of the formulas of the representation language, and (ii) that you understand the meanings of the English sentences. Knowledge of the first kind can be made fully explicit; stating it in a fully explicit fashion is the job of the semantic truth definitions for the representation languages. In fact, translation exercises of this kind in logic textbooks are meant to expand the reader's awareness of the expressive power of the logical representation language by inviting him or her to express an (intuitively) well-understood message in the new medium. Because of this presupposed understanding of the original message, such translations cannot count as *explications* of the concept of meaning for natural language.

As we have seen in Section 6.2, it is possible to make knowledge of the meaning of a fragment of natural language fully explicit. What we gave there is a translation procedure from natural language into predicate logic that can count as an explication of the concept of meaning for natural language. The procedure does not presuppose knowledge of the meaning of complete natural language sentences. Instead, it specifies how sentence meanings are derived from the meanings of smaller building blocks. The meanings of complex expressions are constructed in a systematic fashion from the meanings of the smallest building blocks occurring in those expressions. The meaning of these smallest building blocks is taken as given. We assume that they are given by instructions for linking individual words to the reality outside language. In our example, these links are made by the interpretation instructions for relation and function symbols in a predicate logical model. Computational semantics has little or nothing to say about the interpretation of semantic atoms. It has rather a lot to say, however, about the process of composing complex meanings in a systematic way out of the meanings of components. The intuition that this is always possible can be stated somewhat more precisely; it is called the Principle of Compositionality, which we already encountered in the first chapter:

The meaning of an expression is a function of the meanings of its immediate syntactic components and their syntactic mode of composition.

The principle of compositionality is implicit in the work of Frege on the philosophy of language, and it has been made fully explicit in Richard Montague's approach to natural language semantics. Another key element in Montague-style semantics is the treatment of quantifiers.

7.2 Quantification

An important goal in computational semantics for natural language is to provide an account of *the process of drawing inferences* in natural language. A key role in this process is played by quantifiers, and therefore quantification is a topic of central interest in computational semantics. The first systematic account of quantification is that of Aristotle; see Section 5.7. Impressive though it is, Aristotle's theory of quantification has two logical defects:

(1) Quantifier combinations are not treated; only one quantifier per sentence is allowed.
(2) 'Non-standard' quantifiers such as *most, half of, at least five,* ... are not covered.

A minor additional flaw is the assumption of existential presupposition. In mathematical reasoning, and sometimes also in everyday reasoning, one wants to be able to assert universally quantified statements without the bother of first having to provide existence proofs.

The first of these defects was removed by Frege. Frege's theory of quantification is basically what we now call predicate logic. It is based on the introduction of individual variables bound by the quantifiers $\forall$ ('for all') and $\exists$ ('there exists'). Quantifiers with their associated variables can combine with arbitrarily complex predicate logical formulae to form new predicate logical formulae, so a formula may contain an arbitrary number of quantifiers.

The quantifiers $\forall$ and $\exists$ are called the standard quantifiers. These two quantifiers are interdefinable with the help of negation: *Something stinks* means the same as *It is not the case that it holds for every x that x does not stink*, and *Everything is fine* means the same as *It is not the case that there is a thing x with the property that x is not fine*. More formally: $\exists x Px$ is true if and only if $\neg\forall x\neg Px$ is true, and $\forall x Px$ is true if and only if $\neg\exists x\neg Px$ is true.

If one conveniently forgets about the existential presuppositions, the Aristotelian quantifiers from the Square of Opposition (cf. Figure 5.1 on page 107) can be expressed in terms of the Fregean standard quantifiers as follows (with $\rightsquigarrow$ for 'translates as'):

$$
\begin{array}{lcl}
\textit{All A are B} & \rightsquigarrow & \forall x(Ax \rightarrow Bx) \\
\textit{Some A is/are B} & \rightsquigarrow & \exists x(Ax \wedge Bx) \\
\textit{No A is B} & \rightsquigarrow & \forall x(Ax \rightarrow \neg Bx) \\
\textit{Not all A are B} & \rightsquigarrow & \neg\forall x(Ax \rightarrow Bx)
\end{array}
$$

A thing to note is that different ways of rendering an Aristotelian quantifier in Frege's logic may be equivalent. Another possible translation for *No A is B* is $\neg\exists x(Ax \wedge Bx)$. There is nothing to choose between the two translations because in every situation where the first one is true the second one is true as well, and vice versa.

Using standard quantifiers and equality it is also possible to express numerical constraints like *At least two A are B*:

$$\exists x\exists y(x \neq y \wedge Ax \wedge Ay \wedge Bx \wedge By).$$

It is not difficult to see that all disjunctions and conjunctions of quantifiers of the forms *at least n* and *at most m* can be expressed in terms of standard quantifiers and equality.

To illustrate the claim that first-order logic has no difficulty with quantifier combinations, consider the translation of example (7.1).

Every prince sang a ballad. (7.1)

$\forall x(Prince\ x \rightarrow \exists y(Ballad\ y \land Sing\ x\ y)).$

Observe that the translation does not contain phrases corresponding to the noun phrases *every prince* or *a ballad*. Given a natural language sentence and its translation into first-order logic, it is impossible to pinpoint the sub-expression in the translation that gives the meaning of a particular noun phrase in the original. In the translation into first-order logic, the noun phrases have been syntactically eliminated, so to speak.

The next example, (7.2), with the two possible translations listed below it, can serve to illustrate a few further points.

A ballad was sung by every prince. (7.2)

$\exists y(Ballad\ y \land \forall x(Prince\ x \rightarrow Sing\ x\ y))$

$\forall x(Prince\ x \rightarrow \exists y(Ballad\ y \land Sing\ x\ y))$

The fact that both translations are appropriate for (7.2) shows that the sentence is ambiguous. It also shows that translating into first-order logic can be used to disambiguate natural language sentences. In such cases one says that the different translations express different *readings* of the original sentence.

In an early era of natural language semantics, the time when first-order predicate logic was still considered as the one and only tool for semantic analysis, quantified noun phrases were commonly regarded as systematically misleading expressions. Their natural language syntax did not correspond to their logic, for in natural language they were separate constituents, but they evaporated during the process of translation into first-order logic.

The Fregean view on quantifiers is a vast improvement over the Aristotelean view. Three areas with scope for further improvement remained: (i) finding logical representation languages permitting the preservation of noun phrases as separate constituents, (ii) finding procedures for translating from natural language to logical representations that are not *ad hoc*, and (iii) finding ways to treat non-standard quantifiers such as *most*, preferably in a uniform framework with standard quantifiers.

The relational view of quantifiers

In the relational perspective on quantifiers, first proposed in [Mos57], a quantifier is viewed as a two-place relation on the power set of a domain of discourse (or universe) E satisfying certain requirements. (You can read E as mnemonic for the set of entities, for example.) The power set of a set E, notation $\mathcal{P}(E)$, is the set of all subsets of E. A two-place relation on $\mathcal{P}(E)$ is a set of pairs of subsets of E. The relational perspective on quantification is implicit in Montague grammar. It was first systematically applied to natural language analysis in Barwise and Cooper [BC81]. Below it will be shown that the relational view can be used to remedy the defects of both the Aristotelian and the Fregean theory. It covers non-standard quantifiers, it allows quantifier combinations of arbitrary complexity, it does not syntactically eliminate quantified noun phrases, and it can be used as one of the ingredients in a non *ad hoc* translation procedure from natural language to a language of logical representations.

We will start by demonstrating that in the modern relational perspective the suggestion of misleading form disappears. Two simple example sentences will illustrate that a representation language with generalized quantifier expressions (expressions denoting two-place relations between sets) and a notation for lambda abstraction is eminently suited for the compositional analysis of natural language sentences with quantified noun phrases. First consider example (7.3).

$$\textit{Every princess laughed.} \qquad (7.3)$$

This sentence is composed of a noun phrase *every princess*, composed in turn of a determiner *every* and a noun *princess*, and a verb phrase *laughed*. The determiner *every* translates into an expression **every** denoting a function from properties to a function from properties to truth values. More precisely, **every** denotes the function mapping a property P to the characteristic function of the set of all properties having P as a subset. The noun *princess* translates into $\lambda x \mapsto \textit{Princess } x$, or simply *Princess*. The verb phrase *laughed* translates into $\lambda y \mapsto \textit{Laugh } y$, or simply *Laugh*. The noun phrase *every princess* translates into **every** *Princess*, and, finally, the whole sentence into the expression (**every** *Princess*) *Laugh*. This expression yields true in case the property of being a princess is included in the property of laughing, false otherwise. See Figure 7.1.

Fig. 7.1. Every princess laughed

expression	translation	type
every	**every**	$(e \to t) \to ((e \to t) \to t)$
princess	*Princess*	$(e \to t)$
every princess	**every** *Princess*	$(e \to t) \to t$
laughed	*Laugh*	$(e \to t)$
every princess laughed	(**every** *Princess*) *Laugh*	t

To see how quantifier combinations are dealt with compositionally, consider example (7.4).

Every mermaid hummed a song.   (7.4)

The trick is finding the right translation for the transitive verb. This turns out to be the lambda expression $\lambda X \lambda y \mapsto X (\lambda z \mapsto Hum\ y\ z)$, where X is a variable over noun phrase type expressions. The verb translation is of the right type to take the object noun phrase translation as its argument; this gives translation (7.5) for the verb phrase, which reduces to (7.6). In Section 7.4 we will say more about this reduction process.

$$(\lambda X \lambda y \mapsto X (\lambda z \mapsto Hum\ y\ z))(\mathbf{a}\ Song). \qquad (7.5)$$

$$\lambda y \mapsto (\mathbf{a}\ Song)(\lambda z \mapsto Hum\ y\ z). \qquad (7.6)$$

Here $\mathbf{a}$ denotes the function which maps every property P to (the characteristic function of) the set of all properties having a non-empty overlap with P. Feeding (7.6) as argument to the expression **every** *Mermaid*, the translation of the subject, one gets (7.7) as translation for the whole sentence.

$$(\mathbf{every}\ Mermaid)(\lambda y \mapsto ((\mathbf{a}\ Song)(\lambda z \mapsto Hum\ y\ z))). \qquad (7.7)$$

We can summarize these steps as follows:

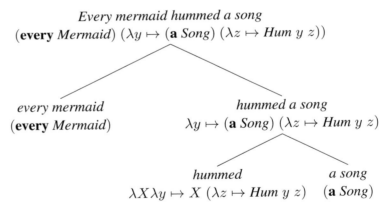

We said in the beginning that we view quantifiers as two-place relations on the power set of some domain E, satisfying certain requirements. So let us now look at these requirements.

Conditions on Quantifier Relations

All dwarfs work is true in a given model if and only if the relation of inclusion holds between the set of dwarfs in the model and the set of workers in the model.

Abstracting from the domain of discourse, we can say that determiner interpretations (henceforth simply called determiners) pick out binary relations on sets of individuals, on arbitrary domains of discourse E. The notation is $D_E AB$. We call A the *restriction* of the quantifier and B its *body*. If $D_E AB$ is the translation of a simple sentence consisting of a quantified noun phrase with an intransitive verb phrase, then the noun denotation is the restriction and the verb phrase denotation the body. So in the example *All dwarfs work*, the NP *all dwarfs* is the restriction of the determiner *all*, and the VP *work* is the body. See Figure 7.2 for a general graphical representation.

Fig. 7.2. Interpretation of $D_E AB$ as a relation between sets A and B

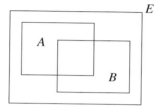

Not all two-place relations on sets of individuals are quantifier relations. The first two requirements that quantifiers must meet are general requirements for denotations of determiners: *extension* and *conservativity*, which will be abbreviated as **EXT** and **CONS**, respectively. Extension is the following:

EXT For all $A, B \subseteq E \subseteq E'$: $D_E AB \Leftrightarrow D_{E'} AB$.

A relation observing **EXT** is stable under growth of the universe. So, given sets A and B, only the objects in the minimal universe $A \cup B$ matter. See Figure 7.3.

Fig. 7.3. The Effect of EXT

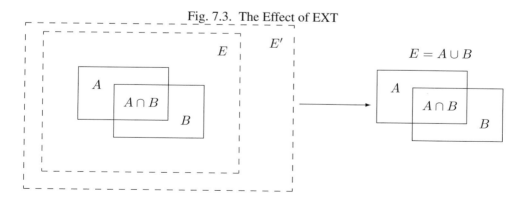

An example is *all*: to determine the truth of *All dwarfs work*, we only need the intersection of the set of dwarfs and the set of workers. It does not matter at all how many or which kind of entities are contained in the rest of the domain.

But not all natural language determiners do satisfy **EXT**. An example of a determiner that does not is *many* in the sense of *relatively many*.

The second requirement for determiners is conservativity:

CONS For all $A, B \subseteq E$: $D_E AB \Leftrightarrow D_E A(A \cap B)$.

This property expresses that the first argument of a determiner relation (the interpretation of the noun) plays a crucial role: everything outside the extension of the first argument is irrelevant. *Some* is an example for a conservative determiner: to determine the truth of *Some dwarfs work*, we only need to check whether the set of dwarfs contains workers – nothing outside the set of dwarfs will have any effect on the truth or falsity of the sentence.

It is also not difficult to think of noun phrase determiners that do not satisfy **CONS**. One example is *only* in the following sentence.

$$\textit{Only dwarfs sing during work.} \qquad (7.8)$$

This example is true in a situation where all singing workers are dwarfs. Starting out from a situation like this, and adding some non-dwarfs to the singing workers will make (7.8) false. This shows non-conservativity. All is still well if it can be argued that noun phrases starting with *only*, *mostly*, or *mainly* (two other sources of non-conservativity) are exceptional syntactically, in the sense that these noun phrase prefixes are not really determiners. In the case of *only*, it could be argued that *only dwarfs* has structure $[_{NP}[_{MOD} \textit{only}][_{NP} \textit{dwarfs}]]$, with *only* not a determiner but a noun phrase modifier, just as in (7.9).

$$\textit{Only Bombur sings during work.} \qquad (7.9)$$

However this may be, separating out the determiners satisfying **CONS** and **EXT** is important, for the two conditions taken together ensure that the truth of $D\,AB$ depends only on $A - B$ and $A \cap B$. Thus, the combined effect of **EXT** and **CONS** boils down to limiting the domain of discourse relevant for the truth or falsity of $D_E AB$ to two sets: the set of things which are A but not B (formally: the set $A - B$), and the set of things which are both A and B (formally: the set $A \cap B$).

Next, the relational perspective suggests a very natural way of distinguishing between expressions of quantity and other relations. Quantifier relations satisfy the following condition of *isomorphy*, formulated in terms of bijections. A bijection is a function that is one-to-one and onto. Where a function $f: A \to B$ is one-to-one if $x \neq y$ implies that $f(x) \neq f(y)$, for all $x, y \in A$, i.e. if no two arguments are mapped to the same output. And $f: A \to B$ is onto if for every $y \in B$ there is some $x \in A$ with $f(x) = y$. If A is finite and $f: A \to A$ is a bijection, then f is just a permutation of A.

ISOM If f is a bijection from E to E', then $D_E AB \Rightarrow D_{E'} f[A] f[B]$.

Here $f[A]$, the image of A under f, is the set of all things which are f-values of things in A. **ISOM** expresses that only the *cardinalities* (numbers of elements) of the sets A and B matter, for the image of a set under a bijection is a set with the same number of elements as the original set. If D satisfies **EXT**, **CONS**, and **ISOM**, it turns out that the truth of $D\,AB$ depends only on the cardinal numbers $|A - B|$ and $|A \cap B|$ (respectively, the number of things which are A but not B, and the number of things which are both A and B). See Figure 7.4 for the combined effect of these three conditions.

A quantifier simply is a relation Q satisfying **EXT**, **CONS**, and **ISOM**.

Fig. 7.4. The Combined Effect of EXT, CONS, ISOM

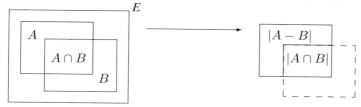

Some examples will make clearer how the semantic effect of a quantifier $Q\,AB$ can always be described in terms of the properties of the numbers $|A - B|$ and $|A \cap B|$: *All A are B* is true if and only if the number of things which are A and not B is 0. *Some A is B* is true if and only if the number of things that are both A and B is at least 1. And *Most A are B* is true if and only if the number of things that are both A and B exceeds the number of things that are A and not B.

We now turn to a way to characterize quantifiers $Q\,AB$ according to the two numbers $|A - B|$ and $|A \cap B|$. We will then use this characterization for the logical representation of quantifiers.

Numerical Trees

Suppose a quantifier Q has A as a first and B as a second argument. Q can then be characterized as a subset of the *tree of numbers* given in Figure 7.5. The first number in each number pair is $|A - B|$, the second one $|A \cap B|$. Some examples of tree patterns for quantifiers are given in Figure 7.6. To interpret these patterns, you first have to identify a tree position, and then check the value. Say the rightmost position of the third row has $+$. This means that the quantifier relation $Q(A, B)$ holds in case A consists of two objects, and both of these objects have property B.

Fig. 7.5. General Format of a Numerical Tree

$$
\begin{array}{lccccccccccc}
|A| = 0 & & & & & & 0,0 & & & & & \\
|A| = 1 & & & & & 1,0 & & 0,1 & & & & \\
|A| = 2 & & & & 2,0 & & 1,1 & & 0,2 & & & \\
|A| = 3 & & & 3,0 & & 2,1 & & 1,2 & & 0,3 & & \\
|A| = 4 & & 4,0 & & 3,1 & & 2,2 & & 1,3 & & 0,4 & \\
|A| = 5 & 5,0 & & 4,1 & & 3,2 & & 2,3 & & 1,4 & & 0,5 \\
\vdots & & & & & & \vdots & & & & & \\
\end{array}
$$

Exercise 7.1 Give a Haskell implementation of the tree of numbers. The call `treeOfNumbers` should yield the (infinite) sequences of number pairs (m, n) that you get by walking through the tree in top-down, left-to-right order. Here is an initial piece of this list:

```
Main> take 10 treeOfNumbers
[(0,0),(1,0),(0,1),(2,0),(1,1),(0,2),(3,0),(2,1),(1,2),(0,3)]
```

To get used to these representations, one should try and answer some questions about numerical trees, such as those in the following exercise.

Exercise 7.2

(1) What are the tree patterns for *all*, *some*, *no*, and *not all*? How are these patterns related?
(2) What are the tree patterns for *at most three* and *exactly three*? How are the patterns for *at most three*, *at least three*, and *exactly three* related?
(3) Which tree operations correspond to taking the negation of a quantifier, the conjunction of two quantifiers, and the disjunction of two quantifiers?

Exercise 7.3 Let the following type specifications be given:

```
type Quant = (Integer -> Bool) -> [Integer] -> Bool
genTree :: Quant -> [(Integer,Integer)]
```

Write the function genTree that yields, for any quantifier function q of the appropriate type, those number pairs (m, n) from the tree of numbers for which quantifier q gives 'true' on a universe of size $m + n$ if and only if n objects from the universe have the quantifier property. For example, $(0, 4)$ is in the sequence for *all* because 4 of the objects in a 4-object domain A have property B if *all A are B* is true. Here are some examples of what you should get:

```
Main> take 10 (genTree all)
[(0,0),(0,1),(0,2),(0,3),(0,4),(0,5),(0,6),(0,7),(0,8),(0,9)]
```

Fig. 7.6. Examples of Numerical Trees
At least three A are B

Less than half of the A are B

```
              −
         +        −       −
       +    +       −       −
     +    +       −     −     −     −
```

An even number of the A are B

```
            +
          +    −
        +    −    +
      +    −    +    −
    +    −    +    −    +
  +    −    +    −    +    −
```

```
Main> take 10 (genTree any)
[(0,1),(1,1),(0,2),(2,1),(1,2),(0,3),(3,1),(2,2),(1,3),(0,4)]
Main> take 10 (genTree (\ p dom -> not (any p dom)))
[(0,0),(1,0),(2,0),(3,0),(4,0),(5,0),(6,0),(7,0),(8,0),(9,0)]
```

Logical Representations for Quantifiers

The pairs of cardinals that characterize a quantifier $Q\,AB$ can be used for representation purposes. Every quantifier is defined by means of an arithmetical expression in two variables m and n, where m is the number of elements in $A - B$, n the number of elements in $A \cap B$. Logical forms for quantified expressions can exploit this fact:

- at least two $\leadsto \lambda mn \mapsto n \geq 2$.
- all $\leadsto \lambda mn \mapsto m = 0$.
- no $\leadsto \lambda mn \mapsto n = 0$.

Here are Haskell versions (after a module declaration for the code of this chapter):

```
module TCOM where

import Data.List
import FSynF
import Model
```

```
allNum, noNum :: Int -> Int -> Bool
allNum = \ m n -> m == 0
noNum  = \ m n -> n == 0

atleastNum, atmostNum :: Int -> Int -> Int -> Bool
atleastNum k = \ m n -> n >= k
atmostNum  k = \ m n -> n <= k
```

Logical operations on quantifiers can now be handled compositionally, by performing the corresponding logical operations on the arithmetical expressions:

- If $Q \rightsquigarrow E$, then *not* $Q \rightsquigarrow \lambda mn \mapsto \neg(Emn)$.
- If $Q_1 \rightsquigarrow E_1$ and $Q_2 \rightsquigarrow E_2$, then Q_1 *and* $Q_2 \rightsquigarrow \lambda mn \mapsto ((E_1 mn) \wedge (E_2 mn))$ and $[Q_1$ *or* $Q_2] \rightsquigarrow \lambda mn \mapsto ((E_1 mn) \vee (E_2 mn))$.

For instance, according to these instructions, the arithmetical expression that translates *at least two but not all* is: $\lambda mn \mapsto n \geq 2 \wedge \neg(m = 0)$. It can be implemented as follows:

```
atleast2butnotall :: Int -> Int -> Bool
atleast2butnotall = \ m n -> m > 0 && n >= 2
```

Relational Properties

As quantifiers are relations, we can study their relational properties and the way in which these properties are reflected in the tree patterns. For example, a quantifier Q is reflexive if and only if $\forall X \, Q \, X X$. E.g. the quantifiers *all* and *some* are reflexive, the quantifiers *no* and *not all* are not.

One can now study questions about tree patterns such as the following. If Q is reflexive, what will its tree pattern be like? Can it be shown that every quantifier with this tree pattern is reflexive? If some quantifier Q has a tree pattern with an outer north east diagonal consisting of minus signs, which relational property of Q does this reflect?

A relational property with linguistic interest is *symmetry*. A quantifier Q is *symmetric* if and only if $\forall X \forall Y \, Q \, XY \Leftrightarrow Q \, YX$.

Exercise 7.4 Give the quantifier tree pattern that corresponds to symmetry.

The linguistic interest of this class lies in the fact that the symmetric quantifiers are precisely the class of quantifiers which can occur at the Q position in *there-existential* sentences (sentences of the form *There are Q*).

Another example of a relational property of quantifiers with linguistic interest (to be illustrated below) is *upward right-monotonicity* in the second argument place:

MON↑ If $Q \, AB$ and $B \subseteq B'$, then $Q \, AB'$.

This means that the truth or falsity of $Q \, AB$ does not change if the set B is extended. Examples of quantifiers that upward right-monotone are *all*, *some*, and *at least five*.

Exercise 7.5 Can you find the quantifier tree pattern that corresponds to **MON↑**?

A quantifier relation is *downward right-monotone* in the second argument if the following holds:

MON↓ If $Q \, AB$ and $B' \subseteq B$, then $Q \, AB'$.

I.e. the truth or falsity of $Q \, AB$ is not affected by a reduction of the set B. Examples are *not all* and *no*.

Exercise 7.6 Can you find a quantifier tree pattern that corresponds to the property **MON↓**?

An example for a quantifier that satisfies neither **MON↑** nor **MON↓** is *an even number of*. (You can see this by inspecting the tree pattern.)

Barwise and Cooper [BC81] observed a certain correlation between the monotonicity properties of conjoined noun phrases on the one hand and the use of *and* versus *but* on the other: noun phrases that are monotone in the same direction are conjoined with *and*; monotonicity in opposite directions triggers conjunction by means of *but*. Examples are the coordinations *all men and some women* and *many English but no Dutch*. Of course, this is only an approximate rule; other factors are at work as well.

A second linguistic application is the account of so-called negative and positive polarity phenomena in natural language. To give an example, *to lift a finger* and *any* are negative polarity items, because they must occur in a 'negative context'.

$$\text{\textit{Few dwarfs lifted a finger to help the elves.}} \tag{7.10}$$

$$\text{* \textit{Many dwarfs lifted a finger to help the elves.}} \tag{7.11}$$

$$\text{\textit{No dwarf liked any of the elves.}} \tag{7.12}$$

$$\text{* \textit{Every dwarf liked any of the elves.}} \tag{7.13}$$

The noun phrases allowing negative polarity items in their scopes turn out to be, roughly at least, the **MON↓** noun phrases.

Negative polarity items have positive counterparts, namely expressions allowed within the scope of a **MON↑** noun phrase but awkward in the scope of a **MON↓** noun phrase:

$$\text{\textit{Some people could hardly believe it.}} \tag{7.14}$$

$$\text{* \textit{Nobody could hardly believe it.}} \tag{7.15}$$

A further linguistic question suggested here is the following. Given some list of positive polarity items in English, is it possible to arrive at more fine-grained classifications by subdividing this list into items that are allowed within the scope of a noun phrase which is neither **MON↑** nor **MON↓** and items that are not allowed in such contexts?

Some questions that can be solved by looking at the tree pattern characterisations of the monotonicity properties are in the next exercises.

Exercise 7.7 What is the effect of negation on monotonicity?

Exercise 7.8 What monotonicity property does the conjunction of two **MON↑** noun phrases have? Same question for the conjunction of two **MON↓** noun phrases.

Exercise 7.9 What is the monotonicity behaviour of the disjunction of two **MON↑** (**MON↓**) noun phrases?

Exercise 7.10 What is the monotonicity property of the conjunction (disjunction) of a **MON↑** and a **MON↓** noun phrase?

The answers to these questions can be tested by substituting the resulting noun phrases in sentences containing negative or positive polarity items.

One can also study monotonicity in the first argument:

↑MON If $Q\,AB$ and $A \subseteq A'$, then $Q\,A'B$.
↓MON If $Q\,AB$ and $A' \subseteq A$, then $Q\,A'B$.

Examples of ↑**MON** determiners are *some* and *not all*. *All* and *no* are ↓**MON** determiners. It is left to the reader to establish the tree patterns corresponding to the ↑**MON** and ↓**MON** properties.

Examples (7.16) and (7.17) illustrate that monotonicity properties in the left argument can be used to explain polarity phenomena within the syntactic restriction of the determiners, i.e. within the noun phrases that have these determiners as their heads.

$$\textit{All dwarfs who liked any of the elves were mistrusted.} \qquad (7.16)$$

$$\textit{* Some dwarfs who liked any of the elves were mistrusted.} \qquad (7.17)$$

Quantifiers, Automata, and Definability Quantifiers correspond to automata that accept strings over a binary alphabet $\{0, 1\}$: a string s with m zeros and n ones in it is accepted if and only if position $(m, n)\rangle$ in the numerical tree for the quantifier has a +. To give an example, the quantifier *all* corresponds to the regular language 1^* (the set of all strings consisting of just 1s). Figure 7.7 gives a finite state machine for this quantifier. The start state of the automaton has an arrow pointing to it; the grey state is the accepting state.

Fig. 7.7. Finite State Machine for Computing *All*

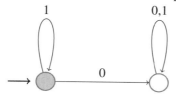

Exercise 7.11 Construct finite state machines for computing *at least two, at most five*, and *between three and seven*. Would these finite state machines still work if one would wish to allow strings of infinite length?

The languages accepted by quantifier automata are closed under permutation: it is the number of zeros and ones in the string that counts, not the order in which they are presented. Call a finite state machine *permutation invariant* if it has the following property: if reading a string s will get the machine from state p to state q, then reading any permutation of s will also get the machine from state p to state q. Quantifier automata must be permutation invariant. A finite state machine is *acyclic* if the machine does never return to a given state once it has left that state (in other words: 1-cycles are allowed, but all other cycles are out). An example of a quantifier that can be computed by a cyclic finite state machine but not by an acyclic one is *an even number of*.

A quantifier is called *first-order definable* if it is definable in terms of the Fregean quantifiers $\forall$ and $\exists$, equality, and the two predicates for the restriction and the body of the quantifier. The question of first-order definability is relevant for the semantics of natural language, because the suitability of logical representation languages for given natural language fragments depends on it. Here is a formal characterization of the first-order definable quantifiers:

The first-order definable quantifiers are exactly those that can be computed by an acyclic permutation-invariant finite state machine [Ben86].

It follows from this that *an even number of* is not first-order definable (a cyclic automaton is needed for its computation), nor are quantifiers like *half* and *most*, which cannot be computed on a finite state machine at all (a memory stack is needed to 'remember' the numbers of elements in $A - B$ and $A \cap B$).

Exercise 7.12 The automata perspective can be exploited to give an account of *semi-quantifiers* involving ordinals:

$$\textit{Every tenth page of a fairy tale is boring.} \tag{7.18}$$
$$\textit{The first ten pages of a fairy tale are boring.} \tag{7.19}$$

Design finite state machines for computing these semi-quantifiers. Next, note that semi-quantifiers do not observe **ISOM**. Formulate a weaker condition that they do satisfy.

7.3 The Language of Typed Logic and Its Semantics

In this section we will give formal definitions of the language of typed logic (or: typed lambda calculus) and its semantics, using Haskell counterparts and implementations to illustrate the theory. We will use it in Section 7.5 below for the composition of meaning in our natural language fragment.

Assume that we have constants and variables available for all types in the type hierarchy. Then the language of typed logic over these is defined as follows.

$$
\begin{aligned}
\textbf{type} \quad &::=\quad e \mid t \mid (\textbf{type} \rightarrow \textbf{type}) \\
\textbf{expression} \quad &::=\quad \textbf{constant}_{\textbf{type}} \\
&\quad\mid\quad \textbf{variable}_{\textbf{type}} \\
&\quad\mid\quad (\lambda\, \textbf{variable}_{\textbf{type}_1} \mapsto \textbf{expression}_{\textbf{type}_2})(\textbf{type}_1 \rightarrow \textbf{type}_2) \\
&\quad\mid\quad (\textbf{expression}_{\textbf{type}_1 \rightarrow \textbf{type}_2}\ \textbf{expression}_{\textbf{type}_1})_{\textbf{type}_2}
\end{aligned}
$$

Note that for an expression of the form $(E_1\ E_2)$ to be *well-typed* the types have to match, and that the type of the resulting expression is fully determined by the types of the components. Similarly, the type of a lambda expression $(\lambda v \mapsto E)$ is fully determined by the types of v and E.

Exercise 7.13 Assume constant A has type $e \rightarrow t$ and constant B has type $(e \rightarrow t) \rightarrow t$. Variable x has type e, variable Y has type $e \rightarrow t$. Which of the following expressions are well-typed?

(1) $(\lambda x \mapsto (A\ x))$
(2) $(B\ (\lambda x \mapsto (A\ x)))$
(3) $(\lambda Y \mapsto (Y\ (\lambda x \mapsto (A\ x))))$
(4) $(\lambda Y \mapsto (B\ Y))$

Often we leave out the type information. The definition of the language then looks like this:

$$
\begin{array}{rcl}
\textbf{expression} & ::= & \textbf{constant} \\
& | & \textbf{variable} \\
& | & (\lambda\ \textbf{variable} \mapsto \textbf{expression}) \\
& | & (\textbf{expression expression})
\end{array}
$$

A model M for typed logic consists of a domain D_e together with an interpretation function I which maps every constant of the language to a function of the appropriate type in the domain hierarchy based on D_e. A variable assignment g for typed logic maps every variable of the language to a function of the appropriate type in the domain hierarchy. The semantics for the language is given by defining a function $[\![\cdot]\!]_g^M$ which maps every expression of the language to a function of the appropriate type.

- $[\![\textbf{constant}]\!]_g^M = I(\textbf{constant})$
- $[\![\textbf{variable}]\!]_g^M = g(\textbf{variable})$
- $[\![(\lambda v_{\tau_1} \mapsto E_{\tau_2})]\!]_g^M = h$,
  where $h : D_{\tau_1} \rightarrow D_{\tau_2}$ is the function given by $\lambda d \mapsto [\![E]\!]_{g[v:=d]}^M$
- $[\![(E_1\ E_2)]\!]_g^M = [\![E_1]\!]_g^M([\![E_2]\!]_g^M)$

Exercise 7.14 Assume that $Give(a, b, c)$ expresses that a gives b to c. What do the following expressions say?

(1) $\lambda x \mapsto Give(x, b, c)$
(2) $\lambda x \mapsto Give(a, x, c)$
(3) $\lambda x \mapsto Give(a, b, x)$
(4) $\lambda x \mapsto Give(x, b, x)$
(5) $\lambda x \mapsto (\lambda y \mapsto Give(y, b, x))$
(6) $\lambda x \mapsto (\lambda y \mapsto Give(x, b, y))$

In fact, the logical constants of predicate logic can be viewed as constants of typed logic, as follows: $\neg$ is a constant of type $t \rightarrow t$ with the following interpretation.

- $[\![\neg]\!] = h$, where h is the function in $t \rightarrow t$ which maps 0 to 1 and vice versa

As we have seen already, $\wedge$ and $\vee$ are constants of type $t \to t \to t$ with the following interpretations.

- $[\![\wedge]\!] = h$, where h is the function in $t \to t \to t$ which maps 1 to $\{(1,1),(0,0)\}$ and 0 to $\{(1,0),(0,0)\}$
- $[\![\vee]\!] = h$, where h is the function in $t \to t \to t$ which maps 1 to $\{(1,1),(0,1)\}$ and 0 to $\{(1,1),(0,0)\}$

Note that $\{(1,1),(0,0)\}$ is the identity function on $\{0,1\}$.

Exercise 7.15 Give the interpretation of the material implication constant $\to$ in typed logic.

Exercise 7.16 Give the interpretation of the material equivalence constant $\leftrightarrow$ in typed logic.

The quantifiers $\exists$ and $\forall$ are constants of type $(e \to t) \to t$, with the following interpretations.

- $[\![\forall]\!] = h$, where h is the function in $(e \to t) \to t$ which maps the function that characterizes D_e to 1 and every other characteristic function to 0
- $[\![\exists]\!] = h$, where h is the function in $(e \to t) \to t$ which maps the function that characterizes $\emptyset$ to 0 and every other characteristic function to 1

It is possible to add constants for quantification over different types. E.g. to express second-order quantification (i.e. quantification over properties of things), one would need quantifier constants of type $((e \to t) \to t) \to t$.

Exercise 7.17 What is the type of binary generalized quantifiers such as the following?

(1) $Q_\forall(\lambda x \mapsto (P\,x))(\lambda x \mapsto (Q\,x))$ (*all P are Q*)
(2) $Q_\exists(\lambda x \mapsto (P\,x))(\lambda x \mapsto (Q\,x))$ (*some P are Q*)
(3) $Q_M(\lambda x \mapsto (P\,x))(\lambda x \mapsto (Q\,x))$ (*most P are Q*)

We will assume that for every type τ built from e and t we have a constant $i_{\tau \to \tau \to t}$ available to express the identity of two objects of type τ.

Then $i_{e \to e \to t}$ denotes identity of individual objects, and it is convenient to abbreviate $((i\,b)\,a)$, for a, b of type e, as $a = b$.

Exercise 7.18 Write out $i_{t \to t \to t}$. Which two-place connective does this constant express?

With these constants added, the language of typed logic defined above contains ordinary predicate logic as a proper fragment. Here are some example expressions of typed logic, with their predicate logical counterparts:

Typed logic	Predicate logic
$(\neg\,(P\,x))$	$\neg P x$
$((\wedge\,(P\,x))\,(Q\,y))$	$P x \wedge Q y$
$(\forall\,(\lambda x \mapsto (P\,x)))$	$\forall x P x$
$(\forall\,(\lambda x \mapsto (\exists\,(\lambda y \mapsto ((R\,x)\,y)))))$	$\forall x \exists y R x y$

It is possible to reduce the difference in syntactic appearance between ordinary predicate logic and typed logic by means of some abbreviation conventions. Occasionally we will write $(\lambda x \mapsto (\lambda y \mapsto E))$ as $\lambda x y \mapsto E$, and similarly for three or more successive lambda abstractions. Also, an expression of the form $(((E\,a)\,b)\,c)$ can be written as $Eabc$ to make it resemble predicate logical notation more closely (similarly for different numbers of arguments). Finally, it is convenient to write $((\wedge\,E_1)\,E_2)$ as $E_1 \wedge E_2$ and similarly for $\vee$, $\rightarrow$ and $\leftrightarrow$. These conventions are similar to the Haskell operator binding conventions. We will also omit outermost parentheses.

Note that although $(((E\,a)\,b)\,c)$ may be written as $Eabc$, this is not the same as $E(a,b,c)$. The difference is that in $Eabc$, the arguments of the function E are consumed one by one, while in $E(a,b,c)$, the function E takes a single argument which is a triple. Technically, the process of converting $(((E\,a)\,b)\,c)$ to $E(a,b,c)$ is done by means of a function that puts the arguments in an ordered triple. This is what the function `uncurry3` (compare this with the `curry3` function on page 137) does for us.

```
uncurry3 :: (a -> b -> c -> d) -> (a, b, c) -> d
uncurry3 f (x,y,z) = f x y z
```

To demonstrate the use of this, here is a definition of a three-place relation in Haskell:

```
rel3 :: Entity -> Entity -> Entity -> Bool
rel3 D x y = love x y
rel3 E x y = not (love x y)
rel3 _ _ _ = False
```

Here is a check of the definition of `rel3`:

```
TCOM> love B S
True
TCOM> rel3 A B S
False
TCOM> rel3 D B S
```

```
True
TCOM> uncurry3 rel3 (D,B,S)
True
```

Assume *Give* is a typed logical constant of type $e \rightarrow e \rightarrow e \rightarrow t$ which is interpreted as the three-place relation of giving something to someone. If $Give(a, b, c)$ is uncurried notation for 'a gives b to c', then $\lambda x \mapsto \exists y \exists z Give(x, y, z)$ expresses 'giving something to someone', and $\lambda x \mapsto \exists y Give(x, b, y)$ expresses 'giving b to someone'. Finally, $\lambda x \mapsto \exists y Give(y, b, x)$ expresses 'receiving b from someone'.

Exercise 7.19 Assume $Give(x, y, z)$ means that x gives y to z. Use this to find a typed logic expression for 'receiving something from someone'.

Suppose we want to translate *Siegfried gave Kriemhild the ring*, which has syntactic structure

$$[_S [_{NP} \textit{Siegfried}] [_{VP} [_{TV} [_{DTV} \textit{gave}] [_{NP} \textit{Kriemhild}]] [_{NP} \textit{the ring}]]],$$

in a compositional way. This means that we want the translation of *gave* to first combine with the translation of the indirect object, then combine with the translation of the direct object, and after that combine with the translation of the subject. So we want to use $\lambda z y x \mapsto Give(x, y, z)$ as translation for *gave*. We construct this expression by first abstracting over the one who receives (z), then abstracting over the thing that is given (y), and finally abstracting over the one who gives (x). In curried notation this would correspond to $\lambda z y x \mapsto Give\, x\, y\, z$ or $\lambda z y x \mapsto (((Give\, x)\, y)\, z)$. In the latter, however, the order in which *Give* takes its arguments does not reflect the argument order that we read off the syntactic structure. That's why in the following chapter we will use constants with a different argument order, such that we can construct the meaning $\lambda z y x \mapsto (((Give\, z)\, y)\, x)$, which reflects that *Give* is first applied to the indirect object meaning, then to the direct object meaning, and then to the subject meaning.

Translating all the combinations of phrases as function argument combination in the sentence above, we arrive at the following translation of the whole sentence:

$$(((\lambda z y x \mapsto Give(x, y, z)\, c)\, b)\, a). \tag{7.20}$$

This does indeed express what we want, but in a rather roundabout way. We would like to reduce this expression to $Give(a, b, c)$. The subject of reducing expressions of typed logic is taken up in the next section.

7.4 Reducing Expressions of Typed Logic

To reduce expression (7.20) from the previous section to its simplest form, three steps of so-called β-conversion are needed. During β-conversion of an expression consisting of a function expression $\lambda v \mapsto E$ followed by an argument expression A, basically the following happens (we will state a *proviso* shortly). The prefix $\lambda v \mapsto$ is removed from the function expression $\lambda v \mapsto E$, leaving E, and next the argument expression A is *substituted* in E for all free occurrences of v. The free occurrences of v in E are precisely the occurrences which were bound by λv in $\lambda v \mapsto E$.

Here is the *proviso*. In some cases, the substitution process described above cannot be applied without further ado, because it will result in unintended capturing of variables within the argument expression A. Consider expression (7.21) (we use unabbreviated notation again, because the syntactic details do matter now).

$$((\lambda x \mapsto (\lambda y \mapsto ((R\ y)\ x)))\ y). \tag{7.21}$$

In this expression, y is bound in the functional part $(\lambda x \mapsto (\lambda y \mapsto ((R\ y)\ x)))$ but free in the argument part y. Reducing (7.21) by β-conversion according to the recipe given above would result in $(\lambda y \mapsto ((R\ y)\ y))$, with capture of the argument y at the place where it is substituted for x. This problem can be avoided by performing β-conversion on an alphabetic variant of the original expression, say on (7.22).

$$((\lambda x \mapsto (\lambda z \mapsto ((R\ z)\ x)))\ y). \tag{7.22}$$

Another example where switching to an alphabetic variant (also called α-conversion) is necessary before β-conversion to prevent unintended capture of free variables is the expression (7.23).

$$((\lambda p \mapsto \forall x((P\ x) \leftrightarrow p))(Q\ x)). \tag{7.23}$$

In (7.23), p is a variable of type t and x one of type e. Variable x is bound inside the functional part $(\lambda p \mapsto \forall x((P\ x) \leftrightarrow p))$ but free in the argument part $(Q\ x)$. Substituting $(Q\ x)$ for p in the function expression would cause x to be captured, with failure to preserve the original meaning. Again, the problem is avoided if β-conversion is performed on an alphabetic variant of the original expression, say on (7.24).

$$((\lambda p \mapsto \forall z((P\ z) \leftrightarrow p))(Q\ x)). \tag{7.24}$$

Performing β-reduction on (7.24) yields $\forall z((P\ x) \leftrightarrow (Q\ x))$, with the argument of B still free, as it should be.

To state all this in a formally precise way, we start with a definition of 'variable v is free in expression E'. v is free in E if the following holds (we use $\approx$ for the relation of being syntactically identical, i.e. for being the same expression):

- $v \approx E$

- $E \approx (E_1\ E_2)$, and v is free in E_1 or v is free in E_2
- $E \approx (\lambda x \mapsto E_1)$, and $v \not\approx x$, and v is free in E_1

Exercise 7.20 Which occurrences of x are free?

(1) $(\lambda x \mapsto (P\ x))$
(2) $((\lambda x \mapsto (P\ x))\ x)$
(3) $(\lambda x \mapsto ((R\ x)\ x))$
(4) $((\lambda x \mapsto ((R\ x)\ x))x)$
(5) $((\lambda y \mapsto ((R\ x)\ y))x)$

Exercise 7.21 Same question for $((\lambda y \mapsto \exists x((R\ x)\ y))\ x)$, where one should bear in mind that $\exists x((R\ x)\ y)$ is shorthand for $(\exists (\lambda x \mapsto ((R\ x)\ y)))$.

Next, we give the definition of substitution of s for free occurrences of v in E, with notation $E[v := s]$.

- If $E \approx v$, then $E[v := s] \approx s$,
  if $E \approx x \not\approx v$ (i.e. E is a variable different from v), then $E[v := s] \approx x$,
  if $E \approx c$ (i.e. E is a constant, and therefore different from v), then $E[v := s] \approx c$.
- If $E \approx (E_1\ E_2)$, then $E[v := s] \approx (E_1[v := s]\ E_2[v := s])$.
- If $E \approx (\lambda x \mapsto E_1)$, then

  – if $v \approx x$, then $E[v := s] \approx E$,
  – if $v \not\approx x$, then there are two cases:

    (1) if x is not free in s or v is not free in E, then
       $E[v := s] \approx (\lambda x \mapsto E_1[v := s])$,
    (2) if x is free in s and v is free in E, then
       $E[v := s] \approx (\lambda y \mapsto E_1[x := y][v := s])$, for some y which is not free in s and not free in E_1.

This definition is rather involved. Especially the distinction within the final case in two subcases (1) and (2) may look like an overcomplication. To see that it is not, consider the following simple example.

$$(\lambda y \mapsto (P\ x))[x := y]. \tag{7.25}$$

The function $(\lambda y \mapsto (P\ x))$ is the function yielding $(P\ x)$ for any argument, i.e. a constant function. If we apply the above definition without taking subcase (2) into account, we get:

$$(\lambda y \mapsto (P\ x))[x := y] \approx (\lambda y \mapsto (P\ x)[x := y]) \approx (\lambda y \mapsto (P\ y)).$$

This is a completely different function, namely the function that assigns to argument a the result of applying P to a. But by using subcase (2) we do get the correct result:

$$\begin{aligned}
(\lambda y \mapsto (P\,x))[x := y] &\approx (\lambda z \mapsto (P\,x)[y := z][x := y]) \\
&\approx (\lambda z \mapsto (P\,x)[x := y]) \\
&\approx (\lambda z \mapsto (P\,y)).
\end{aligned}$$

Finally, here is the definition of *reduction*, which comes in three flavours: β-reduction, α-reduction, and η-reduction, for which we use arrows $\xrightarrow{\beta}$, $\xrightarrow{\alpha}$, and $\xrightarrow{\eta}$. Here are the definitions:

Beta reduction: $((\lambda v \mapsto E)\,s) \xrightarrow{\beta} E[v := s]$
     Condition: v and s are of the same type (otherwise the expression to be reduced is not well-typed).

Alpha reduction: $(\lambda v \mapsto E) \xrightarrow{\alpha} (\lambda x \mapsto E[v := x])$
     Conditions: v and x are of the same type, and x is not free in E.

Eta reduction: $((\lambda v \mapsto E)\,v) \xrightarrow{\eta} E$

The 'real work' takes place during β-reduction. The α-reduction rule serves only to state in an explicit fashion that lambda calculations are insensitive to switches to alphabetic variants. Whether one uses λx to bind occurrences of x or λy to bind occurrences of y is immaterial, just as it is immaterial in the case of predicate logic whether one writes $\forall x Px$ or $\forall y Py$. The η-reduction rule makes a principle explicit that we have used implicitly all the time: if $(P\,j)$ expresses that John is present, then both P and $(\lambda x \mapsto (P\,x))$ express the property of being present. This is so because $((\lambda x \mapsto (P\,x))\,x) \xrightarrow{\eta} (P\,x)$, so P and $(\lambda x \mapsto (P\,x))$ give the same result when applied to argument x, i.e. they express the same function. Applying β-reduction to

$$(((\lambda zyx \mapsto Give(x, y, z)\,c)\,b)\,a),$$

or in unabbreviated notation

$$((((\lambda z \mapsto (\lambda y \mapsto (\lambda x \mapsto Give(x, y, z))))\,c)\,b)\,a)$$

gives:

$$((((\lambda z \mapsto (\lambda y \mapsto (\lambda x \mapsto Give(x, y, z))))\,c)\,b)\,a)$$

$$\xrightarrow{\beta} (((\lambda y \mapsto (\lambda x \mapsto Give(x, y, c)))\,b)\,a)$$

$$\xrightarrow{\beta} (\lambda x \mapsto Give(x, b, c)\,a)$$

$$\xrightarrow{\beta} Give(a,b,c).$$

This is exactly what we want. To be fully precise we have to state explicitly that expressions can be reduced 'in context'. The following principles express this:

$$\frac{E \xrightarrow{\beta} E'}{(F\ E) \xrightarrow{\beta} (F\ E')} \qquad\qquad \frac{E \xrightarrow{\beta} E'}{(E\ F) \xrightarrow{\beta} (E'\ F)}$$

$$\frac{E \xrightarrow{\beta} E'}{(\lambda v \mapsto E) \xrightarrow{\beta} (\lambda v \mapsto E')}$$

Here F is assumed to have the appropriate type, of course. These principles allow β-reductions at arbitrary depth within expressions.

Exercise 7.22 Reduce the following expressions to their simplest forms.

(1) $((\lambda Y \mapsto (\lambda x \mapsto (Y\ x)))\ P)$
(2) $(((\lambda Y \mapsto (\lambda x \mapsto (Y\ x)))\ P)\ y)$
(3) $((\lambda P \mapsto (\lambda Q \mapsto \exists x(Px \wedge Qx)))\ A)$
(4) $(((\lambda P \mapsto (\lambda Q \mapsto \exists x(Px \wedge Qx)))\ A)\ B)$
(5) $((\lambda P \mapsto (\lambda Q \mapsto \forall x(Px \rightarrow Qx)))(\lambda y \mapsto ((\lambda x \mapsto R(x,y))\ j)))$

Our type system with matching lambda language may seem complicated at first sight, but in fact it is a very elegant system, with some special properties that make it easy to handle. In the statement of the following property, we write $E_1 \twoheadrightarrow E_2$ for 'E_1 reduces in a number of α, β, η steps to E_2.'

Confluence property (or: Church-Rosser property):
> For all expressions E, E_1, E_2 of typed logic: if $E \twoheadrightarrow E_1$ and $E \twoheadrightarrow E_2$, then there is an expression F with $E_1 \twoheadrightarrow F$ and $E_2 \twoheadrightarrow F$.

An expression of the form $((\lambda v \mapsto E)\ s)$ is called a β-*redex* (for: β-reducible expression). $E[v := s]$ is called the *contractum* of $((\lambda v \mapsto E)\ s)$. An expression that does not contain any redexes is called a *normal form*.

Normal form property: Every expression of typed logic can be reduced to a normal form.

Combining the confluence property and the normal form property we get that the normal forms of an expression E are identical modulo α-conversion. That is to say, all normal forms of E are alphabetic variants of one another.

The normal form property holds thanks to the restrictions imposed by the typing discipline. Untyped lambda calculus lacks this property. In untyped lambda calculus it is allowed to apply expressions to themselves. In typed lambda calculus this is forbidden, because $(X\ X)$ cannot be consistently typed.

Exercise 7.23 In untyped lambda calculus, expressions like $(\lambda x \mapsto (x\ x))$ are well-formed. Show that $((\lambda x \mapsto (x\ x))(\lambda x \mapsto (x\ x)))$ does not have a normal form.

7.5 Typed Meanings for Natural Language

Now we are ready for another exercise in composition of meaning for natural language. We will illustrate the theory with our fragment from before. Every syntax rule has a semantic counterpart to specify how the meaning representation of the whole is built from the meaning representations of the components. $[\![X]\!]$ is used as notation for the meaning of X.

Sentences are interpreted as function application of the NP meaning to the VP meaning:

$$\mathbf{S} \longrightarrow \mathbf{NP\ VP} \qquad [\![\mathrm{S}]\!] \longrightarrow ([\![\mathrm{NP}]\!]\ [\![\mathrm{VP}]\!])$$

NPs are interpreted as generalized quantifiers, or as determiner meanings applied to common noun meanings:

NP	$\longrightarrow$	*Snow White*	$[\![\mathrm{NP}]\!]$	$\longrightarrow$	$\lambda P \mapsto (P\ s)$
NP	$\longrightarrow$	*Alice*	$[\![\mathrm{NP}]\!]$	$\longrightarrow$	$\lambda P \mapsto (P\ a)$
NP	$\longrightarrow$	*Dorothy*	$[\![\mathrm{NP}]\!]$	$\longrightarrow$	$\lambda P \mapsto (P\ d)$
NP	$\longrightarrow$	*Goldilocks*	$[\![\mathrm{NP}]\!]$	$\longrightarrow$	$\lambda P \mapsto (P\ g)$
NP	$\longrightarrow$	*Little Mook*	$[\![\mathrm{NP}]\!]$	$\longrightarrow$	$\lambda P \mapsto (P\ m)$
NP	$\longrightarrow$	*Atreyu*	$[\![\mathrm{NP}]\!]$	$\longrightarrow$	$\lambda P \mapsto (P\ y)$
NP	$\longrightarrow$	**DET CN**	$[\![\mathrm{NP}]\!]$	$\longrightarrow$	$([\![\mathrm{DET}]\!]\ [\![\mathrm{CN}]\!])$
NP	$\longrightarrow$	**DET RCN**	$[\![\mathrm{NP}]\!]$	$\longrightarrow$	$([\![\mathrm{DET}]\!]\ [\![\mathrm{RCN}]\!])$

Determiners get the following interpretations:

$$\mathbf{DET} \longrightarrow some$$
$$[\![\mathrm{DET}]\!] \longrightarrow \lambda PQ \mapsto \exists x((P\ x) \wedge (Q\ x))$$

$$\mathbf{DET} \longrightarrow a$$
$$[\![\mathrm{DET}]\!] \longrightarrow \lambda PQ \mapsto \exists x((P\ x) \wedge (Q\ x))$$

$$\mathbf{DET} \longrightarrow every$$
$$[\![\mathrm{DET}]\!] \longrightarrow \lambda PQ \mapsto \forall x((P\ x) \rightarrow (Q\ x))$$

$$\mathbf{DET} \longrightarrow no$$
$$[\![\mathrm{DET}]\!] \longrightarrow \lambda PQ \mapsto \forall x((P\ x) \rightarrow \neg(Q\ x))$$

$$\mathbf{DET} \longrightarrow the$$
$$[\![\mathrm{DET}]\!] \longrightarrow \lambda PQ \mapsto \exists x(\forall y((P\ y) \leftrightarrow (x = y)) \wedge (Q\ x))$$

Common nouns are interpreted as one-place predicates:

$$
\begin{array}{llll}
\textbf{CN} & \longrightarrow & \textit{girl} & \quad [\![\textbf{CN}]\!] \longrightarrow \lambda x \mapsto (\textit{Girl } x) \\
\textbf{CN} & \longrightarrow & \textit{boy} & \quad [\![\textbf{CN}]\!] \longrightarrow \lambda x \mapsto (\textit{Boy } x) \\
\textbf{CN} & \longrightarrow & \textit{princess} & \quad [\![\textbf{CN}]\!] \longrightarrow \lambda x \mapsto (\textit{Princess } x) \\
\textbf{CN} & \longrightarrow & \textit{dwarf} & \quad [\![\textbf{CN}]\!] \longrightarrow \lambda x \mapsto (\textit{Dwarf } x) \\
\textbf{CN} & \longrightarrow & \textit{giant} & \quad [\![\textbf{CN}]\!] \longrightarrow \lambda x \mapsto (\textit{Giant } x) \\
\textbf{CN} & \longrightarrow & \textit{wizard} & \quad [\![\textbf{CN}]\!] \longrightarrow \lambda x \mapsto (\textit{Wizard } x) \\
\textbf{CN} & \longrightarrow & \textit{sword} & \quad [\![\textbf{CN}]\!] \longrightarrow \lambda x \mapsto (\textit{Sword } x) \\
\textbf{CN} & \longrightarrow & \textit{dagger} & \quad [\![\textbf{CN}]\!] \longrightarrow \lambda x \mapsto (\textit{Dagger } x)
\end{array}
$$

The interpretation of a common noun with a relative clause is the intersection of the interpretation of the common noun with the interpretation of the relative clause:

$$
\begin{array}{lll}
\textbf{RCN} & \longrightarrow & \textbf{CN } \textit{that} \textbf{ VP} \\
[\![\textbf{RCN}]\!] & \longrightarrow & \lambda x \mapsto ((([\![\textbf{CN}]\!] \; x) \wedge ([\![\textbf{VP}]\!] \; x))
\end{array}
$$

$$
\begin{array}{lll}
\textbf{RCN} & \longrightarrow & \textbf{CN } \textit{that} \textbf{ NP TV} \\
[\![\textbf{RCN}]\!] & \longrightarrow & \lambda x \mapsto ((([\![\textbf{CN}]\!] \; x) \wedge ([\![\textbf{NP}]\!] \; (\lambda y \mapsto ((([\![\textbf{TV}]\!] \; y) \; x))))
\end{array}
$$

Intransitive verbs are interpreted as one-place predicates:

$$
\begin{array}{llll}
\textbf{VP} & \longrightarrow & \textit{laughed} & \quad [\![\textbf{VP}]\!] \longrightarrow \lambda x \mapsto (\textit{Laugh } x) \\
\textbf{VP} & \longrightarrow & \textit{cheered} & \quad [\![\textbf{VP}]\!] \longrightarrow \lambda x \mapsto (\textit{Cheer } x) \\
\textbf{VP} & \longrightarrow & \textit{shuddered} & \quad [\![\textbf{VP}]\!] \longrightarrow \lambda x \mapsto (\textit{Shudder } x)
\end{array}
$$

Other VPs are interpreted as follows:

$$
\begin{array}{lll}
\textbf{VP} & \longrightarrow & \textbf{TV NP} \\
[\![\textbf{VP}]\!] & \longrightarrow & \lambda x \mapsto ([\![\textbf{NP}]\!] \; (\lambda y \mapsto ((([\![\textbf{TV}]\!] \; y) \; x)))
\end{array}
$$

$$
\begin{array}{lll}
\textbf{VP} & \longrightarrow & \textbf{DV NP}_1 \textbf{ NP}_2 \\
[\![\textbf{VP}]\!] & \longrightarrow & \lambda x \mapsto ([\![\textbf{NP}_1]\!] \; (\lambda y \mapsto ([\![\textbf{NP}_2]\!] \; (\lambda z \mapsto (((([\![\textbf{TV}]\!] \; z) \; y) \; x)))))
\end{array}
$$

Transitive verbs are interpreted as two-place predicates:

$$
\begin{array}{llll}
\textbf{TV} & \longrightarrow & \textit{loved} & \quad [\![\textbf{TV}]\!] \longrightarrow \lambda xy \mapsto ((\textit{Love } x) \; y) \\
\textbf{TV} & \longrightarrow & \textit{admired} & \quad [\![\textbf{TV}]\!] \longrightarrow \lambda xy \mapsto ((\textit{Admire } x) \; y) \\
\textbf{TV} & \longrightarrow & \textit{helped} & \quad [\![\textbf{TV}]\!] \longrightarrow \lambda xy \mapsto ((\textit{Help } x) \; y) \\
\textbf{TV} & \longrightarrow & \textit{defeated} & \quad [\![\textbf{TV}]\!] \longrightarrow \lambda xy \mapsto ((\textit{Defeat } x) \; y)
\end{array}
$$

As an example, consider the sentence *Alice admired Dorothy*, which has the following syntactic structure in our fragment:

$$[_S \; [_{NP} \; \textit{Alice }] [_{VP} \; [_{TV} \; \textit{admired }] [_{NP} \; \textit{Dorothy }]]].$$

According to the rules above, this gets assigned the following meaning:

$$(\llbracket Alice \rrbracket \, (\lambda u \mapsto \llbracket Dorothy \rrbracket \, (\lambda v \mapsto (((\lambda x \mapsto (\lambda y \mapsto ((Admire \; x) \; y))) \; v) \; u))))$$

Where $\llbracket Alice \rrbracket = \lambda P \mapsto (P \; a)$ and $\llbracket Dorothy \rrbracket = \lambda P \mapsto (P \; d)$. Reducing this expression gives:

$$\xrightarrow{\beta} (\llbracket Alice \rrbracket \, (\lambda u \mapsto \llbracket Dorothy \rrbracket \, (\lambda v \mapsto ((\lambda y \mapsto ((Admire \; v) \; y)) \; u))))$$

$$\xrightarrow{\beta} ((\lambda P \mapsto (P \; a))(\lambda u \mapsto (\lambda P \mapsto (P \; d))(\lambda v \mapsto ((Admire \; v) \; u))))$$

$$\xrightarrow{\beta} ((\lambda P \mapsto (P \; a))(\lambda u \mapsto ((\lambda v \mapsto ((Admire \; v) \; u)) \; d)))$$

$$\xrightarrow{\beta} ((\lambda P \mapsto (P \; a))(\lambda u \mapsto ((Admire \; d) \; u)))$$

$$\xrightarrow{\beta} ((\lambda u \mapsto ((Admire \; d) \; u)) \; a)$$

$$\xrightarrow{\beta} ((Admire \; d) \; a).$$

Exercise 7.24 Give the compositional translation for *Snow White helped some dwarf*, and reduce it to normal form.

7.6 Implementing Semantic Interpretation

We will proceed by defining for every syntactic category an interpretation function of the appropriate type, using `Entity` for e and `Bool` for t. The interpretation of sentences has type `Bool`, so the interpretation function `intS` gets type `Sent -> Bool`.

Since there is only one rewrite rule for S, the interpretation function `intS` consists of only one equation:

```
intSent :: Sent -> Bool
intSent (Sent np vp) = (intNP np) (intVP vp)
```

The interpretation function `intNP` consists of four equations, one for every rewrite rule for NP in the grammar fragment. The function has type

$$\texttt{NP -> (Entity -> Bool) -> Bool}.$$

Here `Entity -> Bool` is the Haskell counterpart to $e \rightarrow t$, which is the type of the VP interpretation that the NP combines with to form a sentence.

```
intNP :: NP -> (Entity -> Bool) -> Bool
intNP SnowWhite    = \ p -> p snowWhite
intNP Alice        = \ p -> p alice
intNP Dorothy      = \ p -> p dorothy
intNP Goldilocks   = \ p -> p goldilocks
intNP LittleMook   = \ p -> p littleMook
intNP Atreyu       = \ p -> p atreyu
intNP (NP1 det cn)  = (intDET det) (intCN cn)
intNP (NP2 det rcn) = (intDET det) (intRCN rcn)
```

Note the close connection between `\ p -> p alice` and $\lambda P \mapsto (P\ a)$ that we get by employing the Haskell counterpart to λ.

For the interpretation of verb phrases we invoke the information encoded in our first-order model.

```
intVP :: VP -> Entity -> Bool
intVP Laughed   = \ x -> laugh x
intVP Cheered   = \ x -> cheer x
intVP Shuddered = \ x -> shudder x
```

The interpretation of complex VPs is a bit more involved. We have to find a way to make reference to the property of 'standing into the TV relation to the subject of the sentence'. We do this in the same way as in the type logic specification of the semantic clause for [VP TV NP].

```
intVP (VP1 tv np) =
   \ subj -> intNP np (\ obj -> intTV tv subj obj)
intVP (VP2 dv np1 np2) =
   \ subj -> intNP np1 (\ iobj -> intNP np2 (\ dobj ->
                        intDV dv subj iobj dobj))
```

Note that `subj` refers to the sentence subject and `obj` to the sentence direct object.

The interpretation of transitive and ditransitive verbs discloses another bit of information about the world. Again, we invoke the information about the world encoded in our first-order model.

```
intTV :: TV -> Entity -> Entity -> Bool
intTV Loved    = \ x y -> love x y
intTV Admired  = \ x y -> admire x y
intTV Helped   = \ x y -> help x y
intTV Defeated = \ x y -> defeat x y


intDV :: DV -> Entity -> Entity -> Entity -> Bool
intDV Gave = \ x y z -> give x y z
```

The interpretation of CNs is similar to that of VPs.

```
intCN :: CN -> Entity -> Bool
intCN Girl     = \ x -> girl x
intCN Boy      = \ x -> boy x
intCN Princess = \ x -> princess x
intCN Dwarf    = \ x -> dwarf x
intCN Giant    = \ x -> giant x
intCN Wizard   = \ x -> wizard x
intCN Sword    = \ x -> sword x
intCN Dagger   = \ x -> dagger x
```

Next, we get the most involved part of the implementation: the definition of the determiner interpretations. Let us first consider the type. The interpretation of a DET needs two properties (type `Entity -> Bool`): one for the CN and one for the VP, to yield the type of an S interpretation, i.e. `Bool`.

```
intDET :: DET ->
          (Entity -> Bool) -> (Entity -> Bool) -> Bool
```

The interpretation of *some*, for example, just checks whether the two properties corresponding to CN and VP have anything in common. This is what this check looks like in Haskell. Note that this is not an instruction for a translation to logical form, but an instruction to use the Haskell `any` function to check whether two sets of entities have a non-empty intersection.

```
intDET Some p q = any q (filter p entities)
```

Here `filter p entities` gives the list of all members of `entities` that satisfy property p, and `any` is a function taking a property and a list that returns True if the sublist of elements satisfying the property is non-empty, `False` otherwise. Thus, `any q list` checks whether any element of the list satisfies property q.

The interpretation of *every* checks whether the CN property is included in the VP property. Again, this is not a translation to logical form but an instruction for a check whether the appropriate quantifier relation holds between p and q.

```
intDET Every p q = all q (filter p entities)
```

Here `filter p entities` gives the list of all members of `entities` that satisfy property p, and `all q list` checks whether every member of `list` satisfies property q.

The interpretation of *the* consists of two parts (recall Russell's treatment of definites outlined in Section 6.2):

(1) a check that the CN property is unique, i.e. that it is true of precisely one entity in the domain,
(2) a check that the CN and the VP property have an element in common, in other words, the *some* check on the two properties.

```
intDET The p q = singleton plist && q (head plist)
          where
                plist = filter p entities
                singleton [x] = True
                singleton  _  = False
```

The interpretation of *no* is just the negation of the interpretation of *some*:

```
intDET No p q = not (intDET Some p q)
```

Now suppose we also want to give an interpretation for the determiner *most*. It compares the length of the list of entities satisfying the first argument (the restriction) with the length of the list of entities satisfying the second argument (the body).

```
intDET Most p q = length pqlist > length (plist \\ qlist)
      where
            plist   = filter p entities
            qlist   = filter q entities
            pqlist  = filter q plist
```

Exercise 7.25 Implement interpretation functions for `AtLeast` and `AtMost`.

The interpretation of relativized common nouns of the form [*That* CN VP] checks whether an entity has both the CN and the VP property:

```
intRCN :: RCN -> Entity -> Bool
intRCN (RCN1 cn _ vp) =
       \ e -> ((intCN cn e) && (intVP vp e))
```

The interpretation of relativized common nouns of the form [*That* CN NP TV] checks whether an entity has both the CN property as the property of being the object of NP TV.

```
intRCN (RCN2 cn _ np tv) =
   \ e -> ((intCN cn e) &&
           (intNP np (\ subj -> (intTV tv subj e))))
```

Assume you have collected all the code from the book website, and you have loaded the module TCOM.hs. Here are some examples of queries for this code:

```
TCOM> intSent (Sent (NP1 The Princess) Laughed)
True
TCOM> intSent (Sent (NP1 The Giant) Shuddered)
False
TCOM> intSent (Sent (NP1 Some Dwarf) Cheered)
False
TCOM> intSent (Sent (NP1 No Wizard) Laughed)
True
TCOM> intSent (Sent (NP1 Some Dwarf)
                    (VP1 Defeated (NP1 Some Giant)))
True
TCOM> intSent (Sent (NP2 No (RCN1 Boy That
                    (VP1 Admired Goldilocks))) Shuddered)
True
```

It is a bit awkward that we have to provide the data structures of syntax ourselves. The process of constructing syntax data structures from strings of words is called parsing; this topic will be taken up in Chapter 9.

7.7 Handling Ambiguity

It is illuminating to examine the notion of *ambiguity* for fragments of natural language with a compositional semantics. If a natural language expression E is ambiguous, i.e. if E has several distinct meanings, then, under the assumption that these meanings are arrived at in a compositional way, there are three possible sources for the ambiguity (combinations are possible, of course):

(1) The ambiguity is lexical: E contains a word with several distinct meanings. An example is *a splendid ball*.

(2) The ambiguity is structural: E can be assigned several distinct syntactic structures. Examples are *old [men and women]* versus *[old men] and women*, or: *the boy saw the [girl with the binoculars]* versus *the boy saw [the girl] [with the binoculars]*.

(3) The ambiguity is derivational: the syntactic structure that E exhibits can be derived in more than one way. An example is the sentence *Every prince sang some ballad.* It is not structurally ambiguous, but in order to account for the $\exists \forall$ reading one might want to assume that one of the ways in which the structure can be derived is by combining *some ballad* with the incomplete expression *every prince sang ___* .

Lexical ambiguities can be handled in a fragment like ours by means of multiplying lexical entries. The two meanings of *ball* give rise to different translations:

$$\mathbf{CN} \longrightarrow ball \qquad [\![CN]\!] \longrightarrow (\lambda x \mapsto (Ball_1 \ x))$$
$$\mathbf{CN} \longrightarrow ball \qquad [\![CN]\!] \longrightarrow (\lambda x \mapsto (Ball_2 \ x))$$

If we use these translations, then lexical ambiguity shows up in the fact that *The ball was nice* will receive two parses, each with its own translation. An alternative approach would be to allow ambiguities in the logical representation language, by allowing ambiguous translations such as the following:

$$\mathbf{CN} \longrightarrow ball \qquad [\![CN]\!] \longrightarrow (\lambda x \mapsto (?\{Ball_1 \ x, Ball_2 \ x\}))$$

To work this out, such ambiguous translations should of course be given a clear meaning, for otherwise the translation would fail to count as a specification of the semantics.

A correct handling of structural ambiguities should fall out of the matching between syntax and semantics. You already looked at the syntax in Exercise 4.8 on page 69. There we asked you to extend the fragment such that it can handle the structurally ambiguous sentence *A dwarf defeated a giant with a sword.* The next exercise will get you acquainted with the semantic handling of this ambiguity.

Exercise 7.26 Extend the semantics to match the extended fragment from Chapter 4. Hint:

the two readings for the sentence *A dwarf defeated a giant with a sword* that you should aim at are the following (or equivalent reformulations):

$$\exists x((Dwarf\ x) \wedge \exists y((Sword\ y) \wedge ((Have\ y)\ x)) \wedge \exists z((Giant\ z) \wedge ((Defeat\ x)\ z)))$$

$$\exists x((Dwarf\ x) \wedge \exists z((Giant\ z) \wedge \exists y((Sword\ y) \wedge (Have\ y)\ z) \wedge ((Defeat\ z)\ x))).$$

Here *Have* is an $e \rightarrow e \rightarrow t$-type constant for the relation of having. You should use *Have* in the translation of *with*.

Exercise 7.27 Derive the two readings of *Atreyu defeated a giant with a dagger* in the extended fragment, and reduce them both to normal form.

Derivational ambiguities, finally, are very much a logician's ploy. In an essay on philosophical logic by Peter Thomas Geach they are introduced as follows:

[...] when we pass from "Kate / is loved by / Tom" to "Some girl / is loved by / every boy", it does make a big difference whether we first replace "Kate" by "some girl" (so as to get the predicable "Some girl is loved by —" into the proposition) and then replace "Tom" by "every boy" (so as to get the predicable "— is loved by every boy" into the proposition) and then replace "Kate" by "some girl". Two propositions that are reached from the same starting point by the same set of logical procedures (e.g. substitutions) may nevertheless differ in import because these procedures are taken to occur in a different order. [Gea80, Section 64]

This is exactly the mechanism that has been proposed by Richard Montague to account for operator scope ambiguities in natural language. Montague introduces a rule for *quantifying-in* of noun phrases in incomplete syntactic structures. The wide scope $\exists$ reading for the example *Every prince sang some ballad* is derived by using a rule Q_i to quantify in *some ballad* for syntactic index i in the structure *Every prince sang REF$_i$*. In more complex cases, where more than one occurrence of REF$_i$ is present, the appropriate occurrence is replaced by the noun phrase, and the other occurrences are replaced by pronouns or reflexives with the right syntactic agreement features. See [Mon73] for details.

A rudimentary version of quantifying-in, for the present fragment, would look like this. First we extend the syntax with dummy pronouns REF$_i$ (i a natural number which serves as an index), with a matching semantics, where a correspondingly indexed variable of type e is used. Next we add an indexed rule Q_i which combines an NP with a sentence S containing precisely one occurrence of REF$_i$ (notation for this: S[REF$_i$]), and replaces that occurrence by an occurrence of the NP (notation: S[REF$_i$/NP]). The translation instruction uses the fact that the sentence translation contains a free variable x_i resulting from the presence of the dummy pronoun

REF_i. This variable is bound, and the NP translation is applied to the result.

$$\mathbf{NP}_i \qquad \longrightarrow \qquad REF_i$$
$$[\![NP]\!] \qquad \longrightarrow \qquad (\lambda P \mapsto (P\ x_i))$$

$$\mathbf{NP} + \mathbf{S}[REF_i] \quad \Rightarrow Q_i \Rightarrow \quad \mathbf{S}[REF_i/\mathbf{NP}]$$
$$[\![NP + S]\!] \qquad \longrightarrow \qquad ([\![NP]\!]\ (\lambda x_i \mapsto [\![S]\!]))$$

Exercise 7.28 Use the quantifying-in rule to get a reading of *Every boy admired some girl* where *some girl* gets widest scope. Reduce the translation to normal form.

In Chapter 10 we will develop a more principled account of operator scope ambiguities.

7.8 Further Reading

Lewis [Lew70] gives a good introduction to the process of building meanings in a compositional way. Excellent introductions to Montague grammar are Dowty, Wall, and Peters [DWP81] and Gamut [Gam91b]. A nifty implementation of a natural language interpreter with a Montague style semantics as a lazy functional program can be found in [FL89].

The Montagovian approach to scope ambiguities does not account for restrictions on possible scope readings (at least not without further ado). Such restrictions can be imposed by means of constraints regulated by lexical features of determiner words. Imposing the right constraints is not easy, as the scope behaviour of natural language expressions tends to be influenced by the wider syntactic context. In Alshawi [Als92] details are given on how scoping mechanisms can be incorporated in large scale natural language systems.

Richard Montague was murdered in 1971; a stunning novel in which his life and death is a background theme is [Cam08].

8

Extension and Intension

Summary

The semantic treatment we have given up to now consisted of evaluation in a single (predicate logical) model. In this chapter, we will make the distinction between *extensional* and *intensional* evaluation. Extension is interpretation in a single model, intension is interpretation across different possible situations. In the preceding chapters we talked about expressions (signifiers) and their interpretations (referents). In this chapter we will discuss a way to make technical sense of the *sense* or the *signified*, the concept or idea that an expression invokes in a user of the language. The resulting semantics is called *possible world semantics* or *intensional semantics*. It is one of the trademarks of Montague grammar.

8.1 Sense and Reference, Intension and Extension

In his paper *On Sense and Reference* (1892) the German mathematician and philosopher Gottlob Frege made a famous distinction between the *sense* (German: Sinn) of an expression and its *reference* (German: Bedeutung). The reference of a name, according to Frege, is the thing that the name refers to. The sense of the name is the thought that allows us to identify the referent. Frege discusses various examples. If a, b, c denote the lines that connect the vertices of a triangle to the midpoints of the opposite sides, then the intersection of a and b coincides with the intersection of b and c. Thus, 'the intersection of a and b' and 'the intersection of b and c' have the same reference, but not the same sense.

It is natural, now, to think of there being connected with a sign (name, combination of words, letter), besides that to which the sign refers, which may be called the reference of the sign, also what I should like to call the sense of the sign, wherein the mode of presentation is contained. In our example, accordingly, the reference of the expressions 'point of intersection of a and b' and 'point of intersection of b and c' would be the same,

183

but not their senses. The reference of 'evening star' would be the same as that of 'morning star', but not the sense.

> Frege, [Fre92].

If all there is to the meaning of an expression like 'morning star' or 'evening star' is the reference, then it would be hard to explain why 'the morning star is the morning star' and 'the morning star is the evening star' are quite different statements. The truth of the first can be established *a priori* (no observations are needed for it), but the second one describes an astronomical discovery made by the Babylonians that the bright star in the evening and the bright star at other times visible in the morning both refer to the same heavenly object. So there must be more to a name like 'morning star' than its reference. Frege called this the sense.

The famous Swiss linguist Ferdinand de Saussure (1857–1913) distinguished between the *signifier* (the language sign, realized either as a sound image in spoken language or as a string of characters in written language), the *signified* (the concept or idea that the signifier invokes in the language user), and the *referent* (the actual thing or set of things that the sign refers to). With the distinction between *signified* and *referent* he meant roughly the same thing as Frege with the distinction between *sense* and *reference*.

One way to think about the Babylonian discovery that was mentioned by Frege is as follows. Either *morning star* and *evening star* refer to different things, or they refer to the same thing. The pre-Babylonians did not know which of these two views was correct. Or maybe they falsely held the latter view. So imagine two situations w_1 and w_2 where in w_1 a and b both refer to Venus, and in w_2 a refers to Venus and b to some other object, let us say Xenus.

The *extension* of the name b in w_1 is Venus, the *extension* of the name b in w_2 is Xenus. In fact, we could look at the table of extensions in all relevant situations. Such a table or function we call the *intension* of a name. In this case, the intension of b is the function f given by: $f(w_1)$ equals Venus and $f(w_2)$ equals Xenus.

The question how expressions refer to things is a recurring theme in philosophy. The Greek philosopher Plato (428–348 BC) expressed the view that elementary things can only be named, and that there is nothing to their names but their referents:

> But in fact none of the primal elements can be expressed by reason; they can only be named, for they have only a name; but the things composed of these are themselves complex, and so their names are complex and form a rational explanation; for the combination of names is the essence of reasoning. Thus the elements are not objects of reason or of knowledge, but only of perception, whereas the combinations of them are objects of knowledge and expression and true opinion.
>
> Plato's *Theaetetus*, [Pla], 202ab.

This view was shared by philosophers like John Stuart Mill, and opposed, as we have seen, by Gottlob Frege. Frege's view was heralded as the correct solution by Bertrand Russell, by Ludwig Wittgenstein in his later work, and by Willard Quine, to mention but a few. Interestingly, the debate about how names refer is far from over. Frege, Russell, and Quine viewed proper names as a kind of abbreviated descriptions, with the description serving as a handle to get at the referent.

Around 1970, when this was the predominant view among analytic philosophers, Saul Kripke (b. 1940) made an influential plea for the view that names just refer. See his famous paper *Naming and Necessity* [Kri72]. Kripke's message in a slogan: 'Names are rigid designators.' What makes Kripke's analysis of naming interesting is the fact that it has far-reaching consequences for a number of deep issues in philosophy. Epistemology (the philosophy of knowledge) makes a fundamental distinction between *a priori* and *a posteriori* knowledge. *A priori* knowledge is independent from experience. *A posteriori* knowledge depends on experience, or, as philosophers often call it, on empirical evidence. *A priori* knowledge is the kind of knowledge one gets from dictionaries, *a posteriori* knowledge is the kind of knowledge one gets from encyclopedias. If you know English well enough you know that 'Morons are stupid people' has to be true, regardless of the facts of the world.

Another distinction made by philosophers is that between necessary and contingent truths. Necessary truths are true propositions whose negation is a contradiction; contingent truths are true propositions that one can imagine to be false. It was a common assumption among philosophers that the two distinctions more or less coincide. In other words, many philosophers believed that what is *a priori* is necessary and vice versa, and the same for *a posteriori* and contingent.

Kripke argued, however, that the fact that the morning star is the evening star is a *necessary a posteriori truth*. He claimed that the distinction between necessary and contingent is a metaphysical distinction, and that metaphysics is not the same as epistemology.

'The morning star is the evening star' is necessary, for the object called the morning star names the planet Venus, and that object is also named 'evening star'. It is also *a posteriori*, for it is a fact that had to be discovered by the Babyloneans. Another example discussed by Kripke is 'Water is H_2O.' According to Kripke, it is not possible to imagine a situation where this is false, given that we use the name 'water' for that wonderful cool something that at some splendid moment was flowing over Helen Keller's hands (see page 4), for *that stuff* happens to have this particular chemical structure. Still, what the chemical structure was had to be discovered.

One might object that it is possible to imagine a person who is craving for water but mistakenly believes that 'H_2O' refers to some particularly poisonous kind of herbicide. Wouldn't such a person decline a sip of H_2O? No, as a matter of fact he wouldn't. When asked 'Would you like a sample of H_2O?' he would possibly shriek and shout 'Good heavens, no', but that does not mean he therewith declines an offer of what *we all* call 'H_2O'. The confusion is caused by the fact that he uses the word 'H_2O' differently from the way we all use it.

Exercise 8.1 (Courtesy of Albert Visser.) Suppose we would all decide to call tails of cows 'legs.' How many legs would a cow then have?

There is more to say about naming and reference, but we have to return to our main topic now. Richard Montague proposed to use intensions as a systematic way to get at a working definition for *sense*. For this, he used *intensional type logic*, partly developed by himself, partly derived from earlier work by Alonzo Church in type theory and by Rudolf Carnap in intensional logic.

Intensional type logic has a new base type for worlds. We will use s for this type. A function of type $s \rightarrow t$ maps possible worlds to truth values; such a function is called a 'proposition'. A function of type $s \rightarrow e$ maps possible worlds to entities; such a function is called an 'individual concept'.

We will illustrate the main idea of intensional type logic with a tiny implementation. We will use *Snow White* as a term with different reference (different extensions) in different situations (different worlds). This is against the view of Kripke, by the way, for to say that *Snow White* is a rigid designator is to say that the referent has to be the same in all possible worlds. Well, Snow White is a fairy tale princess anyway, so we will let that pass. (Montague himself used the example of *the temperature*, which may refer to different values in different situations.)

Assume there are three possible worlds, call them w_1, w_2, and w_3. We are going to make sure that the name has a different referent in two of these worlds. We first declare a module with a new example model, to serve as an alternative world.

The module is a variation on module `Model`, which we import because we need the declaration of the type `Entity`.

```
module Model2 where

import List
import Model
```

We will allow *Snow White* in the new model to have a different denotation from the denotation that the name has in `Model` (our earlier model introduced in Section 6.3).

```
snowWhite' :: Entity
snowWhite' = T
```

Similarly, we define variations for the denotations of the common nouns. Some of them the same as in the other model, some of them different:

```
girl', boy', princess', dwarf', giant',
   child', person', man', woman', thing' :: OnePlacePred
girl'     = list2OnePlacePred [S,T,A,D,G]
boy'      = list2OnePlacePred [M,Y]
princess' = list2OnePlacePred [E,S]
dwarf'    = list2OnePlacePred [B,R]
giant'    = list2OnePlacePred []
wizard'   = list2OnePlacePred [W,V]
child'    = \ x -> (girl' x || boy' x)
person'   = \ x -> (child' x || princess' x || dwarf' x
                               || giant' x   || wizard' x)
man'      = \ x -> (dwarf' x || giant' x   || wizard' x)
woman'    = \ x -> princess' x
thing'    = \ x -> not (person' x || x == Unspec)
```

Finally, here are variations on the denotations of some verbs:

```
laugh', cheer', shudder' :: OnePlacePred
laugh'   = list2OnePlacePred [A,G,E,T]
cheer'   = list2OnePlacePred [M,D]
shudder' = list2OnePlacePred []
```

8.2 Intensional Interpretation

Our sample intensional interpretation uses two first-order models taken from modules Model and Model2.

```
module EAI where
import FSynF
import Model
import Model2
import TCOM
```

We will identify these 'worlds' as W1 and W2. For purposes of illustration we will throw in a third world W3 that is like W2 except for the fact that all the girls are princesses.

```
data World = W1 | W2 | W3 deriving (Eq,Show)

worlds :: [World]
worlds = [W1,W2,W3]
```

The interpretation of *Snow White* is different in the three worlds. We see from the example that the extensional interpretation of a proper name is of type Entity, but the intensional interpretation is a function of type World -> Entity. The extensional interpretation of a sentence is of type Bool, but the intensional interpretation is of type World -> Bool.

Types that we will need a lot in what follows are the type World -> Entity of individual concepts and the type World -> Bool of propositions. It makes sense to introduce abbreviations for these types.

```
type IEntity = World -> Entity
type IBool   = World -> Bool
```

Intensional interpretation replaces the type Entity by World -> Entity (abbreviated IEntity) and the type Bool by World -> Bool (abbreviated IBool).

Here is the definition of our first intensional function. The interpretation of *Snow White* depends on the world we are in. The intensional meaning of the proper name has type World -> Entity, or abbreviated IEntity:

```
iSnowWhite :: IEntity
iSnowWhite W1 = snowWhite
iSnowWhite W2 = snowWhite'
iSnowWhite W3 = snowWhite'
```

Here are intensions for some lexical CNs:

```
iGirl, iPrincess, iPerson :: World -> Entity -> Bool
iGirl      W1 = girl
iGirl      W2 = girl'
iGirl      W3 = girl'
iPrincess W1 = princess
iPrincess W2 = princess'
iPrincess W3 = girl'
iPerson    W1 = person
iPerson    W2 = person'
iPerson    W3 = person'
```

Here are intensions for some lexical VPs:

```
iLaugh, iShudder :: World -> Entity -> Bool
iLaugh W1 =   laugh
iLaugh W2 =   laugh'
iLaugh W3 =   laugh'
iShudder W1 =   shudder
iShudder W2 =   shudder'
iShudder W3 =   shudder'
```

Here is an intension for a TV:

```
iCatch :: World -> Entity -> Entity -> Bool
iCatch W1 = \ x y -> False
iCatch W2 = \ x y -> False
iCatch W3 = \ x y -> elem x [B,R,T] && girl' y
```

The intensional interpretation of a sentence has the type `World -> Bool`, or abbreviated `IBool`. The intensional interpretation of a sentence consisting of a subject NP followed by a VP consists of the application of the intensional interpretation of the subject to the intensional interpretation of the predicate:

```
iSent :: Sent -> IBool
iSent (Sent np vp) = iNP np (iVP vp)
```

The intension of a noun phrase has the following type:

```
iNP :: NP -> (IEntity -> IBool) -> IBool
```

The NP intension for proper names is obtained by lifting the type of `iSnowWhite` in exactly the same way as in the case of extensional interpretation (but note that the types are different now):

```
iNP SnowWhite = \ p -> p iSnowWhite
```

Intensions of NPs for quantified NPs and NPs starting with a determiner are given by the following definitions:

```
iNP Everyone  = \ p i -> all (\x -> p (\j -> x) i)
     (filter (\y -> iPerson i y) entities)
iNP Someone   = \ p i -> any (\x -> p (\j -> x) i)
     (filter (\y -> iPerson i y) entities)
iNP (NP1 det cn)  = iDET det (iCN cn)
iNP (NP2 det rcn) = iDET det (iRCN rcn)
```

Extensions of determiners have type $(e \to t) \to (e \to t) \to t$. Intensions of determiners have type $((s \to e) \to (s \to t)) \to ((s \to e) \to (s \to t)) \to (s \to t)$.

```
iDET :: DET -> (IEntity -> IBool)
            -> (IEntity -> IBool) -> IBool
iDET Some p q = \ i -> any (\x -> q (\j -> x) i)
     (filter (\x -> p (\j -> x) i) entities)
iDET Every p q = \ i -> all (\x -> q (\j -> x) i)
     (filter (\x -> p (\j -> x) i) entities)
iDET No p q = \ i -> not (any (\x -> q (\j -> x) i)
     (filter (\x -> p (\j -> x) i) entities))
```

Here are intensions for verbs from the lexicon:

```
iVP :: VP -> IEntity -> IBool
iVP Laughed    = \ x i -> iLaugh i (x i)
iVP Shuddered = \ x i -> iShudder i (x i)
```

Below we will discuss the intensional semantics for examples like (8.1).

> *Some giant wanted to catch a princess.* (8.1)

It is commonly assumed that this sentence has two readings: a reading saying that there is some actual princess that is being pursued by some giant, and a reading where some giant is fantasizing about catching princesses. The first of these readings does not really involve intensions, but the second reading does. In what follows, we will derive the second reading. (The first reading could be derived by means of 'quantifying in', but we will not pursue that here.)

For that, we need interpretations for VPs consisting of an attitude verb *want* followed by an infinitive:

```
iVP (VP3 attitude to inf) = iAV attitude (iINF inf)
```

Here are intensions for CNs:

```
iCN :: CN -> IEntity -> IBool
iCN Girl = \ x i -> iGirl i (x i)
iCN Princess = \ x i -> iPrincess i (x i)
```

The rule for intensional interpretation of an ADJ CN combination is given in the following definition:

```
iRCN (RCN3 adj cn) = iADJ adj (iCN cn)
```

We will deal with an example of an RCN consisting of an adjective and a CN in Section 8.3.

For purposes of illustration this is enough. The following evaluation functions demonstrate the outcomes of intensional interpretation.

```
eval1 = iSent (Sent SnowWhite Laughed) W1
eval2 = iSent (Sent SnowWhite Laughed) W2
eval3 = iSent (Sent Someone Shuddered) W1
eval4 = iSent (Sent Someone Shuddered) W2
eval5 = iSent (Sent (NP1 Every Girl) Shuddered) W1
eval6 = iSent (Sent (NP1 Every Girl) Shuddered) W2
eval7 = iSent (Sent (NP1 Some Girl) Shuddered) W1
eval8 = iSent (Sent (NP1 Some Girl) Shuddered) W2
```

Exercise 8.2 Work out what should be the answers to `eval1`, `eval2`, `eval3`, `eval4`, `eval5`, `eval6`, `eval7`, `eval8` by inspecting the models, next check your findings in Haskell.

8.3 Intensional Constructs

A fake princess is someone who in actual fact is not a princess, but pretends to be one. How does one model such pretense? Let us say that in some other world she is a princess. Then here is a definition of the intensional property of being a fake princess (we use i, j to range over possible worlds):

$$\lambda x \lambda i \mapsto \neg \text{ Princess } x \, i \wedge \exists j \text{ Princess } x \, j.$$

Note that now we can also define the meaning of the adjective *fake*. This adjective takes an intensional predicate P and maps it into a new predicate stating that P does not apply in the actual world but does apply in some other world:

$$\lambda P \lambda x \lambda i \mapsto \neg P \, x \, i \wedge \exists j \, P \, x \, j.$$

To illustrate this definition, here is an implementation for our fragment:

```
iADJ :: ADJ -> (IEntity -> IBool) -> IEntity -> IBool
iADJ Fake = \ p x i ->
  not (p x i) && any (\ j -> p x j) worlds
```

Evaluation commands for trying this out:

```
eval9 = iSent
  (Sent (NP1 Some Princess) Shuddered) W1
eval10 = iSent
  (Sent (NP2 Some (RCN3 Fake Princess)) Shuddered) W1
eval11 = iSent
  (Sent (NP2 Some (RCN3 Fake Princess)) Shuddered) W2
```

Exercise 8.3 Work out what the results of `eval9`, `eval10`, and `eval11` should be, by inspecting the models. Next, check your findings in Haskell.

A *former president* is someone who is not president now, but who was president at some earlier period in time. This is quite similar to a fake president, only the status of the alternative possible world that is used for evaluation of the predicate 'president' is different.

Richard Montague, in his fragments, dealt with tense by using pairs (w, t) of a possible world w at some instant in time t. Reference to the past can then be dealt with by means of $\exists t'(t' < t \wedge \cdots)$. Implementing the semantics of tense is beyond the scope of this book.

Attitude verbs like *want* and *hope* also give rise to intensional constructs. Such verbs combine with infinitives to form complex VPs. We will first implement the intensional semantics for infinitives.

```
iINF :: INF -> IEntity -> IBool
iINF Laugh   = \ x i -> iLaugh i (x i)
iINF Shudder = \ x i -> iShudder i (x i)
iINF (INF tinf np) = \ s -> iNP np (\ o -> iTINF tinf s o)
```

We need an interpretation of the appropriate type for *catch*.

```
iTINF :: TINF -> IEntity -> IEntity -> IBool
iTINF Catch = \x y w -> iCatch w (x w) (y w)
```

Next, the intensional meanings of the attitude verbs. An attitude towards an intensional property should map that property to a property that holds in all worlds where the attitude is realized. So for each agent in the model that can hold attitudes, we have to identify the set of worlds for that attitude: desired worlds or hoped-for worlds. Let us assume that in all worlds everyone wants w_2 or w_3 and everyone hopes for w_3.

```
iAttit :: AV -> IEntity -> IBool
iAttit Wanted x = \i -> elem i [W2,W3]
iAttit Hoped  x = \i -> i == W3
```

To check whether a property holds under an attitude we check whether the property holds in all of the designated attitude worlds.

```
iAV :: AV -> (IEntity -> IBool) -> (IEntity -> IBool)
iAV Wanted p = \ x i ->
  and [ p x j | j <- worlds, iAttit Wanted x j ]
iAV Hoped  p = \ x i ->
  and [ p x j | j <- worlds, iAttit Hoped  x j ]
```

Here are some test examples:

```
eval12 = iSent (Sent SnowWhite
  (VP3 Wanted To (INF Catch (NP1 Some Girl)))) W1
eval13 = iSent (Sent SnowWhite
  (VP3 Wanted To (INF Catch (NP1 No Girl)))) W2
```

We have treated infinitival attitudes as propositional attitudes, taking the proposition to be the statement that the subject has the infinitival property. Wanting to catch a princess is wanting the proposition 'I catch a princess' to be true. There is a vast philosophical literature on the semantics of propositional attitudes, and the present analysis is by no means meant as a last word. The implemenation should be viewed as an illustration of one way to construct plausible meanings for sentences involving attitude verbs.

Exercise 8.4 Work out what the results of `eval12` and `eval13` should be, by inspecting the models. Next, check your findings in Haskell.

We have the machinery now to not only make judgements about truth, but also about necessity and contingency.

```
data Judgement = IsTrue Sent
               | IsNec  Sent
               | IsCont Sent deriving Show
```

Whether or not a statement is true in some model depends on what is the *actual world* in that model. The actual world is the world where we evaluate. To check whether a statement is *necessarily true* in an intensional model, we have to check whether it is true in all possible worlds. A statement is *contingently true* if it is true, but it ain't necessarily so: there exists a world where that statement is false.

```
iJudgement :: Judgement -> IBool
iJudgement (IsTrue s) = \ i -> iSent s i
iJudgement (IsNec s) = \ i ->
  all (\j -> iSent s j) worlds
iJudgement (IsCont s) = \ i ->
  iSent s i && not (all (\j -> iSent s j) worlds)
```

Here are some example judgements, evaluated in various worlds:

```
judgement1,judgement2,judgement3,judgement4 :: Bool
judgement1 = iJudgement
  (IsTrue (Sent (NP1 Some Girl) Shuddered)) W1
judgement2 = iJudgement
  (IsTrue (Sent (NP1 Some Girl) Shuddered)) W2
judgement3 = iJudgement
  (IsNec  (Sent (NP1 Some Girl) Shuddered)) W1
judgement4 = iJudgement
  (IsCont (Sent (NP1 Some Girl) Shuddered)) W1
```

Exercise 8.5 Work out what should be the answers to the four judgements, by inspecting the models. Next, check your findings in Haskell.

8.4 Intensionalization

As was mentioned before, intensionalization is the systematic replacement of type e by $s \to e$ and type t by $s \to t$, combined with a lifting of extensional constructions to the new intensional types. In this section we will demonstrate that there is method to this.

Extensional types are all types built from e and t. Notice that every extensional type has the shape

$$\alpha_1 \to \cdots \to \alpha_n \to e$$

or

$$\alpha_1 \to \cdots \to \alpha_n \to t,$$

where each α_i is an extensional type.

As we have seen already in the examples, each extensional type has a corresponding intensional type. Intensional types are built from extensional types by replacing each e by $s \to e$ and each t by $s \to t$. In our implementation, extensional types are built from `Entity` and `Bool`, and the ingredients of the intensional types are built from `IEntity`, shorthand for the implementation of $s \to t$, and `IBool`, shorthand for the implementation of $s \to t$.

If α is an extensional type, we use $\overline{\alpha}$ for the corresponding intensional type, i.e. for the result of replacing each occurrence of e in α by $s \to e$ and each occurrence of t in α by $s \to t$. For example, suppose that α is the extensional type of a determiner. Then α equals

$$(e \rightarrow t) \rightarrow (e \rightarrow t) \rightarrow t.$$

Now $\overline{\alpha}$ equals

$$((s \rightarrow e) \rightarrow (s \rightarrow t)) \rightarrow ((s \rightarrow e) \rightarrow (s \rightarrow t)) \rightarrow s \rightarrow t.$$

This is the intensional type of a determiner. Compare this with the implemenation above.

In the original set-up of Montague grammar (Montague's original papers) treatment of intensional phenomena is dealt with by generalizing to the worst case. Montague assumes that *each* construct is intensional, and then uses meaning postulates for deriving extensional equivalents when appropriate. But we have seen that the intensional interpretations defined in our fragment above are derived in a systematic fashion from the corresponding extensional interpretations. In this section we explain the general mechanism behind this.

Suppose x has type $s \rightarrow \alpha$, where α is an extensional type. Then x is a function from worlds to objects in some extensional domain D_α. If we use a for the basic extensional types e and t, then there are two cases for the shape of α. Base case: α equals a. Recursive case: α equals $\alpha_1 \rightarrow \alpha_2$, where both α_1 and α_2 are extensional types.

In the base case, x is a function that maps worlds to entities, or to truth values. In the recursive case we can say that x is a function that takes a world and produces an object in the following domain:

$$(D_{\alpha_2})^{D_{\alpha_1}}$$

Suppose y has type $\overline{\alpha}$, where α is the extensional type above. Then in the base case,

$$\overline{\alpha} = \overline{a} = s \rightarrow a,$$

while in the recursive case

$$\overline{\alpha} = \overline{\alpha_1 \rightarrow \alpha_2} = s \rightarrow \overline{\alpha_1} \rightarrow \overline{\alpha_2}.$$

Now we define two operations $^\cap$ and $^\cup$, by mutual recursion. The operation $^\cap$ is for intensionalization. The operation $^\cup$ is for extensionalization. Intuitively, what $^\cap$ does is take a function that gives for every world an extension, and map that to an intensional function that, in a sense to be made precise below, 'does the same job.' Intuitively, $^\cup$ cancels the lifting effect of $^\cap$ again. We want these operations to have the following types:

$$\cap \quad :: \quad (s \rightarrow \alpha) \rightarrow \overline{\alpha}$$
$$\cup \quad :: \quad \overline{\alpha} \rightarrow s \rightarrow \alpha.$$

Here α is an arbitrary extensional type. We will define $\cap$ and $\cup$ by mutual recursion on the structure of α. So there are two cases: the base case where α is a (i.e. either t or e), and the recursive case where α equals $\alpha_1 \to \alpha_2$, with α_1 and α_2 simpler extensional types.

In the base case of $\alpha = a$ we put:

$$^{\cap}(x :: s \to a) = x,$$

$$^{\cup}(y :: s \to a) = y.$$

In the recursive case of $\alpha = \alpha_1 \to \alpha_2$, we put:

$$^{\cap}(x :: s \to \alpha_1 \to \alpha_2) = \lambda y_1 :: \overline{\alpha_1} \mapsto {}^{\cap}(\lambda i \mapsto x\, i\, (^{\cup}y_1\, i)), \qquad (8.2)$$

$$^{\cup}(y :: \overline{\alpha_1} \to \overline{\alpha_2}) = \lambda j \lambda x_1 :: \alpha_1 \mapsto {}^{\cup}(y\, {}^{\cap}(\lambda k \mapsto x_1))\, j, \qquad (8.3)$$

where i, j, k are all of type s. There are a few things to note about these definitions. In definition (8.2), $^{\cup}y_1$ is of type $s \to \alpha_1$. Therefore, $(^{\cup}y_1\, i)$ is of type α_1. This is indeed the right type for the second argument of x. Also, in the same definition, $\lambda i \mapsto x\, i\, (^{\cup}y_1\, i)$ has type $s \to \alpha_2$, and $^{\cap}(\lambda i \mapsto x\, i\, (^{\cup}y_1\, i))$ has type $\overline{\alpha_2}$.

In the definition of $^{\cup}y$ (Definition 8.3), the type of x_1 is α_1. Since α_1 is an extensional type, the abstraction in $\lambda k \mapsto x_1$ is vacuous. Therefore, $\lambda k \mapsto x_1$ defines the constant x_1 function, i.e. the function that maps every world to the same object x_1.

Exercise 8.6 Please check that $^{\cap}$ is an operator of type $(s \to \alpha) \to \overline{\alpha}$ and that $^{\cup}$ is an operator of type $\overline{\alpha} \to s \to \alpha$.

We will now prove that for *any* extensional type α and any function x of type $s \to \alpha$, we have that

$$^{\cup\cap}x = x. \qquad (8.4)$$

We will prove this fact by structural induction (see page 72), more in particular, induction on the structure of the type α.

Base case: α equals a and x has type $s \to a$. We have already seen that in this case $^{\cap}x = x$, and $^{\cup\cap}x = {}^{\cup}x = x$. This proves the base case.

Induction step: Assume α has the form $\alpha_1 \to \alpha_2$. Suppose the relation (8.4) holds for functions of component types α_1, α_2. This is the induction hypothesis.

We have to show that the relation (8.4) also holds for x itself. Here is the calculation. We start with $^{\cup\cap}x$, and replace $^{\cap}x$ by its definition. This gives

$$^{\cup\cap}x = {}^{\cup}(\lambda y_1 \mapsto {}^{\cap}(\lambda i \mapsto x\, i\, (^{\cup}y_1\, i))).$$

Next, we replace $^\cup$ by its definition, and apply β reduction:

$$
\begin{aligned}
^{\cap}x &= {}^\cup(\lambda y_1 \mapsto {}^\cap(\lambda i \mapsto x\ i\ (^\cup y_1\ i))) \\
&= \lambda j \lambda x_1 \mapsto {}^\cup((\lambda y_1 \mapsto {}^\cap(\lambda i \mapsto x\ i\ (^\cup y_1\ i)))\ {}^\cap(\lambda k \mapsto x_1))\ j \\
&= \lambda j \lambda x_1 \mapsto {}^{\cup\cap}(\lambda i \mapsto x\ i\ (^{\cup\cap}(\lambda k \mapsto x_1))i)j
\end{aligned}
$$

Now we note that we can apply the induction hypothesis to achieve $^{\cup\cap}$ cancellation. In particular, $\lambda k \mapsto x_1$ is of type $s \to \alpha_1$, so the induction hypothesis applies to $^{\cup\cap}(\lambda k \mapsto x_1)$. And $\lambda i \mapsto x\ i\ (^{\cup\cap}(\lambda k \mapsto x_1)i)$ is of type $s \to \alpha_2$, so the induction hypothesis applies to $^{\cup\cap}(\lambda i \mapsto x\ i\ (^{\cup\cap}(\lambda k \mapsto x_1)i))$. So we get:

$$
\lambda j \lambda x_1 \mapsto {}^{\cup\cap}(\lambda i \mapsto x\ i\ (^{\cup\cap}(\lambda k \mapsto x_1))i)j
$$
$$
\overset{ih}{=} \lambda j \lambda x_1 \mapsto (\lambda i \mapsto x\ i\ ((\lambda k \mapsto x_1))i)j.
$$

As we observed before, the abstraction $\lambda k \mapsto x_1$ is vacuous, and it follows from this that $(\lambda k \mapsto x_1)i = x_1$, so that we get:

$$
\begin{aligned}
&\lambda j \lambda x_1 \mapsto (\lambda i \mapsto x\ i\ ((\lambda k \mapsto x_1))i)j \\
&= \lambda j \lambda x_1 \mapsto (\lambda i \mapsto x\ i\ x_1)j \\
&= \lambda j \lambda x_1 \mapsto x\ j\ x_1 \\
&= x.
\end{aligned}
$$

The final step is by η-reduction (see page 171). This settles the proof.

Next, does it make sense to try to prove the converse property, i.e. $^{\cap\cup}y = y$ for y of type $\overline{\alpha}$? No, it does not, for we can see from a size argument that such an attempt is doomed to fail. In general there are many more functions of type $\overline{\alpha}$ than of type $s \to \alpha$. Consider a simple case, e.g. $\alpha = e \to t$. Suppose there are n objects of type e. Suppose there are m worlds (objects of type s). Then the domain $D_{e \to t}$ has size 2^n, and the domain $D_{s \to e \to t}$ has size $(2^n)^m$. On the other hand, the domain $D_{(s \to e) \to s \to t}$ has size $(2^m)^{(n^m)}$, which, on the assumption that $n \geq 2$ and $m \geq 2$, is much larger. So it is impossible to get a one-to-one correspondence between the two domains. In other words, the functions of the form $^{\cap}x$ constitute a proper subset of the domain of functions $D_{\overline{\alpha}}$. Therefore, not all functions y in $D_{\overline{\alpha}}$ can have a counterpart x in type $s \to \alpha$ with the property that $y = {}^{\cap}x$. At the end of the section we will give a concrete example of a function y with $y \neq {}^{\cap\cup}y$.

To illustrate what is going on with intensionalization and extensionalization, we implement these functions for some specific types. (In this book we stick to standard Haskell, and in standard Haskell it is impossible to define functions like $^\cap$ and $^\cup$ in one go over classes of types.)

Here is an implementation of $^\cap$ for functions of type $s \to e \to t$ (in the implemenation: `World -> Entity -> Bool`).

```
iProp :: (World -> Entity -> Bool) -> IEntity -> IBool
iProp x = \ y i -> x i (y i)
```

This function can be used for automating the lift of extensional CN and VP denotations to intensional ones.

```
vpINT :: VP -> World -> Entity -> Bool
vpINT Laughed   = iLaugh
vpINT Shuddered = iShudder


intensVP :: VP -> IEntity -> IBool
intensVP = iProp . vpINT
```

This defines the same function as iVP.

Exercise 8.7 Use iProp to give an alternative definition for iCN.

Here is the extensionalizing function for properties.

```
eProp :: (IEntity -> IBool) -> World -> Entity -> Bool
eProp y = \ j x -> y (\k -> x) j
```

The function eProp is used to implement $\cap$ for type $s \to (e \to t) \to t$.

```
iPropToB :: (World -> ((Entity -> Bool) -> Bool))
                        -> (IEntity -> IBool) -> IBool
iPropToB x = \ y i -> x i (eProp y i)
```

The corresponding $\cup$ function, for the type $((s \to e) \to s \to t) \to s \to t$ uses iProp. It is implemented like this:

```
ePropToB :: ((IEntity -> IBool) -> IBool) ->
       World -> (Entity -> Bool) -> Bool
ePropToB y = \ j x -> y (iProp (\k -> x)) j
```

Exercise 8.8 Use iPropToB to give an alternative definition of iNP.

These functions can again be used to implement $\cap$ and $\cup$ for still higher types:

```
iPropToPropToB ::
   (World -> (Entity -> Bool) -> (Entity -> Bool) -> Bool)
        -> (IEntity -> IBool) -> (IEntity -> IBool) -> IBool
iPropToPropToB x = \ y1 y2 i ->
   x i (eProp y1 i) (eProp y2 i)
```

```
ePropToPropToB ::
     ((IEntity -> IBool) -> (IEntity -> IBool) -> IBool) ->
     World -> (Entity -> Bool) -> (Entity -> Bool) -> Bool
ePropToPropToB y = \ j x1 x2  ->
   y (iProp (\k -> x1)) (iProp (\k -> x2)) j
```

We will use this for giving an alternative definition for `iDET`. Extensional interpretation of determiners is the same at each possible world:

```
detINT :: DET ->  World ->
     (Entity -> Bool) -> (Entity -> Bool) -> Bool
detINT det = \ i -> intDET det
```

This can be intensionalized by means of $\cap$ lifting, as follows:

```
intensDET :: DET -> (IEntity -> IBool)
                 -> (IEntity -> IBool) -> IBool
intensDET = iPropToPropToB . detINT
```

This defines the same function as `iDET`.

We still owe you an example y for which $\cap\cup y \neq y$. For that, let $y :: (s \to e) \to s \to t$, and assume y maps some particular individual concept $c :: s \to e$ to the function $r :: s \to t$ that characterizes $\{w_1\}$ (assume w_1 is the real world), and every other concept to the function $r' :: s \to t$ that characterizes $\emptyset$ (i.e. the function that maps every world to false).

In the implementation, we first need a function for picking out a particular individual concept, say that of Snow White:

```
isSnoww :: IEntity -> Bool
isSnoww x = and [ x i == iSnowWhite i | i <- worlds ]
```

Next, use this to define the function `myY`:

```
myY :: IEntity -> IBool
myY x | isSnoww x = \i -> i == W1
      | otherwise = \i -> False
```

And here is the counterexample:

```
myY' :: IEntity  -> IBool
myY' = iProp (eProp myY)
```

```
EAI> myY iSnowWhite W1
True
EAI> myY' iSnowWhite W1
False
```

8.5 Intensional Models from Extensional Models

An extensional model is built over extensional types e and t. An intensional model is built over the corresponding intensional types $s \rightarrow e$ and $s \rightarrow t$. Note that an intensional model has to contain a domain D_s of possible worlds.

An extensional model M assigns to each constant c of type α (where α is built from e and t) an object $[\![c]\!]_M$ in D_α. An intensional model M assigns to each constant c of type α an object $[\![c]\!]_M$ in $D_{\overline{\alpha}}$.

Similarly for the interpretation of variables. A variable assignment g for variable v of type α in an extensional model is an object in D_α. A variable assignment g for variable v of (extensional) type α in an intensional model is an object in $D_{\overline{\alpha}}$.

The details of extensional interpretation were explained in Section 7.5 above. In Section 8.2 above we have seen that one can build an intensional model from a set of extensional models that are defined over the same domain of entities D_e. We will now look at that construction in a more systematic way. In particular, we will show how one can use the lifting function $^\cap$ to collect a list of extensional models M_i into a single intensional model.

Let $\mathcal{I} = \{M_i \mid i \in I\}$ be a collection of extensional models with the same base domain D_e. I is a set of indices; in our example in Section 8.2, I consisted of $\{1, 2, 3\}$. We create an intensional model $M_{\mathcal{I}}$ as follows. The domain D_s of worlds equals the set of indices I. If c is an object language constant of (extensional) type α, we interpret c by means of

$$M_{\mathcal{I}}(c) = \cap(\lambda i \mapsto M_i(c)).$$

In other words, we consider the function that gives the extensional interpretation of c at each index, and lift this function to the type $\overline{\alpha}$ by means of $\cap$.

Let g be is an extensional variable assignment, suitable for some extensional model M_i in $\mathcal{I}$. Then it follows from the fact that all extensional models in $\mathcal{I}$ use the same domain D_e that g is a suitable variable assignment for *all* models in $\mathcal{I}$. We can lift such a g to an assignment for $M_{\mathcal{I}}$ by means of

$$g^*(v :: \alpha) = \cap(\lambda k \mapsto g(v)).$$

Note that the abstraction $\lambda k \mapsto g(v)$ is vacuous, so that it defines a function that yields the same value $g(v)$ for every index. In other words, $g^*(v)$ is defined as the $\cap$ lifting of the constant $g(v)$ function.

The following fact is proved in [Kan09]. Consider the language of typed lambda calculus with constants of extensional types. Let ϕ be an expression of this language that is not a λ-abstract.

$$[\![\phi]\!]_{M_{\mathcal{I}},g^*} = \cap(\lambda i \mapsto [\![\phi]\!]_{M_i,g})$$

From this and the properties of $\cap$ it follows directly that for *closed* expressions ϕ of type t or e we have:

$$[\![\phi]\!]_{M_{\mathcal{I}}} = \lambda i \mapsto [\![\phi]\!]_{M_i}$$

This means that the intensional model $M_{\mathcal{I}}$ does indeed behave in the appropriate way, as the intensionalization of the models in $\mathcal{I}$.

The importance of this for natural language semantics is that we can define intensional interpretations of extensional constructs by means of a $\cap$ lift of the corresponding extensional interpretations. This allows for a modular set-up of a natural language fragment dealing with intensional phenomena, where extensional constructs can be cleanly separated from intensional constructs.

8.6 Further Reading

An excellent introduction to the (intensional) logical formalisms behind Montague grammar can be found in [Gam91a] and [Gam91b]. The classical introduction to Montague semantics is [DWP81]. In Montague's *Proper Treatment of Quantification* [Mon73] a typed logical language is employed with the property that every expression has both an extension (a value at the current world) and an intension (a function from worlds to extensions). This 'PTQ fragment' employs a combination of generalization to the worst case and the use of so-called meaning postulates to reduce intricate intensionalities back to extensional objects. Such a set-up was criticized in, among others, [PR83], where it was argued on the basis of evidence concerning scope ambiguities in natural language that a more flexible approach was called for.

For a very thorough study of lifting in Montague grammar, see [Hen93]. Intensionalization is studied from a logical point of view in [KF85]. A more systematic approach is in [Ben88], where the lift from t to $s \to t$ is analysed. A proposal for a modular approach to intensionalization of lexical entries, based on Van Benthem's analysis, can be found in [BAW07]. The treatment in the present chapter is based on an improved proposal that resulted from discussion between De Groote, Kanazawa, and Muskens after a presentation of [BAW07], and that is documented in the unpublished note [Kan09].

All these approaches to intensionality are based on possible worlds. This has a well-known drawback, the so-called logical omniscience problem: if ψ is a logical consequence of ϕ, and ϕ is true in some possible world w, then ψ has to be true in w as well. This is a serious problem for the analysis of propositional attitudes in terms of possible worlds. Take the attitude of knowing. If I know that a prime number is a natural number that has no proper divisors except 1 and itself, does it follow that I know that $2^{31} - 1$ is a prime number? In a possible world approach to knowledge it does, but in reality it does not. That $2^{31} - 1$ is a prime is a mathematical truth, but also a fact that had to be discovered. It was discovered by the great mathematician Leonhard Euler in 1750.

Consider Frege's example of the two descriptions of the centroid of a triangle: 'the intersection of a and b' and 'the intersection of b and c'. In all possible worlds where the Euclidian axioms hold, these two descriptions will refer to the same point, for it is a theorem of Euclidian geometry that the three medians of a triangle intersect in the same point. In possible world semantics, Frege's two descriptions would have the same intension. This means that intension does not work for such cases as an explication of *sense*, for it is clear that the two descriptions have a different sense. It turns out to be possible to give a treatment of intensionality that avoids this problem, within the theory of types. This, however, is beyond the scope of our book. See [Mus07] for further details.

9

Parsing

Summary

In this chapter we will first look at some structural relations between nodes in a syntactic tree. Next, we discuss the general problem of recognizing and parsing context-free languages. Then we introduce the notion of parser combinators, and show how these can be used to create parsers from sets of grammar rules in a principled way. Parser combinators are functions that transform parsers for a language into parsers for a different language. We apply these insights in the construction of a recursive descent parser for a natural language fragment. We use the example of relative clause formation to demonstrate how parser combinators can be used to capture the effects of movement rules. At the end of the chapter we have all ingredients in place for transforming strings expressing English sentences into logical forms, or for directly interpreting strings that express sentences of English in an appropriate database.

```
module P where

import Data.List
import Data.Char
import FPH
```

9.1 Talking About Parse Trees

A parse tree is a tree with lexical information at the leaves and syntactic information at the internal nodes, which represents the structure of the parsed expression. It is convenient to leave the nature of the lexical and syntactic information unspecified. So parse trees are either leaves with lexical information of some kind, or

205

labeled nodes dominating a list of trees. A special case is the empty parse tree, which we call Ep.

```
data ParseTree a b =  Ep | Leaf a | Branch b [ParseTree a b]
                  deriving Eq
```

Given show functions for the types a and b, we define a show function for `ParseTree a b` as follows:

```
instance (Show a, Show b) => Show (ParseTree a b) where
  show Ep           = "[]"
  show (Leaf t)     = show t
  show (Branch l ts) = "[." ++ show l   ++ " "
                              ++ show ts ++ "]"
```

Here is an example syntax tree:

```
snowwhite = Branch "S"
              [Branch "NP" [Leaf "Snow White"],
               Branch "VP" [Branch "TV" [Leaf "loved"],
                            Branch "NP" [Leaf "the dwarfs"]]]
```

Here is what the show function produces for this:

```
P> snowwhite
[."S" [[."NP" ["Snow White"]],
       [."VP" [[."TV" ["loved"]],[."NP" ["the dwarfs"]]]]]]
```

And here is the tree in the more usual tree display format.

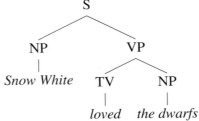

In this first section, we will develop and implement some machinery for talking about syntactic trees.

The first thing one has to grasp is the notion of an occurrence of a subtree in a tree. Take the following tree:

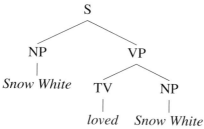

This tree has two occurrences of the subtree [NP *Snow White*]. A natural way to point to these occurrences is by means of *tree positions*. A tree position is a list or string of natural numbers; we use ϵ for the empty string.

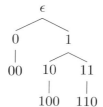

Here is a Haskell function that generates the list of all tree positions in a given syntax tree:

```
type Pos = [Int]

pos ::  ParseTree a b -> [Pos]
pos Ep          = [[]]
pos (Leaf _)    = [[]]
pos (Branch _ ts) = [] : [ i:p | (i,t) <- zip [0..] ts,
                                  p <- pos t ]
```

For our example tree it gives:

```
P> pos snowwhite
[[],[0],[0,0],[1],[1,0],[1,0,0],[1,1],[1,1,0]]
```

The following definition of the *subtree* at a position in a syntax tree uses indexing in a list: `list!!i` gives the item at position i in the list, counting from 0. Incidentally, this is why we count subtrees from 0 onward in the pos function.

```
subtree :: ParseTree a b -> Pos -> ParseTree a b
subtree t              []     = t
subtree (Branch _ ts) (i:is) = subtree (ts!!i) is
```

Notation for the subtree of t at position p is t_p. The list of all subtrees of a syntax tree corresponds to the set $\{t_p \mid p \in \text{Pos}(t)\}$. Here is an implementation:

```
subtrees :: ParseTree a b -> [ParseTree a b]
subtrees t = [ subtree t p | p <- pos t ]
```

If p, q are tree positions, we say that $p \leq q$ if p is a prefix of q. If p, q are positions in a syntax tree t, then $p \leq q$ holds if and only if t_q is a subtree of t_p. If p, q are positions in t with $p \leq q$, position p is said to *dominate* position q. If also $p \neq q$, position p is said to *properly dominate* position q. Proper domination is a relation on the set of tree positions. As in Section 5.7 we call a list of pairs over the same type a relation on that type:

```
type Rel a = [(a,a)]
```

The proper dominance relation on the list of positions in a tree can be implemented as follows:

```
properdominance :: ParseTree a b -> Rel Pos
properdominance t = [ (p,q) | p <- pos t,
                              q <- pos t,
                              p /= q,
                              prefix p q ]
```

The dominance relation on a tree is the result of dropping the inequality constraint:

```
dominance :: ParseTree a b -> Rel Pos
dominance t = [ (p,q) | p <- pos t,
                        q <- pos t,
                        prefix p q ]
```

Exercise 9.1 The relation of dominance can be defined as the transitive closure of the relation of immediate dominance, where position p in a tree immediately dominates position q in that tree if p dominates q, p and q are different, and there is no position r different from both p and q such that p dominates r and r dominates q. Give an implementation of a function `immdominance :: ParseTree a b -> Rel Pos` for immediate dominance.

Two positions p, q are *sister positions* in a tree t, if the subtrees t_p and t_q are different daughters of the same mother. Here is a check:

```
sisters :: Pos -> Pos -> Bool
sisters [i]     [j]    = i /= j
sisters (i:is) (j:js) = i == j && sisters is js
sisters _       _      = False
```

The sisterhood relation in a tree can be implemented like this:

```
sisterhood :: ParseTree a b -> Rel Pos
sisterhood t = [ (p,q) | p <- pos t,
                         q <- pos t,
                         sisters p q ]
```

This gives:

```
P> sisterhood snowwhite
[([0],[1]),([1],[0]),([1,0],[1,1]),([1,1],[1,0])]
```

Now the relation of c-command ([Rei76],[Rei83],[Cho81]) is the relational composition of sisterhood and dominance. Here is the definition of relational composition again (familiar from Section 5.7):

```
(@@) :: Eq a => Rel a -> Rel a -> Rel a
r @@ s = nub [ (x,z) | (x,y) <- r, (w,z) <- s, y == w ]
```

Finally, the definition of the c-command relation is:

```
cCommand :: ParseTree a b -> Rel Pos
cCommand t = (sisterhood t) @@ (dominance t)
```

We can illustrate it with our example tree snowwhite:

```
P> cCommand snowwhite
[([0],[1]),([0],[1,0]),([0],[1,0,0]),([0],[1,1]),
 ([0],[1,1,0]),([1],[0]),([1],[0,0]),([1,0],[1,1]),
 ([1,0],[1,1,0]),([1,1],[1,0]),([1,1],[1,0,0])]
```

A *branching position* in a tree is a position p that immediately dominates two distinct positions in the tree. Here is an implementation of a function that collects all branching positions of a tree in a list:

```
branchingPos :: ParseTree a b -> [Pos]
branchingPos t = let ps = pos t in
  [ p | p <- ps, (p++[0]) 'elem' ps, (p++[1]) 'elem' ps ]
```

This gives:

```
P> branchingPos snowwhite
[[],[1]]
```

Exercise 9.2 Show that it follows from the definitions that if p c-commands q in a tree, then

(1) p does not dominate q,
(2) q does not dominate p,
(3) the lowest branching position that dominates p also dominates q.

Exercise 9.3 Clearly, c-command is not a symmetric relation. But the notion of so-called *mutual c-command*, defined as

$$\{(p,q) \mid p \text{ c-commands } q \text{ and } q \text{ c-commands } p\}$$

is a symmetric relation. Give an implementation. Next show that sisterhood coincides with mutual c-command.

A position p in a syntax tree precedes a position q in that tree if either the first index in p is less than the first index in q, or p and q start with the same index and the tail of p precedes the tail of q. An implementation is the following:

```
precede :: Pos -> Pos -> Bool
precede (i:is) (j:js) = i < j || (i == j && precede is js)
precede  _       _       = False

precedence :: ParseTree a b -> Rel Pos
precedence t = [ (p,q) | p <- pos t,
                         q <- pos t,
                         precede p q ]
```

For our example tree it gives:

```
P> precedence snowwhite
[([0],[1]),([0],[1,0]),([0],[1,0,0]),([0],[1,1]),([0],[1,1,0]),
 ([0,0],[1]),([0,0],[1,0]),([0,0],[1,0,0]),([0,0],[1,1]),
 ([0,0],[1,1,0]),([1,0],[1,1]),([1,0],[1,1,0]),([1,0,0],[1,1]),
 ([1,0,0],[1,1,0])]
```

Exercise 9.4 Define a relation of *immediate precedence* in terms of *precedence*, analogous to the definition of *immediate dominance* in terms of *dominance*. Also give an implementation.

The notion of c-command is a variation on an earlier notion proposed in [Lan69], called *command*. A position p commands a position q in a tree if p and q are parallel (neither position dominates the other), and the closest S position dominating p also dominates q.

Exercise 9.5 Give a simplified implementation of *command*, assuming that the closest S position is the root of the tree.

9.2 Recognizing and Parsing Context-Free Languages

In Chapter 4 we explored how to define languages using context-free grammars. Now we want to look at how to recognize these languages automatically. Thus the focus of this chapter will be on separating the strings that are generated by a grammar from the strings that are not. For example, is the string *Every girl laughed* generated by the grammar of the fragment of English specified in 4.2?

There are two possible answers we could be interested in. On the one hand, we can settle for a simple 'yes' or 'no' to tells us that the grammar either can derive a string or that it cannot. The procedure for arriving at this answer is called *recognition*. On the other hand, we might not only be interested in knowing that a string is derivable but also want to know *how* it was derived, i.e. which syntactic structure it has. Generating this kind of answer is called *parsing*.

Let us start with a simple example grammar to demonstrate how to build a recognizer, namely the following context-free grammar for the set of palindromes (strings that are equal to their reversal) over $\{a, b, c\}$:

$$\mathbf{A} \longrightarrow \epsilon \mid a \mid b \mid c \mid a\mathbf{A}a \mid b\mathbf{A}b \mid c\mathbf{A}c. \qquad (9.1)$$

One of the ingredients for building a recognizer that is general enough to be applicable to all context-free grammars is a function for splitting strings in substrings. The following function gives all possible ways of splitting a string into two substrings:

```
split2 :: [a] -> [([a],[a])]
split2 []     = [([],[])]
split2 (x:xs) = [([],(x:xs))]
              ++ (map (\(ys,zs) -> ((x:ys),zs)) (split2 xs))
```

This gives:

```
P> split2 "Jan"
[("","Jan"),("J","an"),("Ja","n"),("Jan","")]
```

The following function generalizes this to giving all possible ways of splitting a string into n substrings, for $n \geq 2$. The function uses split2 for the case $n = 2$, and split2 plus recursion for the case $n > 2$.

```
splitN :: Int -> [a] -> [[[a]]]
splitN n xs
   | n <= 1    = error "cannot split"
   | n == 2    = [ [ys,zs] | (ys,zs) <- split2 xs ]
   | otherwise = [ ys:rs   | (ys,zs) <- split2 xs,
                             rs      <- splitN (n-1) zs ]
```

This gives:

```
P> splitN 3 "Jan"
[["","","Jan"],["","J","an"],["","Ja","n"],["","Jan",""],
 ["J","","an"],["J","a","n"],["J","an",""],["Ja","","n"],
 ["Ja","n",""],["Jan","",""]]
```

Now the function for recognizing whether a string is generated by the grammar above can be given as follows.

```
recognize :: String -> Bool
recognize = \ xs ->
    null xs || xs == "a" || xs == "b" || xs == "c"
    || or [ recognize ys | ["a",ys,"a"] <- splitN 3 xs ]
    || or [ recognize ys | ["b",ys,"b"] <- splitN 3 xs ]
    || or [ recognize ys | ["c",ys,"c"] <- splitN 3 xs ]
```

This gives:

```
P> recognize "aabcbbcbaa"
True
P> recognize "aabcbbcba"
False
```

It should be clear that the above recipe for recognizer construction works for any set of context-free rules. For a rewrite rule of the form $\mathbf{V} \longrightarrow T_1 \cdots T_n$, the split function `splitN` should be used with argument n, for splitting the input into n substrings.

From recognition to generation is a simple step. First, here are tools for generating all strings over a given alphabet:

```
gener :: Int -> String -> [String]
gener 0 alphabet = [[]]
gener n alphabet = [ x:xs | x  <- alphabet,
                            xs <- gener (n-1) alphabet ]

gener' :: Int -> String -> [String]
gener' n alphabet = gener   n    alphabet
                 ++ gener' (n+1) alphabet

generateAll  :: String -> [String]
generateAll alphabet = gener' 0 alphabet
```

Combining this with the recognizer, we get a brute force generation function for the language, which first generates all possible strings over the alphabet and then filters out those that are recognized.

```
generate = filter recognize (generateAll alphabet)
  where alphabet = ['a','b','c']
```

The function `generate` generates the infinite list of all palindromes over $\{a, b, c\}$. With the predefined Haskell function `take`, that takes a specified number of elements from a list, we can get a finite prefix of this list:

```
P> take 15 generate
["","a","b","c","aa","bb","cc","aaa","aba","aca","bab","bbb",
"bcb","cac","cbc"]
```

Parsing with a context-free grammar is the process of constructing syntax trees. Let the types for the terminal symbols and the rewrite symbols of a grammar simply be `String`. Then the data type of syntax trees for our grammar of palindromes can be taken to be `ParseTree String String`. A parser for a grammar is a function that takes strings as input; for each string `xs` it returns the list of all syntax trees that the grammar allows for `xs`.

Here are the appropriate changes to `recognize` to create a parser for the example grammar:

```
parse :: String -> [ParseTree String String]
parse = \ xs ->
    [Leaf "[]" | null xs ]
 ++ [Leaf "a"  | xs == "a" ]
 ++ [Leaf "b"  | xs == "b" ]
 ++ [Leaf "c"  | xs == "c" ]
 ++ [Branch "A" [Leaf "a", t, Leaf "a"] |
                ["a",ys,"a"] <- splitN 3 xs,
                t            <- parse ys    ]
 ++ [Branch "A" [Leaf "b", t, Leaf "b"] |
                ["b",ys,"b"] <- splitN 3 xs,
                t            <- parse ys    ]
 ++ [Branch "A" [Leaf "c", t, Leaf "c"] |
                ["c",ys,"c"] <- splitN 3 xs,
                t            <- parse ys    ]
```

Again, it should be clear that this procedure works for any context-free grammar. Here is a demo, again for the example grammar of palindromes in (9.1).

```
P> parse "aabaa"
[[.A [a,[.A [a,b,a]],a]]]
P> parse "aabbaa"
[[.A [a,[.A [a,[.A [b,[],b]],a]],a]]]
P> parse "aabcbbcbaa"
[[.A [a,[.A [a,[.A [b,[.A [c,[.A [b,[],b]],c]],b]],a]],a]]]
P> parse "aabcbbcba"
[]
```

Exercise 9.6 For context-free grammars without ϵ-productions, i.e. without rules of the form $\mathbf{V} \longrightarrow \epsilon$, the functions for recognition and parsing can be made more efficient by suitable modifications of the functions `split2` and `splitN`. How?

Exercise 9.7 Explain why the approach to parsing context-free grammars with `split2` and `splitN` has no trouble with so-called left-recursive rules, i.e. rules of the form $\mathbf{V} \longrightarrow \mathbf{V}T_2 \cdots T_n$.

9.3 Parsers and Parser Combinators

In this section we are going to develop a more general perspective on the process of parsing with context-free grammars. A context-free grammar has rules of the form $A \to B_1 \cdots B_n$, where the B_i can be either terminals or nonterminals. Also, context-free grammar rules with the same left-hand side symbol can be combined using | for choice. So it is enough if we have a treatment for |, a treatment for $B_1 \cdots B_n$ in the right-hand side of a rule, and a treatment for terminal symbols.

For a general treatment, we assume that terminal symbols have type a, and parse objects have type b. Never mind what a parse object is; a parse object is simply a thing produced by a parser (e.g. a tree). We will assume that the parser works in a *recursive descent* fashion, as follows. The parser scans a list of tokens (objects of type a), and tries to construct parse objects of type b from a prefix of the input list, leaving the remainder of the input list for further processing. The outcome of the parse process is the list of all pairs (b, [a]) that the parser can construct. Parse failure is indicated by return of []. This gives the following type for a parser of tokens of type a:

```
type Parser a b = [a] -> [(b,[a])]
```

The parser uses the grammar rules in a recursive way, starting from the start symbol of the grammar, and working towards the terminals. It will turn out that this can be done by means of a small set of elementary parsing functions and combinations of such parsing functions. We will only use standard functional language constructs, so we will not need anything that was not already introduced earlier.

To make this concrete, assume the terminals of the grammar are strings, and the nonterminals are characters. Then the parse objects could be objects of type ParseTree String Char, the type of parse trees with characters at the internal nodes and strings at the leaf nodes. So a parser for a grammar with strings as terminals and characters as nonterminals would have the following type:

$$\text{[String]} \rightarrow \text{[(ParseTree String Char,[String])]}$$

Such a grammar takes a list of strings as input and produces a list of parse trees with characters (representing the nonterminals) at the internal nodes and strings (representing the terminals) at the leaf nodes. Each parse tree is produced from a prefix of the input; this is why the output consists of pairs of parse trees and lists of strings. These string lists are for the part of the input string that is left unparsed.

For thinking a bit further about what the parser has to do, assume the example grammar of Figure 9.1. When processing a list of strings, the parser will not only yield a parse tree but there will also be a part of the list of strings that is still left unprocessed. For example, when parsing the list of strings [*every,wizard,smiled*], the parser would start by building a syntax tree for **S**, and for that it would have to start building a syntax tree for **NP**, with *every wizard smiled* as input. This will succeed, with a tree for *every wizard* as parse result, and the remainder *smiled* left for further processing. The obvious way to handle this is by letting a parser not

Fig. 9.1. Example Grammar

S	$\longrightarrow$	**NP VP**
NP	$\longrightarrow$	*Alice* | *Dorothy* | **D N**
VP	$\longrightarrow$	*smiled* | *laughed*
D	$\longrightarrow$	*every* | *some* | *no*
N	$\longrightarrow$	*dwarf* | *wizard*

just give parse trees as a result, but pairs consisting of a parse tree and a list of remainder strings.

Let us look at some simple parsers that will be the building blocks for more complex parsers which can handle context-free grammar rules.

Two very elementary parsers are the parsers that always succeed or always fail, respectively.

```
succeed :: b -> Parser a b
succeed r xs = [(r,xs)]

failp :: Parser a b
failp xs = []
```

The parser succeed does not consume any input, and it always returns a given, fixed result r. The parser failp also does not consume any input, but it always fails. Since parse failure corresponds to an empty list of parses, the result of failp is simply the empty list. These parsers may not look very interesting, but the point of having them is to use them as ingredients for more interesting parsers.

Here is a parser for recognizing individual symbols c.

```
symbol :: Eq a => a -> Parser a a
symbol c []                   = []
symbol c (x:xs) | c == x      = [(x,xs)]
                | otherwise = []
```

We can easily generalize this to a parser that recognizes not only single symbols but lists of symbols. A list of symbols is called a *token*, so this parser is called token. It uses the predefined functions take and drop for taking and dropping prefixes of a given length n from a list.

```
token :: Eq a => [a] -> Parser a [a]
token cs xs | cs == take n xs   = [(cs,drop n xs)]
            | otherwise         = []
       where n = length cs
```

A function to check whether the first element of a list of items satisfies a given property p is `satisfy`.

```
satisfy :: (a -> Bool) -> Parser a a
satisfy p []              = []
satisfy p (x:xs) | p x         = [(x,xs)]
                 | otherwise = []
```

As an example, here is a parser that checks whether the first symbol of a string is a digit. This uses the predefined function `isDigit`.

```
digit :: Parser Char Char
digit = satisfy isDigit
```

Exercise 9.8 Show how the function `symbol` can be defined in terms of the function `satisfy`.

Now, these elementary parsers can be taken as parsers for terminal symbols of our grammar. If we take our terminals to be characters, we can recognize the terminal string *Alice* with the parser `token "Alice"`, the terminal string *laughed* with the parser `token "laughed"`, and so on. Alternatively, we can take our terminals to be strings. Then we can recognize the terminal symbol *Alice* with the parser `symbol "Alice"`. It all depends on the choice of type for the inputs.

But what we cannot handle yet are rules with nonterminal symbols in the right-hand sides, for example **S** $\longrightarrow$ **NP VP**. For that, we need a means for combining parsers into more complex ones by sequential composition. Or consider a rule with a choice operator in the right-hand side, like **VP** $\longrightarrow$ *smiled* | *laughed*. What this rule says is that a **VP** is either the token *smiled* or the token *laughed*. We already have parsers for recognizing *smiled* and for recognizing *laughed*. What we need to do is to combine these two parsers into one that makes a choice between the *smiled*-parser and the *laughed*-parser. Functions that combine parsers into a new parser, or transform parsers into new parsers, are called *parser combinators*. For example, here is a parser combinator that takes a parser and returns a parser that does the same as the input parser, except for the fact that it also insists that the remainder list is empty:

```
just :: Parser a b -> Parser a b
just p = filter (null.snd) . p
```

For parsing one of our grammars, we first need a parser combinator for choice, i.e. a function that takes two parsers as arguments and returns a new parser that recognizes everything that either one of the parsers recognizes. It is called <|>. Here are its fixity declaration and definition:

```
infixr 4 <|>

(<|>) :: Parser a b -> Parser a b -> Parser a b
(p1 <|> p2) xs = p1 xs ++ p2 xs
```

For example, the rule **VP** $\longrightarrow$ *smiled* | *laughed* might correspond to the following parser:

```
vp = token "smiled" <|> token "laughed"
```

Next, what to do with rules like **S** $\longrightarrow$ **NP VP**? Intuitively, we want to parse an NP, then want to parse a VP, and finally combine the results. That is, we want a parser combinator <*> for sequential composition, such that a parser for the grammar rule **S** $\longrightarrow$ **NP VP** could simply be s = np <*> vp, with np a parser for NPs and vp a parser for VPs. Here is a general definition of this parser combinator:

```
(p <*> q) xs = [ (combine r1 r2,zs) | (r1,ys) <- p xs,
                                      (r2,zs) <- q ys ]
```

That is, the new parser (p <*> q) first applies p to the input. This returns a result r1 and a remainder ys. Then q is applied to that remainder. This, again, returns a remainder and a result. Finally, (p <*> q) returns that second remainder, zs, and a combination of the two results r1 and r2. How combine is defined depends on how we define our parse objects. For example, if we simply take them to be strings, we can use (++) for combining r1 and r2. The definition of <*> would then be:

```
(<*>) :: Parser a [b] -> Parser a [b] -> Parser a [b]
(p <*> q) xs = [ (r1 ++ r2,zs) | (r1,ys) <- p xs,
                                 (r2,zs) <- q ys ]
```

Now we can construct parser functions for our grammar in (9.1), by starting from elementary parsers for terminals and by combining them into more complex parsers for nonterminals.

```
pS,pNP,pVP,pD,pN :: Parser String String

pS  = pNP <*> pVP
pNP = symbol "Alice"  <|> symbol "Dorothy" <|> (pD <*> pN)
pVP = symbol "smiled" <|> symbol "laughed"
pD  = symbol "every"  <|> symbol "some"    <|> symbol "no"
pN  = symbol "dwarf"  <|> symbol "wizard"
```

Note that these definitions are completely in parallel to our grammar rules. The parser combinator for choice, <|>, corresponds to |, and the parser combinator for sequencing, <*>, corresponds to listing symbols on the right-hand side.

However, we are not quite there yet, because these parsers do not return parse trees as a result, but only return the parsed string. In order to construct parse trees, we turn to do postprocessing on the results of a parse. For that we introduce a new parser combinator <$>. It takes a function and a parser as arguments, and applies the function to the result of the parse. The fixity declaration infixl 7 determines the binding precedence of the combinator.

```
infixl 7 <$>

(<$>) :: (a -> b) -> Parser s a -> Parser s b
(f <$> p) xs = [ (f x,ys) | (x,ys) <- p xs ]
```

This combinator can be used, e.g., to map the result of a parse to a suitable value. Here is a simple example: the function digitize is the parser digit defined above, which checks whether the first character is a digit, together with the postprocessing function f, which turns a digit of type Char into the corresponding integer of type Int. For example, digitize "42" results in [(4,"2")].

```
digitize :: Parser Char Int
digitize = f <$> digit
  where f c = ord c - ord '0'
```

We will use <$> for constructing parse trees. So first, let us think about a general type for parsers that create parse trees. Such parsers take as input a list of items of type a, and produce lists of parse trees for such items. Assuming labels of type b for the labels of the parse trees, we see that

`Parser a (ParseTree a b)`

is a reasonable type. It is convenient to define a type synonym for this type:

```
type PARSER a b = Parser a (ParseTree a b)
```

The type variable a can be instantiated in various ways. It could be String, but it could also be Char. Note that the a in PARSER a b is the type of terminal symbols of the grammar, and the b is the type of nonterminal symbols of the grammar.

The following parser maps the null input string to the parse tree Ep:

```
epsilonT :: PARSER a b
epsilonT = succeed Ep
```

When parsing a symbol there are two possibilities: (i) the symbol is a terminal (of type a), or (ii) the symbol is a nonterminal (of type b). In case (i) the parse should produce a leaf tree, in case (ii) a non-leaf tree. To handle case (i) we will use a parser symbolT, which recognizes a token and returns an appropriate leaf parse tree.

```
symbolT :: Eq a => a -> PARSER a b
symbolT s = (\ x -> Leaf x) <$> symbol s
```

For case (ii), we need postprocessing on sequential composition of parsers. For example, a parser like pNP <*> pVP should output a branch with the results of the parser pNP and pVP as daughter nodes. In the general case, the right-hand side of a rule can be any list of terminals and nonterminals, so we need to be able to decompose such lists. In order to account for this general case, we switch to a version of sequential composition of parsers that combines a parser of type Parser a b with a parser of type Parser a [b] to a parser of type Parser a [b]:

```
infixl 6 <:>

(<:>) :: Parser a b -> Parser a [b] -> Parser a [b]
(p <:> q) xs = [ (r:rs,zs) | (r,ys)  <- p xs,
                             (rs,zs) <- q ys ]
```

We use it for defining a function that collects the results of a list of parsers operating one after the other:

```
collect :: [Parser a b] -> Parser a [b]
collect []     = succeed []
collect (p:ps) = p <:> collect ps
```

Instead of defining an S-parser as pNP `<*>` pVP, like above, we can now define it as `collect [pNP,pVP]`. Finally, we also want to construct a parse tree. For that, we use a parser `parseAs`, which builds and labels non-leaf nodes. The parser `parseAs` takes as its first argument a nonterminal (the label), and as second argument a list of parsers. To handle a rule rule $A \longrightarrow B_1 \cdots B_n$, the function `parseAs` takes as its label input A, and assumes that a list of parsers for $B_1 \cdots B_n$ has been constructed.

```
parseAs :: b -> [PARSER a b] -> PARSER a b
parseAs label ps = (\ xs -> Branch label xs) <$> collect ps
```

The first argument of `parseAs` is a nonterminal from the grammar, i.e. an item of type b.

Now we can implement a parser for the grammar given in (9.1) as follows.

```
sent, np, vp, det, cn :: PARSER String Char
sent =  parseAs 'S' [np,vp]
np   =  symbolT "Alice" <|> symbolT "Dorothy"
     <|> parseAs 'N' [det,cn]
det  =  symbolT "every" <|> symbolT "some" <|> symbolT "no"
cn   =  symbolT "man"   <|> symbolT "woman"
vp   =  symbolT "smiled" <|> symbolT "laughed"
```

Parser combinator style parsing with the palindrome grammar (9.1) goes like this:

```
palindrome :: PARSER Char Char
palindrome =
  epsilonT <|> symbolT 'a' <|> symbolT 'b' <|> symbolT 'c'
            <|> parseAs 'A' [symbolT 'a', palindrome, symbolT 'a']
            <|> parseAs 'A' [symbolT 'b', palindrome, symbolT 'b']
            <|> parseAs 'A' [symbolT 'c', palindrome, symbolT 'c']
```

In a similar way we can implement a parser for our Mastermind grammar. Recall that this EBNF grammar in Section 4.1 also used the extra metasymbols { and }, with the convention that {A} indicates that A may occur zero or more times. The following parser combinator `many` handles this 'parse arbitrary many copies' operator. It produces the longest match first.

```
many :: Parser a b -> Parser a [b]
many p = (p <:> many p) <|> (succeed [])
```

If we want to construct a parse tree for this, we will have to put it under a label:

```
parseManyAs :: b -> PARSER a b -> PARSER a b
parseManyAs l p = (\ xs -> Branch l xs) <$> many p
```

As an example of parsing EBNF, here is a parser for the language of Mastermind.

```
colour, answer, guess, reaction, turn, game
   :: PARSER String String

colour    =  symbolT "red"    <|> symbolT "yellow"
          <|> symbolT "blue"   <|> symbolT "green"
answer    =  symbolT "black" <|> symbolT "white"
guess     =  parseAs "GUESS" [colour,colour,colour,colour]
reaction  =  parseManyAs "REACTION" answer
turn      =  parseAs "TURN" [guess,reaction]
game      =  turn <|> parseAs "GAME" [turn,game]
```

To sum up, each nonterminal symbol **N** gets a corresponding parser `parseAs n`, and each terminal symbol T gets a corresponding parser `symbolT t`. Choice is handled by means of `<|>`, and concatenation in the right-hand side of a rule as list concatenation of parsers, inside a definition of `parseAs n`. EBNF repetition symbols {A} are handled by `parseManyAs newlabel a`, where `newlabel` is some suitable label to put in the syntax tree.

Exercise 9.9 Does the approach to parsing context-free grammars with parser combinators, along the lines sketched in this section, work for all context-free grammars? (Hint: look at left-recursive rules, i.e. rules of the form $\mathbf{A} \longrightarrow \mathbf{A} T_2 \cdots T_n$.)

9.4 Features and Categories

Syntactic features are important in most syntactic formalisms for natural language analysis. We will develop a simple feature system for a small fragment of English.

There are two opposing views of feature agreement. According to the first view, the features of a syntactic component are computed in some way from the features of a 'controlling' component. Call this the derivational view on feature agreement. On this view there is a strict distinction between source and target of feature agreement. According to the second view, features of syntactic structures are partially specified by the constituents of the structure by means of a constraint handling mechanism. On this view, feature agreement has neither source nor target, but is the result of certain compatibility checks between syntactic constituents. The second view is prevalent in so-called unification based approaches to syntax. See, e.g., [PS87, PS94]. It is also possible to combine the two mechanisms, and let feature agreement be a mix of compatibility checking and control.

Implementing the control view is easy in a functional approach: just define the feature set of a component in terms of a function from the feature set of the source of the agreement. To implement the constraint view we need a function for checking compatibility between feature lists. In the implementation below, we will mix the two approaches.

Whatever mechanism we implement, if we add it to a context-free grammar, the result will again be a context-free grammar. Consider the simple case where there is just a feature for number. Then the single rule **S** $\longrightarrow$ **NP VP** is replaced by the following set:

$$\mathbf{S}_\emptyset \longrightarrow \mathbf{NP}_{\{Sg\}}\ \mathbf{VP}_\emptyset$$
$$\mathbf{S}_\emptyset \longrightarrow \mathbf{NP}_{\{Sg\}}\ \mathbf{VP}_{\{Sg\}}$$
$$\mathbf{S}_\emptyset \longrightarrow \mathbf{NP}_{\{Pl\}}\ \mathbf{VP}_\emptyset$$
$$\mathbf{S}_\emptyset \longrightarrow \mathbf{NP}_{\{Pl\}}\ \mathbf{VP}_{\{Pl\}}$$

Adding a feature mechanism to a context-free grammar boils down to replacing rules of the form $A \longrightarrow B\ C$ by rules of the form $A_f \longrightarrow B_g\ C_h$, and similarly for rules with different numbers of right-hand side items. Here, f, g, and h are sets of features, with the feature handling mechanism determining their shapes. Since the feature sets are all finite, this boils down to replacing each terminal T by a finite set of new terminals T_f, and each nonterminal **N** by a finite set of new nonterminals $\mathbf{N}_f$. The resulting grammar will still be a finite set of context-free rules. This shows that a context-free grammar with features can be seen as an abbreviation of a context-free grammar without features but with a much larger rule set.

We will start with defining a number of useful features. A principled approach would be to distinguish various types of feature values, e.g. to put `Masc` and `Neutr` in type `Gender`, to put `Sg` and `Pl` in type `Number`, and so on. For present purposes it is more convenient, however, to put all feature values in the same data type. This will make the system easier to use and modify, at the cost of making feature coding errors slightly more difficult to detect (at least they will not be caught by the type checking).

```
data Feat = Masc  | Fem  | Neutr | MascOrFem
          | Sg    | Pl
          | Fst   | Snd  | Thrd
          | Nom   | AccOrDat
          | Pers  | Refl | Wh
          | Tense | Infl
          | On    | With | By | To | From
          deriving (Eq,Show,Ord)
```

Declare the type `Agreement` as a list of features:

```
type Agreement = [Feat]
```

The following functions pick out the gender, number, person, case, pronoun type, tense, and preposition features, respectively:

```
gender, number, person, gcase, pronType, tense, prepType
  :: Agreement -> Agreement
gender   = filter (`elem` [MascOrFem,Masc,Fem,Neutr])
number   = filter (`elem` [Sg,Pl])
person   = filter (`elem` [Fst,Snd,Thrd])
gcase    = filter (`elem` [Nom,AccOrDat])
pronType = filter (`elem` [Pers,Refl,Wh])
tense    = filter (`elem` [Tense,Infl])
prepType = filter (`elem` [On,With,By,To,From])
```

Two different features of the same type clash, except in the case of `MascOrFem` versus `Masc` or `Fem`. The following function removes the `MascOrFem` feature if necessary. This will ensure that `MascOrFem` expresses the disjunction of `Masc` and `Fem`: it will clash with `Neutr` but not with `Masc` or `Fem` (in the latter case, it is instead replaced by `Masc` or `Fem`, respectively).

```
prune :: Agreement -> Agreement
prune fs = if   (Masc 'elem' fs || Fem 'elem' fs)
           then (delete MascOrFem fs)
           else fs
```

Now that we have features, we can define a data type for syntactic categories. Syntactic categories have four components. The first component gives the phonological representation, the second the category label, the third the set of agreement features, and the fourth the so-called subcatorization list. The subcategorization list of a category C is the list of categories that C combines with.

```
type CatLabel = String
type Phon     = String

data Cat       = Cat Phon CatLabel Agreement [Cat]
               deriving Eq
```

Only the categories that directly correspond with lexical items have phonological content. The other categories have a blank in this position, represented by "_".

```
instance Show Cat where
  show (Cat "_"  label agr subcatlist) = label ++ show agr
  show (Cat phon label agr subcatlist) = phon  ++ " "
                                       ++ label ++ show agr
```

Here are functions for getting the components out of a category:

```
phon :: Cat -> String
phon (Cat ph _ _ _) = ph

catLabel :: Cat -> CatLabel
catLabel (Cat _ label _ _) = label

fs :: Cat -> Agreement
fs (Cat _ _ agr _) = agr

subcatList :: Cat -> [Cat]
subcatList (Cat _ _ _ cats) = cats
```

The following function `combine` combines the feature lists of two categories.
Failure is indicated by `[]`.

```
combine :: Cat -> Cat -> [Agreement]
combine cat1 cat2 =
 [ feats | length (gender   feats) <= 1,
           length (number   feats) <= 1,
           length (person   feats) <= 1,
           length (gcase    feats) <= 1,
           length (pronType feats) <= 1,
           length (tense    feats) <= 1,
           length (prepType feats) <= 1 ]
   where
     feats = (prune . nub . sort) (fs cat1 ++ fs cat2)
```

Two categories agree if the attempt to combine them does not yield `[]`. The
`agree` function implements a compatibility check.

```
agree :: Cat -> Cat -> Bool
agree cat1 cat2 = not (null (combine cat1 cat2))
```

Certain syntactic rules will assign a new feature to a category, e.g. the rule that
combines a syntactic subject with a predicate will assign the feature `Nom` to the
subject. The function `assign` implements a control mechanism for features.

```
assign :: Feat -> Cat -> [Cat]
assign f c@(Cat phon label fs subcatlist) =
  [Cat phon label fs' subcatlist |
        fs' <- combine c (Cat "" "" [f] []) ]
```

Note that the assignment can fail if the category already has an incompatible
feature. In the implementation below we will use a mix of `agree` (feature compatibility checking) and `assign` (feature control).

9.5 Lexical Lookup and Scanning

Our lexicon is a function from words (strings) to lists of syntactic categories. Here
is the type:

```
lexicon :: String -> [Cat]
```

Personal pronouns are the following:

```
lexicon "i"   = [Cat "i"   "NP" [Pers,Fst,Sg,Nom]            []]
lexicon "me"  = [Cat "me"  "NP" [Pers,Fst,Sg,AccOrDat]      []]
lexicon "we"  = [Cat "we"  "NP" [Pers,Fst,Pl,Nom]           []]
lexicon "us"  = [Cat "us"  "NP" [Pers,Fst,Pl,AccOrDat]      []]
lexicon "you" = [Cat "you" "NP" [Pers,Snd]                  []]
lexicon "he"  = [Cat "he"  "NP" [Pers,Thrd,Sg,Nom,Masc]     []]
lexicon "him" = [Cat "him" "NP" [Pers,Thrd,Sg,AccOrDat,Masc]
  []]
lexicon "she" = [Cat "she" "NP" [Pers,Thrd,Sg,Nom,Fem]      []]
lexicon "her" = [Cat "her" "NP" [Pers,Thrd,Sg,AccOrDat,Fem]
  []]
lexicon "it"  = [Cat "it"  "NP" [Pers,Thrd,Sg,Neutr]        []]
lexicon "they" = [Cat "they" "NP" [Pers,Thrd,Pl,Nom]        []]
lexicon "them" = [Cat "them" "NP" [Pers,Thrd,Pl,AccOrDat]
  []]
```

Reflexive pronouns are:

```
lexicon "myself"     =
 [Cat "myself"     "NP" [Refl,Sg,Fst,AccOrDat] []]
lexicon "ourselves" =
 [Cat "ourselves"  "NP" [Refl,Pl,Fst,AccOrDat] []]
lexicon "yourself"   =
 [Cat "yourself"   "NP" [Refl,Sg,Snd,AccOrDat] []]
lexicon "yourselves" =
 [Cat "yourselves" "NP" [Refl,Pl,Snd,AccOrDat] []]
lexicon "himself"    =
 [Cat "himself"    "NP" [Refl,Sg,Thrd,AccOrDat,Masc]  []]
lexicon "herself"    =
 [Cat "herself"    "NP" [Refl,Sg,Thrd,AccOrDat,Fem]   []]
lexicon "itself"     =
 [Cat "itself"     "NP" [Refl,Sg,Thrd,AccOrDat,Neutr] []]
lexicon "themselves" =
 [Cat "themselves" "NP" [Refl,Pl,Thrd,AccOrDat] []]
```

Wh-pronouns and relatives are:

```
lexicon "who"    = [Cat "who" "NP"  [Wh,Thrd,MascOrFem] [],
      Cat "who" "REL" [MascOrFem]         []]
lexicon "whom"   =
 [Cat "whom" "NP"  [Sg,Wh,Thrd,AccOrDat,MascOrFem] [],
   Cat "whom" "REL" [Sg,MascOrFem,AccOrDat]         []]
lexicon "what"   =
 [Cat "what" "NP"  [Wh,Thrd,AccOrDat,Neutr]     []]
lexicon "that"   = [Cat "that"  "REL" []          [],
                     Cat "that"  "DET" [Sg]       []]
lexicon "which"  = [Cat "which" "REL" [Neutr] [],
                     Cat "which" "DET" [Wh]       []]
```

Proper names are:

```
lexicon "snowwhite"  =
 [Cat "snowwhite"  "NP" [Thrd,Fem,Sg]   []]
lexicon "alice"      =
 [Cat "alice"      "NP" [Thrd,Fem,Sg]   []]
lexicon "dorothy"    =
 [Cat "dorothy"    "NP" [Thrd,Fem,Sg]   []]
lexicon "goldilocks" =
 [Cat "goldilocks" "NP" [Thrd,Fem,Sg]   []]
lexicon "littlemook" =
 [Cat "littlemook" "NP" [Thrd,Masc,Sg]  []]
lexicon "atreyu"     =
 [Cat "atreyu"     "NP" [Thrd,Masc,Sg]  []]
```

Determiners are:

```
lexicon "every"   = [Cat "every"   "DET" [Sg]  []]
lexicon "all"     = [Cat "all"     "DET" [Pl]  []]
lexicon "some"    = [Cat "some"    "DET" []    []]
lexicon "several" = [Cat "several" "DET" [Pl]  []]
lexicon "a"       = [Cat "a"       "DET" [Sg]  []]
lexicon "no"      = [Cat "no"      "DET" []    []]
lexicon "the"     = [Cat "the"     "DET" []    []]
```

```
lexicon "most"     = [Cat "most"    "DET" [Pl]  []]
lexicon "many"     = [Cat "many"    "DET" [Pl]  []]
lexicon "few"      = [Cat "few"     "DET" [Pl]  []]
lexicon "this"     = [Cat "this"    "DET" [Sg]  []]
lexicon "these"    = [Cat "these"   "DET" [Pl]  []]
lexicon "those"    = [Cat "those"   "DET" [Pl]  []]
```

To be able to treat complex determiners we also define a category of determiner functions:

```
lexicon "less_than" = [Cat "less_than" "DF" [Pl]  []]
lexicon "more_than" = [Cat "more_than" "DF" [Pl]  []]
```

Common nouns are:

```
lexicon "thing"     = [Cat "thing"    "CN" [Sg,Neutr,Thrd] []]
lexicon "things"    = [Cat "things"   "CN" [Pl,Neutr,Thrd] []]
lexicon "person"    = [Cat "person"   "CN" [Sg,Masc,Thrd]  []]
lexicon "persons"   = [Cat "persons"  "CN" [Pl,Masc,Thrd]  []]
lexicon "boy"       = [Cat "boy"      "CN" [Sg,Masc,Thrd]  []]
lexicon "boys"      = [Cat "boys"     "CN" [Pl,Masc,Thrd]  []]
lexicon "man"       = [Cat "man"      "CN" [Sg,Masc,Thrd]  []]
lexicon "men"       = [Cat "men"      "CN" [Pl,Masc,Thrd]  []]
lexicon "girl"      = [Cat "girl"     "CN" [Sg,Fem,Thrd]   []]
lexicon "girls"     = [Cat "girls"    "CN" [Pl,Fem,Thrd]   []]
lexicon "woman"     = [Cat "woman"    "CN" [Sg,Fem,Thrd]   []]
lexicon "women"     = [Cat "women"    "CN" [Pl,Fem,Thrd]   []]
lexicon "princess"  = [Cat "princess" "CN" [Sg,Fem,Thrd]   []]
lexicon "princesses" = [Cat "princesses" "CN" [Pl,Fem,Thrd] []]
lexicon "dwarf"     = [Cat "dwarf"    "CN" [Sg,Masc,Thrd]  []]
lexicon "dwarfs"    = [Cat "dwarfs"   "CN" [Pl,Masc,Thrd]  []]
lexicon "dwarves"   = [Cat "dwarves"  "CN" [Pl,Masc,Thrd]  []]
lexicon "giant"     = [Cat "giant"    "CN" [Sg,Masc,Thrd]  []]
lexicon "giants"    = [Cat "giants"   "CN" [Pl,Masc,Thrd]  []]
```

More common nouns:

```
lexicon "wizard"   = [Cat "wizard"   "CN" [Sg,Masc,Thrd]  []]
lexicon "wizards"  = [Cat "wizards"  "CN" [Pl,Masc,Thrd]  []]
lexicon "sword"    = [Cat "sword"    "CN" [Sg,Neutr,Thrd] []]
lexicon "swords"   = [Cat "swords"   "CN" [Pl,Neutr,Thrd] []]
lexicon "dagger"   = [Cat "dagger"   "CN" [Sg,Neutr,Thrd] []]
lexicon "daggers"  = [Cat "daggers"  "CN" [Pl,Neutr,Thrd] []]
```

Auxiliaries are:

```
lexicon "did"    = [Cat "did"    "AUX" [] []]
lexicon "didn't" = [Cat "didn't" "AUX" [] []]
```

Intransitive verb phrases have an empty subcategorization list:

```
lexicon "smiled"    = [Cat "smiled"    "VP" [Tense] []]
lexicon "smile"     = [Cat "smile"     "VP" [Infl]  []]
lexicon "laughed"   = [Cat "laughed"   "VP" [Tense] []]
lexicon "laugh"     = [Cat "laugh"     "VP" [Infl]  []]
lexicon "cheered"   = [Cat "cheered"   "VP" [Tense] []]
lexicon "cheer"     = [Cat "cheer"     "VP" [Infl]  []]
lexicon "shuddered" = [Cat "shuddered" "VP" [Tense] []]
lexicon "shudder"   = [Cat "shudder"   "VP" [Infl]  []]
```

Transitive verb phrases have a single noun phrase with the feature AccOrDat on their subcatorisation list:

```
lexicon "loved"     =
 [Cat "loved"    "VP" [Tense] [Cat "_" "NP" [AccOrDat] []]]
lexicon "love"      =
 [Cat "love"     "VP" [Infl]  [Cat "_" "NP" [AccOrDat] []]]
lexicon "admired"   =
 [Cat "admired"  "VP" [Tense] [Cat "_" "NP" [AccOrDat] []]]
lexicon "admire"    =
 [Cat "admire"   "VP" [Infl]  [Cat "_" "NP" [AccOrDat] []]]
```

More transitive verbs:

```
lexicon "helped"      =
 [Cat "helped"    "VP" [Tense] [Cat "_" "NP" [AccOrDat] []]]
lexicon "help"        =
 [Cat "help"      "VP" [Infl]  [Cat "_" "NP" [AccOrDat] []]]
lexicon "defeated"      =
 [Cat "defeated" "VP" [Tense] [Cat "_" "NP" [AccOrDat] []]]
lexicon "defeat"        =
 [Cat "defeat"    "VP" [Infl]  [Cat "_" "NP" [AccOrDat] []]]
```

Ditransitive verb phrases have an NP and a *to*-PP on their subcategorization list:

```
lexicon "gave"          =
 [Cat "gave" "VP" [Tense] [Cat "_" "NP" [AccOrDat] [],
                  Cat "_" "PP" [To]        []],
  Cat "gave" "VP" [Tense] [Cat "_" "NP" [AccOrDat] [],
                  Cat "_" "NP" [AccOrDat]  []]]
lexicon "give"          =
 [Cat "give" "VP" [Infl]  [Cat "_" "NP" [AccOrDat] [],
                    Cat "_" "PP" [To]        []],
  Cat "give" "VP" [Infl]  [Cat "_" "NP" [AccOrDat] [],
                    Cat "_" "NP" [AccOrDat]  []]]
lexicon "sold" =
 [Cat "sold" "VP" [Tense] [Cat "_" "NP" [AccOrDat] [],
                    Cat "_" "PP" [To]        []],
  Cat "sold" "VP" [Tense] [Cat "_" "NP" [AccOrDat] [],
                    Cat "_" "NP" [AccOrDat]  []]]
lexicon "sell" =
 [Cat "sell" "VP" [Infl]  [Cat "_" "NP" [AccOrDat] [],
                    Cat "_" "PP" [To]        []],
  Cat "sell" "VP" [Infl]  [Cat "_" "NP" [AccOrDat] [],
                    Cat "_" "NP" [AccOrDat]  []]]
```

We can use the subcategorization lists to define other subcategorization patterns. Here is an example of a verb which takes an NP and an optional instrumental *with*-PP:

```
lexicon "kicked" =
  [Cat "kicked" "VP" [Tense] [Cat "_" "NP" [AccOrDat] [],
                              Cat "_" "PP" [With]      []],
   Cat "kicked" "VP" [Tense] [Cat "_" "NP" [AccOrDat] []]]
lexicon "kick" =
  [Cat "kick"   "VP" [Infl]  [Cat "_" "NP" [AccOrDat] [],
                              Cat "_" "PP" [With]      []],
   Cat "kick"   "VP" [Infl]  [Cat "_" "NP" [AccOrDat] []]]
```

And here is an example of a verb which takes an NP and an optional *from*-PP:

```
lexicon "took" =
  [Cat "took" "VP" [Tense] [Cat "_" "NP" [AccOrDat] [],
                            Cat "_" "PP" [From]      []],
   Cat "took" "VP" [Tense] [Cat "_" "NP" [AccOrDat] []]]
lexicon "take" =
  [Cat "take" "VP" [Infl]  [Cat "_" "NP" [AccOrDat] [],
                            Cat "_" "PP" [From]      []],
   Cat "take" "VP" [Infl]  [Cat "_" "NP" [AccOrDat] []]]
```

Here are some prepositions:

```
lexicon "on"   = [Cat "on"   "PREP" [On]    []]
lexicon "with" = [Cat "with" "PREP" [With]  []]
lexicon "by"   = [Cat "by"   "PREP" [By]    []]
lexicon "to"   = [Cat "to"   "PREP" [To]    []]
lexicon "from" = [Cat "from" "PREP" [From]  []]
```

The following entries implement conjunctions and conditionals. Note that we treat period (full stop) as sentence conjunction.

```
lexicon "and"  = [Cat "and"  "CONJ" [] []]
lexicon "."    = [Cat "."    "CONJ" [] []]
lexicon "if"   = [Cat "if"   "COND" [] []]
lexicon "then" = [Cat "then" "THEN" [] []]
```

Finally, we say that there is nothing else in the lexicon:

```
lexicon _ = []
```

Now, the `scan` function scans an input string and puts whitespace in front of punctuation marks.

```
scan :: String -> String
scan []                          = []
scan (x:xs) | x 'elem' ".,?" = ' ':x:scan xs
            | otherwise     =     x:scan xs
```

The lexer will produce lists of words (strings). Here is the data type for such lists:

```
type Words = [String]
```

The lexer creates lists of words from the input string. For robustness, we convert everything to lowercase. The `lexer` function uses the predefined function `words` to split the input into separate words. The function `preprocess` is defined below.

```
lexer :: String -> Words
lexer = preproc . words . (map toLower) . scan
```

It is useful to do some preprocessing on the list of input words. We will disregard commas anywhere in the input, and periods and question marks at the end of the input.

```
preproc :: Words -> Words
preproc []              = []
preproc ["."]           = []
preproc ["?"]           = []
preproc (",":xs)        = preproc xs
```

While we are at it, we can also use preprocessing for adjusting the break-up of words in the input:

```
preproc ("did":"not":xs)      = "didn't" : preproc xs
preproc ("nothing":xs)        = "no"     : "thing"  : preproc xs
preproc ("nobody":xs)         = "no"     : "person" : preproc xs
preproc ("something":xs)      = "some"   : "thing"  : preproc xs
preproc ("somebody":xs)       = "some"   : "person" : preproc xs
preproc ("everything":xs)     = "every"  : "thing"  : preproc xs
preproc ("everybody":xs)      = "every"  : "person" : preproc xs
preproc ("less":"than":xs)    = "less_than" : preproc xs
preproc ("more":"than":xs)    = "more_than" : preproc xs
preproc ("at":"least":xs)     = "at_least"  : preproc xs
preproc ("at":"most":xs)      = "at_most"   : preproc xs
preproc (x:xs)                = x : preproc xs
```

The lexicon is a lexical database of type `String -> [Cat]`. The `lookupWord` function fetches a list of categories for a word.

```
lookupWord :: (String -> [Cat]) -> String -> [Cat]
lookupWord db w = [ c | c <- db w ]
```

Finally, we collect a list of lists of categories for a list of words. An error is generated on encounter of a word that is not in the lexical database.

```
collectCats :: (String -> [Cat]) -> Words -> [[Cat]]
collectCats db words =
  let
    listing = map (\ x -> (x,lookupWord db x)) words
    unknown = map fst (filter (null.snd) listing)
  in
    if unknown /= [] then
      error ("unknown words: " ++ show unknown)
    else initCats (map snd listing)

initCats :: [[Cat]] -> [[Cat]]
initCats []         = [[]]
initCats (cs:rests) = [ c:rest | c    <- cs,
                                 rest <- initCats rests ]
```

This gives:

```
P> collectCats lexicon ["i","loved","her"]
[[i NP[Pers,Fst,Sg,Nom],loved VP[Tense],
her NP[Pers,Thrd,Sg,Acc,Fem]]]
P> collectCats lexicon ["she","despised","me"]

Program error: unknown words: ["despised"]
```

9.6 Parsing Categories

We will now develop the tools for parsing with categories. The input list for the parsing process will consist of categories, and the parsers will build parse trees with categories at the leaf nodes and at the internal nodes. To start with, here is a function for getting the category out of a parse tree (a map from trees to categories):

```
t2c :: ParseTree Cat Cat -> Cat
t2c (Leaf   c)   = c
t2c (Branch c _) = c
```

It is convenient to lift the `agree` function to parse trees:

```
agreeC :: ParseTree Cat Cat -> ParseTree Cat Cat -> Bool
agreeC t1 t2 = agree (t2c t1) (t2c t2)
```

Our parsing functions will take a list of categories and produce a list of pairs consisting of a parse tree and a remainder list of categories. The simplest possible parser is the one for constructing a leaf tree of a given category:

```
leafP :: CatLabel -> PARSER Cat Cat
leafP label []     = []
leafP label (c:cs) = [(Leaf c,cs) | catLabel c == label ]
```

For smooth handling of feature assignment it is useful to also lift the `assign` function to the level of parse trees:

```
assignT :: Feat ->  ParseTree Cat Cat
                    -> [ParseTree Cat Cat]
assignT f (Leaf    c)   = [Leaf    c' | c' <- assign f c]
assignT f (Branch c ts) = [Branch c' ts | c' <- assign f c]
```

Sentences are all constructed by means of the subject–predicate rule. Here is the corresponding parser. Note that the subject and the predicate have to agree in their feature lists, that the subject agreement list must allow the assignment of the feature Nom, and that the predicate must have combined with all its complements, i.e. its subcategorization list has to be empty.

```
sRule :: PARSER Cat Cat
sRule = \ xs ->
        [ (Branch (Cat "_" "S" [] []) [np',vp],zs) |
          (np,ys) <- parseNP xs,
          (vp,zs) <- parseVP ys,
          np'     <- assignT Nom np,
          agreeC np vp,
          subcatList (t2c vp) == [] ]
```

A sentence can only be parsed in this one way, so here is our parser for sentences:

```
parseSent :: PARSER Cat Cat
parseSent = sRule
```

Noun phrases can either be formed according to a rule or found on the input category list:

```
npRule :: PARSER Cat Cat
npRule = \ xs ->
  [ (Branch (Cat "_" "NP" fs []) [det,cn],zs) |
    (det,ys) <- parseDET xs,
    (cn,zs)  <- parseCN  ys,
    fs       <- combine (t2c det) (t2c cn),
    agreeC det cn ]

parseNP :: PARSER Cat Cat
parseNP = leafP "NP" <|> npRule
```

Preposition phrases are always constructed by a rule. Note that the rule uses feature control: the preposition assigns `AccOrDat` case to the NP.

```
ppRule :: PARSER Cat Cat
ppRule = \ xs ->
   [ (Branch (Cat "_" "PP" fs []) [prep,np'],zs) |
     (prep,ys) <- parsePrep xs,
     (np,zs)   <- parseNP ys,
      np'      <- assignT AccOrDat np,
      fs       <- combine (t2c prep) (t2c np') ]

parsePP :: PARSER Cat Cat
parsePP = ppRule
```

The subcategorization lists of verbs consist of NPs and PPs, so it makes sense to construct a parser for such lists.

```
parseNPorPP :: PARSER Cat Cat
parseNPorPP = parseNP <|> parsePP

parseNPsorPPs :: [Cat] -> [([ParseTree Cat Cat],[Cat])]
parseNPsorPPs = many parseNPorPP
```

Determiners are always lexical:

```
parseDET :: PARSER Cat Cat
parseDET = leafP "DET"
```

Exercise 9.10 Add a rule for complex determiners consisting of a determiner function and a numeral. This should cater for *less than n, more than n. at least n, at most n,* and *exactly n.* Preprocessing makes all determiner functions available as single words. You will also need a parser for numerals, of course.

For now, common nouns are always in the lexicon, so their categories will be found on the input category list. Below, in Section 9.7, we will extend this to common nouns with relative clauses.

```
parseCN :: PARSER Cat Cat
parseCN = leafP "CN"
```

All prepositions and all auxiliaries are lexical:

```
parsePrep :: PARSER Cat Cat
parsePrep = leafP "PREP"

parseAux :: PARSER Cat Cat
parseAux = leafP "AUX"
```

Verb phrases are either parsed with a rule for finite VPs, or with a rule for auxiliaries combining with an infinitive VP.

```
parseVP :: PARSER Cat Cat
parseVP = finVpRule <|> auxVpRule
```

Both of these rules use a parser for combining a verb with its subcategorization list:

```
vpRule :: PARSER Cat Cat
vpRule = \xs ->
  [ (Branch (Cat "_" "VP" (fs (t2c vp)) []) (vp:xps),zs) |
    (vp,ys)      <- leafP "VP" xs,
    subcatlist   <- [subcatList (t2c vp)],
    (xps,zs)     <- parseNPsorPPs ys,
    match subcatlist (map t2c xps) ]
```

This uses a function for matching a subcategorization list with a list of NPs and PPs. Not only the feature lists have to agree, but the category labels should be the same: NPs should match with NPs, PPs with PPs.

```
match :: [Cat] -> [Cat] -> Bool
match []     []      = True
match _      []      = False
match []     _       = False
match (x:xs) (y:ys) = catLabel x == catLabel y
      && agree x y
      && match xs ys
```

For a finite VP, just check that tense can be assigned to the VP:

```
finVpRule :: PARSER Cat Cat
finVpRule = \xs -> [(vp',ys) | (vp,ys) <- vpRule xs,
vp'    <- assignT Tense vp ]
```

For a VP consisting of an auxiliary and an infinitive form, parse the auxiliary, parse the VP, and check that the VP is in infinitive form. For this, check that `Inf` can be assigned to the VP.

```
auxVpRule :: PARSER Cat Cat
auxVpRule = \xs ->
 [(Branch (Cat "_" "VP" (fs (t2c aux)) []) [aux,inf'],zs) |
  (aux,ys) <- parseAux xs,
  (inf,zs) <- vpRule ys,
  inf'    <- assignT Infl inf ]
```

Parsing is the process of constructing a list of parse trees for a string. Each parse tree will correspond to a possible parse of the string. If a string does not parse, the list of parse trees is empty.

```
prs :: String -> [ParseTree Cat Cat]
prs string = let ws = lexer string
     in  [ s | catlist <- collectCats lexicon ws,
         (s,[])  <- parseSent catlist ]
```

You can try this out with `prs "I loved her."`, and so on.

9.7 Handling Extractions

Left extraction in natural language occurs when a subconstituent of some constituent is missing, and some other constituent to the left of the incomplete constituent represents that missing constituent in some way, for example in the sentence *Who did some dwarf defeat.* In the generative tradition, such dislocations are accounted for by means of transformations that *move* a constituent while leaving a trace. Computational and logic-oriented approaches to natural language processing replace the transformational account with an *in situ* analysis, through gap threading (lexical functional grammar, categorial grammar) and/or through extension of the context-free rule format with wrapping operations (extraposition grammars, tuple-based and tree-based extensions of context-free grammars).

An example of this is relative clause formation. The intuition about relative clauses is that they are sentences with an NP missing. To write a parser that parses the internal structure of a relative clause correctly, we will extend our parsers with an extra component: a stack of gaps or missing constituents. This comes close to the gap threading mechanism of *Generalized Phrase Structure Grammar* (GPSG) [GKPS85] and *Head-Driven Phrase Structure Grammar* (HPSG) [PS94].

Above we have seen that extension of context-free rules with a feature agreement mechanism was possible within the context-free rule format. The case of extraction is different. Formally, adding an extraction mechanism to context-free rules gets us outside the context-free rule format. The grammar class we get in is that of sequentially indexed grammars. Sequentially indexed grammars use indices that get pushed to an arbitrary nonterminal in the right-hand side of a rule. Rules have the form $A_X \longrightarrow B \ldots C$ to indicate that X gets consumed in the production of $B \ldots C$, or the form $A \longrightarrow B \ldots C_X \ldots D$ to indicate that X gets pushed to C in the production. A sequentially indexed grammar for a toy fragment of natural language might look like this:

$$
\begin{aligned}
\mathbf{S} &\rightarrow \mathbf{NP\ VP} \\
\mathbf{VP} &\rightarrow \mathbf{TV\ NP} \mid \textit{laughed} \\
\mathbf{NP} &\rightarrow \mathbf{DET\ CN} \mid \textit{Alice} \mid \textit{Dorothy} \\
\mathbf{TV} &\rightarrow \textit{admired} \mid \textit{helped} \\
\mathbf{DET} &\rightarrow \textit{the} \mid \textit{some} \\
\mathbf{CN} &\rightarrow \textit{boy} \mid \textit{girl} \mid \mathbf{CN}\ \textit{that}\ \mathbf{S_{NP}} \\
\mathbf{NP_{NP}} &\rightarrow \epsilon
\end{aligned}
$$

This uses index the $_{\mathbf{NP}}$ to handle NP gaps in relative clauses. We will not give a precise formal definition of sequentially indexed grammars and sequentially indexed languages here, as formal grammar theory is outside the scope of this book. A full account can be found in [Eij07b].

As we will see now, treatment of extraction phenomena with extraction stacks remains close to the spirit of a movement analysis. Relative clause formation in English is a simple example of left extraction. The structure of the relative clause in (9.2) is represented by the annotation that links the relative pronoun *that* to its trace t_i.

> *Dorothy admired the princess that$_i$ Goldilocks gave the sword to t_i.*   (9.2)

Our grammar will give the example the parse in Figure 9.2, with # indicating the NP gap.

Fig. 9.2. Parse tree for example (9.2)

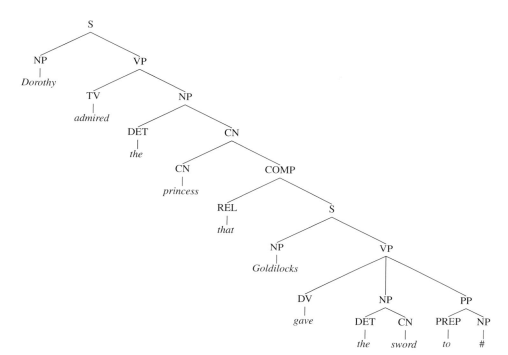

The stack parser that handles NPs should take the so-called island constraints on extraction (first proposed in [Ros67]) into account. Islands are domains out of which extraction is not possible. One example are relative clauses inside an NP. Ross proposed the *Complex NP Constraint*, which rules out configurations of the form

$$\ldots that_i \ldots [_{NP} \ldots [_{REL} \; that_j \; [_S \ldots t_i \ldots t_j \ldots]]].$$

The constraint is imposed to rule out examples like (9.3).

*Dorothy admired the princess that$_i$ [Goldilocks helped [$_{NP}$ the boy that$_j$
[t$_i$ gave the sword to t$_j$]]].   (9.3)

Exercise 9.11 Some linguists would claim that the complex NP constraint *explains* the ungrammaticality of (9.3). Other linguists might counter that the complex NP constraint is just a *description*, and descriptions never explain anything. Which side are you on in this debate? Discuss.

As you can check, example (9.3) does not receive a parse in the fragment that we will present, but (9.4) does.

> *Dorothy admired the princess that$_i$ [t$_i$ helped [$_{NP}$ the boy that$_j$*
>
> *[Goldilocks gave the sword to t$_j$]]].*   (9.4)

Each occurrence of # gets bound by the closest *that* above it. Note that this follows directly from the island constraint, for if an occurrence of # is not bound by the closest *that* above it the island constraint is violated.

To treat dependencies, we will enrich our parsers with a stack of 'extracted material'. We call this a stack parser.

```
type StackParser a b = [a] -> [a] -> [(b,[a],[a])]
```

We will be interested in the special version of this where the yield of the parser consists of parse trees.

```
type SPARSER a b = StackParser a (ParseTree a b)
```

As in the previous sections, we will first build a few special purpose stack parsers. A new version of the choice operator is the following:

```
infixr 4 <||>

(<||>) :: StackParser a b -> StackParser a b
  -> StackParser a b
(p1 <||> p2) stack xs = p1 stack xs ++ p2 stack xs
```

A new version of the sequential composition operator (<:>) is:

```
infixl 6 <:>

(<:>) :: StackParser a b  -> StackParser a [b]
                          -> StackParser a [b]
(p <:> q) us xs = [(r:rs,ws,zs) | (r,vs,ys)  <- p us xs,
                                  (rs,ws,zs) <- q vs ys ]
```

The function succeedS implements a stack parser for immediate success:

```
succeedS :: b -> StackParser a b
succeedS r us xs = [(r,us,xs)]
```

The operation <::> and the function succeedS can be used to construct the stack parser version of the many parser:

```
manyS :: StackParser a b -> StackParser a [b]
manyS p = (p <::> manyS p) <||> succeedS []
```

The two fundamental stack operations are (i) pushing a new item on the stack, and (ii) popping the top item from a non-empty stack. Push creates a new stack parser from a category and an existing stack parser:

```
push :: Cat -> SPARSER Cat Cat -> SPARSER Cat Cat
push c p stack = p (c:stack)
```

Pop checks the whether the category label of the top element on the stack matches a given label and, if so, creates a leaf tree for that element. If the extraction stack is empty, the parse fails.

```
pop :: CatLabel -> SPARSER Cat Cat
pop c []      xs                    = []
pop c (u:us) xs | catLabel u == c = [(Leaf u, us, xs)]
                | otherwise       = []
```

A stack parser for recognizing a category on the input list can be implemented as follows.

```
leafPS :: CatLabel -> SPARSER Cat Cat
leafPS l _ []         = []
leafPS l s (c:cs) = [(Leaf c,s,cs) | catLabel c == l ]
```

Texts are conjunctions of sentences:

```
prsTXT :: SPARSER Cat Cat
prsTXT = conjR <||> prsS

conjR :: SPARSER Cat Cat
conjR = \ us xs ->
    [ (Branch (Cat "_" "TXT" [] []) [s, conj, txt], ws, zs) |
        (s,vs,ys)       <- prsS us xs,
        (conj,vs1,ys1) <- leafPS "CONJ" vs ys,
        (txt,ws,zs)     <- prsTXT vs1 ys1                    ]
```

Exercise 9.12 Note that texts are right-branching. That is, we parse a three-sentence conjunction *S and S and S* as

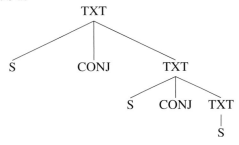

rather than

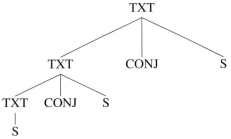

Predict what would happen if we modify the rule to make it left-branching. Then make the
modification and check your prediction.

Parsing a sentence is done with the subject–predicate rule or with one of the two
rules for conditional sentences.

```
prsS :: SPARSER Cat Cat
prsS = spR <||> cond1R <||> cond2R
```

The subject–predicate rule can be implemented as follows:

```
spR :: SPARSER Cat Cat
spR = \ us xs ->
  [ (Branch (Cat "_" "S" (fs (t2c np)) []) [np',vp],ws,zs) |
       (np,vs,ys) <- prsNP us xs,
       (vp,ws,zs) <- prsVP vs ys,
        np'        <- assignT Nom np,
      agreeC np vp,
      subcatList (t2c vp) == [] ]
```

The first rule for conditional sentences treats examples like (9.5).

If a princess admired a dwarf, he loved her. (9.5)

```
cond1R :: SPARSER Cat Cat
cond1R = \ us xs ->
   [ (Branch (Cat "_" "S" [] []) [cond,s1,s2], ws, zs) |
       (cond,vs,ys) <- leafPS "COND" us xs,
       (s1,vs1,ys1) <- prsS vs ys,
       (s2,ws,zs)   <- prsS vs1 ys1 ]
```

The second rule for conditional sentences treats examples like (9.6).

If a princess admired a dwarf, then he loved her. (9.6)

```
cond2R :: SPARSER Cat Cat
cond2R = \ us xs ->
    [ (Branch (Cat "_" "S" [] []) [cond,s1,s2], ws, zs) |
        (cond,vs,ys) <- leafPS "COND" us xs,
        (s1,vs1,ys1) <- prsS vs ys,
        (_,vs2,ys2)  <- leafPS "THEN" vs1 ys1,
        (s2,ws,zs)   <- prsS vs2 ys2 ]
```

The semantics of conditionals like (9.5) and (9.6) will be handled in Chapter 12.

Parsing an NP can be done in three ways: by finding the NP on the input list, by application of the rule NP → DET CN, and by popping an NP from the extraction stack.

```
prsNP :: SPARSER Cat Cat
prsNP = leafPS "NP" <||> npR <||> pop "NP"
```

The rule should be implemented in such manner that gaps from outside are passed on to the next constituent, never consumed inside the NP. This is in order to impose the Complex NP Constraint. So we pass on the contents of the incoming stack us to the output extraction stack.

```
npR :: SPARSER Cat Cat
npR = \ us xs ->
  [ (Branch (Cat "_" "NP" fs []) [det,cn], (us++ws), zs) |
      (det,vs,ys) <- prsDET [] xs,
      (cn,ws,zs)  <- prsCN vs ys,
       fs         <- combine (t2c det) (t2c cn),
      agreeC det cn ]
```

Determiner categories are always found on the input list:

```
prsDET :: SPARSER Cat Cat
prsDET = leafPS "DET"
```

Exercise 9.13 Implement a rule for determiners consisting of a determiner function and a numeral, to treat complex determiners like *at least 5* (compare Exercise 9.10).

Common nouns are lexical, or are formed with a relative clause rule:

```
prsCN :: SPARSER Cat Cat
prsCN = leafPS "CN" <||> cnrelR
```

VPs are either finite forms or auxilaries plus infinitive forms:

```
prsVP :: SPARSER Cat Cat
prsVP = finVpR <||> auxVpR
```

Both rules use the following stack parser version of the key VP rule:

```
vpR :: SPARSER Cat Cat
vpR = \us xs ->
  [(Branch (Cat "_" "VP" (fs (t2c vp)) []) (vp:xps),ws,zs) |
            (vp,vs,ys)  <- leafPS "VP" us xs,
            subcatlist  <- [subcatList (t2c vp)],
            (xps,ws,zs) <- prsNPsorPPs vs ys,
            match subcatlist (map t2c xps) ]
```

Here is a parser for finite VPs:

```
finVpR :: SPARSER Cat Cat
finVpR = \us xs -> [(vp',vs,ys) | (vp,vs,ys) <- vpR us xs,
                                  vp' <- assignT Tense vp ]
```

The parser for VPs consisting of an auxiliary plus an infinitive form can be implemented as follows:

```
auxVpR :: SPARSER Cat Cat
auxVpR = \us xs ->
     [ (Branch (Cat "_" "VP" (fs (t2c aux)) [])
               [aux,inf'], ws, zs) |
                 (aux,vs,ys) <- prsAUX us xs,
                 (inf,ws,zs) <- vpR vs ys,
                  inf'       <- assignT Infl inf ]
```

Auxiliaries are found on the input list, or popped from the extraction stack. The second case handles the left dislocation of auxiliaries in yes/no questions and wh-questions (see below).

```
prsAUX :: SPARSER Cat Cat
prsAUX = leafPS "AUX" <||> pop "AUX"
```

PPs are constructed with a rule or popped from the extraction stack:

```
prsPP :: SPARSER Cat Cat
prsPP = ppR <||> pop "PP"
```

The PP rule combines a preposition with an NP.

```
ppR :: SPARSER Cat Cat
ppR = \us xs ->
  [ (Branch (Cat "_" "PP" fs []) [prep,np'], ws, zs) |
      (prep,vs,ys) <- prsPREP us xs,
      (np,ws,zs)   <- prsNP vs ys,
      np'          <- assignT AccOrDat np,
      fs           <- combine (t2c prep) (t2c np') ]
```

Prepositions are all found on the input list:

```
prsPREP :: SPARSER Cat Cat
prsPREP = leafPS "PREP"
```

The verb subcategorization lists consist of NPs or PPs. Here is how to handle them:

```
prsNPorPP :: SPARSER Cat Cat
prsNPorPP = prsNP <||> prsPP

prsNPsorPPs :: [Cat] -> [Cat]
       -> [([ParseTree Cat Cat],[Cat],[Cat])]
prsNPsorPPs = manyS prsNPorPP
```

Complex CNs use a parser `prsREL` for relative clauses:

```
cnrelR :: SPARSER Cat Cat
cnrelR = \us xs ->
    [ (Branch (Cat "_" "CN" (fs (t2c cn)) [])
              [cn,rel], ws, zs) |
              (cn,vs,ys)  <- leafPS "CN" us xs,
              (rel,ws,zs) <- prsREL vs ys,
              agreeC cn rel ]
```

Exercise 9.14 Suppose we replace the `leafPS "CN"` in this definition with `prsCN`. What would happen, and why?

There are two relative clause rules: one for relative clauses starting with a relative pronoun and one for relative clauses without such a pronoun.

```
prsREL :: SPARSER Cat Cat
prsREL = relclauseR <||> thatlessR
```

Regular relative clauses consist of a relative plus a sentence with an NP gap. The sentence with NP gap is created by pushing the gap on a parser for sentences.

```
relclauseR :: SPARSER Cat Cat
relclauseR = \us xs ->
  [(Branch (Cat "_" "COMP" fs []) [rel,s], ws, zs) |
      (rel,vs,ys) <- leafPS "REL" us xs,
      fs          <- [fs (t2c rel)],
      gap         <- [Cat "#" "NP" fs []],
      (s,ws,zs)   <- push gap prsS vs ys ]
```

That-less relatives do not have a relative pronoun, or, equivalently, they start with a zero relative pronoun. Constraints are that the extracted NP cannot be the subject, and that the subject of the embedded sentence does not have a feature Wh. This takes care of relatives like *the princess I admired* and *the prince I gave the sword to*.

```
thatlessR :: SPARSER Cat Cat
thatlessR = \ us xs ->
      [ (Branch (Cat "_" "COMP" [] []) [s], vs, ys) |
          gap       <- [Cat "#" "NP" [AccOrDat] []],
          (s,vs,ys) <- push gap prsS us xs,
          notElem Wh (fs (t2c s))                    ]
```

As a bonus, we can use the extraction stack for other purposes than extracting NPs. To deal with yes/no questions, we extract an auxiliary from a sentence. This analyses examples like *Did she love me?* as Did_i *she* $\#_i$ *love me*.

```
prsYN :: SPARSER Cat Cat
prsYN = \us xs ->
   [(Branch (Cat "_" "YN" [] []) [aux,s], ws,zs) |
      (aux,vs,ys) <- prsAUX us xs,
      gap         <- [Cat "#" "AUX" (fs (t2c aux)) [] ],
      (s,ws,zs)   <- push gap prsS vs ys ]
```

From yes/no questions it is but a small step to wh-questions. We analyse a wh-question as a yes/no question with an extracted NP or PP carrying a feature Wh. This analyses *Who did she love?* as *Who$_i$ did$_j$ she #$_j$ love #$_i$*.

```
isWH :: ParseTree Cat Cat -> Bool
isWH tr = Wh 'elem' (fs (t2c tr))


prsWH :: SPARSER Cat Cat
prsWH = \us xs ->
   [ (Branch (Cat "_" "WH" [] []) [wh,yn], ws,zs) |
      (wh,vs,ys) <- prsNPorPP us xs,
      isWH wh,
      gapfs      <- [filter (/= Wh) (fs (t2c wh))],
      gap        <- [Cat "#" (catLabel (t2c wh)) gapfs []],
      (yn,ws,zs) <- push gap prsYN vs ys ]
```

The parsing function for parsing a string with a stack parser is just like the parsing function prs from Section 9.6.

```
parses :: String -> [ParseTree Cat Cat]
parses str = let ws = lexer str
             in [ s | catlist   <- collectCats lexicon ws,
                     (s,[],[]) <- prsTXT [] catlist
                                ++ prsYN  [] catlist
                                ++ prsWH  [] catlist ]
```

Here is a test suite of sentences that should parse:

```
testSuite1 :: [String]
testSuite1 =
 [ "Alice admired Dorothy.",
   "Did Alice admire Dorothy?",
   "Who did Alice admire?",
   "Atreyu gave the sword to the princess.",
   "Did Atreyu give the sword to the princess?",
   "Who did Atreyu give the sword to?",
   "To whom did Atreyu give the sword?",
   "Goldilocks helped the girl "
    ++ "that Atreyu gave the sword to.",
  "Did Goldilocks help the girl "
    ++ "that Atreyu gave the sword to.",
   "Goldilocks helped the boy that helped the princess "
    ++ "that Atreyu gave the sword to." ]
```

And here is a test suite of strings that should not parse.

```
testSuite2 :: [String]
testSuite2 =
 [ "Dorothy admired the boy that Alice helped Atreyu",
   "Dorothy admired the boy that helped",
   "Dorothy admired the girl that "
    ++ "Atreyu helped the princess that gave the sword to" ]
```

9.8 Adding Semantics

If we want to put parse trees to use in computational semantics, we need functions for mapping them to logical forms, or functions for direct interpretation of parse trees in appropriate models. To illustrate the interpretation process for parse trees, we will define a function from parse trees to logical forms. We will not provide full semantic coverage of our grammar. The semantics of conditional sentences, sentence conjunctions and multiple sentence texts will be taken up in Chapter 12. Some other extensions will be left to the reader.

Our logical form language will have terms, generalized quantifiers, abstracts, and formulas. The terms are either constants or variables:

```
data Term = Const String | Var Int deriving (Eq,Ord)
```

The generalized quantifiers are:

```
data GQ = Sm | All | Th | Most | Many | Few
          deriving (Eq,Show,Ord)
```

An abstract is an LF representation of a lambda term:

```
data Abstract = MkAbstract Int LF deriving (Eq,Ord)
```

Abstracts occur in the logical forms for quantifications. A quantification consists of a generalized quantifier and two abstracts, one for the restriction of the quantifier and one for its body.

```
data LF = Rel String [Term]
        | Eq    Term Term
        | Neg   LF
        | Impl LF LF
        | Equi LF LF
        | Conj [LF]
        | Disj [LF]
        | Qt GQ Abstract Abstract
     deriving (Eq,Ord)
```

It is convenient to define show functions for these data types:

```
instance Show Term where
  show (Const name) = name
  show (Var i)      = 'x': show i

instance Show Abstract where
  show (MkAbstract i lf) =
    "(\\ x" ++ show i ++ " " ++ show lf ++ ")"
```

```
instance Show LF where
  show (Rel r args)    = r ++ show args
  show (Eq t1 t2)      = show t1 ++ "==" ++ show t2
  show (Neg lf)        = '~': (show lf)
  show (Impl lf1 lf2)  = "(" ++ show lf1 ++ "==>"
                             ++ show lf2 ++ ")"
  show (Equi lf1 lf2)  = "(" ++ show lf1 ++ "<=>"
                             ++ show lf2 ++ ")"
  show (Conj [])       = "true"
  show (Conj lfs)      = "conj" ++ concat [ show lfs ]
  show (Disj [])       = "false"
  show (Disj lfs)      = "disj" ++ concat [ show lfs ]
  show (Qt gq a1 a2)   = show gq ++ (' ' : show a1)
                                 ++ (' ' : show a2)
```

Next, we will match the parse rule for each category with a logical form translation rule. All sentences are of the form [s NP VP], so we only need to check for one type of parse tree:

```
transS :: ParseTree Cat Cat -> LF
transS (Branch (Cat _ "S" _ _) [np,vp]) =
  (transNP np) (transVP vp)
```

Translations for yes/no questions are of the same type as those for sentences. There is no difference in interpretation; the difference is in use: the LF translations of declarative sentences are for making assertions, those of yes/no questions are for querying. Therefore we add the following:

```
transS (Branch (Cat _ "YN" _ _)
       [Leaf (Cat "did"    "AUX" _ []),s]) = transS s
transS (Branch (Cat _ "YN" _ _)
       [Leaf (Cat "didn't" "AUX" _ []),s]) = Neg (transS s)
```

NPs can be formed in three ways, so we have to check three patterns:

```
transNP :: ParseTree Cat Cat ->
                 (Term -> LF) -> LF
transNP (Leaf (Cat "#"  "NP" _ _)) = \ p -> p (Var 0)
transNP (Leaf (Cat name "NP" _ _)) = \ p -> p (Const name)
transNP (Branch (Cat _ "NP" _ _) [det,cn]) =
                                (transDET det) (transCN cn)
```

Determiners are building blocks for generalized quantifications. Here are the determiners for the Aristotelean quantifiers, and some other determiners:

```
transDET :: ParseTree Cat Cat -> (Term -> LF)
                              -> (Term -> LF)
                              -> LF
transDET (Leaf (Cat "every" "DET" _ _)) =
  \ p q -> let i = fresh[p,q] in
  Qt All      (MkAbstract i (p (Var i)))
              (MkAbstract i (q (Var i)))
transDET (Leaf (Cat "all" "DET" _ _)) =
  \ p q -> let i = fresh[p,q] in
  Qt All      (MkAbstract i (p (Var i)))
              (MkAbstract i (q (Var i)))
transDET (Leaf (Cat "some" "DET" _ _)) =
  \ p q -> let i = fresh[p,q] in
  Qt Sm       (MkAbstract i (p (Var i)))
              (MkAbstract i (q (Var i)))
transDET (Leaf (Cat "a" "DET" _ _)) =
  \ p q -> let i = fresh[p,q] in
  Qt Sm       (MkAbstract i (p (Var i)))
              (MkAbstract i (q (Var i)))
transDET (Leaf (Cat "several" "DET" _ _)) =
  \ p q -> let i = fresh[p,q] in
  Qt Sm       (MkAbstract i (p (Var i)))
              (MkAbstract i (q (Var i)))
transDET (Leaf (Cat "no" "DET" _ _)) =
  \ p q -> let i = fresh[p,q] in
  Neg (Qt Sm (MkAbstract i (p (Var i)))
              (MkAbstract i (q (Var i))))
```

```
transDET (Leaf (Cat "the" "DET" _ _)) =
  \ p q -> let i = fresh[p,q] in
  Qt Th         (MkAbstract i (p (Var i)))
                (MkAbstract i (q (Var i)))
transDET (Leaf (Cat "most" "DET" _ _)) =
  \ p q -> let i = fresh[p,q] in
  Qt Most       (MkAbstract i (p (Var i)))
                (MkAbstract i (q (Var i)))
transDET (Leaf (Cat "many" "DET" _ _)) =
  \ p q -> let i = fresh[p,q] in
  Qt Many       (MkAbstract i (p (Var i)))
                (MkAbstract i (q (Var i)))
transDET (Leaf (Cat "few" "DET" _ _)) =
  \ p q -> let i = fresh[p,q] in
  Neg (Qt Many (MkAbstract i (p (Var i)))
                (MkAbstract i (q (Var i))))
```

A special case is the determiner *which*. It will be used to abstract over a variable
`Var 0`:

```
transDET (Leaf (Cat "which" "DET" _ _)) =
  \ p q -> Conj [p (Var 0),q (Var 0)]
```

Common nouns can be either lexical or complex. Here are translations for these
two cases:

```
transCN :: ParseTree Cat Cat -> Term -> LF
transCN (Leaf    (Cat name "CN" _ _))          = \ x ->
                                                 Rel name [x]
transCN (Branch (Cat _    "CN" _ _) [cn,rel]) = \ x ->
                      Conj [transCN cn x, transREL rel x]
```

Relative clauses can be of two kinds: with an explicit relative pronoun or without
one.

```
transREL :: ParseTree Cat Cat -> Term -> LF
transREL (Branch (Cat _ "COMP" _ _ ) [rel,s]) =
  \ x -> sub x (transS s)
transREL (Branch (Cat _ "COMP" _ _ ) [s])       =
  \ x -> sub x (transS s)
```

There are two kinds of PPs: simple ones with gaps on the extraction stack, and complex ones.

```
transPP :: ParseTree Cat Cat -> (Term -> LF) -> LF
transPP (Leaf    (Cat "#" "PP" _ _)) = \ p -> p (Var 0)
transPP (Branch (Cat _    "PP" _ _) [prep,np]) = transNP np
```

Some of the patterns for VPs are the following:

```
transVP :: ParseTree Cat Cat -> Term -> LF
transVP (Branch (Cat _ "VP" _ _)
                [Leaf (Cat name "VP" _ [])]) =
       \ t -> Rel name [t]
transVP (Branch (Cat _ "VP" _ _)
                [Leaf (Cat name "VP" _ [_]),np]) =
       \ subj -> transNP np (\ obj -> Rel name [subj,obj])
```

```
transVP (Branch (Cat _ "VP" _ _)
                [Leaf (Cat name "VP" _ [_,_]),np,pp]) =
       \ subj   -> transNP np
       (\ obj    -> transPP pp
        (\ iobj -> Rel name [subj,obj,iobj]))
transVP (Branch (Cat _ "VP" _ _)
                [Leaf (Cat "did" "AUX" _ []),vp]) =
       transVP vp
transVP (Branch (Cat _ "VP" _ _)
                [Leaf (Cat "didn't" "AUX" _ []),vp]) =
       \x -> Neg ((transVP vp) x)
transVP (Branch (Cat _ "VP" _ _)
                [Leaf (Cat "#" "AUX" _ []),vp]) =
       transVP vp
```

Exercise 9.15 Which cases are not covered by the above? Check the lexicon and write translations for the remaining cases.

Wh-questions contain an embedded sentence with a Wh-gap. If we assume that this gap is translated by the variable `Var 0`, then we can translate the Wh-question as an abstraction over this variable:

```
transWH :: ParseTree Cat Cat -> Abstract
transWH (Branch (Cat _ "WH" _ _ ) [wh,s]) =
  MkAbstract 0 (Conj [transW wh, transS s])
```

This leaves us with the following translation of Wh-NPs:

```
transW :: ParseTree Cat Cat -> LF
transW (Branch (Cat _ "NP" fs _) [det,cn]) =
                            transCN cn (Var 0)
transW (Leaf (Cat _ "NP" fs _))
      | Masc        `elem` fs = Rel "man"    [Var 0]
      | Fem         `elem` fs = Rel "woman"  [Var 0]
      | MascOrFem   `elem` fs = Rel "person" [Var 0]
      | otherwise             = Rel "thing"  [Var 0]
```

```
transW (Branch (Cat _ "PP" fs _) [prep,np])
      | Masc        `elem` fs = Rel "man"    [Var 0]
      | Fem         `elem` fs = Rel "woman"  [Var 0]
      | MascOrFem   `elem` fs = Rel "person" [Var 0]
      | otherwise             = Rel "thing"  [Var 0]
```

Some unfinished business remains. The rule for translation of relative clauses uses a substitution function that replaces unbound occurrences of `Var 0` by a new term. The result is that `sub x lf` has type LF, and `\ x -> sub x lf` has type `Term -> LF`.

```
subst :: Term -> Term -> Term
subst x (Const name)      = Const name
subst x (Var n) | n == 0  = x
                | otherwise = Var n
                | x == Var n = error "bad substitution"
```

```
sub :: Term -> LF -> LF
sub x (Rel name ts)     = Rel name (map (subst x) ts)
sub x (Eq t1 t2)        = Eq (subst x t1) (subst x t2)
sub x (Neg lf)          = Neg (sub x lf)
sub x (Impl lf1 lf2)    = Impl (sub x lf1) (sub x lf2)
sub x (Equi lf1 lf2)    = Equi (sub x lf1) (sub x lf2)
sub x (Conj lfs)        = Conj (map (sub x) lfs)
sub x (Disj lfs)        = Disj (map (sub x) lfs)
sub x (Qt gq abs1 abs2) = Qt gq (sb x abs1) (sb x abs2)

sb :: Term -> Abstract -> Abstract
sb x (MkAbstract 0 lf) = MkAbstract 0 lf
sb x (MkAbstract n lf) = MkAbstract n (sub x lf)
```

The next functions are for collecting the lists of indices that have bound occurrences in an LF.

```
bInLF :: LF -> [Int]
bInLF (Rel _ _)         = []
bInLF (Eq _  _)         = []

bInLF (Neg lf)          = bInLF lf
bInLF (Impl lf1 lf2)    = bInLFs [lf1,lf2]
bInLF (Equi lf1 lf2)    = bInLFs [lf1,lf2]
bInLF (Conj lfs)        = bInLFs lfs
bInLF (Disj lfs)        = bInLFs lfs
bInLF (Qt gq abs1 abs2) = bInAs [abs1,abs2]

bInLFs :: [LF] -> [Int]
bInLFs = nub . concat . map bInLF
```

List of indices that have bound occurrences in an abstract:

```
bInA :: Abstract -> [Int]
bInA (MkAbstract i lf) = i: bInLF lf

bInAs :: [Abstract] -> [Int]
bInAs = nub . concat . map bInA
```

The function `bInLFs` is used for computing a fresh index for a list of predications. Note that the function `fresh` is used in the definition of `transDET`.

```
freshIndex  :: [LF] -> Int
freshIndex lfs = i+1
  where i       = foldr max 0 (bInLFs lfs)

fresh :: [Term -> LF] -> Int
fresh preds    = freshIndex (map ($ dummy) preds)
  where dummy = Const ""
```

The following function parses and translates declarative sentences.

```
process :: String -> [LF]
process string = map transS (parses string)
```

Wh-questions get a different treatment, for they translate into abstracts.

```
processW :: String -> [Abstract]
processW string = map transWH (parses string)
```

Here are some example calls:

```
P> process "Alice admired the princess that Atreyu gave
             the sword to."
[The (\ x2 conj[princess[x2],The (\ x1 sword[x1])
                    (\ x1 gave[atreyu,x1,x2])])
                    (\ x2 admired[alice,x2])]
P> processW "To whom did Atreyu give the dwarf that shuddered?"
[(\ x0 conj[person[x0],The (\ x1 conj[dwarf[x1],shuddered[x1]])
                    (\ x1 give[atreyu,x1,x0])])])]
```

The final step in the process from parsing to interpretation is left to you.

Exercise 9.16 Write functions for interpreting the logical forms from this section in an appropriate model.

9.9 Further Reading

Logics for talking about tree relations were proposed in [BGMV93] (modal logic) and in [BRVs95] (first-order logic). The binary relations on positions that were used in Section 9.1 can readily be described in logical terms.

Natural language parsing is assimilated to logical deduction in [PW83]. The bible of parsing in the context of formal language theory is [AU72]. Parsing natural language fragments with Prolog is the topic of [PS87]. Parser combinators in the context of functional programming are introduced in [Wad85] and receive further discussion in [Hut92]. Examples of parser combinators can also be found in [JS01]. The approach to the treatment of gaps with parser combinators in Section 9.7 is based on [Eij03].

Formally, extraction grammars are more powerful than context-free grammars, for they allow the definition of sequentially indexed languages. Sequentially indexed languages are a proper extension of context-free languages, and also of the linear indexed languages of [Gaz88]. We refer to [Eij07b] for further details.

A special-purpose programming language for developing multilingual natural language applications, with parsing at the core, is Grammatical Framework, or GF. GF is similar to Haskell, but specialized to grammar writing. See [Ran09] and `http://www.grammaticalframework.org`.

10

Handling Relations and Scoping

Summary

In this chapter we will interpret verb phrases as relations of various arities, using a type of arbitrary arity relations. The problem of encoding relations in type theory in such a way that the usual logical operations can be applied to them (relations should be 'conjoinable', as the jargon has it) has been studied extensively in the semantic literature. We will define conjunction, disjunction, and complementation on our relational types. Next we turn to the interpretation of determiner phrases as functions from $(n + 1)$-ary relations to n-ary relations, the interpretation of m-ary sequences of determiner phrases as functions from $(n + m)$-ary relations to n-ary relations, and to the handling of scope reversal for such functions.

10.1 Interpreting NP Lists

Instead of analysing the sentence *Every unicorn ate a lettuce leaf* as a relation between the CN property of being a unicorn and the VP property of eating lettuce leaves (namely the relation of inclusion), it is also possible to look at the complex expression *Every unicorn __ a lettuce leaf*, and interpret that as a function that takes a relation (a denotation of a transitive verb) and produces a truth value. Similarly, *Every unicorn was fed a lettuce leaf by some fairy* can be analysed as stating that the set of unicorns is included in the set of entities that were fed a lettuce leaf by some fairy, but it is also possible to look at the complex expression *Every unicorn __ a lettuce leaf by some fairy*, and even at *Every unicorn __ a lettuce leaf __ some fairy*. The interpretation of *Every unicorn __ a lettuce leaf by some fairy* is again a function from binary relations to truth values, the interpretation of *Every unicorn __ a lettuce leaf __ some fairy* is a function from ternary relations to truth values.

Following Keenan [Kee92] we call a function from properties (unary relations) to truth values a type $\langle 1 \rangle$ function, a function from binary relations to truth values

261

a type $\langle 2 \rangle$ function, and, in general, a function from n-ary relations to truth values a type $\langle n \rangle$ function.

A type $\langle 1 \rangle$ function f can be lifted to a function f' from $(n+1)$-ary relations R to n-ary relations $f'(R)$ by means of

$$f'(R) = \{\langle d_1, \ldots, d_n \rangle \mid f(\{d \mid \langle d_1, \ldots, d_n, d \rangle \in R\}) = 1\}.$$

These lifted type $\langle 1 \rangle$ functions can then be composed by means of

$$f' \circ g' = \lambda R \mapsto f'(g'(R)).$$

Here it is assumed, of course, that R has arity ≥ 2. The lifted type $\langle 2 \rangle$ function $f' \circ g'$ maps $(n+2)$-ary relations to n-ary relations.

Similarly, a type $\langle n \rangle$ function F can be lifted to a function from $(m+n)$-ary relations to m-ary relations, by means of

$$
\begin{aligned}
F'(R) \;=\; & \{\langle d_1, \ldots, d_m \rangle \mid \\
& F(\{\langle d_{m+1}, \ldots, d_{m+n} \rangle \mid \\
& \langle d_1, \ldots, d_m, d_{m+1}, \ldots, d_{m+n} \rangle \in R\}) = 1\}.
\end{aligned}
$$

Many type $\langle 2 \rangle$ functions can be decomposed in this way into pairs of type $\langle 1 \rangle$ functions. E.g. the type $\langle 2 \rangle$ function F that interprets the complex expression *Every unicorn __ a lettuce leaf* can be decomposed into a type $\langle 1 \rangle$ function g that interprets *a lettuce leaf* and a type $\langle 1 \rangle$ function f that interprets *every unicorn*, for $f' \circ g'$ equals F'. To illustrate this, we start with f and g; both are functions that map unary relations to truth values.

$$f = \lambda P \mapsto \forall x (\textit{Unicorn } x \to Px)$$
$$g = \lambda Q \mapsto \exists y (\textit{LettuceLeaf } y \wedge Qy)$$

Next we lift these functions to functions f' and g' that map $(n+1)$-ary relations to n-ary relations.

$$f' = \lambda R \mapsto \{\langle d_1, \ldots, d_n \rangle \mid f(\{d \mid \langle d_1, \ldots, d_n, d \rangle \in R\}) = 1\}$$
$$g' = \lambda R \mapsto \{\langle d_1, \ldots, d_n \rangle \mid f(\{d \mid \langle d_1, \ldots, d_n, d \rangle \in R\}) = 1\}$$

Now we can combine g' with a binary relation (e.g. *to eat*) in order to get a unary relation (expressing *to eat a lettuce leaf*), which we then can combine with f' in order to get a nullary relation, i.e. a truth value. Both these combinations decrease the arity of the input relation by one, or in other terms: both quantifiers bind one argument position. Alternatively, we can compose f' and g' to a function F' that maps $(n + 2)$-ary relations to n-ary relations in one step. This interprets the complex expression *Every unicorn ___ a lettuce leaf*. As an illustration, let us look at the concrete case of composing the two type $\langle 1 \rangle$ functions f and g, that map unary relations to truth values, into a type $\langle 2 \rangle$ function $f \circ g$, that maps binary relations to truth values. The result is

$$f \circ g = \lambda R \mapsto \forall x(Unicorn\ x \to \exists y(LettuceLeaf\ y \wedge Rxy)).$$

So *Every unicorn ___ a lettuce leaf* can be seen as a compound quantifier that is decomposable into the two quantifiers *every unicorn* and *a lettuce leaf*.

In [Kee92] it is demonstrated that there are cases where compound quantifiers are *not* decomposable. Keenan shows that the following sentence exhibits an example of non-decomposable type $\langle 2 \rangle$ quantification:

Different djinnis satisfied different wishes. (10.1)

For sentence (10.1) to make sense, we have to assume that there are at least two djinnis. The sentence is true if there is a one-to-one correspondence between djinnis and sets of wishes they satisfied. Thus, *Different djinnish ___ different wishes* is interpreted as the type $\langle 2 \rangle$ function expressing that its argument relation R satisfies the property that all the aR, with a ranging over djinnis, are different (here aR is used as shorthand for $\{x \mid Rax\}$), i.e. the set of objects that a bears R to. So, intuitively, *different djinnis* and *different wishes* cannot be interpreted independently, so *Different djinnis ___ different wishes* is not decomposable. Keenan has an ingenious method to prove this fact. He states and proves a theorem to the effect that for any two type $\langle 2 \rangle$ functions F, G that are reducible it holds that these functions are equal iff they act the same on Cartesian products, i.e. if for all subsets P, Q of the domain of discourse U it holds that $F(P \times Q) = G(P \times Q)$.

How can this be used to show that a type $\langle 2 \rangle$ function F is non-reducible? Here is how, for the example of (10.1). Let F be the type $\langle 2 \rangle$ function that interprets *different djinnis ___ different wishes*. Pick a universe containing at least three djinnis d_1, d_2, d_3 and at least two wishes w_1, w_2. Let $P \times Q$ be a product relation, i.e. a relation that links every object in P to every object in Q. If there are two djinnis not in P, then they bear $P \times Q$ to the same wishes, namely no wishes. If there are two djinnis in P, then the wishes they bear $P \times Q$ to are again the same, namely $Q \cap Wish$. Again, $F(P \times Q) = 0$. Let $\mathbf{0}$ be the type $\langle 1 \rangle$ function that is false for any argument. Then, by the above, $F(R) = \mathbf{0} \circ \mathbf{0}(R)$ for any product relation R. But obviously, F is different from the composition $\mathbf{0} \circ \mathbf{0}$, for F is true of $\{\langle d_1, w_1 \rangle, \langle d_2, w_2 \rangle\}$, and $\mathbf{0} \circ \mathbf{0}$ is not. Thus, by Keenan's theorem, F is not reducible.

Here are some further examples of quantifiers that Keenan shows to be not reducible.

> *Three knights in the castle dated the same princess.*   (10.2)
>
> *The women at the wedding all wore different hats.*   (10.3)
>
> *The trolls gave different answers to different questions.*   (10.4)

In this chapter we will interpret determiner phrase clusters as relation reducers, with a cluster consisting of n NPs interpreted as a type $\langle n \rangle$ function. In the cases where such an NP cluster interpretation is reducible to n type $\langle 1 \rangle$ functions, the reduction $f_1 \circ \cdots \circ f_n$ imposes a scope ordering on the NPs. This means that quantifier scoping can be handled by considering different orderings of the reducing type $\langle 1 \rangle$ functions, while taking care that the scope reorderings respect the relevant argument binding constraints. E.g. recall the interpretation of *Every unicorn ___ a lettuce leaf* above. The composition $f \circ g$ gave the scope order of the universal quantifier having scope over the existential quantifier. To reorder the scoping of $f \circ g$, we first define a swap operation S by means of

$$\mathbf{S} := \lambda R \lambda x \lambda y \mapsto (R\, y)\, x.$$

This reorders the outermost two argument places of a relation. The inverse scope reading of f and g can now be expressed as $g \circ f \circ \mathbf{S}$. This corresponds to

$$\lambda R \mapsto \exists y (\textit{LettuceLeaf } y \wedge \forall x (\textit{Unicorn } x \to Rxy)).$$

We will look at this way of reversing scope in a bit more detail in Section 10.5 below.

10.2 Generalized Relations

A binary relation on a set A can be viewed as a function of type $A \to \mathcal{P}(A)$. It maps elements a of A to subsets aR of A, where aR is again shorthand for

$$\{x \in A \mid Rax\}.$$

Equivalently, a binary relation can be viewed as a function of type $A \to A \to t$. It maps elements a of A to characteristic functions χ_a on A, where χ_a is given by $\chi_a(b) = 1$ iff Rab.

Similarly, a unary relation on a set A is a function of type $A \to t$, a ternary relation on a set A is a function of type $A \to A \to A \to t$, and so on. A special case is a nullary relation: this is just a truth value. Note that an $(n+1)$-ary relation on A can be viewed as a function from A to the type of n-ary relations over A.

What we want is a data type for arbitrary arity relations. Each instance of the data type should have a definite arity, but two instances may well have different arities.

But first, we declare the chapter module and import some relevant modules that were defined before. With the keyword `hiding` we specify functions that we don't want to be imported.

```
module HRAS where

import Data.List
import Model
import FSynF hiding (Form,Term,Var,Eq,Neg,
                     Impl,Equi,Conj,Disj)
import TCOM
import P
```

We will use the following auxiliary data type `RL a r`.

```
data RL a r = Zero r
            | Succ (RL a (a -> r))
```

This allows us to build relations starting from a given r. The two cases are r and $a \to r$. If we apply the constructor a second time, for `RL a (a -> r)`, we get $a \to r$ and $a \to a \to r$. If we apply the constructor for `RL a (a -> a -> r)` we get $a \to a \to r$ and $a \to a \to a \to r$, and so on.

The data type we need is a particular case of this where we start out from `Bool`:

```
type REL a = RL a Bool
```

What this says is that a relation either is nullary, in which case it is just a Boolean preceded by the tag `Zero`, or it is n-ary, with $n \geq 1$. This is indicated by the tag `Succ`. If a relation over objects of type a is n-ary, with $n \geq 1$, then it can be viewed as a function of type $a \to R_{n-1}$, where R_{n-1} indicates the type of $(n-1)$-ary relations. The arity of a relation can be determined by counting the occurrences of `Succ`:

```
arity :: RL a b -> Int
arity (Zero _) = 0
arity (Succ r) = succ (arity r)
```

Here is a general function for applying a relation to an argument. Precondition is that the relation is at least unary.

```
apply :: REL a -> a -> REL a
apply (Zero _) _ = error "no argument position left"
apply (Succ r) x = apply' r x

apply' :: RL a (a -> r) -> a -> RL a r
apply' (Zero f) x = Zero (f x)
apply' (Succ r) x = Succ (apply' r x)
```

The function illustrates the need for the auxiliary data type `RL a r`. At the point where `apply' (Zero f) x` gets defined, `Zero f` is not of type `REL a` but of type `RL a (a -> r)`, for `f` is a function, not a Boolean.

We will also need an operation for abstraction. Note that abstraction increases the arity by one. If `f` is a function that yields relations of arity 0, then we know that `f x` is of the form `Zero b`, where the Boolean `b` indicates whether `x` is in the relation or not. Note the extra argument for arity, and the use of an auxiliary function `abstract'`, of a more general type than `abstract`.

```
abstract :: Int -> (a -> REL a) -> REL a
abstract = abstract'

abstract' :: Int -> (a -> RL a b) -> RL a b
abstract' 0 f = Succ (Zero (\ x -> charF (f x)))
  where charF :: RL a r -> r
        charF (Zero f) = f
        charF (Succ _) = error "arity error"
abstract' n f = Succ (abstract' (n-1) (\ x -> relF (f x)))
  where relF :: RL a r -> RL a (a -> r)
        relF (Zero _) = error "nullary rel"
        relF (Succ r) = r
```

Exercise 10.1 Explain why the auxiliary function `abstract'` is necessary.

A binary relation over objects of type a can be viewed as a function of type $a \rightarrow a \rightarrow t$, or, uncurried, of type $(a, a) \rightarrow t$, a ternary relation over objects of type a as a function of type $a \rightarrow a \rightarrow a \rightarrow t$, or, uncurried, of type $(a, a, a) \rightarrow t$,

and so on. Here are functions for encoding relations of various fixed arities into
RELs (it is assumed that the relations are curried).

```
encode0 :: Bool -> REL a
encode0 b = Zero b

encode1 :: (a -> Bool) -> REL a
encode1 f = Succ (Zero f)

encode2 :: (a -> a -> Bool) -> REL a
encode2 f = Succ (Succ (Zero f))

encode3 :: (a -> a -> a -> Bool) -> REL a
encode3 f = Succ (Succ (Succ (Zero f)))
```

Conversely, we can map 0-ary relations to type `Bool`, unary relations to type
`a -> Bool`, and so on. Note that we need a separate decoding function for each
arity, because the decoding fixes the result type. Here are two examples:

```
decode0 :: REL a -> Bool
decode0 (Zero b) = b
decode0 r        = error ("relation of arity " ++ ar)
        where ar = show (arity r)

decode1 :: REL a -> a -> Bool
decode1 (Succ (Zero f)) = f
decode1 r                   = error ("relation of arity " ++ ar)
                where ar = show (arity r)
```

We can think of `REL a` as curried: relations of this type take their arguments
one by one. Here is a general function for list-uncurrying them. A list-uncurried
function for an arbitrary arity relation is a function that takes it arguments as a list,
where the length of the list is the arity. The general type is `[a] -> Bool`.

```
listUncurry :: REL a -> [a] -> Bool
listUncurry    (Zero b) []     = b
listUncurry r@(Succ _) (x:xs) = listUncurry (apply r x) xs
```

If there is a finite domain, it is of course also possible to represent a function of arity n as a list of lists, with the element lists all of length n. The following function gives a flexible means of representing a relation as a list of lists.

```
rel2lists :: [a] -> REL a -> [[a]]
rel2lists domain (Zero b) = [[] | b ]
rel2lists domain (Succ r) =
   [ x: tuple | x      <- domain,
                tuple <-
                  rel2lists domain (apply (Succ r) x) ]
```

Exercise 10.2 Explain why the last line of the code of `rel2lists` does apply (Succ r) instead of just `r`.

So why didn't we use the type `[[a]]` as the type of arbitrary arity relations in the first place? The trouble is that the type `[[a]]` does not guarantee a fixed arity in the way `REL a` does. Translating from `REL a` to `[[a]]` yields lists that are all of the same length, with the length determined by the arity of the relation. But the type `[[a]]` is more general than that. List members can have different lengths, which is undesirable for the representation of relations.

For good measure, here are conversions from unary, binary and ternary predicates to lists of lists:

```
upred2lists :: [a] -> (a -> Bool) -> [[a]]
upred2lists domain p = [ [x]     | x <- filter p domain ]

bpred2lists :: [a] -> (a -> a -> Bool) -> [[a]]
bpred2lists domain p = [ [x,y]   | x <- domain,
                                   y <- domain,
                                   p x y            ]
tpred2lists :: [a] -> (a -> a -> a -> Bool) -> [[a]]
tpred2lists domain p = [ [x,y,z] | x <- domain,
                                   y <- domain,
                                   z <- domain,
                                   p x y z          ]
```

This gives:

```
HRAS> tpred2lists entities give
[[A,E,S],[T,S,X]]
```

How do we convert from lists of lists (all of the same length) to RELs? First note that for this we have to know the arity, for if the arity is unknown, there is no way of dealing with the empty list of lists. The following function gives the conversion.

```
lists2rel ::  Eq a => Int -> [[a]] -> REL a
lists2rel 0 [[]] = Zero True
lists2rel 0 []   = Zero False
lists2rel n xss  = abstract (n-1) r
      where r x = let yss = filter (\ xs -> head xs == x) xss
                  in  lists2rel (n-1) (map tail yss)
```

When this is applied to a list of lists that are not all of the same length, a program error is generated (because of the attempt to access the head of an empty list). Finally, here is a converse to list uncurrying:

```
listCurry :: Int -> ([a] -> Bool) -> REL a
listCurry 0 f = Zero (f [])
listCurry n f = abstract (n-1) g
  where g x    = listCurry (n-1) (h x)
        h x xs = f (x:xs)
```

10.3 Boolean Algebras of Relations

In this section we define generalizations of the Boolean operations to relations. Conjoining of relations of the same arity is a generalization of conjunction for Booleans. The result of conjoining relations r and s is called the Boolean meet of r and s, and is often denoted with $r \sqcap s$. It is implemented in terms of a general function for lifting relations (of the same arity) for a given Boolean operation:

```
liftOp :: (Bool -> Bool -> Bool) -> REL a -> REL a -> REL a
liftOp op (Zero b)   (Zero c)   = Zero (op b c)
liftOp op r@(Succ _) s@(Succ _) =
  abstract n (\ x -> liftOp op (apply r x) (apply s x))
    where n = arity r - 1
liftOp op _          _          = error "arity mismatch"
```

In terms of this, relation conjunction is defined by doing a relational lift with conjunction:

```
conjR :: REL a -> REL a -> REL a
conjR = liftOp (&&)
```

Disjoining relations works the same way. The result of disjoining r and s is called the Boolean join of r and s, and is denoted with $r \sqcup s$.

```
disjR :: REL a -> REL a -> REL a
disjR = liftOp (||)
```

Finally, here is an operation for taking the complement of a relation. The complement (negation) of a relation r is often written as $\bar{r}$.

```
negR :: REL a -> REL a
negR (Zero b)   = Zero (not b)
negR r@(Succ _) = abstract n (\x -> negR (apply r x))
      where n = arity r - 1
```

These definitions illustrate that relations of the same arity form a Boolean algebra [DP90, Hal63].

These operations are what is needed for performing logical relations on complex VPs, to get interpretations for *to hurt but not kill*, *to love or admire*, *to give or sell*, and so on. If *Hurt* is the binary relation that interprets *to hurt*, and *Kill* the binary relation that interprets *to kill*, then *Hurt* $\sqcap$ $\overline{Kill}$ interprets *to hurt but not kill*, and so on.

Here is an illustration using the implementation:

```
HRAS> rel2lists entities (disjR (encode2 love) (encode2 help))
[[B,S],[D,M],[R,S],[S,B],[V,V],[W,W],[Y,E]]
```

Note that the generalized operations for conjunction, disjunction, and negation are in fact generalizations of conjunction, disjunction, and negation for Booleans. Booleans can be viewed as 0-ary relations, and we have generalized the operations to n-ary relations, for arbitrary n.

Exercise 10.3 Define and implement the relation of entailment between n-ary relations.

10.4 Flexible Types for NP Interpretations

There is extensive semantic literature on the need for flexible type assignment to syntactic categories (see, e.g., [Hen93]). Many of the arguments for this have to do with the need to account for various scoping ambiguities resulting from the interaction of quantified NPs with other quantified NPs or with intensional verb contexts.

Now note that the type REL a is flexible, for this type can do duty for the whole family of types t, $a \to t$, $a \to a \to t$, and so on. We intend to use the flexible type REL a for the interpretations of verbs, and we will perform a 'flexible lift' on NP interpretations, so that an NP can be viewed as an operation on verb meanings, i.e. as a function of type REL a -> REL a. For this perspective on the semantics of NPs, compare [Kee87, Kee92].

Let's define a type for generalized quantifier operations. We will call them KQ, for *Keenan quantifier*:

```
type KQ a = REL a -> REL a
```

An important conversion function that we need is that from a characteristic function of properties to a function that maps relations to relations. We will use this to lift the type of NP interpretations.

Consider the problem of applying a function of type (a -> Bool) -> Bool not to a property (type a -> Bool), but to a relation with arity > 1. Note that a -> Bool can be viewed as the type of a relation of arity 1, and Bool as the type of a relation of arity 0. Thus, (a -> Bool) -> Bool is the type of reduction of 1-ary to 0-ary relations.

So how about the general case: the reductions of $(n + 1)$-ary relations to n-ary relations? The general shape of a relation of arity $(n + 1)$ is

$$\lambda x_1 \ldots \lambda x_n \lambda y \mapsto r. \tag{10.5}$$

Here, r is a Boolean expression (i.e. of type Bool).

Converting a property function f into a relation transformer is done by reducing that relation by recursion. If the argument relation has the form $\lambda y \mapsto r$, with r of type Bool, then property function f can be applied to it, yielding a Boolean $f (\lambda y \mapsto r)$. If the argument relation has the form $\lambda x_1 \ldots \lambda x_n \lambda y \mapsto r$, the new relation is given by (10.6).

$$\lambda x_1 \ldots \lambda x_n \mapsto f (\lambda y \mapsto r) \tag{10.6}$$

So this is what reduction of a relation $\lambda x_1 \ldots \lambda x_n \lambda y \mapsto r$ should yield. Our obvious next question is: how is the operation defined that yields this result?

The recursion that defines the operation **R** that reduces f with $\lambda x_1 \ldots \lambda x_n \lambda y \mapsto r$ can be expressed as follows:

$$
\begin{aligned}
\mathbf{R}\, f\, (\lambda y \mapsto r) &:= f\, (\lambda y \mapsto r) \\
\mathbf{R}\, f\, (\lambda x_1 \ldots \lambda x_n \lambda y \mapsto r) &:= \lambda x \mapsto \mathbf{R}\, f\, ((\lambda x_1 \ldots \lambda x_n \lambda y \mapsto r)\, x).
\end{aligned}
$$

This is precisely the conversion that we need for lifting the type of generalized quantifiers to that of relation transformers. Hence the name `liftQ` of the implementation.

```
liftQ :: ((a -> Bool) -> Bool) -> KQ a
liftQ f r
  | arity r == 0 = error "no argument position left"
  | arity r == 1 = Zero (f (decode1 r))
  | otherwise    = abstract (n-1) g
    where g x    = liftQ f (apply r x)
          n      = arity r - 1
```

Note that if `rel` has arity $(n+1)$, then `liftQ f rel` has arity n. Thus, `liftQ f` is indeed a reducer of $(n + 1)$-arity relations to n-ary relations.

10.5 Scope Reversal of Quantifiers

We have defined generalized negation and generalized quantification as maps from relations to relations, i.e. operators of type `REL a -> REL a`. A difference between these two kinds of operators is that generalized negation does not reduce the arity of its argument relation, whereas generalized quantification does. The relational operator interpretation of an NP reduces the arity of its argument relation by 1, for applying the generalized quantifier to the relation consumes one of the arguments of the relation.

Now suppose we want to swap the scopes of two generalized quantifier operations, as sketched in Section 10.1 above. We can view the scope swap as an operation that takes two Keenan quantifiers and produces a new Keenan quantifier that has the effect of applying the quantifiers with their order reversed. Thus, the swap takes two operators Q_1 and Q_2 and creates a new operator that should express the effect of giving Q_2 scope over Q_1.

Recall that we could not simply define the scope swapping operation as $Q_2 \cdot Q_1$, for performing Q_2 after Q_1 and thereby giving Q_2 wide scope. The problem was that this switches the argument positions that the operators work on. Look at it like this. In $Q_1(Q_2 R)$, Q_2 gets applied to R first, so it applies to the outermost argument of R. Suppose R has arity n, then Q_2 applies to the n-th argument, and produces a new relation $Q_2 R$ of arity $(n-1)$. Next, Q_1 applies to the outermost argument of $Q_2 R$, and produces a new relation $Q_1(Q_2 R)$ of arity $(n-2)$.

Now suppose we want to perform the applications in the opposite order. Then Q_1 has to apply to R first, but Q_1 still should apply to the $(n-1)$-th argument position of R. Next, we should get a new relation $Q_1 R$, and Q_2 should apply to what used to be the n-th argument of R. To bring this about, we have to define the reverse scoping as follows:

$$Q_2 \cdot Q_1 \cdot \mathbf{S},$$

where S is the swap operation as defined in Section 10.1:

$$\mathbf{S} := \lambda R \lambda x \lambda y \mapsto (R \ y) \ x.$$

Since we have implementations of abstraction and application of relations, it is easy to give an implementation of this argument swap operation:

```
swap :: REL a -> REL a
swap r    = abstract n (\ x ->
                abstract (n-1) (\ y ->
                   (apply (apply r y) x)))
  where n = arity r - 1
```

And here is the implementation of quantifier scope reversal itself:

```
qscopeReversal :: KQ a -> KQ a -> KQ a
qscopeReversal q1 q2 = q2 . q1 . swap
```

This says that for scope reversal, we first swap the two outermost argument places of the relation, and next apply the two quantifiers in reversed order.

For a scope reversal of a quantifier and a negation no argument swapping is needed, as the negation operation is not an arity reducer.

10.6 Interpreting Verbs as Arbitrary Arity Relations

We will interpret verbs as arbitrary arity relations, type REL a. In a full-fledged theory of thematic role assignment, the arity of the relation will depend on the number of realized theta roles of the verb, but we will gloss over the details.

Theta theory is the theory of the way in which thematic roles like *Agent*, *Patient* or *Theme*, *Cause*, *Instrument*, and so on, function in the thematic structure of predicates in the lexicon and, more generally, in syntax. In Government and Binding theory [Cho81] and in the later Minimalist Program [Cho92], lexical entries for verbs are provided with a *theta grid* in which the thematic roles are given that the verb assigns. The verb *give*, e.g., would assign three thematic roles, one for *Agent*, one for *Goal*, and one for *Theme*.

Although thematic relations have been with us for a long time – early references for an analysis in terms of 'abstract thematic roles' are [Gru65] and [Jac72] – it seems fair to say that most linguistic work in theta theory is informal and speculative. Also, the theory of thematic roles has received relatively little attention from formal semanticists (with [Dow89] as one of the exceptions). There is no general agreement on the number of theta roles that should be distinguished. [Rei00] came up with the proposal to link theta roles to feature clusters defined in terms of $\pm c$ (c for 'cause') and $\pm m$ (m for 'mental'). There are 9 consistent subsets of the feature set $\{+c, -c, +m, -m\}$, and they can get linked to the following nine theta roles:

Agent	$[+c+m]$	Instrument	$[+c-m]$
Experiencer	$[-c+m]$	Patient, Theme	$[-c-m]$
Cause	$[+c]$	Animate	$[+m]$
Source, Subject Matter	$[-m]$	Goal	$[-c]$
None	$[\,]$		

The thematic role assignments of a verb are part of the link between language and reality (the realm of things outside language that language is about). To implement thematic roles by means of type constraints in semantics would be a mistake, for in *Little Mook kicked the door* and *Little Mook kicked Alice*, *the door* and *Alice* are both in the thematic role of *Patient*, but this cannot be taken to imply that *the door* and *Alice* have to be things of the same kind (except in the trivial sense of being the type of things that can receive kicks).

Verb interpretations have a number of roles, identifiable by indices $1, \ldots, n$. Here is an example of a predicate:

give	1	2	3
	Agent	Goal	Theme

If Atreyu gives Dorothy a sword, then Atreyu is the agent, Dorothy is the goal, and the sword is the theme. Of course, this is just for illustration. There may also be a theta role for location or time, and perhaps there are still other roles. In general, to interpret a predicate with n thematic roles, the predicate will get as its denotation an n-ary relation.

For a rudimentary version of Theta Theory it is enough to be able to extract a new relation from a given relation by specifying a list of argument positions. For the implementation we need to be able to pick the entity at an index from a list. For this, we use a predefined Haskell function. The only snag is that !! computes from index 0, whereas we would like to start at index 1.

```
role :: Int -> [a] -> a
role n es = es !! (n-1)
```

Extracting a list of roles from a list:

```
roles :: [Int] -> [a] -> [a]
roles []      _  = []
roles (i:is) es = role i es : roles is es
```

Using this, we implement the extraction function first for lists of lists:

```
extr :: Eq a => [Int] -> [[a]] -> [[a]]
extr is ess = nub [ roles is es | es <- ess ]
```

The following exercise explains why nub is necessary in this definition.

Exercise 10.4 Find an example of a list of lists relList, without duplicates, and with all members of relList of the same length, and an example of a list of positive integers is, such that [roles is es | es <- relList] has duplicates.

Next, we can convert this to the type Rel by means of rel2lists and lists2rel, as follows:

```
extract :: Eq a => [a] -> [Int] -> REL a -> REL a
extract domain is r =
  lists2rel n (extr is (rel2lists domain r))
      where n = length is
```

Thus, if r is a ternary relation, then extract [2,1,3] r is the relation that is like r except for the fact that its first two argument positions are swapped. We will use the extraction function below in the implementation of scope reversals.

```
extr2lists :: Eq a => [a] -> [Int] -> REL a -> [[a]]
extr2lists domain is =
  rel2lists domain . extract domain is
```

Some examples to check what we have done:

```
HRAS> extr2lists entities [1,2]    (encode2 love)
[[B,S],[R,S],[Y,E]]
```

```
HRAS> extr2lists entities [2,1]    (encode2 love)
[[E,Y],[S,B],[S,R]]
HRAS> extr2lists entities [1,1]    (encode2 love)
[[B,B],[R,R],[Y,Y]]
HRAS> extr2lists entities [1,2,3] (encode3 give)
[[A,E,S],[T,S,X]]
HRAS> extr2lists entities [2,3,1] (encode3 give)
[[E,S,A],[S,X,T]]
```

Next, we turn to the relational interpretation of verb phrases. First we lump all kinds of verbs together in a single data type.

```
data VerbPhrase = V1 VP | V2 TV | V3 DV

instance Show VerbPhrase where
  show (V1 vp) = show vp
  show (V2 vp) = show vp
  show (V3 vp) = show vp
```

And here is how to interpret them all as arbitrary arity relations:

```
relVP :: VerbPhrase -> REL Entity
relVP (V1 Laughed)   = encode1 laugh
relVP (V1 Cheered)   = encode1 cheer
relVP (V1 Shuddered) = encode1 shudder
relVP (V2 Loved)     = encode2 love
relVP (V2 Admired)   = encode2 admire
relVP (V2 Helped)    = encode2 help
relVP (V2 Defeated)  = encode2 defeat
relVP (V3 Gave)      = encode3 give
```

10.7 Relational Interpretation of NPs

Generalized quantifier interpretations of NPs were given in Chapter 7, by means of the function intNP. All we have to do now is to lift these to the type of Keenan quantifiers:

```
relNP :: NP -> KQ Entity
relNP = liftQ . intNP
```

The next step is to interpret a list of NPs as a Keenan quantifier. If the NP list is empty, the Keenan quantifier is just the identity function on relations (note that this is a Keenan quantifier). If the NP list is non-empty, we use function composition. This works because each NP is interpreted as a Keenan quantifier, and these Keenan quantifiers are relation transforming functions. So it does make sense to apply these functions one by one.

```
relNPs :: [NP] -> KQ Entity
relNPs [] = id
relNPs (np:nps) = relNP np . relNPs nps
```

This definition has the effect of giving the first NP on the list scope over the other NPs, for the relation transformer that is applied last will have widest scope. So in fact what we have done is implement a fixed scoping mechanism where the first element on the list outscopes the next, and so on. If the order of the NP list reflects surface word order, our scoping mechanism gives surface scope order. For generating other possible scopings, this will need to be modified. But first we give an interpretation mechanism for sentences. We will assume, just for simplicity of exposition, that a sentence consists of a list of NPs and a VP.

```
relSent :: [NP] -> VerbPhrase -> REL Entity
relSent nps vp = (relNPs nps) (relVP vp)
```

If all goes well and the arity of the verb phrase relation matches the length of the NP list, the outcome of `relSent` is a nullary relation, i.e. a Boolean. This gives the following evaluation function:

```
eval :: [NP] -> VerbPhrase -> Bool
eval nps vp
  | length nps == arity (relVP vp) = decode0 (relSent nps vp)
  | otherwise                      = error "arity mismatch"
```

Here are some examples:

```
HRAS> eval [NP1 Some Dwarf] (V1 Cheered)
False
```

```
HRAS> eval [NP1 Every Dwarf,SnowWhite] (V2 Loved)
True
HRAS> eval [NP1 Every Dwarf,NP1 Some Giant] (V2 Loved)
False
HRAS> eval [NP1 Some Giant,NP1 Every Dwarf] (V2 Loved)
False
HRAS> eval [NP1 Some Giant,NP1 Every Dwarf] (V2 Helped)
False
HRAS> eval [NP1 Some Giant,NP1 Some Dwarf] (V2 Helped)
False
HRAS> eval [NP1 Every Dwarf,NP1 Some Girl] (V2 Admired)
True
HRAS> eval [NP1 Some Girl,NP1 Every Dwarf] (V2 Admired)
False
HRAS> eval [NP1 Some Girl,NP1 Some Sword,NP1 The Giant]
      (V3 Gave)
False
```

10.8 Quantifier Scoping

We show in this section that the ordered list of realized theta roles on a verb concept allows us to formalize and implement a particularly simple and elegant quantifier scoping algorithm. Our approach to scoping can be viewed as a 'clean' version of Richard Montague's quantifying-in rule (cf. page 181). The cleanup is made possible by the fact that our relational approach avoids the use of free variables in syntax or semantics. Our quantifier scoping algorithm can also be viewed as a 'clean' version of the quantifier storage approach proposed in [Coo75, Coo83] (cleaner, again, because no free variables are involved).

If we want to consider all different scope orders of n quantifiers, then we have to look at the $n! = 1 \times \cdots \times n$ different permutations of the quantifiers. We start out from a general function that gives all the permutations of a finite list:

```
perms :: [a] -> [[a]]
perms []     = [[]]
perms (x:xs) = concat (map (insrt x) (perms xs))
  where
    insrt :: a -> [a] -> [[a]]
    insrt x []     = [[x]]
    insrt x (y:ys) = (x:y:ys) : map (y:) (insrt x ys)
```

This gives:

```
HRAS> perms [1,2,3]
[[1,2,3],[2,1,3],[2,3,1],[1,3,2],[3,1,2],[3,2,1]]
```

In our case, where we have verb concepts with realized theta roles together with lists of NPs corresponding to the realized roles, all we have to do is permute the theta role list and the NP list in parallel.

```
permsInPar :: [a] -> [b] -> [([a],[b])]
permsInPar xs ys = map unzip (perms (zip xs ys))
```

This gives:

```
HRAS> permsInPar [1,2,3] [5,6,7]
[([1,2,3],[5,6,7]),([2,1,3],[6,5,7]),([2,3,1],[6,7,5]),
 ([1,3,2],[5,7,6]),([3,1,2],[7,5,6]),([3,2,1],[7,6,5])]
```

Now we can permute NP lists and adjust relations to the permutation, in parallel, as follows.

```
permRelNPs :: Eq a  =>
                [a]     ->
                REL a ->
                [NP]    -> [([Int],REL a,[NP])]
permRelNPs domain rel nps =
  [ (perm,extract domain perm rel,pnps) |
      (perm,pnps) <- permsInPar [1..length nps] nps   ]
```

The first element of the result triple is a list indicating the way surface scope order got permuted, the second element gives the relation with permuted theta roles, and the third element gives the permuted NP list.

The scope algorithm will produce a list of pairs consisting of an indication of the way in which surface order got permuted, and a Boolean for the truth value of the interpretation of the sentence under this scope ordering. To generate all scopings of a simple sentence we permute its NP list (the list of NPs consisting of the sentence subject together with the list of verb complements) in parallel with the roles of the relation interpreting the verb, and evaluate the results.

```
allScopings :: [NP] -> VerbPhrase -> [([Int],Bool)]
allScopings nps vp =
 [(perm, decode0 ((relNPs pnps) newrel))
    | (perm, newrel, pnps) <-
           permRelNPs entities (relVP vp) nps,
           arity (relVP vp) == length nps        ]
```

This gives:

```
HRAS> allScopings [NP1 No Dwarf,NP1 Some Girl] (V2 Admired)
[([1,2],False),([2,1],True)]
```

This indicates that under the surface scope order reading of the NPs the sentence is false in the example model, but under the reverse scope order reading of the NPs ('For some girl there is no dwarf who admires her') the sentence is true.

Exercise 10.5 In our treatment of the semantics, we do direct interpretation in the model. As an alternative to this, implement a translation function from NP lists and Verb Phrases to lists of logical forms, with different logical forms for different scopings.

10.9 Underspecified Logical Form

Instead of direct interpretation we can also look at scoping at the level of logical forms. We will reuse the logical forms from Chapter 9. The counterpart of an arbitrary arity relation is a relational logical form:

```
data RForm = MkRForm [Int] LF deriving Eq

instance Show RForm where
   show (MkRForm [] lf) = show lf
   show (MkRForm is lf) = " \\" ++ show (map Var is)
                               ++ " -> " ++ show lf
```

A relational form is basically a lambda abstract over a list of individual variables in a logical form, and the show function is designed to make this clear. It is important to be able to compute fresh variable indices for relational forms.

```
freshIdx :: RForm -> Int
freshIdx (MkRForm _ lf) = freshIndex [lf]
```

Keenan quantifiers at the logical form level are functions from relational forms to relational forms:

```
type KQLF   = RForm -> RForm
```

Such functions cannot be displayed directly. To remedy this, we define a data type KOp of Keenan operators, and implement a show function for them. We can display them by means of relational abstraction, where the abstracted relation has an arbitrary type. The Int argument of the operator sets the Keenan type of the operation.

```
data KOp = MkKOp Int KQLF

instance Show KOp where
  show (MkKOp n q) =
   "\\ R -> " ++ show (q (MkRForm is (Rel "R" is')))
      where k     = freshIdx rform
            rform = q (MkRForm js (Rel "R" js'))
            js    = take n (repeat 0)
            js'   = map Var js
            is    = map (+k) [0..n-1]
            is'   = map Var is
```

To see what this does, consider the operation of negation, viewed as a Keenan quantifier of type $\langle 0 \rangle$.

```
neg :: KQLF
neg (MkRForm is lf) = MkRForm is (Neg lf)

ng :: KOp
ng = MkKOp 0 neg
```

The operator can be displayed, as follows:

```
HRAS> ng
\ R -> ~R[]
```

Lifting a NP logical form to a Keenan quantifier logical form is done by:

```
liftKQLF :: ((Term -> LF) -> LF) -> KQLF
liftKQLF np (MkRForm [] lf)
   = error "No argument position left"
liftKQLF np (MkRForm (i:is) lf)
   = MkRForm is (np (\ x -> (subi i x lf)))
```

This uses substitution for an index, which is a generalization of the substitution function subst from Chapter 9.

```
substi :: Int -> Term -> Term -> Term
substi i x (Const name)           = Const name
substi i x (Var n) | n == i       = x
                   | otherwise    = Var n
                   | x == Var n = error "bad substitution"

subi :: Int -> Term -> LF -> LF
subi i x (Rel name ts)  = Rel name (map (substi i x) ts)
subi i x (Eq t1 t2)     = Eq (substi i x t1) (substi i x t2)
subi i x (Neg lf)       = Neg (subi i x lf)
subi i x (Impl lf1 lf2) = Impl (subi i x lf1) (subi i x lf2)
subi i x (Equi lf1 lf2) = Equi (subi i x lf1) (subi i x lf2)
subi i x (Conj lfs)     = Conj (map (subi i x) lfs)
subi i x (Disj lfs)     = Disj (map (subi i x) lfs)
subi i x (Qt gq abs1 abs2) =
               Qt gq (sbi i x abs1) (sbi i x abs2)

sbi :: Int -> Term -> Abstract -> Abstract
sbi i x (MkAbstract j lf)
  | i == j    = MkAbstract 0 lf
  | otherwise = MkAbstract j (subi i x lf)
```

Logical forms for verb phrases are constructed as usual:

```
lfVerbPhrase :: VerbPhrase -> RForm
lfVerbPhrase (V1 Laughed)   =
  MkRForm [1]    (Rel "laugh"    [Var 1])
lfVerbPhrase (V1 Cheered)   =
  MkRForm [1]    (Rel "cheer"    [Var 1])
```

```
lfVerbPhrase (V1 Shuddered) =
  MkRForm [1]     (Rel "shudder" [Var 1])
lfVerbPhrase (V2 Loved)      =
  MkRForm [1,2]   (Rel "love"    [Var 2,Var 1])
lfVerbPhrase (V2 Admired)    =
  MkRForm [1,2]   (Rel "admire"  [Var 2,Var 1])
lfVerbPhrase (V2 Helped)     =
  MkRForm [1,2]   (Rel "help"    [Var 2,Var 1])
lfVerbPhrase (V2 Defeated)   =
  MkRForm [1,2]   (Rel "defeat"  [Var 2,Var 1])
lfVerbPhrase (V3 Gave)       =
  MkRForm [1,2,3] (Rel "give"    [Var 3,Var 2,Var 1])
```

These can be displayed nicely:

```
HRAS> lfVerbPhrase (V3 Gave)
 \[x1,x2,x3] -> give[x3,x2,x1]
```

Translation of Noun Phrases proceeds by lifting their Montague-style logical forms to the level of Keenan quantifiers.

```
trNP :: NP -> KQLF
trNP = liftKQLF . lfNP
```

Montague style logical forms are given by:

```
lfNP :: NP -> (Term -> LF) -> LF
lfNP SnowWhite    = \ p -> p (Const "SnowWhite" )
lfNP Alice        = \ p -> p (Const "Alice"     )
lfNP Dorothy      = \ p -> p (Const "Dorothy"   )
lfNP Goldilocks   = \ p -> p (Const "Goldilocks" )
lfNP LittleMook   = \ p -> p (Const "LittleMook" )
lfNP Atreyu       = \ p -> p (Const "Atreyu"    )
lfNP (NP1 det cn) = (lfDET det) (lfCN cn)
```

Again, if we make these Keenan quantifiers into operators of the right type, we can display them:

```
opNP :: NP -> KOp
opNP = MkKOp 1 . trNP
```

This gives:

```
HRAS> opNP Alice
\ R -> R[Alice]
HRAS> opNP (NP1 Some Dwarf)
\ R -> Some (\ x1 dwarf[x1]) (\ x1 R[x1])
```

Logical forms for CNs are as usual:

```
lfCN :: CN -> Term -> LF
lfCN Girl     = \ t -> Rel "girl"     [t]
lfCN Boy      = \ t -> Rel "boy"      [t]
lfCN Princess = \ t -> Rel "princess" [t]
lfCN Dwarf    = \ t -> Rel "dwarf"    [t]
lfCN Giant    = \ t -> Rel "giant"    [t]
lfCN Wizard   = \ t -> Rel "wizard"   [t]
lfCN Sword    = \ t -> Rel "sword"    [t]
lfCN Dagger   = \ t -> Rel "dagger"   [t]
```

Logical forms for determiners are the following:

```
lfDET :: DET -> (Term -> LF) -> (Term -> LF) -> LF
lfDET Some = \ p q -> let i = fresh[p,q] in
              Qt Sm (MkAbstract i (p (Var i)))
                    (MkAbstract i (q (Var i)))
lfDET Every = \ p q -> let i = fresh[p,q] in
               Qt All (MkAbstract i (p (Var i)))
                      (MkAbstract i (q (Var i)))
lfDET No = \ p q -> let i = fresh[p,q] in
            Neg (Qt Sm (MkAbstract i (p (Var i)))
                       (MkAbstract i (q (Var i))))
lfDET The = \ p q -> let i = fresh[p,q] in
             Qt Th (MkAbstract i (p (Var i)))
                   (MkAbstract i (q (Var i)))
```

Again, we consider a list of NPs followed by a verb phrase as a sentence. Here are logical forms for sentences.

```
lfSent :: [NP] -> VerbPhrase -> RForm
lfSent []         vp = lfVerbPhrase vp
lfSent (np:nps) vp = trNP np (lfSent nps vp)
```

This gives:

```
HRAS> lfSent [Alice] (V1 Shuddered)
shudder[Alice]
HRAS> lfSent [Alice,Dorothy] (V2 Loved)
love[Alice,Dorothy]
HRAS> lfSent [NP1 Some Dwarf,SnowWhite] (V2 Loved)
Some (\ x1 dwarf[x1]) (\ x1 love[x1,SnowWhite])
```

The advantage of the present approach is that we can also represent underspecified logical forms, like this:

```
uForm :: [NP] -> VerbPhrase -> ([KOp],RForm)
uForm nps vp = (f nps, lfVerbPhrase vp)
    where f = map (MkKOp 1 . trNP)
```

An underspecified form consists of a list of Keenan operators followed by a relational form that the operators have to apply to. By permuting the order in tandem with adjustment of the relational form, all the possible readings are created.

```
HRAS> uForm [NP1 Some Dwarf,NP1 Every Princess] (V2 Loved)
([\ R -> Some (\ x1 dwarf[x1]) (\ x1 R[x1]),
  \ R -> All (\ x1 princess[x1]) (\ x1 R[x1])],
 \[x1,x2] -> love[x2,x1])
```

10.10 Further Reading

In [Mus89a, Mus89b] it is shown that relations instead of functions can be taken as the basic ingredients of type theory. Our approach is slightly different, for our implementation of relations is based on recursive data types. Recursive data types are treated in any textbook on functional programming. See, e.g., [RL99] for an account of recursive data types in Haskell.

The linguist Ed Keenan pointed out the importance of type $\langle n \rangle$ functions for natural language semantics. See [Kee92] for many examples of irreducible type $\langle n \rangle$ functions, i.e. functions of type $\langle n \rangle$ that cannot be represented as compositions of unary functions. See [BS94] for graphical representations of irreducibility arguments. The notion of (ir)reducibility is generalized in [Eij05], extending work of [Dek03]. A quantifier is reducible if it can be represented as a composition of quantifiers of lesser, but not necessarily unary, types. [Eij05] proposes a direct criterion for reducibility, and establishes a normal form theorem for reduction. With these formal tools it can be established that natural language has examples of type $\langle n \rangle$ quantificational expressions that cannot be reduced to any composition of quantifiers of lesser degree. A comprehensive overview of the semantics of quantification, in natural language and in logic, is given in [PW06].

There is a vast literature on ambiguity, underspecification, and logical form, with fancy names like Underspecified Discourse Representation Theory and Minimal Recursion Semantics; see [DP96] for an overview. We believe that the sketch in Section 10.9 captures the essence of the issues involved. It certainly makes clear that claims to the effect that lambda calculus is unsuitable for representing underspecification are unfounded.

11

Continuation Passing Style Semantics

Summary

In this chapter we are going to show an alternative way of treating quantifiers and their scoping, based on the concept of continuations. Continuations in computer science abstract over the state of the computation, and add the future computation from the present state as an extra parameter. The chapter starts with a section on continuation style programming. Next, we move to applications in computational semantics. Continuations in computational linguistics abstract over the linguistic context of an expression and introduce it as an explicit parameter in the meaning computation. We will see how computing with continuations will allow quantifiers in object position to take scope over the whole sentence, and how quantifier scope ambiguities can be derived by imposing different regimes on the order in which the quantifier meanings are computed.

```
module CPSS where

import FSynF
import Model
import MCWPL
```

11.1 Continuation Passing Style Programming

To see how continuations work in Haskell, let us start with the simplest possible example: a function of type `a -> b`.

To lift a function f of this type to a continuation passing style (CPS) function means that instead of just letting f compute its value for some argument x, we pass

287

that value to some arbitrary *other* function that encodes 'what to do next'. Here is a general way of doing that:

```
mkc :: (a -> b) -> a -> (b -> r) -> r
mkc f x next = next (f x)
```

Let us use this for applying the powers of two function (2^) to an argument, and next show the result:

```
CPSS> mkc (2^) 4 show
"16"
```

Similarly, we can apply the function to an argument, and next apply it again:

```
CPSS> mkc (2^) 4 (2^)
65536
```

If we look more closely at `mkc`, we see that this function can be viewed as a combination of application and argument raising, as follows:

```
raise :: a -> (a -> r) -> r
raise x = \ f ->  f x

mkc' ::  (a -> b) -> a -> (b -> r) -> r
mkc' f x = raise (f x)
```

We see that `raise` lifts types to CPS value types, the type of a CPS value being `(a -> r) -> r`. In other words: a CPS value is a thing that you have to apply a function of type `a -> r` to in order to get a result of type `r`.

Where have we seen this argument raising before? Exactly, this is how Montague grammar deals with proper names to assimilate them to the type of generalized quantifiers. So if it is the case, as Reynolds [Rey93] claims, that continuations were invented over and over again in computer science, then the person who reinvented them first for natural language semantics was, without doubt, Richard Montague.

A typical use of continuation passing style programming is for implementing computations which can be interrupted. Error handling is a prime example. To see how this is done in Haskell we advise you to have a look at the Haskell Continuation monad.

11.2 Continuations as Abstractions over Context

In the semantics we gave in 7.5, a quantificational NP like *every dwarf* denotes a function of type $(e \rightarrow t) \rightarrow t$. Also the denotation of non-quantificational NPs is lifted to that type. As an example, recall the denotation of *Alice*:

$$\lambda P \mapsto (P\, a)$$

This term denotes a function that takes the linguistic context of the NP *Alice* and plugs the individual constant corresponding to Alice into that context.

The treatment of NP denotations as abstractions over NP contexts was devised by Montague in order to give a unified treatment of quantificational and non-quantificational NPs. But we do not need to restrict this strategy to NPs; we can extend it to expressions of other categories as well.

Suppose we are computing the meaning of

$$[_S\ Alice\ [_{VP}\ helped\ Dorothy]].$$

Let us start with the NP *Alice* again. Its linguist context is __ *helped Dorothy*. It denotes a predicate with one free argument slot. During the meaning computation this slot will be filled with the individual constant corresponding to Alice. Abstracting over this predicate we reach at the denotation we mentioned above: $\lambda P \mapsto (P\, a)$, with P being of type $e \rightarrow t$. We already know that we can do this for every NP. So the NP *Dorothy* has a very similar denotation: $\lambda P \mapsto (P\, d)$. It is an abstraction over the linguistic context of *Dorothy*, which, in this case, is *Alice helped* __, i.e. again a predicate which only needs to be applied to an NP denotation in order to yield a full sentence.

Now we can apply exactly the same treatment to the verb *helped*: we can say that the meaning of *helped* is an abstraction over the linguistic context it appears in, thus a function that takes something that requires a verb meaning in order to yield a full sentence. So analogous to NPs, we can specify the meaning of *helped* as $\lambda \mathcal{P} \mapsto (\mathcal{P}\, Help)$, where *Help* is the two-place predicate that *helped* denotes, and $\mathcal{P}$ is the linguistic context of *helped*. In the above sentence this is *Alice* __ *Dorothy*. Now this context is of course of another type than the context of an NP, because it is applied to a verb of type $e \rightarrow e \rightarrow t$. A meaning we could assign to *Alice* __ *Dorothy*, that instantiates this type, is $\lambda P \mapsto ((P\, d)\, a)$, i.e. a function that takes a predicate of type $e \rightarrow e \rightarrow t$ (a transitive verb denotation) and applies it to the individual constants corresponding to Dorothy and Alice. The type of this function is $(e \rightarrow e \rightarrow t) \rightarrow t$. So this is the type of the linguistic context of a transitive verb, thus the type of the $\mathcal{P}$ in the denotation of *helped* above. The denotation of *helped* then is a function from this context type to t, i.e. $((e \rightarrow e \rightarrow t) \rightarrow t) \rightarrow t$.

Exercise 11.1 In a similar manner, we can look at the meaning of *helped Dorothy*. Its linguistic context is *Alice __*. Specify the denotation of *helped Dorothy* and its type along the above lines, and do the same also for *Alice helped*.

We will call the meaning of the linguistic context of an expression its *continuation*. The notion stems from computer science. There continuations are used for giving a compositional semantics of programs that exhibit apparent non-compositional side effects like jumps and exceptions. It serves the same purpose we used it for: it captures the context of an expression and provides it to the computation as a function.

The general type of the continuation of an expression of type τ is a function of type $\tau \to r$, with r being the type of result values.

At this point two remarks are in order. First, note that the continuation of an expression is not fixed. For example the linguistic context of *Alice* in the sentence *Alice helped Dorothy* differs from the linguistic context of *Alice* in *The princess that admired Alice laughed.*

Second, we need to ask what exactly the linguistic context is. Up to now we implicitly assumed that it is the sentence the expression occurs in. However, this is not precise enough. Consider the following sentence:

$$\text{If Alice helped Dorothy, then she cheered.} \qquad (11.1)$$

What is the sentence that the expression *Alice* appears in? Is it the whole sentence (11.1), or is it only the embedded sentence *Alice helped Dorothy*? If we decide for the former, we will not have solved our problem but encounter it again in the following sentence:

$$\text{If Alice helped Dorothy, then she cheered,} \qquad (11.2)$$
$$\text{and if Alice kicked Dorothy, then she did not cheer.}$$

Do we now decide for the *if-then*-clause we had before, or do we again decide for the whole sentence (11.2)? Then, is (11.3) the same like (11.2)? And if so, aren't we actually talking about texts and not about single sentences?

$$\text{If Alice helped Dorothy, then she cheered.} \qquad (11.3)$$
$$\text{If Alice kicked Dorothy, then she did not cheer.}$$

In order to avoid those ramblings and instead have a precise delimitation of the linguistic context of an expression, we specify the linguistic context as being the linguistic context up to the nearest enclosing sentence node. So in all three examples above, the linguistic context of the first occurrence of *Alice* is the embedded sentence *Alice helped Dorothy*.

Specifying the linguistic context as the next enclosing sentence now also specifies the result values as sentence denotations. This, in turn, specifies the result type

r as being type t. For example, starting from a not lifted NP of type e, an NP-continuation is of type $e \to t$. The continuation of an intransitive verb is of type $(e \to t) \to t$, and the continuation of a transitive verb is of type $(e \to e \to t) \to t$. This might seem a natural choice, but it is neither necessary nor the only one that makes sense for the analysis of natural language. We will see other useful examples of result types later in this chapter and also in the course of the next chapter.

We specified the denotation of an expression as a function from the continuation of that expression to the result type t. We will call such functions from continuations to result values *computations*. For example, the meaning of *Alice*, $\lambda P \mapsto (P\, a)$, is the computation of *Alice*. This computation tells us what role the sub-expression *Alice* plays in the whole expression, i.e. what is going to be done with it when computing the meaning of the whole expression (in this case it is plugged into a VP-meaning). Under this view, a continuation is an instruction of what to do next.

Here are general type synonyms in Haskell, for continuations (functions from values a to a result type r), and for computations (functions from continuations to the result type r):

```
type Cont a r = a -> r
type Comp a r = Cont a r -> r
```

As already mentioned, we will assume that r is our sentence type t, so in the implementation we will only work with continuation types `Cont a Bool`.

Here is a list of examples:

category	value type	continuation type	computation type
NP	e	$e \to t$	$(e \to t) \to t$
IV, CN	$e \to t$	$(e \to t) \to t$	$((e \to t) \to t) \to t$
TV	$e \to e \to t$	$(e \to e \to t) \to t$	$((e \to e \to t) \to t) \to t$

This schema applies to every type.

Exercise 11.2 What are the continuation and computation types for adjectives of type $(e \to t) \to (e \to t)$?

Now we will turn to systematically lifting the denotation of expressions from the type they had in Chapter 7 to the type of a computation. The resulting semantics is called *continuation passing style semantics*, because during the whole meaning computation we will keep passing continuations around. The lifting is called *continuation passing style transformation*, or CPS transformation for short. There are several different possibilities to perform this lift. We will pick a particularly simple one (e.g. used in [Bar02],[Bar04]).

11.3 Continuizing a Grammar

Our CPS transformation will lift expression denotations to functions that take their continuation as an extra argument. This, however, will not change the meaning of the expressions. For a big part of our fragment the semantics will turn out to work exactly like before. But as a consequence of this lifting, each expression will have access to its linguistic context (in other words: to a later stage in the meaning computation). We will exploit this for the semantics of quantifiers.

In order to continuize our gammar, we have to proceed in two steps. First we need to lift the denotation of every basic expression in our grammar, i.e. the meaning of the terminal symbols. Second we will also have to lift our rule for functional application, because once we have lifted all denotations to computations, they are not of the right type to simply apply to each other.

Let us start with the first step. In the previous section we already lifted the denotations of *Alice*, *Dorothy*, and *helped*. What we got were $\lambda P \mapsto (P\ a)$, $\lambda P \mapsto (P\ d)$, and $\lambda \mathcal{P} \mapsto (\mathcal{P}\ \mathit{Help})$, respectively. The pattern is very easy: the lifted denotation of a basic expression is a function from the continuation of that expression to the result of applying that continuation to the original denotation. Stating this as a general rule for all terminals of our grammar, we get the first part of our CPS transformation:

$$\bar{c} = \lambda k \mapsto (k\ c) \quad \text{for all constants } c \tag{11.4}$$

We denote the CPS transformation of a lambda expression by overlining it.

Implementing this rule in Haskell gives us the following function for continuizing terminals:

```
cpsConst :: a -> Comp a r
cpsConst c = \ k -> k c
```

In fact, these lifted denotations do not make use of the continuation but just pass it around. This can be seen from the fact that the continuation is always the outermost function. It is applied to the original denotation without being modified. So for this part of the fragment, the transformed one and the original one are equivalent. In order to get the original denotation from the continuized one, we simply apply the latter to the trivial continuation, the identity function. For example, applying the lifted denotation of *helped* to the identity function results in the two-place predicate *Help*:

$$(\lambda k \mapsto (k \; Help)) \; (\lambda x \mapsto x)$$
$$= (\lambda x \mapsto x) \; Help$$
$$= Help$$

On the contrary, quantificational NPs will make use of having access to their context. In particular we allow them to take scope over that context. These are the meanings of the two quantifiers *everyone* and *someone*:

$$[\![everyone]\!] = \lambda k \mapsto \forall x((Person \; x) \to (k \; x))$$
$$[\![someone]\!] = \lambda k \mapsto \exists x((Person \; x) \land (k \; x))$$

Just like other NPs, their denotation is a function that takes an NP continuation and plugs in a value of type e. Unlike NPs like *Alice*, this is not an individual constant but a variable bound by a universal or existential quantifier. The most important detail is that the quantifiers $\forall$ and $\exists$ take scope over the continuation k. So if this linguistic context k is the rest of the sentence, the quantifier will end up having wide scope over the whole sentence – even when it appears in object position.

Extending this strategy to quantificational determiners, we get the following meaning assignments:

$$[\![every]\!] = \lambda k \lambda P \mapsto k \; (\lambda Q \mapsto \forall x(Qx \to Px))$$
$$[\![some]\!] = \lambda k \lambda P \mapsto k \; (\lambda Q \mapsto \exists x(Qx \land Px))$$
$$[\![the]\!] = \lambda k \lambda P \mapsto k \; (\lambda Q \mapsto \iota x(Qx \land Px))$$
$$[\![no]\!] = \lambda k \lambda P \mapsto k \; (\lambda Q \mapsto \neg \exists x(Qx \land Px))$$

Now quantificational NPs are expressions whose continuized interpretation cannot be reduced to the original one because it crucially relies on the presence of continuations.

After continuizing the denotations of the terminals of our grammar, we also need a rule for a continuized functional application. To see why this necessary, consider a transitive verb and an NP: we cannot apply the lifted denotation of the transitive verb to the lifted denotation of the NP, because the type of the former is $((e \to e \to t) \to t) \to t$, and the type of the latter is $(e \to t) \to t$. What we need is a lifted functional application that combines a function computation and an argument computation into a computation of the application of the function to the argument. The following CPS transformation rule does that:

$$\overline{(M\ N)} = \lambda k \mapsto \overline{N}\ (\lambda n \mapsto \overline{M}\ (\lambda m \mapsto k\ (m\ n)))\qquad(11.5)$$

Here m is an M continuation and n is an N continuation. You can understand the rule as follows: in order to evaluate the application of M to N, first evaluate N and bind the result to the variable n, then evaluate M and bind the result to the variable m, finally apply m to n and pass the result to the continuation k.

This illustrates the three general ingredients of a CPS transformation: name all intermediate results, sequence the evaluations, and introduce continuations as an extra parameter.

This CPS transformation results in the fixed evaluation order of first evaluating N and then evaluating M. To illustrate how this comes about, let us consider the following pseudo program consisting of only two instructions:

```
(4+2); square 6
```

In principle, a compiler could decide in which order to evaluate these two instructions. Whichever order it choses, the result will be the same. However, this is different if we introduce a dependency:

```
x=4+2; square x
```

Here the evaluation of the square function depends on the successful evaluation of the variable assignment. Because of this dependency the compiler is forced to evaluate the two instructions in order. A similar thing happens with a CPS transformation: when we name the intermediate results and sequence them, we introduce a dependency that forces a certain order of evaluation.

You can also think of the continuation as the function that has to be called next with the result of the actual evaluation. In our functional application rule above, the continuation of N is the term $\lambda n \mapsto \overline{M}\ (\lambda m \mapsto k\ (m\ n))$. This function constitutes what to do next after evaluating N. Since it contains the evaluation of M, we fixed the order of first evaluating N and then evaluating M.

However, be aware that the evaluation order should not be confused with the order of reductions when reducing a lambda term. When we apply the above rule to terms M and N, it does not matter at all, which parts of the whole expression we reduce first. But although all possibilities will reduce to the same result, this result will mimic the order of having evaluated N before having evaluated M.

Order of evaluation is something we did not care about yet, and that we could not express before. But now that we have continuized our grammar, we were able to fix it in in a certain way. Actually we could also have fixed it in the other way, such that M is evaluated before N. We will use that fact for scope reversal later in Section 11.5.

The Haskell function corresponding to lifted functional application is:

```
cpsApply :: Comp (a -> b) r -> Comp a r -> Comp b r
cpsApply m n = \ k -> n (\ b -> m (\ a -> k (a b)))
```

What does that mean with respect to our grammar? Recall two basic rules using application, that we had in our fragment in Chapter 7, Section 7.5:

$$\mathbf{S} \longrightarrow \mathbf{NP}\ \mathbf{VP} \qquad [\![\mathbf{S}]\!] = ([\![\mathbf{VP}]\!]\ [\![\mathbf{NP}]\!])$$
$$\mathbf{VP} \longrightarrow \mathbf{TV}\ \mathbf{NP} \qquad [\![\mathbf{VP}]\!] = ([\![\mathbf{TV}]\!]\ [\![\mathbf{NP}]\!])$$

Instead of using non-continuized denotations $[\![\cdot]\!]$ and functional application, we now use continuized denotations and lifted function application:

$$\mathbf{S} \longrightarrow \mathbf{NP}\ \mathbf{VP} \qquad \overline{\mathbf{S}} = \overline{(\mathbf{VP}\ \mathbf{NP})}$$
$$\mathbf{VP} \longrightarrow \mathbf{TV}\ \mathbf{NP} \qquad \overline{\mathbf{VP}} = \overline{(\mathbf{TV}\ \mathbf{NP})}$$

Let us see how semantic composition along these lines proceeds. To keep it simple, we stick to our example from the beginning:

$$[_{\mathrm{S}}\ \textit{Alice}\ [_{\mathrm{VP}}\ \textit{helped Dorothy}\,]]$$

We start with computing the meaning of the VP, according to the interpretation rules just stated:

$$\overline{([\![\textit{helped}]\!]\ [\![\textit{Dorothy}]\!])}$$
$$= \lambda k \mapsto \overline{[\![\textit{Dorothy}]\!]}\ (\lambda n \mapsto \overline{[\![\textit{helped}]\!]}\ (\lambda m \mapsto (k\ (m\ n))))$$
$$= \lambda k \mapsto \overline{[\![\textit{Dorothy}]\!]}\ (\lambda n \mapsto (\lambda k' \mapsto k'\ \textit{Help})\ (\lambda m \mapsto (k\ (m\ n))))$$
$$= \lambda k \mapsto \overline{[\![\textit{Dorothy}]\!]}\ (\lambda n \mapsto (\lambda m \mapsto (k\ (m\ n)))\ \textit{Help})$$
$$= \lambda k \mapsto \overline{[\![\textit{Dorothy}]\!]}\ (\lambda n \mapsto (k\ (\textit{Help}\ n)))$$
$$= \lambda k \mapsto (\lambda P \mapsto (P\ d)\ (\lambda n \mapsto (k\ (\textit{Help}\ n))))$$
$$= \lambda k \mapsto (\lambda n \mapsto (k\ (\textit{Help}\ n))\ d)$$
$$= \lambda k \mapsto (k\ (\textit{Help}\ d))$$

Next, we apply this VP denotation to the denotation of *Alice*. The reduction proceeds analogously:

$$\overline{((\llbracket \mathit{helped} \rrbracket \, \overline{\llbracket \mathit{Dorothy} \rrbracket}) \, \overline{\llbracket \mathit{Alice} \rrbracket})}$$
$$= \lambda k \mapsto \overline{\llbracket \mathit{Alice} \rrbracket} \, (\lambda n \mapsto \overline{(\llbracket \mathit{helped} \rrbracket \, \overline{\llbracket \mathit{Dorothy} \rrbracket})} \, (\lambda m \mapsto (k \, (m \, n))))$$
$$= \lambda k \mapsto \overline{\llbracket \mathit{Alice} \rrbracket} \, (\lambda n \mapsto \lambda k' \mapsto (k' \, (\mathit{Help} \, d)) \, (\lambda m \mapsto (k \, (m \, n))))$$
$$= \lambda k \mapsto \overline{\llbracket \mathit{Alice} \rrbracket} \, (\lambda n \mapsto (\lambda m \mapsto (k \, (m \, n))) \, (\mathit{Help} \, d))$$
$$= \lambda k \mapsto \overline{\llbracket \mathit{Alice} \rrbracket} \, (\lambda n \mapsto (k \, ((\mathit{Help} \, d) \, n)))$$
$$= \lambda k \mapsto (\lambda P \mapsto (P \, a)) \, (\lambda n \mapsto (k \, ((\mathit{Help} \, d) \, n)))$$
$$= \lambda k \mapsto (\lambda n \mapsto (k \, ((\mathit{Help} \, d) \, n))) \, a$$
$$= \lambda k \mapsto (k \, ((\mathit{Help} \, d) \, a))$$

Applying the result $\lambda k \mapsto (k \, ((\mathit{Help} \, d) \, a))$ to the trivial continuation, the identity function, would give us $((\mathit{Help} \, d) \, a)$. So in fact we did exactly what we would have done in our original, non-continuized semantics, with the only difference that we have this extra layer of continuation parameters, which are passed around the whole time. Now you rightly may ask: Why we are doing all this if nothing else comes out in the end but the usual meaning? After all, we could have arrived at that much easier. The answer is that as soon as we involve quantifiers, this extra parameter will play an indispensable role. The semantics of quantifiers that was given above makes crucial use of it. Since we allowed quantifiers to take scope over their linguistic context, they can take scope over the whole sentence from whatever position they occur in. You already have all the means you need to check that.

Exercise 11.3 Compute the meanings of the following sentences.

Everyone admired Goldilocks.   (11.6)

Goldilocks admired someone.   (11.7)

11.4 Implementing a Continuized Grammar

We now implement interpretation functions based on our continuized grammar.

In Chapter 7 sentences were interpreted by applying the VP denotation to the NP denotation. Now we take the continuized denotation of the VP and apply it with our lifted functional application to the continuized denotation of the NP.

```
intSent_CPS :: Sent -> Comp Bool Bool
intSent_CPS (Sent np vp) =
   cpsApply (intVP_CPS vp) (intNP_CPS np)
```

For interpreting non-quantificational NPs, we take the original interpretations from Chapter 7 and lift them according to the rule (11.4) for constants.

```
intNP_CPS :: NP -> Comp Entity Bool
intNP_CPS SnowWhite  = cpsConst snowWhite
intNP_CPS Alice      = cpsConst alice
intNP_CPS Dorothy    = cpsConst dorothy
intNP_CPS Goldilocks = cpsConst goldilocks
intNP_CPS LittleMook = cpsConst littleMook
intNP_CPS Atreyu     = cpsConst atreyu
```

Quantificational NPs get interpretations as we specified them in the previous section, with the only difference that we do not build a predicate logic formula but rather base them on our direct interpretation from Chapter 7.

```
intNP_CPS Everyone = \ k -> all k (filter person entities)
intNP_CPS Someone  = \ k -> any k (filter person entities)
```

The continuized interpretation of determiners is of a form such that it can be applied directly to a common noun (the interpretation function for determiners is given below):

```
intNP_CPS (NP1 det cn) = (intDET_CPS det) (intCN_CPS cn)
```

VPs are either constants, which are interpreted again according to the rule (11.4), or they consist of a transitive verb followed by an NP, whose continuized interpretations are applied with lifted functional application.

```
intVP_CPS :: VP -> Comp (Entity -> Bool) Bool
intVP_CPS Laughed      = cpsConst laugh
intVP_CPS Cheered      = cpsConst cheer
intVP_CPS Shuddered    = cpsConst shudder
intVP_CPS (VP1 tv np) = cpsApply (intTV_CPS tv) (intNP_CPS np)
```

Transitive verbs and common nouns only comprise constants.

```
intTV_CPS :: TV -> Comp (Entity -> Entity -> Bool) Bool
intTV_CPS Loved    = cpsConst love
intTV_CPS Admired  = cpsConst admire
intTV_CPS Helped   = cpsConst help
intTV_CPS Defeated = cpsConst defeat


intCN_CPS :: CN -> Comp (Entity -> Bool) Bool
intCN_CPS Girl     = cpsConst girl
intCN_CPS Boy      = cpsConst boy
intCN_CPS Princess = cpsConst princess
intCN_CPS Dwarf    = cpsConst dwarf
intCN_CPS Giant    = cpsConst giant
intCN_CPS Sword    = cpsConst sword
intCN_CPS Dagger   = cpsConst dagger
```

Determiners are interpreted as specified in the previous section. As with *every-one* and *someone*, we base their continuation semantics on our direct interpretation from Chapter 7.

```
intDET_CPS :: DET -> (Comp (Entity -> Bool) Bool)
                        -> (Comp Entity Bool)
intDET_CPS Some  = \ k p -> k (\ q ->
                   any p (filter q entities))
intDET_CPS Every = \ k p -> k (\ q ->
                   all p (filter q entities))
intDET_CPS No    = \ k p -> k (\ q ->
                   not (any p (filter q entities)))
intDET_CPS The   = \ k p -> k (\ q ->
                   singleton (filter q entities)
                   && p (head (filter q entities)))
                 where
                   singleton [x] = True
                   singleton _   = False
```

Exercise 11.4 In Exercise 7.25 you implemented interpretation functions for AtLeast and AtMost. Continuize these interpretation functions.

Here are a few example computations based on this implementation.

```
compSent s = intSent_CPS s id

ex1 = compSent (Sent Everyone Laughed)
ex2 = compSent (Sent Someone Laughed)
ex3 = compSent (Sent Everyone (VP1 Admired Goldilocks))
ex4 = compSent (Sent Goldilocks (VP1 Admired Everyone))
ex5 = compSent (Sent Goldilocks (VP1 Admired Someone))
ex6 = compSent (Sent (NP1 Some Boy) Laughed)
ex7 = compSent (Sent (NP1 The Princess) Laughed)
```

We interpret sentences using the function `intSent_CPS`. The result of that function is a sentence computation, i.e. a function of type `(Bool -> Bool) -> Bool`, that takes a sentence continuation (representing the linguistic context of the sentence) and returns a result value of type `Bool`. An example of a possible sentence continuation is negation: if we had a negated sentence, we could apply the computation of the unnegated sentence to the negation function `neg`. But here we do not want to bother about the linguistic context of sentences and instead want the sentence computation to return a result value of type `Bool`. Therefore we apply the sentence computation to the trivial continuation, the identity function `id`.

Exercise 11.5 In Exercise 4.6 we asked you to extend the fragment of Chapter 4 to also include adjectives, for which you were supposed to give a semantics in Exercise 7.26. Continuize this semantics of adjective phrases, such that the CPS fragment of this chapter can interpret sentences like:

```
Sent Goldilocks (VP1 Admired (NP1 Some (AP Evil Princess)))
```

11.5 Scope Reversal by Means of Continuations

Above we gave the following rule for continuized functional application, which fixes the evaluation order in a way such that N is evaluated before M is.

$$\overline{(M\ N)} = \lambda k \mapsto \overline{N}\ (\lambda n \mapsto \overline{M}\ (\lambda m \mapsto k\ (m\ n)))$$

Now we will see how this evaluation order results in linear scope of quantifiers. Consider the sentence:

Everyone helped someone.

According to our interpretation rules, we have to compute

$$\overline{(([\![helped]\!]\ [\![someone]\!])\ [\![everyone]\!])}$$

Here $\overline{\llbracket someone \rrbracket}$ is $\lambda k \mapsto \exists x(k\ x)$, and $\overline{\llbracket everyone \rrbracket}$ is $\lambda k \mapsto \forall x(k\ x)$, as specified before. The end result will be:

$$\lambda k \mapsto \forall x((Person\ x) \to \exists y((Person\ y) \wedge (k\ ((Help\ y)\ x)))).$$

Because of the evaluation order determined by the rule for functional application, *everyone* turns out to take scope over *someone*. To see this, let us spell out the derivation in some detail. First we apply the verb denotation to the quantified NP *someone*:

$(\overline{\llbracket helped \rrbracket}\ \overline{\llbracket someone \rrbracket})$

$\to\ \lambda k \mapsto \overline{\llbracket someone \rrbracket}\ (\lambda n \mapsto \overline{\llbracket helped \rrbracket}\ (\lambda m \mapsto k\ (m\ n)))$

$\to\ \lambda k \mapsto (\lambda k' \mapsto \exists x((Person\ x) \wedge (k'\ x)))\ (\lambda n \mapsto \overline{\llbracket helped \rrbracket}\ (\lambda m \mapsto k\ (m\ n)))$

$\to\ \lambda k \mapsto \exists x((Person\ x) \wedge (\overline{\llbracket help \rrbracket}\ (\lambda m \mapsto k\ (m\ x))))$

$\to\ \lambda k \mapsto \exists x((Person\ x) \wedge ((\lambda k' \mapsto (k'\ Help))\ (\lambda m \mapsto k\ (m\ x))))$

$\to\ \lambda k \mapsto \exists x((Person\ x) \wedge (k\ (Help\ x)))$

Note that the order of beta reductions does not play a role. (You can check this by first reducing $\overline{\llbracket helped \rrbracket}$ and only after that reducing $\overline{\llbracket someone \rrbracket}$.)

Next we apply the result to $\overline{\llbracket everyone \rrbracket}$, using $(P\ x)$ as an abbreviation for $(Person\ x)$:

$(\overline{\llbracket helped\ someone \rrbracket}\ \overline{\llbracket everyone \rrbracket})$

$\overset{\beta}{\longrightarrow} \lambda k \mapsto \overline{\llbracket everyone \rrbracket}\ (\lambda n \mapsto \overline{\llbracket helped\ someone \rrbracket}\ (\lambda m \mapsto k\ (m\ n)))$

$\overset{\beta}{\longrightarrow} \lambda k \mapsto (\lambda k' \mapsto \forall x((P\ x) \to (k'\ x)))\ (\lambda n \mapsto \overline{\llbracket helped\ someone \rrbracket}\ (\lambda m \mapsto k\ (m\ n))$

$\overset{\beta}{\longrightarrow} \lambda k \mapsto \forall x((P\ x) \to (\overline{\llbracket helped\ someone \rrbracket}\ (\lambda m \mapsto k\ (m\ x))))$

$=\ \lambda k \mapsto \forall x((P\ x) \to ((\lambda k' \mapsto \exists y((P\ y) \wedge (k'\ (Help\ y))))\ (\lambda m \mapsto k\ (m\ x))))$

$\to\ \lambda k \mapsto \forall x((P\ x) \to (\exists y((P\ y) \wedge (k\ (Help\ y)\ x))))$

Crucial is the step from the third to the fourth line. There the denotation of *everyone* is applied to the term $(\lambda n \mapsto \overline{\llbracket helped\ someone \rrbracket}\ (\lambda m \mapsto k\ (m\ n)))$, and hence this term is substituted for k'. This means that the denotation of *helped someone* is plugged into the denotation of *everyone*. *Everyone* therefore turns out to have wider scope.

This was determined by our rule for functional application. But instead of enforcing the order of first evaluating the argument and then evaluating the function, we also could have chosen to let application work the other way around: first evaluate the function, then evaluate the argument. The rule would then read like this:

$$\overline{\overline{(M\ N)}} = \lambda k \mapsto \overline{\overline{M}}\ (\lambda m \mapsto \overline{\overline{N}}\ (\lambda n \mapsto k\ (m\ n)))$$

If M and N are terminals, then $\overline{\overline{M}}$ and $\overline{\overline{N}}$ are the same like $\overline{M}$ and $\overline{N}$.
The corresponding Haskell function is:

```
cpsApply' :: Comp (a -> b) r -> Comp a r -> Comp b r
cpsApply' m n = \ k -> m (\ a -> n (\ b -> k (a b)))
```

A consequence of this rule is that deriving the meaning of *everybody helped someone* will result in scope reversal. This is because now the order between the denotation of *everyone* and the denotation of *helped someone* is switched, so the denotation of *everyone* will be plugged into the denotation *helped someone*. This will eventually lead to the existential quantifier having scope over the universal quantifier. The result of the derivation is:

$$\lambda k \mapsto \exists y((Person\ y) \wedge \forall x((Person\ x) \rightarrow k\ ((Help\ y)\ x)))$$

Exercise 11.6 Verify this result by writing down the derivation in detail.

Here are two examples from our fragment, using this other functional application rule:

```
example_linearScope = (cpsApply  (cpsApply
  (intTV_CPS Helped) (intNP_CPS Someone))
  (intNP_CPS (NP1 Every Wizard))) id

example_inverseScope = (cpsApply' (cpsApply'
  (intTV_CPS Helped) (intNP_CPS Someone))
  (intNP_CPS Everyone)) id
```

11.6 Further Reading

The concept of continuations arose in theoretical computer science during the 1960s and 1970s. An overview of the discovery of continuations and pointers to the classic literature is given in [Rey93]. As it turns out, continuations were introduced by Aad van Wijngaarden, in a talk given in 1964, and next rediscovered again and again in computer science. Van Wijngaarden proposed the new concept in a sketch of a translation of Algol 60 to a restricted sub-language without labels or goto statements:

[...] if you do this trick I devised, then you will find that the actual execution of the program is equivalent to a set of statements; no procedure ever returns because it always calls for another one before it ends, and all of the ends of all of the procedures will be at the end of the program: one million or two million ends. If one procedure gets to the end, that is the end of all; therefore, you can stop. That means you can make the procedure implementation so that it does not bother to enable the procedure to return. That is the whole difficulty with procedure implementation. That's why this is so simple; it's exactly the same as a goto, only called in other words. [Wij66] (quoted in [Rey93])

The trick van Wijngaarden described was in fact a CPS transformation of Algol 60 programs, which is somewhat different from an actual example of a CPS program. Many such examples were given around 1970.

As we have seen, Richard Montague was the one who introduced continuation style evaluation in natural language semantics, by his stratagems for lifting of denotations. This was also around 1970. The lift from names (type 'entity') to functions from predicates to truth values is a prime example. Among the other rediscoverers in natural language semantics we must certainly mention Hans Kamp and Irene Heim, who invented continuation style text processing, in order to treat donkey anaphora and anaphoric linking across sentence boundaries. See Chapter 12 below, and the references given there.

New linguistic applications of continuations were proposed by Chung-chieh Shan and Chris Barker. They use continuation semantics for quantifier scope, for treatment of focus, for licensing of negative polarity items, and for deriving interactions between scope and binding. References are [Bar02],[Bar04],[BS06], [Sha07], and Shan's thesis [Sha05].

Continuation semantics also seems promising for intensional semantics, in order to explain the difference between the two readings of (11.8): the reading where Dorothy has a particular prince in mind and the reading where any prince will do. This kind of ambiguity is already treated in Montague's papers.

$$\textit{Dorothy believes a prince will marry her.} \qquad (11.8)$$

We end with a word of warning. In programming, continuation style processing is very powerful, but used without proper care it can easily lead to programs that are hard to understand. Something similar holds for linguistics. Descriptions of syntactic and semantic phenomena in terms of continuations run the danger of just providing complex reformulations.

12

Discourse Representation and Context

Summary

This chapter sketches a dynamic incremental semantics for natural language that starts out from Discourse Representation Theory (DRT), and extends this into type theory. This type-theoretic version of DRT can be viewed as a reconstruction that does justice to the incrementality and the finite domain semantics of the original.

12.1 The Dynamics of Pronoun Linking

Basic ingredients for a dynamic account of pronoun linking are contexts and constraints on contexts. An example of such a dynamic account is Discourse Representation Theory (DRT) [Kam81]. A DRT-style representation for a piece of text consists of a context, plus a list of constraints on that context. In the characteristic box notation of DRT this looks like:

context
constraints
on context

In DRT, the context consists of a list of *reference markers* or *discourse referents*. The constraints are assertions about these markers. Together they represent the information that a text provides, plus information about the anaphoric possibilities of the text. As the information conveyed by a piece of text grows, the corresponding representation structures get 'updated'. This happens roughly as follows:

To make this picture precise, one has to say more about how contexts and constraints are represented. Let us look at how this is done in DRT. You can hardly get simpler than the following example:

$$A \text{ man entered.} \tag{12.1}$$

Still, the example serves to illustrate one of the purposes of context: to enable anaphoric reference. Once (12.1) has been uttered, it should be possible to pick up a reference to *a man* (or better: to *that man*) by means of a pronoun.

One of the key points of DRT is that a standard first-order logic representation does not allow us to do this. A standard first-order logic representation of the meaning of (12.1) would be (12.2).

$$\exists x (\textit{Man } x \wedge \textit{Enter } x). \tag{12.2}$$

The scope of the quantifier $\exists x$ is closed, and there is no way to 'break into it' again.

This is why the DRT representation for (12.1) is different; it has a discourse marker x, and two constraints on that marker. The marker x constitutes the context that is created by the mention of *a man*. This marker remains available for future reference.

x
Man x
Enter x

Now suppose the discourse gets on with (12.3) and (12.4).

$$A \text{ woman entered.} \tag{12.3}$$

$$He \text{ smiled at her.} \tag{12.4}$$

This leads to the following successive updates of the representation. First, a new marker is introduced for the NP *a woman* in (12.3). Next, the two pronouns in (12.4) are resolved to the two reference markers.

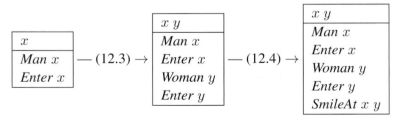

Note that reference resolution for the two pronouns has taken place in the construction of this representation structure, but we have not explained how this goes about. We now have to see how the account can be made more formal. It is reasonable to assume that a sentence to be added to an existing representation has a representation of its own. So we get a picture with a representation structure for

the first sentence and a representation structure for the second sentence, with • for
the as yet unspecified operation of combining two representation structures.

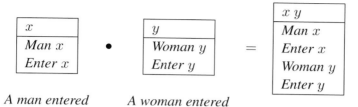

A man entered   A woman entered

How are reference markers selected? In [Kam81] and in the DRT textbook
[KR93], the representation construction algorithm simply states 'take a fresh reference marker', and leaves it at that. The Classic DRT construction algorithms
always parses new sentences in the context of an existing representation structure. What this means is that Classic DRT never *merges* representation structures.
Another way of saying this is that the semantics of Classic DRT is a kind of continuation semantics: processing new discourse is the 'what to do next' of the continuation.

We will set our aim a bit higher than Classic DRT, by developing a compositional
reconstruction. Using • for representation merge, a lexical entry for the indefinite
determiner *a* in DRT style might look like this:

$$\lambda PQ \mapsto \boxed{\begin{array}{|c|}\hline x \\ \hline \\ \hline\end{array}} \bullet Px \bullet Qx.$$

What this says is that an indefinite article *a* gives rise to the introduction of a
new reference marker x to the context, and that this marker x is predicated both of
the restriction P and the body Q of the determiner. Restriction and body are abstracted over in the lexical entry. The introduction of the marker is merged with the
representation for the restriction, and this is in turn merged with the representation
for the body.

The lexical entry for determiner *every* has a different structure. It uses the symbol $\Rightarrow$ for discourse implication. A precise definition of its meaning will be given
below.

$$\lambda PQ \mapsto \left(\boxed{\begin{array}{|c|}\hline x \\ \hline \\ \hline\end{array}} \bullet Px \right) \Rightarrow Qx$$

Again, how to pick a reference marker x? And how to define •? A proposal for
a straightforward solution is given in the compositional version of DRT in [Zee89],

where compositional discourse representation structures (DRSs) are defined like this. It is assumed that U is the set of reference markers, so M^U is the set of all functions from markers to members of the discourse domain. The set of DRSs is given by:

$$\delta \ ::= \ B \mid \delta \bullet \delta \mid \delta \to \delta,$$

where B is a basic DRS, and where basic DRSs, merger of DRSs, and implication of DRSs are defined by:

- Basic DRSs are $(\emptyset, \emptyset)$, $(\emptyset, \{Pr_0 \cdots r_{n-1}\})$, $(\emptyset, \{\bot\})$, and $(\{r\}, \emptyset)$.
- Merger of DRSs, $\delta \bullet \delta'$, is defined as $(V_\delta \cup V_{\delta'}, C_\delta \cup C_{\delta'})$.
- Implication of DRSs, $\delta \to \delta'$, is defined as $(\emptyset, \{\delta \Rightarrow \delta'\})$.

Here the DRSs are represented as pairs; V_δ picks the left component of the pair (the set of discourse markers), and C_δ picks its right component (the set of constraints).

These definitions can also be given in more suggestive (but slightly less precise) box notation, as follows.

- Basic DRSs:

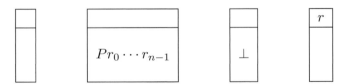

- Merger of DRSs:

- Implication of DRSs:

Assume we have a first-order model $\mathcal{M} = (M, I)$, where M is the domain and I the interpretation for the predicates. Then the semantics for these structures is given by:

$$\llbracket (\emptyset, \emptyset) \rrbracket = (\emptyset, M^U)$$
$$\llbracket (\emptyset, \{Pr_0 \cdots r_{n-1}\}) \rrbracket = (\emptyset, \{f \in M^U \mid \mathcal{M} \models_f Pr_0 \cdots r_{n-1}\})$$
$$\llbracket (\emptyset, \{\bot\}) \rrbracket = (\emptyset, \emptyset)$$
$$\llbracket (\{r\}, \emptyset) \rrbracket = (\{r\}, M^U)$$
$$\llbracket \delta \bullet \delta' \rrbracket := \llbracket \delta \rrbracket \oplus \llbracket \delta' \rrbracket$$
$$\llbracket \delta \Rightarrow \delta' \rrbracket := \llbracket \delta \rrbracket \to \llbracket \delta' \rrbracket$$

where

$$(X, F) \oplus (Y, G) := (X \cup Y, F \cap G)$$
$$(X, F) \to (Y, G) := (\emptyset, \{h \in M^U \mid \forall f \in F \ (\text{if } h[X]f \text{ then } \exists g \in G \text{ with } f[Y]g)\})$$

One piece of notation is still in need of explanation: if f and g are functions in M^U, and if $Y \subseteq U$, then $f[Y]g$ holds iff $f(u) = g(u)$ is the case for all $u \in Y$. Thus, $f[Y]g$ expresses that f and g agree on the values of the markers in Y.

This setup suggests that merging representation structures works as follows:

But this is not quite the outcome one would like. As a further illustration of the problem, the following sentence exhibits an unsolved puzzle with coordination:

$$A \ man \ entered \ and \ a \ man \ left. \tag{12.5}$$

Representations for the lexical entries:

a man: $\lambda Q \mapsto \boxed{\begin{array}{c} x \\ \hline Man\ x \end{array}} \bullet Qx$

entered: $\lambda y \mapsto \boxed{\begin{array}{c} \\ \hline Enter\ y \end{array}}$

left: $\lambda y \mapsto \boxed{\begin{array}{c} \\ \hline Leave\ y \end{array}}$

and: $\lambda pq \mapsto p \bullet q$

Applying these definitions gives:

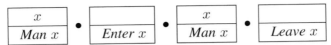

Combining these representations using the definition of • that was given above yields an unintuitive result, for it merges the two men:

12.2 Abstraction over Context

The essence of the solution to the merge problem is *abstraction over context*. If we take contexts to be simply finite lists of reference markers, then context abstraction can take the following form:

$$\lambda \boxed{\text{context}} \mapsto \left(\boxed{\text{context}} + \boxed{\begin{array}{c} \text{context extension} \\ \hline \text{constraints} \end{array}} \right)$$

Contexts are lists of reference markers; these reference markers serve to encode discourse information, and allow the discourse participants to keep track of the topics of discourse.

Order of discourse topics is relevant: topics mentioned most recently are (other things being equal) more readily accessible for reference resolution. Order of reference markers can be used as a measure for *salience*. A topic (or its marker) is more salient than another if it is more prominent on the list of candidates for reference resolution. For reference resolution, additional information of the following kinds is also needed:

- gender and number information,
- actor focus (agent of the sentence),
- discourse focus ('what is talked about' in the sentence).

Instead of giving a full account, we will sketch the basics, but in such a way that the reader can easily work out further details.

So how does abstraction over context work? Starting out from Incremental Dynamics [Eij01], which is in fact the one-variable version of Vermeulen's sequence semantics [Ver93], we represent a context as a stack of items. Here is an example:

| c_0 | c_1 | c_2 | c_3 | c_4 | $\cdots$ | |

Existential quantification is context extension, i.e. it pushes a new item on the stack:

| c_0 | c_1 | c_2 | c_3 | $+ d =$ | c_0 | c_1 | c_2 | c_3 | d |

We will use indices to refer to the items:

0	1	2	3	4	$\cdots$	$n-1$	n
c_0	c_1	c_2	c_3	c_4	$\cdots$	c_{n-1}	d

If c is a context, $c[0]$ is its first element, and $|c|$ is its length. So the context elements are $c[0]$ up to $c[k]$ where $k = |c| - 1$.

Discourse merge can now be implemented as context composition, as follows. As types of contexts, we can take $[e]$, the type of lists of entities. Context transitions get the type $[e] \rightarrow [e] \rightarrow t$; they are characteristic functions of binary relations on contexts.

Assume $c, c' :: [e]$ and $x :: e$. Then we use $\hat{c}x$ to denote the result of extending context c with item x. Note that the type of ($\hat{\ }$) is $[e] \rightarrow e \rightarrow [e]$, and that $\hat{c}x$ is a new context with $|\hat{c}x| = |c| + 1$. Now we can define dynamic existential quantification as follows:

$$\exists \quad := \quad \lambda cc' \mapsto \exists x(\hat{c}x = c')$$

What this says is that the quantifier $\exists$ has the effect of extending an input context c with an element x from the domain, and creating an output context $\hat{c}x$.

Exercise 12.1 What is the type of $\exists$?

Next, assume $\phi, \psi :: [e] \rightarrow [e] \rightarrow t$ (ϕ and ψ are context transitions) and $c, c' :: [e]$ (c and c' are contexts), and define context composition:

$$\phi \, ; \, \psi \quad := \quad \lambda cc' \mapsto \exists c''(\phi cc'' \wedge \psi c''c')$$

This defines context composition of context transitions ϕ and ψ as a relation between an input context c and an output context c', where c is fed as input to ϕ, yielding an output c'', which is fed as input to ψ, yielding output c' in turn.

Exercise 12.2 What is the type of (;)?

Let us consider what the lexical entries for determiners might look like in this setup. Assume $P, Q :: \mathbb{N} \rightarrow [e] \rightarrow [e] \rightarrow t$. Abbreviate this type as K. Then the lexical entry for determiner a has type $K \rightarrow K \rightarrow [e] \rightarrow [e] \rightarrow t$.

$$\lambda PQc \mapsto (\exists \, ; \, Pi \, ; \, Qi)c \text{ where } i = |c|. \tag{12.6}$$

This is very compact notation indeed, and it is worthwhile to have a closer look at what happens in (12.6). P and Q are variables for the restriction and the body of the indefinite determiner. These variables are of the type of pointers into context transitions, abbreviated as K. The input context is represented by c, and $\exists$ extends this input context with a new element. The index i points to this new element, for the input context c runs from $c[0]$ to $c[|c| - 1]$, and i is set equal to $|c|$, the length of c. So what the entry for the indefinite determiner says is that the input context c can be extended with a new element, and this new element will satisfy both P and Q, and it will remain accessible for future reference.

Here is an operation that blocks future reference: context negation or dynamic negation. One way to express this in DRT is this:

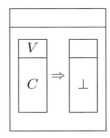

The typed logical version is the following, where ϕ represents the embedded representation structure.

$$\neg\phi \quad := \quad \lambda cc' \mapsto (c = c' \wedge \neg\exists c'' \phi cc'')$$

This defines a relation between input context c and output context c' where the input context equals the output context, and where there is no extension c'' of context c for which ϕ holds.

Similarly, we can define dynamic implication:

$$\phi \Rightarrow \psi \quad := \quad \lambda cc' \mapsto (c = c' \wedge \forall c_2 (\phi cc_2 \rightarrow \exists c_3 \psi c_2 c_3)).$$

Now the lexical entry for the determiner *every* can be phrased in terms of dynamic implication, as follows:

$$\lambda PQc \mapsto (\exists \, ; \, Pi \Rightarrow Qi)c \text{ where } i = |c|. \tag{12.7}$$

Exercise 12.3 Here is another way to phrase the lexical entry for the determiner *every*:

$$\lambda PQc \mapsto (\neg(\exists \, ; \, Pi \, ; \, \neg Qi))c \text{ where } i = |c|.$$

Show that this is equivalent to the definition in (12.7).

We will now check that this approach handles the coordination puzzle all right. Here are the representations for *a man*, *entered*, and *left*:

$$\begin{aligned}
\textit{a man}: & \quad \lambda Qcc' \mapsto \exists x(\textit{Man } x \wedge Qi(\hat{c}x)c')c & \text{where } i = |c| \\
\textit{entered}: & \quad \lambda jcc' \mapsto (c = c' \wedge \textit{Enter } c[j]) & \text{where } j \in |c| \\
\textit{left}: & \quad \lambda jcc' \mapsto (c = c' \wedge \textit{Leave } c[j]) & \text{where } j \in |c|
\end{aligned}$$

The notation $j \in |c|$ is shorthand for $j \in \{0, \ldots, |c| - 1\}$.

Remark. The notation $j \in |c|$ is based on John von Neumann's definition of natural numbers. Von Neumann (1903–1957) proposed the following set-theoretic definition:

- For 0, take the empty set, $\emptyset$.
- For the successor operation $n \mapsto s(n)$, take take $x \mapsto x \cup \{x\}$.

This gives:

- $0 = \emptyset$,
- $1 = s(0) = \emptyset \cup \{\emptyset\} = \{\emptyset\} = \{0\}$,
- $2 = s(1) = 1 \cup \{1\} = \{0\} \cup \{1\} = \{0, 1\}$,
- $3 = s(2) = 2 \cup \{2\} = \{0, 1\} \cup \{2\} = \{0, 1, 2\}$,
- and so on.

So every natural number n equals the set of all its predecessor numbers. Therefore, if n is a natural number, then $j \in n$ means the same as $j \in \{0, \ldots, n-1\}$. But if you don't care about Von Neumann numbers, that is perfectly fine with us. In that case, just remember that $j \in n$ is shorthand for $j \in \{0, \ldots, n-1\}$.

Back to the example now. The above entries for *a*, *man*, and *entered* yield the following representation for *A man entered*:

$$\lambda cc' \mapsto \exists x(\textit{Man } x \wedge \textit{Enter } (\hat{c}x)[i] \wedge \hat{c}x = c') \tag{12.8}$$

This reduces to (12.9).

$$\lambda cc' \mapsto \exists x(\textit{Man } x \wedge \textit{Enter } x \wedge \hat{c}x = c') \tag{12.9}$$

Similarly, we get the following as representation for *A man left*:

$$\lambda cc' \mapsto \exists x(\textit{Man } x \wedge \textit{Leave } x \wedge \hat{c}x = c') \tag{12.10}$$

Combining (12.9) and (12.10) by means of *and* (translated as $\lambda pq \mapsto p \,;\, q$) gives the following representation for *A man entered and a man left*:

$$\lambda cc' \mapsto \exists x(\textit{Man } x \wedge \textit{Enter } x \wedge \hat{c}x = c') \,;\, \lambda cc' \mapsto \exists x(\textit{Man } x \wedge \textit{Leave } x \wedge \hat{c}x = c')$$

This reduces to the following (note the renaming of variables):

$$\lambda cc_1 \mapsto \exists x(\textit{Man } x \wedge \textit{Enter } x \wedge \hat{c}x = c_1) \,;\, \lambda c_2 c' \mapsto \exists y(\textit{Man } y \wedge \textit{Leave } y \wedge \hat{c_2}y = c')$$

Applying the ; combinator and using β reduction gives:

$$\lambda cc' \quad \mapsto \quad \exists c'' \exists x (\textit{Man } x \wedge \textit{Enter } x \wedge \hat{c}x = c''$$
$$\wedge \exists y (\textit{Man } y \wedge \textit{Leave } y \wedge c''\hat{}y = c')).$$

By simple equality reasoning, this reduces to:

$$\lambda cc' \mapsto \exists x (\textit{Man } x \wedge \textit{Enter } x \wedge \exists y (\textit{Man } y \wedge \textit{Leave } y \wedge \hat{c}x\hat{}y = c')).$$

This is indeed a correct rendering, for it sets up an appropriate context with references to two men, with the right constraints.

12.3 Continuizing the Account

The following combinator G lifts the type of context transitions $[e] \to [e] \to t$ to the type of a map from contexts to context continuations $[e] \to ([e] \to t) \to t$.

$$G = \lambda \phi c P \mapsto \exists c' (\phi cc' \wedge Pc')$$

Call this a continuized context transition. A continuized context transition can be viewed as a relation between contexts and context properties (type $[e] \to t$). Its first argument is an input context, and its second argument is a property of output contexts, for encoding 'what to do next with the output context'.

The recipe for composing continuized context transitions is as follows:

$$\lambda \Phi \Psi c P \mapsto (\Phi c (\lambda c \mapsto \Psi c P)) \tag{12.11}$$

So let us lift the context transition (12.9) to its continuized counterpart:

$$G(\lambda cc' \mapsto \exists x (\textit{Man } x \wedge \textit{Enter } x \wedge \hat{c}x = c'))$$

This reduces to:

$$\lambda c P \mapsto \exists c' \exists x (\textit{Man } x \wedge \textit{Enter } x \wedge \hat{c}x = c' \wedge Pc')$$

By equality reasoning, we can simplify this further, to:

$$\lambda c P \mapsto \exists x (\textit{Man } x \wedge \textit{Enter } x \wedge P(\hat{c}x))$$

In a similar fashion, continuizing (12.10) will give us:

$$\lambda c P \mapsto \exists x (\textit{Man } x \wedge \textit{Leave } x \wedge P(\hat{c}x))$$

Next, combine these two continuized context transitions with recipe (12.11) for composing them:

$$\lambda c P \quad \mapsto \quad (\lambda c P \mapsto \exists x (\textit{Man } x \wedge \textit{Enter } x \wedge P(\hat{c}x))c$$
$$(\lambda c \mapsto (\lambda c P \mapsto \exists x (\textit{Man } x \wedge \textit{Leave } x \wedge P(\hat{c}x)))cP)$$

η-conversion yields:

$$\lambda cP \;\; \mapsto \;\; (\lambda P \mapsto \exists x (Man\; x \wedge Enter\; x \wedge P(\hat{c}x)))$$
$$(\lambda c \mapsto \exists x (Man\; x \wedge Leave\; x \wedge P(\hat{c}x)))$$

Before we can do further η-conversion we need an α-conversion step, as follows:

$$\lambda cP \;\; \mapsto \;\; (\lambda P \mapsto \exists x (Man\; x \wedge Enter\; x \wedge P(\hat{c}x)))$$
$$(\lambda c \mapsto \exists y (Man\; y \wedge Leave\; y \wedge P(\hat{c}y)))$$

Further η-conversion now yields:

$$\lambda cP \mapsto \exists x (Man\; x \wedge Enter\; x \wedge \exists y (Man\; y \wedge Leave\; y \wedge P(\hat{c}x\hat{\;}y)))$$

We have created a new context transition that tells us 'what to do next' with a context containing two men, one of them entering and the other one leaving.

Exercise 12.4 invites you to further explore the relation between context transitions and continuized context transitions.

Exercise 12.4 Consider the following combinator E for mapping continuized context transitions into context transitions.

$$E = \lambda \Phi cc' \mapsto \exists P (\Phi cP \wedge Pc')$$

Assuming $\Phi :: [e] \to ([e] \to t) \to t$, check that the type of E equals

$$([e] \to ([e] \to t) \to t) \to [e] \to [e] \to t.$$

Next, assume ϕ is a context transition, and compute $E(G\phi)$.

12.4 Implementing Discourse Representation

In this section we will start implementing our version of compositional DRT. Here is the module declaration, together with some imports.

```
module DRAC where

import Data.List
import Model
import P hiding (person)
```

We will give implementations of $\exists$, ; , $\Rightarrow$, and $\hat{}$. Also, it is useful to define an operation $\Downarrow$ of type $([e] \to t) \to t$ to indicate that the context set $[e] \to t$ is not empty. Thus, $\Downarrow$ serves as an indication of success. Assuming p to be an expression of type $[e] \to t$, the definition of $\Downarrow p$ is:

$$\Downarrow p \quad := \quad \exists c \mapsto pc$$

We have imported a first-order model Model where the lexical meanings of CNs and VPs are given as one-place predicates (type $e \to t$), those of TVs as two-place predicates (type $e \to e \to t$), and so on. We therefore define blow-up operations for lifting one-place and two-place predicates to the dynamic level. Assume A to be an expression of type $e \to t$, and B an expression of type $e \to e \to t$; we use c, c' as variables of type $[e]$, and j, j' as variables of type $\mathbb{N}$, and we employ postfix notation for the lifting operations:

$$
\begin{aligned}
A^\circ &:= \quad \lambda jcc' \mapsto (c = c' \wedge Ac[j]) \\
B^\bullet &:= \quad \lambda jj'cc' \mapsto (c = c' \wedge Bc[j]c[j'])
\end{aligned}
$$

The encodings of the ID operations in typed logic and the blow-up operations for one- and two-place predicates are employed in the semantic specification of the fragment. The semantic specifications employ variables j, j' of type $\mathbb{N}$, variables c, c' of type $[e]$, and variables P, Q of type $\mathbb{N} \to [e] \to [e] \to t$.

Let us start with the basic types we need for our Haskell implementation. Contexts get represented as lists of entities, and propositions are lists of contexts. Transitions are maps from contexts to propositions. Indices are simply integers.

```
type Context = [Entity]
type Prop    = [Context]
type Trans   = Context -> Prop
type Idx     = Int
```

The index lookup $c[i]$ is implemented by lookupIdx.

```
lookupIdx :: Context -> Idx -> Entity
lookupIdx []     i = error "undefined context element"
lookupIdx (x:xs) 0 = x
lookupIdx (x:xs) i = lookupIdx xs (i-1)
```

The context extension $\hat{c}x$ is implemented by extend.

```
extend :: Context -> Entity -> Context
extend = \ c e -> c ++ [e]
```

The dynamic context operations for negation, conjunction, and implication are the following:

```
neg :: Trans -> Trans
neg = \ phi c -> if phi c == [] then [c] else []

conj :: Trans -> Trans -> Trans
conj = \ phi psi c -> concat [ psi c' | c' <- (phi c) ]

impl :: Trans -> Trans -> Trans
impl = \ phi psi ->  neg (phi 'conj' (neg psi))
```

Dynamic quantifiers can be implemented like this:

```
exists :: Trans
exists = \ c -> [ (extend c x) | x <- [minBound..maxBound]]

forAll :: Trans -> Trans
forAll = \ phi -> neg (exists 'conj' (neg phi))
```

Anchors for proper names are extracted from an initial context, that we simply call `context`:

```
context :: Context
context = [A,D,G,M,Y]

anchor :: Entity -> Context -> Idx
anchor = \ e c -> anchor' e c 0 where
  anchor' e []      i = error (show e ++ " is not anchored")
  anchor' e (x:xs) i | e == x    = i
                     | otherwise = anchor' e xs (i+1)
```

Next we give a sketch of direct discourse interpretation on the basis of the parse trees from Chapter 9. First we associate strings with the predicates they denote (you can look up the predicates in Chapter 6). Then we will define blow-up functions that lift these predicates to the dynamic level.

In the lexicon, proper names are strings. The following function maps them to entities:

```
name2entity :: String -> Entity
name2entity "snowwhite"  = snowWhite
name2entity "alice"      = alice
name2entity "dorothy"    = dorothy
name2entity "goldilocks" = goldilocks
name2entity "littlemook" = littleMook
name2entity "atreyu"     = atreyu
```

Also intransive VPs are strings in the lexicon. The following function maps them to unary predicates:

```
name2pred :: String -> OnePlacePred
name2pred "laugh"     = laugh
name2pred "laughed"   = laugh
name2pred "cheer"     = cheer
name2pred "cheered"   = cheer
name2pred "shudder"   = shudder
name2pred "shuddered" = shudder
```

Common noun denotations are of the same type as intransitive VPs. Here are mappings to unary predicates for common nouns in the lexicon:

```
name2pred "thing"      = thing
name2pred "things"     = thing
name2pred "person"     = person
name2pred "persons"    = person
name2pred "boy"        = boy
name2pred "boys"       = boy
name2pred "man"        = man
name2pred "men"        = man
name2pred "girl"       = girl
name2pred "girls"      = girl
name2pred "woman"      = woman
name2pred "women"      = woman
name2pred "princess"   = princess
name2pred "princesses" = princess
```

```
name2pred "dwarf"      = dwarf
name2pred "dwarfs"     = dwarf
name2pred "dwarves"    = dwarf
name2pred "giant"      = giant
name2pred "giants"     = giant
name2pred "wizard"     = wizard
name2pred "wizards"    = wizard
name2pred "sword"      = sword
name2pred "swords"     = sword
name2pred "dagger"     = dagger
name2pred "daggers"    = dagger
```

In the lexicon, transitive verbs are strings. The following function maps them to characteristic functions of binary relations:

```
name2binpred :: String -> TwoPlacePred
name2binpred "love"      = love
name2binpred "loved"     = love
name2binpred "admire"    = admire
name2binpred "admired"   = admire
name2binpred "help"      = help
name2binpred "helped"    = help
name2binpred "defeat"    = defeat
name2binpred "defeated"  = defeat
```

Similarly for ditransitive verbs. These are mapped to characteristic functions of ternary relations:

```
name2terpred :: String -> ThreePlacePred
name2terpred "give" = give
name2terpred "gave" = give
```

The function `name2pred`, `name2binpred`, and `name2terpred` constitute the interface between the lexicon and the database model.

The lexical meanings of VPs and CNs are one-place predicates, those of TVs two-place predicates. Now let us define functions for blowing up these lexical meanings to the appropriate discourse types. Mapping one-place predicates to functions from indices to context transitions (or: context predicates) is done by:

```
blowupPred :: OnePlacePred -> Idx -> Trans
blowupPred = \ pred i c -> if   pred (lookupIdx c i)
                           then [c]
                           else []
```

Discourse blow-up for two-place and three-place predicates is done by the following two functions:

```
blowupPred2 :: TwoPlacePred -> Idx -> Idx -> Trans
blowupPred2 = \ pred i1 i2 c ->
                    let l1 = lookupIdx c i1
                        l2 = lookupIdx c i2
                    in if   pred l1 l2
                       then [c]
                       else []

blowupPred3 :: ThreePlacePred -> Idx -> Idx -> Idx -> Trans
blowupPred3 = \ pred i1 i2 i3 c ->
                       let l1 = lookupIdx c i1
                           l2 = lookupIdx c i2
                           l3 = lookupIdx c i3
                       in if   pred l1 l2 l3
                          then [c]
                          else []
```

Now let us turn to the dynamic interpretation of texts (including single sentences). It can be given by:

```
dintTXT :: ParseTree Cat Cat -> Trans
dintTXT (Branch (Cat "_" "TXT" _ _) [s,cnj,txt])  =
            (dintTXT s) `conj` (dintTXT txt)
dintTXT (Branch (Cat "_" "S" _ _)   [cond,s1,s2]) =
            (dintTXT s1) `impl` (dintTXT s2)
dintTXT (Branch (Cat "_" "S" _ _)   [np,vp])      =
            (dintNP np) (dintVP vp)
```

Here is the interpretation of simple relative clauses:

```
dintREL :: ParseTree Cat Cat -> Idx -> Trans
dintREL (Branch (Cat  _   "COMP" _ _) [rel,s]) = dintREL s
dintREL (Branch (Cat  _   "COMP" _ _) [s])     = dintREL s
dintREL (Branch (Cat "_" "S"    _ _)
         [Leaf (Cat "#" "NP"    _ _),vp])       = dintVP vp
dintREL (Branch (Cat "_" "S"    _ _) [np,vp]) =
                    \ i -> (dintNP np) (dintVPgap vp i)
```

For the interpretation of VPs with gaps, we just give the case of TVs with an object NP gap. The interpretation of VPs with a ditransitive verb and a direct object gap or an indirect object gap works similarly:

```
dintVPgap :: ParseTree Cat Cat -> Idx -> Idx -> Trans
dintVPgap (Branch (Cat  _   "VP" _ _)
           [Leaf (Cat name "VP" _ [_]),
            Leaf (Cat "#"  "NP" _ _ )]) =
       blowupPred2 (name2binpred name)
```

Interpretation functions for NPs and CNs are the following:

```
dintNP :: ParseTree Cat Cat -> (Idx -> Trans) -> Trans
dintNP (Leaf (Cat name "NP" _ _)) =
  \ p c -> p (anchor (name2entity name) c) c
dintNP (Branch (Cat _ "NP" _ _) [det,cn]) =
  (dintDET det) (dintCN cn)

dintCN :: ParseTree Cat Cat -> Idx -> Trans
dintCN (Leaf (Cat name "CN" _ _)) =
   blowupPred (name2pred name)
dintCN (Branch (Cat _ "CN" _ _) [cn,rel]) = \ i ->
  (dintCN cn i) `conj` (dintREL rel i)
```

Now, the interpretation of determiners is where all the dynamics happens:

```
dintDET :: ParseTree Cat Cat ->
           (Idx -> Trans) -> (Idx -> Trans) -> Trans
dintDET (Leaf (Cat "every" "DET" _ _)) =
  \ phi psi c -> let i = length c in
       neg (exists 'conj' (phi i) 'conj' (neg (psi i))) c
dintDET (Leaf (Cat "some" "DET" _ _)) =
  \ phi psi c -> let i = length c in
       (exists 'conj' (phi i) 'conj' (psi i)) c
dintDET (Leaf (Cat "a" "DET" _ _)) =
  \ phi psi c -> let i = length c in
       (exists 'conj' (phi i) 'conj' (psi i)) c
dintDET (Leaf (Cat "no" "DET" _ _)) =
  \ phi psi c -> let i = length c in
       neg (exists 'conj' (phi i) 'conj' (psi i)) c
dintDET (Leaf (Cat "the" "DET" _ _)) =
  \ phi psi c -> let i = length c in
               ((unique (phi i)) 'conj'
                  exists 'conj' (phi i) 'conj' (psi i)) c
```

The interpretation of the determiner *the* uses a function unique, that checks that a discourse predicate is unique. Here is its definition:

```
singleton :: [a] -> Bool
singleton [x] = True
singleton _   = False

unique :: Trans -> Trans
unique phi c | singleton xs = [c]
             | otherwise    = []
    where xs = [ x | x <- entities,
                     phi (extend c x) /= [] ]
```

Regarding the interpretation of VPs, we first give the cases of intransitive, transitive, and ditransitive verbs:

```
dintVP :: ParseTree Cat Cat -> Idx -> Trans
dintVP (Branch (Cat _     "VP" _ _ )
        [Leaf (Cat name "VP" _ [])])            =
       blowupPred (name2pred name)
dintVP (Branch (Cat _     "VP" _ _)
        [Leaf (Cat name "VP" _ [_]),np])        =
       \ subj -> dintNP np (\ obj ->
       (blowupPred2 (name2binpred name)) subj obj)
dintVP (Branch (Cat _     "VP" _ _  )
        [Leaf (Cat name "VP" _ [_,_]),np,pp]) =
       \ subj -> dintNP np (\ iobj -> dintPP pp (\ dobj ->
       (blowupPred3 (name2terpred name)) subj iobj dobj))
```

Next we turn to the interpretation of VPs with auxiliaries:

```
dintVP (Branch (Cat _        "VP" _ _ )
        [Leaf (Cat "did"    "AUX" _ []),vp]) = dintVP vp
dintVP (Branch (Cat _        "VP" _ _)
        [Leaf (Cat "didn't" "AUX" _ []),vp]) =
                            \ i -> neg (dintVP vp i)
```

Here is the interpretation of PPs:

```
dintPP :: ParseTree Cat Cat -> (Idx -> Trans) -> Trans
dintPP (Branch (Cat _ "PP" _ _) [prep,np]) = dintNP np
```

Now we can specify a function for evaluation in a context:

```
evl :: ParseTree Cat Cat -> Prop
evl = \ txt -> dintTXT txt context
```

This evaluation function can be combined with the parsing function from Chapter 9.

```
prc :: String -> [Prop]
prc string = map evl (parses string)
```

You can try this out with a few examples.

```
DRAC> prc "every dwarf that shuddered laughed"
[[[A,D,G,M,Y]]]
DRAC> prc "some dwarf that shuddered did not laugh"
[[]]
DRAC> prc "some dwarf that did not shudder did not laugh"
[[[A,D,G,M,Y,B],[A,D,G,M,Y,R]]]
```

Carrying out this program further is left to the reader.

Exercise 12.5 Interpretation of pronouns in context is not yet part of the fragment. Extend this fragment with singular pronouns *he*, *him*, *she*, *her*, *it*, and interpret each pronoun as a random element from the available context. (A more sophisticated reference resolution method will be given in the fragment in Section 12.7.)

```
lift :: Trans -> Context -> (Context -> Bool) -> Bool
lift phi c p = any p (phi c)
```

In the next section we switch to the use of special purpose syntactic data structures, which will be convenient for pronoun interpretation and reference resolution.

12.5 From Structure Trees to Dynamic Interpretation

We will now make a fresh start with special purpose data structures for syntax. We will assume that pronouns are the only NPs that carry indices. The topic of pronoun reference resolution in context will be taken up below, in our second fragment.

First, we give an interpretation for the categories we will use.

Sentences are, as usual, interpreted as function application of the NP meaning to the VP meaning. *If-then*-sentences are interpreted with the help of dynamic implication, and the sequence of two sentences with the help of context composition. NPs are interpreted in a familiar way as generalized quantifiers or as determiner meanings applied to common noun meanings.

S	$\longrightarrow$	**NP VP**	$[\![S]\!]$	$\longrightarrow$	$([\![NP]\!]\,[\![VP]\!])$
S	$\longrightarrow$	*if* **S** *then* **S**	$[\![S]\!]$	$\longrightarrow$	$[\![S_1]\!] \Rightarrow [\![S_2]\!]$
S	$\longrightarrow$	**S . S**	$[\![S]\!]$	$\longrightarrow$	$[\![S_1]\!]\,;\,[\![S_2]\!]$
NP	$\longrightarrow$	*Alice*	$[\![NP]\!]$	$\longrightarrow$	$\lambda Pcc' \mapsto \exists j((c[j]=a) \wedge Pjcc')$
NP	$\longrightarrow$	*PRO^j*	$[\![NP]\!]$	$\longrightarrow$	$\lambda Pcc' \mapsto Pjcc'$
NP	$\longrightarrow$	**DET CN**	$[\![NP]\!]$	$\longrightarrow$	$([\![DET]\!]\,[\![CN]\!])$
NP	$\longrightarrow$	**DET RCN**	$[\![NP]\!]$	$\longrightarrow$	$([\![DET]\!]\,[\![RCN]\!])$

Here are interpretations for determiners:

DET $\longrightarrow$ *every*
$[\![\text{DET}]\!]$ $\longrightarrow$ $\lambda PQc \mapsto (\neg(\exists\, ;\, P|c|\, ;\, \neg Q|c|))c$

DET $\longrightarrow$ *some*
$[\![\text{DET}]\!]$ $\longrightarrow$ $\lambda PQc \mapsto (\exists\, ;\, P|c|\, ;\, Q|c|)c$

DET $\longrightarrow$ *no*
$[\![\text{DET}]\!]$ $\longrightarrow$ $\lambda PQc \mapsto (\neg(\exists\, ;\, P|c|\, ;\, Q|c|))c$

DET $\longrightarrow$ *the*
$[\![\text{DET}]\!]$ $\longrightarrow$ $((\lambda c' \mapsto c = c' \wedge \exists x \forall y (\Downarrow (P|c|\ \hat{}\ y) \leftrightarrow x = y))$
$\qquad\qquad\qquad ;\, \exists\, ;\, P|c|\, ;\, Q|c|)c$

Common nouns are interpreted as lifted one-place predicates:

CN	$\longrightarrow$	*boy*	$[\![\text{CN}]\!]$	$\longrightarrow$	*Boy$^\circ$*
CN	$\longrightarrow$	*girl*	$[\![\text{CN}]\!]$	$\longrightarrow$	*Girl$^\circ$*
CN	$\longrightarrow$	*princess*	$[\![\text{CN}]\!]$	$\longrightarrow$	*Princess$^\circ$*

And common nouns with relative clauses are interpreted as follows:

RCN $\longrightarrow$ **CN** *that* **VP**
$[\![\text{RCN}]\!]$ $\longrightarrow$ $\lambda j \mapsto (([\![\text{CN}]\!]\, j)\, ;\, ([\![\text{VP}]\!]\, j))$

RCN $\longrightarrow$ **CN** *that* **NP TV**
$[\![\text{RCN}]\!]$ $\longrightarrow$ $\lambda j \mapsto (([\![\text{CN}]\!]\, j)\, ;\, ([\![\text{NP}]\!](\lambda j' \mapsto (([\![\text{TV}]\!]\, j')j))))$

Intransitive and transitive verbs are interpreted as lifted one-place and two-place predicates, respectively. VPs made up of a transitive verb and an NP are interpreted as composition of the NP meaning with the verb meaning.

VP	$\longrightarrow$	*laughed*	$[\![\text{VP}]\!]$	$\longrightarrow$	*Laugh$^\circ$*
VP	$\longrightarrow$	*shuddered*	$[\![\text{VP}]\!]$	$\longrightarrow$	*Shudder$^\circ$*
VP	$\longrightarrow$	**TV NP**	$[\![\text{VP}]\!]$	$\longrightarrow$	$\lambda j \mapsto ([\![\text{NP}]\!]\, ;\, \lambda j' \mapsto (([\![\text{TV}]\!]\, j')j))$

TV	$\longrightarrow$	*admired*	$[\![\text{TV}]\!]$	$\longrightarrow$	*Admire$^\bullet$*
TV	$\longrightarrow$	*defeated*	$[\![\text{TV}]\!]$	$\longrightarrow$	*Defeat$^\bullet$*

Note that it is assumed that proper names are linked to anchored elements in context. The setup of the context extension mechanism ensures that no anchored elements can ever be overwritten.

In the implementation below we also throw in reflexive pronouns; the formulation of the abstract interpretation rule for those is left as an exercise for the reader.

Exercise 12.6 Give a rule for the interpretation of reflexive pronouns.

Note that the syntax of the fragment is only a slight variation of the syntax of the fragment in Section 4.2. There is no index information on NPs, except for pronouns. And now we will use NPs He, She, and It.

```
data Sent = Sent NP VP | If Sent Sent | Txt Sent Sent
            deriving (Eq,Show)
data NP   = SnowWhite  | Alice | Dorothy | Goldilocks
            | LittleMook | Atreyu
            | PRO Idx    | He | She | It
            | NP1 DET CN | NP2 DET RCN
            deriving (Eq,Show)
data DET  = Every | Some | No | The
            deriving (Eq,Show)
data CN   = Girl   | Boy     | Princess | Dwarf | Giant
            | Wizard | Sword   | Poison
            deriving (Eq,Show)
data RCN  = RCN1 CN That VP | RCN2 CN That NP TV
            deriving (Eq,Show)
data That = That deriving (Eq,Show)
data REFL = Self deriving (Eq,Show)
```

Verb phrases are like follows:

```
data VP   = Laughed | Cheered | Shuddered
            | VP1 TV NP      | VP2 TV REFL
            | VP3 DV NP NP | VP4 DV REFL NP
            | VP5 AUX INF
            deriving (Eq,Show)
data TV   = Loved    | Admired | Helped | Defeated
            deriving (Eq,Show)
data DV   = Gave deriving (Eq,Show)
```

We also define an auxiliary for VP negation, and infinitives:

```
data AUX  = DidNot deriving (Eq,Show)
```

```
data INF  = Laugh | Cheer  | Shudder
          | INF1  TINF NP  | INF2  DINF NP NP
          deriving (Eq,Show)
data TINF = Love  | Admire | Help | Defeat
          deriving (Eq,Show)
data DINF = Give deriving (Eq,Show)
```

For the interpretation of VPs containing a reflexive pronoun we use the relation reducer `self` from Section 6.3. However, we will use the relation reducer on relations in type `Idx -> Idx -> Trans` rather than `Entity -> Entity -> Bool`. This works without further ado because `self` was defined with a polymorphic type.

The interpretation of sentences is of type `Sent -> Trans`:

```
intS :: Sent -> Trans
intS (Sent np vp) = (intNP np) (intVP vp)
intS (If   s1 s2) = (intS s1) `impl` (intS s2)
intS (Txt  s1 s2) = (intS s1) `conj` (intS s2)
```

Interpretations of proper names and pronouns are the following:

```
intNP :: NP -> (Idx -> Trans) -> Trans
intNP SnowWhite  = \ p c -> p (anchor snowWhite  c) c
intNP Alice      = \ p c -> p (anchor alice      c) c
intNP Dorothy    = \ p c -> p (anchor dorothy    c) c
intNP Goldilocks = \ p c -> p (anchor goldilocks c) c
intNP LittleMook = \ p c -> p (anchor littleMook c) c
intNP (PRO i)    = \ p   -> p i
```

Interpretation of complex NPs are given as expected:

```
intNP (NP1 det cn)  = (intDET det) (intCN cn)
intNP (NP2 det rcn) = (intDET det) (intRCN rcn)
```

Also the interpretation of (`VP1 TV NP`) is as expected, while the interpretation of (`VP2 TV REFL`) uses the relation reducer `self`. Finally, the interpretation of lexical VPs uses discourse blow-up from the lexical meanings:

```
intVP :: VP -> Idx -> Trans
intVP Laughed              = blowupPred laugh
intVP Cheered              = blowupPred cheer
intVP Shuddered            = blowupPred shudder
intVP (VP1 tv np)          = \s -> intNP np (\o -> intTV tv s o)
intVP (VP2 tv _)           = self (intTV tv)
intVP (VP3 dv np1 np2) = \s -> intNP np1 (\io -> intNP np2
                                 (\o -> intDV dv s io o))
intVP (VP4 dv _ np)        = self (\s io -> intNP np (\o ->
                                                intDV dv s io o))
intVP (VP5 _not inf)       = \s -> neg (intINF inf s)
```

The interpretation of TVs uses discourse blow-up of two-place predicates:

```
intTV :: TV -> Idx -> Idx -> Trans
intTV Loved    = blowupPred2 love
intTV Admired  = blowupPred2 admire
intTV Helped   = blowupPred2 help
intTV Defeated = blowupPred2 defeat

intDV :: DV -> Idx -> Idx -> Idx -> Trans
intDV Gave = blowupPred3 give
```

The interpretation of infinitives is the same as that of the corresponding VPs:

```
intINF :: INF -> Idx -> Trans
intINF Laugh               = intVP Laughed
intINF Cheer               = intVP Cheered
intINF Shudder             = intVP Shuddered
intINF (INF1 tinf np)      = \s -> intNP np (\o ->
                                       intTINF tinf s o)
intINF (INF2 dinf np1 np2) = \s -> intNP np1 (\io ->
                                       intNP np2 (\o ->
                                       intDINF dinf s io o))
```

Interpretations for TINFs and DINFs are the same as their tensed counterparts:

```
intTINF :: TINF -> Idx -> Idx -> Trans
intTINF Love   = intTV Loved
intTINF Admire = intTV Admired
intTINF Help   = intTV Helped
intTINF Defeat = intTV Defeated


intDINF :: DINF -> Idx -> Idx -> Idx -> Trans
intDINF Give   = intDV Gave
```

Like the interpretation of intransitive verbs, the interpretation of CNs uses discourse blow-up of one-place predicates:

```
intCN :: CN -> Idx -> Trans
intCN Girl     = blowupPred girl
intCN Boy      = blowupPred boy
intCN Princess = blowupPred princess
intCN Dwarf    = blowupPred dwarf
intCN Giant    = blowupPred giant
intCN Wizard   = blowupPred wizard
intCN Sword    = blowupPred sword
```

The discourse type of determiners is the combination of two context predicates into a transition:

```
intDET :: DET -> (Idx -> Trans) -> (Idx -> Trans) -> Trans
```

Determiners are interpreted in terms of dynamic quantification `exists`, dynamic negation `neg`, dynamic conjunction `conj`, and dynamic uniqueness check `unique`. Note that the values of the indices are derived from the input context.

```
intDET Some  = \ phi psi c -> let i = length c in
                 (exists 'conj' (phi i) 'conj' (psi i)) c
intDET Every = \ phi psi c -> let i = length c in
         neg (exists 'conj' (phi i) 'conj' (neg (psi i))) c
```

```
intDET No    = \ phi psi c -> let i = length c in
                  neg (exists `conj` (phi i) `conj` (psi i)) c
intDET The   = \ phi psi c -> let i = length c in
                  ((unique (phi i)) `conj`
                      exists `conj` (phi i) `conj` (psi i)) c
```

Exercise 12.7 Give an alternative definition of intDET Every in terms of impl.

The interpretation of relativized common nouns is as expected:

```
intRCN :: RCN -> Idx -> Trans
intRCN (RCN1 cn _ vp)  = \i -> conj (intCN cn i)
                                     (intVP vp i)
intRCN (RCN2 cn _ np v) = \i -> conj (intCN cn i)
                                     (intNP np (intTV v i))
```

Testing It Out

The initial context from which evaluation can start is given by context, defined on page 315.

```
eval :: Sent -> Prop
eval = \ s -> intS s context
```

Here is set of example sentences, for use as a test suite:

```
ex1  = Sent Dorothy Cheered
ex2  = Sent Dorothy Laughed
ex3  = Sent Dorothy (VP5 DidNot Laugh)
ex4  = Txt  (Sent Dorothy Cheered)
            (Sent LittleMook Cheered)
ex5  = Txt  (Sent Dorothy Cheered)
            (Sent (PRO 1) (VP1 Admired (NP1 Some Girl)))
ex6  = Sent (NP1 Some Boy) (VP1 Loved (NP1 Some Princess))
ex7  = Sent (NP1 Some Boy) (VP1 Loved (NP1 The Princess))
```

```
ex8  = Sent (NP1 Some Boy) (VP1 Defeated (NP1 No Giant))
ex9  = Sent (NP1 The  Boy) (VP1 Defeated (NP1 No Giant))
ex10 = Sent (NP1 Some Boy) (VP1 Loved (NP1 The Princess))
```

If these examples evaluate to false, an empty context set is returned. This is an example:

```
DRAC> eval ex2
[]
```

If they evaluate to true, a list of context sets is returned. Here is an example where the original context gets extended with a new referent:

```
DRAC> eval ex5
[[A,D,G,M,Y,G]]
```

Here are some more example sentences:

```
ex11 = Sent (NP1 No   Boy) (VP1 Loved Goldilocks)
ex12 = Sent (NP1 Some Boy) (VP1 Loved SnowWhite)
ex13 = Sent LittleMook (VP1 Loved   (NP1 Some Princess))
ex14 = Sent LittleMook (VP1 Defeated (NP2 Some (RCN1 Giant
                                  That (VP1 Loved Alice))))
ex15 = Sent (NP1 No Wizard) (VP1 Loved Dorothy)
ex16 = Sent (NP2 No (RCN1 Giant That
                (VP1 Defeated LittleMook)))
            (VP1 Loved Dorothy)
ex17 = Sent (NP2 Some(RCN1 Princess That
                (VP1 Admired LittleMook)))
            (VP1 Loved Dorothy)
ex19 = Sent (PRO 2) (VP1 Loved   (PRO 1))
ex20 = Sent (PRO 2) (VP1 Admired (PRO 1))
ex18 = Sent (NP1 The  Boy)  (VP1 Loved SnowWhite)
ex21 = Sent (NP1 Some Girl) (VP2 Admired Self)
ex22 = Sent (NP1 No   Boy)  (VP2 Admired Self)
```

12.6 Salience

Anaphoric reference resolution is incremental. Information needed to determine the reference of a pronoun in a text is determined 'on the go', on the basis of:

- syntactic properties of the sentence that contains the pronoun,
- information conveyed in the previous discourse, and
- background information shared by speaker and hearer (the *common ground*).

Surface syntactic form is an important determinant for salience. It is usually assumed that a subject is more salient than an object. For example, the first choice for resolving *he* in (12.12) is *Little Mook*. And the first choice for resolving *he* in (12.13) is *the dwarf*.

Little Mook hit the dwarf. He was upset. (12.12)

The dwarf got kicked by Little Mook. He was upset. (12.13)

In these two examples, *Little Mook* and *the dwarf* are the two obvious candidates for resolving the reference of the pronoun *he*, because both *Little Mook* and *the dwarf* have been made salient by the preceding text.

To illustrate how this process of salience update can be made explicit, consider the following context:

Alice	Snow White	Goldilocks

Salience update in context is a reshuffle of the order of importance of the items in a context list. This may make Goldilocks the most salient item:

Goldilocks	Snow White	Alice

To allow reshuffling of a context with Goldilocks in it, in such a way that we do not lose track of her, we represent contexts as lists of indexed objects, with the indices running from 0 to the length of the context minus 1:

0	1	2
Goldilocks	Snow White	Alice

Reshuffling this to make Alice most salient gives:

2	0	1
Alice	Goldilocks	Snow White

Note that the indices $0, \ldots, n - 1$ determine a permutation of the context list. We call these lists of indexed objects contexts under permutation.

Context Manipulation

In a context c, the entity with index i is given by $c[*i]$.

$[*0] = $ Goldilocks

If c is a context under permutation, let $(i)c$ be the result of placing the item $(i, c[*i])$ upfront. Here is an example:

$$(1) \quad \begin{pmatrix} \overset{2}{\boxed{\text{Alice}}} \; \overset{0}{\boxed{\text{Goldilocks}}} \; \overset{1}{\boxed{\text{Snow White}}} \end{pmatrix} = \overset{1}{\boxed{\text{Snow White}}} \; \overset{2}{\boxed{\text{Alice}}} \; \overset{0}{\boxed{\text{Goldilocks}}}$$

$(i)c$ is the result of moving the item with index i to the head position of the context list. Successive applications of this operation can generate all permutations of a context. If d is an object and c a context, then $d : c$ is the result of putting item $(|c|, d)$ at the head position of the context list.

$$\text{Dorothy} : \begin{pmatrix} \overset{2}{\boxed{\text{Alice}}} \; \overset{0}{\boxed{\text{Goldilocks}}} \; \overset{1}{\boxed{\text{Snow White}}} \end{pmatrix} = \overset{3}{\boxed{\text{Dorothy}}} \; \overset{1}{\boxed{\text{Snow White}}} \; \overset{2}{\boxed{\text{Alice}}} \; \overset{0}{\boxed{\text{Goldilocks}}}$$

The operation $(:)$ is used for adding a new element to the context, in most salient position.

Further Refinement of Entries for Determiners

Let $p[e]$ be the type of contexts under permutation. Assume c, c' are variables of type $p[e]$, and P, Q are variables of type $\mathbb{N} \to p[e] \to p[e] \to t$. Our new definition of context extension runs as follows:

$$\exists \quad := \quad \lambda c c' \mapsto \exists x ((x : c) = c').$$

Lexical entries for determiners now use this new definition instead of the old one. The new translation of *a man* effects a salience reshuffle:

$$\lambda Q c c' \mapsto \exists x (Man\ x \land Qi(x : c)c') \text{ where } i = |c|.$$

The referent for the indefinite that gets introduced appears in most salient position in the new context. Note that $(x : c)[*i]$ points to the newly introduced referent x. In any c' that is an extension or permutation of $(x : c)$, the expression $c'[*i]$ will continue to point to x.

Discussion

It may seem that the integration of salience reshuffling in dynamic semantics precludes an account of the role of surface syntax in establishing salience. This impression is mistaken, however. The context semantics is flexible enough to take syntactic effects on salience ordering into account.

Lambda abstraction allows us to make flexible use of the salience updating mechanism. In systems of typed logic, predicate argument structure is a feature of the 'surface syntax' of the logic. Consider the difference between the following formulas:

$$(\lambda xy \mapsto Kxy)\, l\, d$$
$$(\lambda xy \mapsto Kyx)\, d\, l$$
$$(\lambda x \mapsto Klx)\, d$$

All of these reduce to Kld, but the predicate argument structure is different.

Surface predicate argument structure of lambda expressions can be used to encode the relevant salience features of surface syntax. We can get the right salience effects from the surface word order of examples like the following:

Little Mook kicked the dwarf.	(12.14)
The dwarf got kicked by Little Mook.	(12.15)
The dwarf, Little Mook kicked.	(12.16)

To get the desired salience effect, we first make sure that the sentence gets translated into a lambda expression with the appropriate predicate argument structure. Next, we use this expression for the salience update of the appropriate contexts.

Reference Resolution

Reference resolution picks the indices of the entities satifying the appropriate gender constraint from the current state, in order of salience. The result of reference resolution is a list of indices, in an order of preference determined by the salience ordering of the state. The meaning of a pronoun, given a state, is an invitation to pick indices from the state, and use those indices to link pronouns to entities. This can be further refined, of course, in a setup that also stores syntactic information (about gender, case, and so on) as part of the contexts.

Names are resolved by picking the most salient index to the named entity from the current state, by looking for an index in a state where all the entities at the index are referents for the name. Naming ambiguity is treated as a kind of special case of pronoun reference resolution. If a name has no index in context, the contexts in the state are extended with an index for the named object.

To conclude, the proposed reference resolution mechanism provides an ordering of resolution options determined by syntactic structure, semantic structure, and discourse structure. This illustrates that pronoun reference resolution can be brought within the compass of dynamic semantics in a relatively straightforward way. The proposed mechanism can be viewed as an extension of pronoun reference resolution mechanisms proposed for discourse representation theory [WA86, BB05].

With minimal modification, the proposal also takes the so-called 'actor focus' from the *centering theory* of local coherence in discourse [GS86, GJW95] into account. Contexts ordered by salience are a suitable data structure for further refinement of the reference resolution mechanism by means of modules for discourse focus and world knowledge [WJP98].

12.7 Implementing Reference Resolution

We turn to the implementation. As we are going to do pronoun resolution, we need more informative contexts, for the context should reveal which pronoun got resolved to which context element. For this, we define a language of constraints, as follows:

```
data Constraint = C1 VP Idx
                | C2 TV Idx Idx
                | C3 DV Idx Idx Idx
                | C4 VP Idx
                | C5 TV Idx Idx
                | C6 DV Idx Idx Idx
                deriving Eq
```

Constraints C1, C2, and C3 are for unnegated verbs, and constraints C4, C5, and C6 are for negated verbs. Examples of constraints are `C1 Laughed 3` and `C2 Helped 4 5`. These are displayed on the screen as `Laughed 3` and `Helped 4 5`, respectively. The following function takes care of the display:

```
instance Show Constraint where
  show (C1 vp i)    = show vp ++ (' ':show i)
  show (C2 tv i j)  = show tv ++ (' ':show i)
                             ++ (' ':show j)
  show (C3 dv i j k) = show dv ++ (' ':show i)
                             ++ (' ':show j)
                             ++ (' ':show k)
```

```
show (C4 vp i)      = '-':show vp ++ (' ':show i)
show (C5 tv i j)    = '-':show tv ++ (' ':show i)
                                   ++ (' ':show j)
show (C6 dv i j k) = '-':show dv ++ (' ':show i)
                                   ++ (' ':show j)
                                   ++ (' ':show k)
```

To keep track of the indices in a constraint we define a function that retrieves its largest index.

```
maxIndex   :: Constraint -> Idx
maxIndex (C1 vp i)     = i
maxIndex (C2 tv i j)   = max i j
maxIndex (C3 dv i j k) = maximum [i,j,k]
maxIndex (C4 vp i)     = i
maxIndex (C5 tv i j)   = max i j
maxIndex (C6 dv i j k) = maximum [i,j,k]
```

To keep track of the modifications, we use `Context'` for the type of contexts in the new style, and similarly for `Prop'` and `Trans'`. Contexts in the new style have constraint lists built into them.

```
type Context' = ([(Idx,Entity)],[Constraint])
type Prop'    = [Context']
type Trans'   = Context' -> Bool -> Prop'
```

The new data type for transitions allows for the specification of positive and negative transitions: if `phi :: Trans'` and `c :: Context'`, then `phi c True` specifies the positive transition for c, and `phi c False` specifies the negative transition for c.

For the new kind of context we need a new function to retrieve its size:

```
size :: Context' -> Int
size (c,co) = length c
```

New Utility Functions

We define two utility functions. The first one is `lookupIdx'`, that looks up at an index to retrieve an entity, where `lookupIdx' c i` is the implementation of $c[*i]$.

```
lookupIdx' :: Context' -> Idx -> Entity
lookupIdx' ([],co)       j = error "undefined context item"
lookupIdx' ((i,x):xs,co) j | i == j    = x
                           | otherwise = lookupIdx' (xs,co) j
```

The second one is `adjust`, that adjusts the context by putting a discourse item up front, thus permutes the salience ordering.

```
adjust :: (Idx,Entity) -> Context' -> Context'
adjust (i,x) (c,co)
    | elem (i,x) c = (((i,x):(filter (/=(i,x)) c)),co)
    | otherwise    = error "item not found in context"
```

Here is a new version of `extend`:

```
extend' :: Context' -> Entity -> Context'
extend' = \ (c,co) e -> let i = length c in (((i,e):c),co)
```

The following function `success` checks if a given transition is possible from some given context.

```
success :: Context' -> Trans' -> Bool
success = \ c phi -> phi c True /= []
```

Now we define a function `cutoff cs i`, that cuts off all context elements in the list of contexts `cs` with index $\geq i$. This is the implementation of $\lceil i \rceil\ C$, the operation used to cut all contexts in C down to size i. The constraints that employ indices $\geq i$ are removed.

```
cutoff :: [Context'] -> Idx -> [Context']
cutoff []           i = []
cutoff ((c,co):cs) i = (cutoffc c i,cutoffco co i)
                     :(cutoff cs i)
  where
    cutoffc []           i          = []
    cutoffc ((j,x):xs) i | j >= i    = cutoffc xs i
                         | otherwise = (j,x):(cutoffc xs i)

    cutoffco []           i          = []
    cutoffco (co:cos)  i
                   | maxIndex co >= i = cutoffco cos i
                   | otherwise        = co:(cutoffco cos i)
```

The result of a cutoff may be that we end up with multiple copies of the same context. To remedy this, we need the function nub for removing superfluous copies.

New Versions of the Dynamic Operations

The neg' of a transition in the new style is got by swapping the truth value, and doing a cutoff for the negative transition relation.

```
neg' :: Trans' -> Trans'
neg' = \ phi c b -> if b then phi c False
                          else cutoff (phi c True) (size c)
```

If conj' succeeds, then the result is as before, and if conj' fails, the salience order of the input gets adjusted by cutting a counterexample context back to its original size.

```
conj' :: Trans' -> Trans' -> Trans'
conj' = \ phi psi c b -> if b
     then concat [ psi c' True | c' <- phi c True ]
     else if any (\c' -> psi c' True /= []) (phi c True)
         then []
         else if  (phi c True) == [] then (phi c False)
             else nub (cutoff (concat [psi c' False |
                                 c' <- phi c True])
                           (size c))
```

The implication function `impl'` can now simply be defined in terms of `neg'` and `conj'`.

```
impl' :: Trans' -> Trans' -> Trans'
impl' = \ phi psi -> neg' (phi 'conj'' (neg' psi))
```

The function `exists'` takes into account that the quantifier action always succeeds.

```
exists' :: Trans'
exists' = \ c b -> if   b
                   then [ (extend' c e) | e <- entities ]
                   else []
```

Syntax and Lexical Semantics

The only new thing that happens now is that pronouns do not carry indices anymore. Besides, the procedure for predicate blow-up is modified, for this is the spot where salience gets reset. Note that the salience relations of the context are adjusted even if the predicate does not hold.

```
blowupPred' :: (Entity -> Bool) -> Idx -> Trans'
blowupPred' = \ pred i c b ->
    let
        e  = lookupIdx' c i
        c' = adjust (i,e) c
    in
        if  b
        then if   pred e
             then [c']
             else []
        else if   pred e
             then []
             else [c']
```

For blow-up of VPs we add an extra touch to this, by including the relevant constraint in the context if the predicate holds. If the negated predicate holds, the constraint is modified accordingly.

```
blowupVP :: VP -> OnePlacePred -> Idx -> Trans'
blowupVP = \ vp pred i c b ->
        let
             e         = lookupIdx' c i
             (c',cos) = adjust (i,e) c
             co        = C1 vp i
             co'       = C4 vp i
        in
             if   b
             then if   pred e
                  then [(c',co:cos)]
                  else []
             else if   pred e
                  then []
                  else [(c',co':cos)]
```

The new definition of TV blow-up for two-place predicates ensures that subject is more salient than object. We also need to add the relevant constraint to the context if the predicate holds.

```
blowupTV :: TV -> TwoPlacePred -> Idx -> Idx -> Trans'
blowupTV = \ tv pred subj obj c b ->
        let
             e1        = lookupIdx' c subj
             e2        = lookupIdx' c obj
             (c',cos) = adjust (subj,e1) (adjust (obj,e2) c)
             co        = C2 tv subj obj
             co'       = C5 tv subj obj
        in
             if   b
             then if   pred e1 e2
                  then [(c',co:cos)]
                  else []
             else if pred e1 e2
                  then []
                  else [(c',co':cos)]
```

Similarly for ditransitive verbs:

```
blowupDV :: DV  -> ThreePlacePred ->
            Idx -> Idx -> Idx -> Trans'
blowupDV = \ dv pred subj iobj dobj c b ->
       let
           e1       = lookupIdx' c subj
           e2       = lookupIdx' c iobj
           e3       = lookupIdx' c dobj
           (c',cos) = adjust (subj,e1)
                      (adjust (iobj,e2)
                      (adjust (dobj,e3) c))
           co       = C3 dv subj iobj dobj
           co'      = C6 dv subj iobj dobj
       in
           if   b
           then if   pred e1 e2 e3
                then [(c',co:cos)]
                else []
           else if   pred e1 e2 e3
                then []
                else [(c',co':cos)]
```

Reference Resolution

The following code implements a simple but powerful reference resolution mechanism. It just picks the indices of the entities satisfying the gender constraint from the current context, in order of salience.

```
resolveMASC :: Context' -> [Idx]
resolveMASC (c,co)  = resolveMASC' c where
  resolveMASC' []                        = []
  resolveMASC' ((i,x):xs) | male x     = i : resolveMASC' xs
                          | otherwise = resolveMASC' xs

resolveFEM :: Context' -> [Idx]
resolveFEM (c,co)  = resolveFEM' c where
  resolveFEM' []                        = []
  resolveFEM' ((i,x):xs) | female x   = i : resolveFEM' xs
                         | otherwise = resolveFEM' xs
```

```
resolveNEU :: Context' -> [Idx]
resolveNEU (c,co)  = resolveNEU' c where
  resolveNEU'  []                       = []
  resolveNEU'  ((i,x):xs) | thing x    = i : resolveNEU' xs
                          | otherwise = resolveNEU' xs
```

Names are resolved by picking the most salient index to the named entity from the current context. If the name has no index in context, the context is extended with an index for the named object.

```
resolveNAME :: Entity -> Context' -> (Idx,Context')
resolveNAME x c | i /= -1   = (i,c)
                | otherwise = (j,extend' c x)
   where i                             = index x c
         j                             = size c
         index x ([],co)               = -1
         index x ((i,y):xs,co) | x == y    = i
                               | otherwise = index x (xs,co)
```

As matters stand now, we will still get wrong results for examples like *he respected him*, where a constraint should be imposed that *he* and *him* do not corefer (see, e.g., Reinhart [Rei83]). This constraint on coreference can be imposed with the following 'irreflexivizer':

```
nonCoref :: (Idx -> Idx -> Trans') -> Idx -> Idx -> Trans'
nonCoref = \ p i j c b -> if   i /= j
                          then (p i j c b)
                          else []
```

When imposed on [vpTV NP] where NP is not a reflexive pronoun, this has the desired effect of blocking coreference. In [Rei83], it is argued that the constraint on coreference is a pragmatic constraint, and that there are exceptions to this rule. Our implementation takes this into account, for the non-coreference constraint is implemented as a constraint on context, not on the underlying reality, where the relation that interprets the TV need not be irreflexive.

Here is a version of the irreflexivizer for ditransitive verbs:

```
nonCoref2 :: (Idx -> Idx -> Idx -> Trans') ->
              Idx -> Idx -> Idx -> Trans'
nonCoref2 = \ p i j k c b -> if   i /= j && j /= k && i /= k
                             then (p i j k c b)
                             else []
```

A New Version of Dynamic Interpretation

Again nothing really new happens, except for the fact that now we can do pronoun resolution in context. To ensure that the old test suite still runs, we also provide a rule for PRO^i.

The interpretation function for sentences is the following:

```
intS' :: Sent -> Trans'
intS' (Sent np vp) = (intNP' np) (intVP' vp)
intS' (If   s1 s2) = (intS' s1) 'impl'' (intS' s2)
intS' (Txt  s1 s2) = (intS' s1) 'conj'' (intS' s2)
```

And now we give an interpretation function for NPs, that uses the resolution functions:

```
intNP' :: NP -> (Idx -> Trans') -> Trans'
intNP' SnowWhite  = \p c ->
                        let (i,c') = resolveNAME snowWhite c
                        in  p i c'
intNP' Alice      = \p c ->
                        let (i,c') = resolveNAME alice c
                        in  p i c'
intNP' Dorothy    = \p c ->
                        let (i,c') = resolveNAME dorothy c
                        in  p i c'
intNP' Goldilocks = \p c ->
                        let (i,c') = resolveNAME goldilocks c
                        in  p i c'
intNP' LittleMook = \p c ->
                        let (i,c') = resolveNAME littleMook c
                        in  p i c'
```

```
intNP' He  = \p c b -> concat [p i c b | i <- resolveMASC c]
intNP' She = \p c b -> concat [p i c b | i <- resolveFEM  c]
intNP' It  = \p c b -> concat [p i c b | i <- resolveNEU  c]
intNP' (PRO i)          = \ p c -> p i c
intNP' (NP1 det cn)  = (intDET' det) (intCN' cn)
intNP' (NP2 det rcn) = (intDET' det) (intRCN' rcn)
```

In the VP interpretation rule for (VP1 tv np) we now impose the non-coreference constraint. For the interpretation of (VP1 tv refl), we use the polymorphic self, this time as an operation that takes in input of type Idx -> Idx -> Trans'.

```
intVP' :: VP -> Idx -> Trans'
intVP' (VP1 tv np)      = \ s -> intNP' np (\ o ->
                               nonCoref (intTV' tv) s o)
intVP' (VP2 tv refl)   = self (intTV' tv)
intVP' (VP3 dv np1 np2) = \ s -> intNP' np1 (\ io ->
                               intNP' np2 (\ o  ->
                               nonCoref2 (intDV' dv) s io o))
intVP' (VP4 dv refl np) = self (\ s io -> intNP' np (\ o ->
                                         intDV' dv s io o))
intVP' (VP5 _not inf)   = \ s -> neg' (intINF' inf s)
```

```
intVP' Laughed   = blowupVP Laughed   laugh
intVP' Cheered   = blowupVP Cheered   cheer
intVP' Shuddered = blowupVP Shuddered shudder
```

Here are interpretation functions for transitive and ditransitive verbs:

```
intTV' :: TV -> Idx -> Idx -> Trans'
intTV' Loved    = blowupTV Loved    love
intTV' Admired  = blowupTV Admired  admire
intTV' Helped   = blowupTV Helped   help
intTV' Defeated = blowupTV Defeated defeat

intDV' :: DV -> Idx -> Idx -> Idx -> Trans'
intDV' Gave     = blowupDV Gave     give
```

The interpretation of infinitives is same as that of the corresponding VPs:

```
intINF' :: INF -> Idx -> Trans'
intINF' Laugh               = intVP' Laughed
intINF' Cheer               = intVP' Cheered
intINF' Shudder             = intVP' Shuddered
intINF' (INF1 tinf np)      = \ s -> intNP' np  (\ o ->
                                     intTINF' tinf s o)
intINF' (INF2 dinf np1 np2) = \ s -> intNP' np1 (\ io ->
                                     intNP' np2 (\ o  ->
                                     intDINF' dinf s io o))
```

Interpretations for TINFs and DINFs are the same as their tensed counterparts:

```
intTINF' :: TINF -> Idx -> Idx -> Trans'
intTINF' Love   = intTV' Loved
intTINF' Admire = intTV' Admired
intTINF' Help   = intTV' Helped
intTINF' Defeat = intTV' Defeated

intDINF' :: DINF -> Idx -> Idx -> Idx -> Trans'
intDINF' Give   = intDV' Gave
```

The interpretation function for common nouns is given as follows:

```
intCN' :: CN -> Idx -> Trans'
intCN' Girl     = blowupPred' girl
intCN' Boy      = blowupPred' boy
intCN' Princess = blowupPred' princess
intCN' Dwarf    = blowupPred' dwarf
intCN' Giant    = blowupPred' giant
intCN' Wizard   = blowupPred' wizard
intCN' Sword    = blowupPred' sword
```

Now we also adjust the uniqueness check to the new data structures:

```
unique' :: Idx -> Trans' -> Trans'
unique' i phi c b =
 if b == singleton xs then [c] else []
   where xs = [ x | x <- entities, success (extend' c x) phi ]
```

Interpretation functions for determiners are given as follows:

```
intDET' :: DET -> (Idx -> Trans')
                  -> (Idx -> Trans') -> Trans'
intDET' Some  = \ phi psi c -> let i = size c in
                  (exists' 'conj'' (phi i) 'conj'' (psi i)) c
intDET' Every = \ phi psi c -> let i = size c in
                  (impl' (exists' 'conj'' (phi i))
                         (psi i)) c
intDET' No    = \ phi psi c -> let i = size c in
                  (impl' (exists' 'conj'' (phi i))
                         (neg' (psi i))) c
intDET' The   = \ phi psi c -> let i = size c in
                  (conj' (unique' i (phi i))
                           exists' 'conj'' (phi i)
                                   'conj'' (psi i)) c
```

Here are interpretation functions for common nouns with relative clauses:

```
intRCN' :: RCN -> Idx -> Trans'
intRCN' (RCN1 cn _ vp)    = \i -> conj' (intCN' cn i)
                                        (intVP' vp i)
intRCN' (RCN2 cn _ np tv) = \i -> conj' (intCN' cn i)
                                        (intNP' np (intTV' tv i))
```

Initiatization and Evaluation in the New Style

For evaluation, we use propositions (lists of contexts) in the new style. First we give a function for the conversion from contexts in the old style to contexts in the new style. This function adds indices and keeps the order of the elements in the old context. This has the effect of making the first element of the old context the most salient item of the new context.

```
convert :: Context -> Context'
convert c = (convert' c (length c - 1),[])
      where convert' []      i = []
            convert' (x:xs) i = (i,x):(convert' xs (i-1))
```

Then we define an evaluation function for sentences in the initial context, checking for truth:

```
eval' :: Sent -> Prop'
eval' s = intS' s (convert context) True
```

We also give an evaluation function for sentences in an empty context, checking for truth:

```
evalFresh :: Sent -> Prop'
evalFresh s = intS' s ([],[]) True
```

Examples

Recall that the position at the front of the context list is the most salient one. We give some variations on the earlier test examples that can be used to check pronoun resolution. Let us first have a look at the initial context.

```
DRAC> convert context
([(4,A),(3,D),(2,G),(1,M),(0,Y)],[])
```

This context contains the females A, D, G, and the males M and Y. A is the most salient individual. Now suppose we use this context to process sentence (12.17).

He admired some girl.   (12.17)

Glossing over the parsing step, here is the syntax tree for this example:

```
nex1 = Sent He (VP1 Admired (NP1 Some Girl))
```

In a context where referents for the pronoun are available, *he* can be resolved to any referent that satisfies the property. And this is what we get:

```
DRAC> eval' nex1
[([(1,M),(5,G),(4,A),(3,D),(2,G),(0,Y)],[Admired 1 5]),
 ([(0,Y),(5,G),(4,A),(3,D),(2,G),(1,M)],[Admired 0 5])]
```

As it turns out, the two males in the current context both admire some girl. In fact, they both admire G. Note that in the new context the admiring boy (either M or Y) and the admired girl G have become the most salient context items.

Next, consider sentence (12.18), where two new discourse elements get introduced.

Some dwarf defeated the giant.   (12.18)

The syntax tree of (12.18):

```
nex2 = Sent (NP1 Some Dwarf) (VP1 Defeated (NP1 The Giant))
```

The result of evaluation in the empty context:

```
DRAC> evalFresh nex2
[([(0,B),(1,T)],[Defeated 0 1]),([(0,R),(1,T)],[Defeated 0 1])]
```

As it turns out, both B and R are dwarfs who defeated the giant, T. The result of evaluation is two new contexts, one for each choice of victorious dwarf, where the dwarf and the giant have become the most salient context items.

Now suppose we continue the text with a sentence where a masculine pronoun is used, as in (12.19).

Some dwarf defeated the giant. He cheered.   (12.19)

Here is the syntax tree:

```
nex2a = Sent (NP1 Some Dwarf) (VP1 Defeated (NP1 The Giant))
        'Txt' (Sent He Cheered)
```

Result of evaluation:

```
DRAC> evalFresh nex2a
[]
```

Hmm, this is strange. One would expect the pronoun to pick up a reference to the most salient male in context, i.e. to the victorious dwarf. Why doesn't that happen? The answer is that in the model of evaluation none of the victorious dwarfs happen to cheer. So let us modify the example:

```
nex2b = Sent (NP1 Some Dwarf) (VP1 Defeated (NP1 The Giant))
        'Txt' (Sent He (VP5 DidNot Cheer))
```

This gives:

```
DRAC> evalFresh nex2b
[([[(0,B),(1,T)],[-Cheered 0,Defeated 0 1]),
 ([(1,T),(0,B)],[-Cheered 1,Defeated 0 1]),
 ([(0,R),(1,T)],[-Cheered 0,Defeated 0 1]),
 ([(1,T),(0,R)],[-Cheered 1,Defeated 0 1])]
```

Here the pronoun gets resolved either to the dwarf, or to the giant, and there are two possible choices for the dwarf. In any case, the referent of the pronoun ends up as the most salient item in context.

Let us look at some more examples.

```
nex3 = (Sent LittleMook Cheered) 'Txt'
       (Sent He (VP1 Admired (NP1 Some Girl)))
```

Interpretation in our standard context yields:

```
DRAC> eval' nex3
[([[(1,M),(5,G),(4,A),(3,D),(2,G),(0,Y)],
  [Admired 1 5,Cheered 1]),
 ([(0,Y),(5,G),(1,M),(4,A),(3,D),(2,G)],
  [Admired 0 5,Cheered 1])]
```

Interpretation in an empty context gets rid of the interpretation of *he* as Y:

```
DRAC> evalFresh nex3
[([[(0,M),(1,G)],[Admired 0 1,Cheered 0]])]
```

```
nex4 = Txt (Sent (NP1 Some Dwarf) (VP5 DidNot Shudder))
           (Sent He (VP1 Defeated (NP1 Some Giant)))
```

This time there are no spurious referents for the pronoun in context. We get:

```
DRAC> eval' nex4
[([[(5,B),(6,T),(4,A),(3,D),(2,G),(1,M),(0,Y)],
  [Defeated 5 6,-Shuddered 5]),
 ([(5,R),(6,T),(4,A),(3,D),(2,G),(1,M),(0,Y)],
  [Defeated 5 6,-Shuddered 5])]
```

Evaluation in the empty context gives:

```
DRAC> evalFresh nex4
[([[(0,B),(1,T)],[Defeated 0 1,-Shuddered 0]),
 ([(0,R),(1,T)],[Defeated 0 1,-Shuddered 0])]
```

```
nex5 = (Sent LittleMook (VP5 DidNot (INF1 Admire Dorothy)))
        'Txt' (Sent He Cheered)
```

The pronoun gets resolved as expected:

```
DRAC> evalFresh nex5
[([(0,M),(1,D)],[Cheered 0,-Admired 0 1])]
```

Here is an example where the context gets extended in different ways:

```
nex6 = Txt (Sent (NP1 Some Dwarf)
                 (VP5 DidNot (INF1 Admire Dorothy)))
           (Sent He (VP5 DidNot Cheer))
```

The evaluation result is:

```
DRAC> evalFresh nex6
[([(0,B),(1,D)],[-Cheered 0,-Admired 0 1]),
 ([(0,R),(1,D)],[-Cheered 0,-Admired 0 1])]
```

An example involving existential quantification and negation is the following:

```
nex7 = Sent (NP1 Some Giant)
            (VP5 DidNot (INF1 Admire (NP1 Some Princess)))
```

The evaluation result is:

```
DRAC> evalFresh nex7
[([(0,T)],[])]
```

The evaluation creates a context with a giant T in it, but there are no further context elements. The reason for this becomes clear if we reflect on the example. The sentence is true. It is evaluated with surface scope order, which means that there is some giant such that there is no princess he admires. So listing princesses admired by T makes no sense, and listing princesses that T does not admire does not make sense either.

Exercise 12.8 Check the evaluation results for the following example list, and comment on your findings.

```
nex8  = (Sent (NP1 The Princess) (VP1 Defeated (NP1 The Giant)))
          'Txt' (Sent She (VP1 Admired He))
nex9  = Sent He (VP1 Loved He)
nex10 = Sent He (VP2 Admired Self)
nex11 = Sent He (VP1 Admired He)
nex12 = Sent (NP1 The Giant ) (VP2 Admired Self)
nex13 = Txt (Sent (NP1 The Princess ) (VP2 Admired Self))
            (Sent She (VP1 Loved (NP1 The Giant)))
nex14 = Txt (Sent (NP1 Some Boy) (VP2 Admired Self))
            (Sent (NP1 Some Princess) (VP1 Loved He))
nex15 = If  (Sent (NP1 Some Boy) (VP2 Admired Self))
            (Sent (NP1 Some Giant) (VP1 Loved He))
nex16 = Txt (Sent (NP1 No Girl) (VP1 Helped LittleMook))
            (Sent (NP1 Some Princess) (VP1 Loved He))
```

12.8 Further Reading

Dynamic semantics for natural language started with Hans Kamp's paper on Discourse Representation Theory [Kam81] and with the closely related PhD thesis of Irene Heim [Hei82]. Semanticists working in the Montague tradition had qualms about the compositionality of this approach. This led to a rational reconstruction by Groenendijk and Stokhof called dynamic predicate logic (or short: DPL) [GS91]. The dynamic predicate logic version od DRT became the choice tool for incorporating discourse representation theory into Montague semantics; see, e.g., [Mus94, Mus96]. A synthesis proposal along slightly different lines can be found in [EK97]. The mathematics of context and context extension has developed into a topic in its own right; see, e.g., [VV96].

Incremental dynamics, as presented in [Eij01], remains closer to Kamp's original proposal. This framework can be viewed as the one-variable version of sequence semantics for dynamic predicate logic proposed in [Ver93]. Incremental dynamics is described in terms of polymorphic type theory in [Eij00]. This system makes clear how the instruction to take fresh discourse referents when needed can be made fully precise by using the standard toolset of (polymorphic) type theory. Such a reconstruction of DRT in type theory does justice to the incrementality and the finite state semantics of the original.

The proposal for the treatment of salience in the second fragment is an extension of the basic context logic. It should be compared with the treatment of pronoun resolution in DRT proposed in the second volume of [BB05], as well as with the earlier proposal for pronoun resolution in DRT in [WA86].

Central claim of the *centering theory* of local coherence in discourse [GS86, GJW95] is that pronouns are used to signal to the hearer that the speaker continues to talk about the same thing. See [WJP98] for extensions and variations that take world knowledge into account, and [BLSW04] for a reformulation in terms of optimality theory. The reference resolution mechanism proposed above is meant as a demonstration that reference resolution can be brought within the compass of dynamic semantics in a relatively straightforward way, and that very simple means are enough to implement something quite useful.

In the second fragment in this Chapter we have demonstrated pronoun reference resolution related to a fixed background model. More realistic is a setup where the 'compatible' models grow incrementally with the discourse. This can be achieved, e.g., by using a tableau unfolding mechanism for model generation (cf. [BE82, Koh00]).

As was mentioned already, discourse semantics in the style of Kamp and Heim can be viewed as a form of continuation passing style semantics for texts. This connection is worked out further in [dG04] and [BS08].

13

Communication as Informative Action

Summary

A theory of communication should provide accounts of changes in the state of information of a group of discourse participants, on the basis of message exchange within the group. This chapter gives an introduction to the way this is done in dynamic epistemic logic, focussing on the relevance of this work for semantics and pragmatics of natural language.

13.1 Knowledge and Communication

> *Suppose I try saying something.*
>
> *What way do I have of knowing*
> *that if I say I know something*
> *I don't really not know it?*
>
> *Or what way do I have of knowing*
> *that if I say I don't know something*
> *I don't really in fact know it?*
>
> Chuang Tzu *(around 350 BC)*

Imagine a typical discourse situation where *we* are talking to *you*. Outside is the realm of things and people that are not included in the discourse situation, the *they*, *he*, *she*, *it*. Here is a rough picture of what this looks like from our point of view:

351

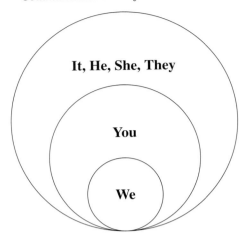

Aim of a communicative discourse is to create common knowledge between *us* and *you*. What does it mean to create common knowledge? If we inform you that something is the case, say that there is a party on tonight, then not only do you know that there is a party on, but also we know that you know, and you know that we know that you know. And so on, *ad infinitum*. This is common knowledge.

To see that common knowledge is different from mere knowledge, consider the example of cash withdrawal from a bank. You withdraw a large amount of money from your bank account and have it paid out to you in cash by the cashier. What happens? The cashier looks at you earnestly to make sure she has your full attention, and then she slowly counts out the banknotes for you: five hundred (counting ten notes), one thousand (counting another ten notes), fifteen hundred (ten notes again), and two thousand (another ten notes). This ritual creates common knowledge that forty banknotes of fifty euros were paid out to you. To see that this is different from mere knowledge, consider the alternative where the cashier counts out the money out of sight, puts it in an envelope, and hands it over to you. At home you open the envelope and count the money. Then the cashier and you have knowledge about the amount of money that is in the envelope. But the amount of money is not common knowledge among you. In order to create common knowledge you will have to insist on counting the money while the cashier is looking on, making sure that you have her full intention. For suppose you fail to do that. On recounting the money at home you discover there has been a mistake. One banknote is missing. Then the situation is as follows: the cashier believed that she knew there were forty banknotes. You now know there are only thirty-nine. How are you going to convince your bank that a mistake has been made, and that it is their mistake?

Exercise 13.1 When money is paid out to you by an ATM, does this create common knowledge between you and the machine? Why (not)?

The branch of logic that studies knowledge is called *epistemic logic*. The basic ingredient is the notion of a possible world or a possible state of affairs. The basic concept is the relation of indistinguishability between worlds. Here is an example. Consider the case where there are two agents, Alice (a) and Bob (b), and a coin has been tossed. In fact, the coin has landed heads, but neither of the agents has observed this. This situation can be modelled like this:

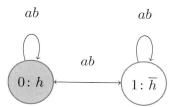

On the left we have the actual world, shaded gray. In the actual world h is true because the coin has landed heads up. The agents a and b cannot distinguish this situation from the situation on the right, where the coin has landed tails up; $\overline{h}$ indicates that the valuation in this situation makes h false. The epistemic indistinguishability relation is an equivalence relation, i.e. it is reflexive, symmetric, and transitive. In the following we will omit the reflexive loops and write $\longleftrightarrow$ as —. The picture above then looks like this:

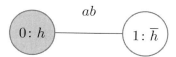

In this example knowledge and common knowledge coincide, for the epistemic relations are the same for both agents.

So let us add a second proposition letter p and a new agent c. Suppose a, b are still ignorant about h and c is ignorant also about p:

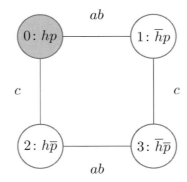

Now in the actual world it is common knowledge between a and b that p. But it is not common knowledge between a, b, c that p. Similarly, in the actual world it is known to c that h, but it is not common knowledge between a, b, c that h.

Next, consider the effect of communicative updates. There is a whole range of them, such as public announcements, group announcements, private communications, public and private lies, and so on. For simplicity we will confine attention in this chapter to public announcements. A public announcement is a true message conveyed to all agents in a communicative situation. In many cases, public announcement of ϕ will make ϕ common knowledge. If, for example, someone announces 'the coin has landed heads', then all the agents come to know it, and since the announcement was public, they also know that all the others know and so on.

However, it is not generally the case that ϕ will be true and common knowledge after the announcement. For consider the coin situation again. Suppose an outside observer would publicly announce 'the coin has landed heads, but you guys do not know it yet'. This would have been a true announcement. But its effect is that *after the announcement* the agents know that the coin has landed heads. The snag is that the announcement states something that is true *before the announcement*.

The crucial logical operation for modelling the effect of public announcement is *elimination* of possibilities. Imagine an information state involving several agents, with several worlds connected by agent accessibilities. Then the effect of a public announcement A is that all non-A worlds get eliminated from the picture. Here is the effect of public announcement of h in the above epistemic situation:

In the next section we will have a close look at two interesting examples of reasoning about (common) knowledge and ignorance.

13.2 Reasoning About Knowledge and Ignorance

As a first example of reasoning about knowledge and ignorance, we consider the so-called riddle of the wise men (or: riddle of the caps). Four men are standing in line. Counting from left to right, the first three are facing left and the last one is facing right. No man can see his own cap. The second man can see the first man's cap, the third man can see the first and the second man's cap, the first and the fourth man can see nothing. Here is a picture of the situation:

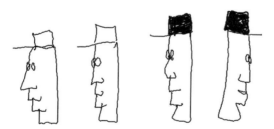

Now suppose it is common knowledge that there are two white caps and two black caps. Then, clearly, the third man knows the colour of his cap, and no other man knows the colour of his cap. For the third man reasons as follows: I see two white caps in front of me. I know that there are only two white caps. So my cap must be black. Now assume the third man announces this, without revealing the colour: 'I know the colour of my cap.' Then this will allow the second man to figure out the colour of *his* cap. For the second man reasons as follows: I know the guy behind me knows that there are only two white caps. I know that because it is common knowledge. I see a white cap in front of me. Suppose my own cap is black. Then the guy behind would see two different caps, and he would not have known his colour. But he knows. So my own cap must be white.

Exercise 13.2 State as precisely as you can what the fourth man learns from this exchange.

Now assume the situation is slightly different: the third man sees a white and a black cap in front of him.

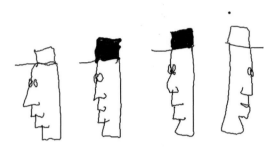

Then, obviously, the third man cannot figure out the colour of his cap. As soon as he announces this, by saying 'I do not know the colour of my cap', the second man knows the colour of his cap. For he reasons as follows: The guy behind me does not know his colour. This must mean he sees two different colours in front of him. I can see that the guy before me is wearing a white cap, so the colour of my own cap must be black.

A similar example is the puzzle of the muddy children. Four children have been playing outside. When they get indoors, the father announces: 'At least one of you is muddy.' The children can see the mud on each other's forehead, but not on their own. The following shows an example scenario, with a and b clean and c and d muddy.

a	b	c	d
○	○	●	●
?	?	?	?
?	?	!	!
!	!	!	!

The first line of question marks shows the initial situation, where nobody knows whether they are muddy. The reason nobody knows is that each child sees at least one other child with mud. Suppose this ignorance is made public. They all say: 'I do not know whether I am muddy.' This provides new information, for now child *c* (or *d*) reasons as follows: Suppose I am clean. Then *d* (or *c*, respectively) would have known in the first round that she was dirty. But she didn't. So I am muddy. This is the second round. If *c* and *d* now say 'I know that I am muddy', then this provides new information for *a* and *b*. For *a* (or *b*) can now reason as follows: Suppose I am dirty. Then *c* and *d* would not have known in the second round that they were dirty. But they knew. So I am clean.

13.3 A Language for Talking About (Common) Knowledge

A suitable logic for talking about knowledge and common knowledge is *epistemic PDL*, or *E-PDL*. PDL is short for propositional dynamic logic. It was invented as a language for computer program specification, but the nice thing about logical tools is that they can be reinterpreted and put to use in different domains. For example, PDL has an operation of program composition: first execute program *P*, next execute program *Q*. We can reinterpret this to express the epistemic relation of what Alice knows about Bob's knowledge. Similarly, PDL has a construction for non-deterministic choice between two programs *P* and *Q*. We can reinterpret this as the relation of what Alice and Bob both know. Finally, PDL can express reflexive transitive closure, for executing a program *P* an arbitrary finite number of times. We reinterpret that as the reflexive transitive closure of a knowledge relation. So if *a* denotes Alice's accessibility relation and *b* Bob's, and we use $\cup$ for union of relations, and $*$ for reflexive transitive closure, then $(a \cup b)^*$ expresses the common knowledge of Alice and Bob.

Here is a language for knowledge and public announcement. Assume that *a* ranges over the accessibility relations for individual agents and that *p* ranges over a set of basic propositions *P*.

$$\phi \quad ::= \quad \top \mid p \mid \neg\phi \mid \phi_1 \wedge \phi_2 \mid [\alpha]\phi \mid [!\phi_1]\phi_2$$
$$\alpha \quad ::= \quad a \mid ?\phi \mid \alpha_1; \alpha_2 \mid \alpha_1 \cup \alpha_2 \mid \alpha^*$$

To interpret this language we need a formal definition of epistemic models. Here it is. Let a set *P* of basic propositions and a set *A* of agents be given. Then an epistemic model *M* for *P* and *A* is a triple (W, V, R), where

- *W* is a non-empty set of worlds (the universe of the model),
- *V* is a function from *W* to $\mathcal{P}(P)$ (the valuation function of the model),
- *R* is a function from *A* to $\mathcal{P}(W \times W)$ that assigns to each $a \in A$ an equivalence relation $\overset{a}{\to}$ on *W* (the accessibility relation for agent *a*).

We use this to define interpretations for formulas ϕ and epistemic expressions α. Let a model $M = (W, V, R)$ be given. The formulas of E-PDL are interpreted as subsets of W, and the epistemic expressions of E-PDL as binary relations on W, as follows.

$$
\begin{aligned}
[\![\top]\!]^M &= W \\
[\![p]\!]^M &= \{w \in W \mid p \in V(w)\} \\
[\![\neg\phi]\!]^M &= W - [\![\phi]\!]^M \\
[\![\phi_1 \wedge \phi_2]\!]^M &= [\![\phi_1]\!]^M \cap [\![\phi_2]\!]^M \\
[\![[\alpha]\phi]\!]^M &= \{w \in W \mid \forall v(\text{ if }(w,v) \in [\![\alpha]\!]^M \text{ then } v \in [\![\phi]\!]^M)\}
\end{aligned}
$$

$$
\begin{aligned}
[\![[!\phi_1]\phi_2]\!]^M &= (W - [\![\phi_1]\!]^M) \cup [\![\phi_2]\!]^{M|\phi_1} \\
\text{where } \quad & M \mid \phi_1 = (W', V', R'), \text{with} \\
& W' = [\![\phi_1]\!]^M, \\
& V' = V \text{ restricted to } W', \\
& R'(a) = R(a) \text{ restricted to } W' \text{ for each } a,
\end{aligned}
$$

$$
\begin{aligned}
[\![a]\!]^M &= R(a) \\
[\![?\phi]\!]^M &= \{(w,w) \in W \times W \mid w \in [\![\phi]\!]^M\} \\
[\![\alpha_1;\alpha_2]\!]^M &= [\![\alpha_1]\!]^M \circ [\![\alpha_2]\!]^M \\
[\![\alpha_1 \cup \alpha_2]\!]^M &= [\![\alpha_1]\!]^M \cup [\![\alpha_2]\!]^M \\
[\![\alpha^*]\!]^M &= ([\![\alpha]\!]^M)^*
\end{aligned}
$$

Note that in this definition $\circ$ is used for relational composition, and $*$ for reflexive transitive closure of a binary relation.

If $w \in W$, then we use $M \models_w \phi$ for $w \in [\![\phi]\!]^M$. Intuitively, $M \models_w \phi$ expresses that ϕ is true at world w of model M.

Here are some example formulas, with their meanings:

- $[a]p$ expresses that agent a knows p. This is true in a world w of model M if all $v \in W$ with $(w,v) \in R(a)$ satisfy $M \models_{w'} p$.
- $\neg[a]\neg p$ expresses that agent a does not know p, i.e. that p is compatible with what a knows.
- $[(a \cup b)^*]p$ expresses that it is common knowledge between a and b that p. Technically, $[(a \cup b)^*]p$ holds in w if for all $v \in W$ with $(w,v) \in (R(a) \cup R(b))^*$ it is the case that p is true.
- $[!\phi_1]\phi_2$ expresses that after the public announcement of ϕ_1, ϕ_2 holds. The effect of the announcement of ϕ_1 is that the model is restricted with respect to ϕ_1.

An important fact is that everything that can be expressed in this logical language can already be expressed in E-PDL. In other words: the addition of public announcements $[!\phi_1]\phi_2$ to the language does not increase expressive power. To show this, we will establish that for every ϕ and every α there is a $T^\phi(\alpha)$ with the following property (see Exercise 13.3):

$$M \models_w [!\phi][\alpha]\psi \text{ iff } M \models_w [T^\phi(\alpha)][!\phi]\psi.$$

Use EE for the type of epistemic expression. Then the function T^ϕ is of type EE $\to$ EE. Here is the definition of this function.

$$
\begin{aligned}
T^\phi(a) &= \ ?\phi\,;a \\
T^\phi(?\psi) &= \ ?(\phi \wedge [!\phi]\psi) \\
T^\phi(\alpha_1;\alpha_2) &= \ T^\phi(\alpha_1)\,;T^\phi(\alpha_2) \\
T^\phi(\alpha_1 \cup \alpha_2) &= \ T^\phi(\alpha_1) \cup T^\phi(\alpha_2) \\
T^\phi(\alpha^*) &= \ (?\phi\,;T^\phi(\alpha))^*
\end{aligned}
$$

Exercise 13.3 Show by induction on the structure of α that

$$M \models_w [!\phi][\alpha]\psi \text{ iff } M \models_w [T^\phi(\alpha)][!\phi]\psi.$$

Exercise 13.3 provides the crucial information for the following axiomatization of the behaviour of public announcements $!\phi$:

$$
\begin{aligned}
[!\phi]\top &\leftrightarrow \phi \\
[!\phi]p &\leftrightarrow \phi \to p \\
[!\phi]\neg\psi &\leftrightarrow \phi \to \neg[!\phi]\psi \\
[!\phi](\psi_1 \wedge \psi_2) &\leftrightarrow [!\phi]\psi_1 \wedge [!\phi]\psi_2 \\
[!\phi][\alpha]\psi &\leftrightarrow [T^\phi(\alpha)][!\phi]\psi
\end{aligned}
$$

Exercise 13.4 Checking that these axioms are sound boils down to checking that their left-hand sides and right-hand sides always evaluate to the same value, using the semantics of the logic. The most important check was already carried out in Exercise 13.3. Carry out the other checks.

Note that the axioms have the form of equivalences, and that there is a crucial difference between the left-hand sides and the right-hand sides of these equivalences. In the left-hand sides, the operator $[!\phi]$ has wide scope, but if the operator occurs in the right-hand side, then it occurs with lower complexity: its scope is a proper subformula of the scope in the left-hand side. This shows that the equivalences have the form of *reduction* axioms: they can be used to reduce the language of E-PDL with public announcements to that of E-PDL simpliciter. This is an example of a much broader phenomenon. In [BvEK06] it is proved that E-PDL with an operator for general communicative action (public announcement, private announcement, group messages, deceptive announcements, but also actions that change the world, and much more besides) can be reduced to E-PDL. This shows that E-PDL is a stable basis for a very general logic of communication and action. In the next section we will use this logic to analyse presuppositions in terms of common knowledge.

13.4 Presuppositions and Common Knowledge

A presupposition of an utterance is an implicit assumption about the world or a background belief shared by speaker and hearer in a discourse. For example, an utterance of (13.1) presupposes that the dragon was not spitting fire before. (13.2) presupposes that you already asked the wizard. And the question in (13.3) presupposes that the name *Jan* refers to a male adult.

The dragon began to spit fire.   (13.1)

You should ask the wizard again.   (13.2)

Is Jan a bachelor?   (13.3)

When these examples occur as parts of more complex sentences, their presuppositions behave in a very systematic way. If a sentence is embedded under a modal like in (13.4), its presupposition remains unchanged. Also negating a sentence, like in (13.5), does not affect the presupposition. However, once we explicitly state the presupposition as the condition of an implication, the presupposition disappears: (13.6) no longer presupposes that you have asked the wizard before.

Maybe the dragon began to spit fire.   (13.4)

You should not ask the wizard again.   (13.5)

If you already asked the wizard, you should not ask him again. (13.6)

If a complex sentence inherits a presupposition from one of its parts, we say that the presupposition *projects*. We will now give a formal analysis of presuppositions and presupposition projection, but restricted to the propositional case. The only reason for this restriction is to keep things simple in our exposition.

Recall that $[!\phi]\psi$ expresses that after public announcement of ϕ, ψ holds. Formally, $M \models_w [!\phi]\psi$ iff $M \models_w \phi$ implies $M \mid \phi \models_w \psi$.

Now consider the special case of an update of the form 'it is common knowledge between i and j that ϕ'. This is expressed as $![(i \cup j)^*]\phi$. It is not difficult to see that the following hold:

- In case ϕ is already common knowledge, this update does not change the model.
- In case ϕ is not yet common knowledge, the update leads to a model without actual worlds.

Take the following picture as an example. Solid lines express i-links, dashed lines i, j-links. In the actual world Jan is male, adult, and unmarried, i.e. the propositions m, a, u hold.

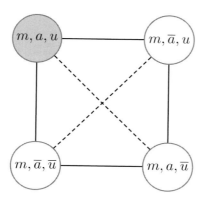

On one hand, the agents i and j know that Jan is male. This is even common knowledge, because $[(i \cup j)^*]m$ holds in the actual world. In fact, it holds in all four worlds – therefore an update with $[(i \cup j)^*]m$ would not eliminate any world or connection. On the other hand, i and j are not aware of the u distinction, i.e. do not know whether Jan is unmarried. Furthermore j is aware of the a distinction but i is not. Therefore $[(i \cup j)^*]a$ and $[(i \cup j)^*]u$ do not hold in the actual world. Updating with either of them would therefor eliminate the actual world.

Now let us look at the following epistemic situation, where both m and a are common knowledge.

We can specify a presupposition as a piece of common knowledge between speaker and hearer in a discourse. For example, *Jan is a bachelor* presupposes that he is a male adult, i.e. an update with *Jan is bachelor* presupposes that $m \wedge a$ is common knowledge. The update would be the following:

$$[(i \cup j)^*](m \wedge a) \wedge u$$

That is, an utterance has two parts: the presuppositional part, which announces that something is common knowledge (here: $m \wedge a$), and the assertional part (here: u).

In the situation depicted above, $m \wedge a$ is indeed common knowledge. Thus the update is possible and would result in the following situation:

Here is a useful fact about public announcement of common knowledge:

$$M \models_w [!([i \cup j)^*]\phi]\psi \text{ iff } M \models_w [(i \cup j)^*]\phi \rightarrow \psi.$$

What the fact says is that public announcement of common knowledge has the force of an implication.

Exercise 13.5 Use induction on the structure of ϕ to show that this fact is true.

Another useful fact about public announcements with a common knowledge component is that it makes no difference if the common knowledge component is announced first:

$$M \models_w [!([(i \cup j)^*]\phi \wedge \phi')]\psi \text{ iff } M \models_w [!([i \cup j)^*]\phi][!\phi']\psi.$$

In other words: uttering a presupposition before an assertion has the same effect as lumping them together. With respect to our example it says that uttering *Jan is a bachelor* has the same effect as first uttering *Jan is a male adult* and then uttering *Jan is unmarried*.

Studying how this works in more detail turns out to give us a grip on the problem of presupposition projection (see, e.g., [Hei92]), i.e. the problem of working out the presuppositions and assertions of complex phrases from those of their components. Consider, e.g., the difference between the following two sentences:

Jan is a bacholor.   (13.7)

If Jan is male, then Jan is a bachelor.   (13.8)

It is commonly held that the first example has as a presupposition that Jan is male, but the second example does not. We can now rely on epistemic logic to work out the difference in presupposition between the two examples. The first one has as associated update

$$[!([(i \cup j)^*](m \wedge a) \wedge u)],$$

and the second has as associated update

$$[!m][!([(i \cup j)^*](m \wedge a) \wedge u)].$$

To appreciate the difference, we simplify the first one as follows:

$$[!([(i \cup j)^*](m \wedge a) \wedge u)]\top$$
$$\leftrightarrow \quad [(i \cup j)^*](m \wedge a) \wedge u$$
$$\leftrightarrow \quad [(i \cup j)^*]m \wedge [(i \cup j)^*]a \wedge u.$$

Thus an update with *Jan is bachelor* presupposes m and a (because this is required to be common knowledge), and asserts u.

On the other hand, first stating that Jan is male, and then updating with *Jan is a bachelor*, gives the following:

$$[!m][!([(i \cup j)^*](m \wedge a) \wedge u)]\top$$
$$\leftrightarrow \quad [!m]([(i \cup j)^*]m \wedge [(i \cup j)^*]a \wedge u)$$
$$\leftrightarrow \quad [!m][(i \cup j)^*]m \wedge [!m][(i \cup j)^*]a \wedge [!m]u$$
$$\leftrightarrow \quad [!m][(i \cup j)^*]a \wedge [!m]u$$
$$\leftrightarrow \quad [(?m; i \cup j)^*]a \wedge (m \to u).$$

The presuppositional part is expressed in terms of so-called *restricted common knowledge*: 'restricted to m it is common knowledge between i and j that a'. The assertional part is an implication $m \to u$, which is indeed what we would expect for (13.8).

This must suffice to demonstrate how dynamic epistemic logic can be used as a calculus of presupposition projection (never mind the exact details of the calculation).

To close off this section on presupposition, we briefly consider the phenomenon of *presupposition accommodation*. Suppose p is common knowledge, say between i and j. Then updating with statement $!([(i \cup j)^*]p \wedge q)$ has the same effect as updating with $!q$. Suppose on the other hand that p is true in the actual world of a model, but not yet common knowledge. Then updating with $!([(i \cup j)^*]p \wedge q)$ will lead to an inconsistent state. Updating with $!p$ followed by an update with $!([(i \cup j)^*]p \wedge q)$ will remain consistent.

Accommodation of the presupposition would consist of replacement of

$$[!([(i \cup j)^*]p \wedge q)] \tag{13.9}$$

by

$$[!p][!([(i \cup j)^*]p \wedge q)]. \tag{13.10}$$

By invoking the Gricean maxim 'be informative' one can explain why (13.10) is not appropriate in contexts where p is common knowledge.

13.5 Adding Public Change

In this section we will look at another tool that proves useful for a formal study of pragmatics: public change.

A propositional substitution σ is list of propositional bindings $p := \phi$ satisfying the following properties:

- if $p := \phi$ is in the list, then ϕ is different from p,
- if $p := \phi$ is in the list, then no other item in the list has p as its left-hand side.

Examples of substitutions are $[p := \neg p]$ and $[p := q, q := p]$. Non-examples are $[p := p]$ (violates the first property) and $[p := q, p := \neg p]$ (violates the second property).

We will use σ to range over substitutions. Each substitution σ determines a function from the set of basic propositions P to the set of formulas of the language. Let σ be a substitution and let $p \in P$. Then if there is a binding $p := \phi$ in σ, we let $\sigma(p)$ equal ϕ, and otherwise we let $\sigma(p)$ equal p.

These substitutions can be used to model actions that change the world. Let $M = (W, V, R)$ be an epistemic model, and let σ be a substitution. Then M^σ is the result of changing M, as follows. We define $M^\sigma = (W, V', R)$, where

$$V'(w) = \{p \in P \mid M \models_w \sigma(p)\}.$$

So the valuation function in the new model assigns to each world those basic propositions for which the σ substitution is true in the old model. This takes the change expressed by the substitution into account. E.g. in $M^{[p:=\neg p]}$, p is true in precisely those worlds where p was false in M.

Next we can extend the epistemic language with operations for public change. If σ is a substitution, then $[\sigma]\phi$ is an expression of the language. The intended interpretation is this:

$$M \models_w [\sigma]\phi \text{ iff } M^\sigma \models_w \phi.$$

Thus $[\sigma]\phi$ expresses the effect of changing the world according to the recipe given in σ.

Again, we can show that this extension of the language does not increase expressive power. This time, we define substitutions on formulas and epistemic expressions, as follows:

$$\top^\sigma = \top \qquad\qquad a^\sigma = a$$
$$p^\sigma = \sigma(p) \qquad\qquad (?\phi)^\sigma = ?\phi^\sigma$$
$$(\neg\phi)^\sigma = \neg\phi^\sigma \qquad\qquad (\alpha_1; \alpha_2)^\sigma = \alpha_1^\sigma; \alpha_2^\sigma$$
$$(\phi_1 \wedge \phi_2)^\sigma = \phi_1^\sigma \wedge \phi_2^\sigma \qquad\qquad (\alpha_1 \cup \alpha_2)^\sigma = \alpha_1^\sigma \cup \alpha_2^\sigma$$
$$([\alpha]\phi)^\sigma = [\alpha^\sigma]\phi^\sigma \qquad\qquad (\alpha^*)^\sigma = (\alpha^\sigma)^*$$

Exercise 13.6 Show by simultaneous induction on ϕ and α that

(1) $M \models_w \phi^\sigma$ iff $M^\sigma \models_w \phi$
(2) $(w, w') \in [\![\alpha^\sigma]\!]^M$ iff $(w, w') \in [\![\alpha]\!]^{M^\sigma}$

Exercise 13.6 shows that the following reduction axiom is sound:

$$[\sigma]\phi \leftrightarrow \phi^\sigma.$$

Since we can use this to remove occurrences of $[\sigma]$ from the language, the addition of the public change operator has not increased expressive power.

Public change is interesting for natural language analysis, for it can be used to analyse important examples of so-called *performative speech acts*. Here are examples.

I call you Adam. (13.11)

I herewith pronounce you husband and wife. (13.12)

(13.11) is different from a mere invitation to use a certain name (such as 'Call me Ishmael'); rather, it changes the world by adding a new name to it, together with a link to the person who gets the name. Similarly, (13.12) creates a new fact of marriage. The following gives a picture of the effect of (13.12), or rather, part of the effect. First consider the following situation (with solid lines for i-links, and dashed lines for i, j-links).

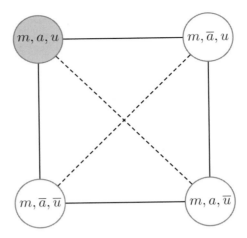

The utterance of (13.12) has the effect of flipping the status of unmarried u to $\bot$ for our male adult. Note that it is a precondition of the marriage act that the people about to be engaged in marriage are not currently married. So the operation for public change has as a precondition that u currently holds:

The update result is:

13.6 Yes/No Questions and Their Answers

We will now proceed to use public changes for the epistemic analysis of yes/no questions. Yes/no questions indicate that the context is undecided with respect to a particular proposition. An answer settles the issue by announcing the truth or falsity of the proposition.

For our analysis we want to adopt the well-known idea of Groenendijk and Stokhof [GS84] that a question partitions the logical space into all the possibilities that constitute a possible answer. In particular, yes/no questions divide the logical space into two possibilities. It therefore suffices to add a designated propositional variable f to our model, that represents the *question focus*. This focus will be reset by a question. More precisely, we analyse a yes/no question ϕ? as an update that changes the denotation of f to ϕ:

The answer *yes* can now be analysed as announcing the truth of f:

Accordingly, the answer *no* can be analysed as announcing the negation of f:

Interestingly, this perspective leads to a natural notion of *appropriate answerhood*. Consider the following exchange:

Question: *Will Atreyu come on his horse?*	(13.13)
Answer 1: *No.*	(13.14)
Answer 2: *It died in the swamps.*	(13.15)

The question will set f to the proposition 'Atreyu will come on his horse.' Now both answers are appropriate. The first one obviously is: updating with it corresponds to announcing the negation of f. This update makes 'Atreyu will not come on his horse' common knowledge. The second answer has the same effect. Since the death of the horse entails that Atreyu cannot and thus will not come on it (i.e. the negation of f), answer 2 entails the answer *no*.

In general, an answer ψ to a question ϕ? is *appropriate* if either updating with ψ has the effect that f becomes common knowledge, or updating with ψ has the effect that $\neg f$ becomes common knowledge.

Exercise 13.7 Which effect do the following answers have? Are they appropriate?

Question: *Did you see a racing snail or a luck dragon?*   (13.16)

Answer: *I saw a racing snail.*

Question: *Is Goldilocks married?*   (13.17)

Answer: *She is not adult.*

Question: *Is Little Mook a bachelor?*   (13.18)

Answer: *He is not adult.*

13.7 Epistemic Model Checking

We will close off the book by implementing a so-called epistemic model checker, a program that can keep track of the epistemic effects caused by public announcements and public changes.

```
module CAIA where

import Data.List
```

Let's keep our set of agents limited to five, and give them some easy-to-use names:

```
data Agent = A | B | C | D | E deriving (Eq,Ord,Enum)

a,alice, b,bob, c,carol, d,dave, e,ernie  :: Agent
a = A; alice = A
b = B; bob   = B
c = C; carol = C
d = D; dave  = D
e = E; ernie = E

instance Show Agent where
   show A = "a"; show B = "b";
   show C = "c"; show D = "d";
   show E = "e"
```

Basic propositions are p_i, q_i, r_i, where i is an appropriate index:

```
data Prop = P Int | Q Int | R Int deriving (Eq,Ord)

instance Show Prop where
  show (P 0) = "p"; show (P i) = "p" ++ show i
  show (Q 0) = "q"; show (Q i) = "q" ++ show i
  show (R 0) = "r"; show (R i) = "r" ++ show i
```

The implementation of epistemic models closely follows their definition. We add two extra parameters: a list of agents that occur in the model, and a list of actual worlds. Obviously, from inside a model it is impossible to say which world is the *real* world. Still, we impose the constraint that the real world must be among the actual worlds.

```
data EpistM state = Mo {
        dom       :: [state],
        agents    :: [Agent],
        valuation :: [(state,[Prop])],
        rels      :: [(Agent,state,state)],
        actual    :: [state]
                    } deriving (Eq,Show)
```

This uses Haskell *record syntax*. The data type for an epistemic model has five fields, and each of these fields can be accessed with an appropriate function. The record syntax makes for a more compact definition, because the access functions for the fields are part of the definition of the data type. To see how this works, consider the following example model.

```
exampleModel :: EpistM Integer
exampleModel =
 Mo [0..3]
    [a..c]
    [(0,[]),(1,[P 0]),(2,[Q 0]),(3,[P 0, Q 0])]
    ([ (a,x,x) | x <- [0..3] ] ++
     [ (b,x,x) | x <- [0..3] ] ++
     [ (c,x,y) | x <- [0..3], y <- [0..3] ])
    [1]
```

We can access the valuation of this model by means of

```
CAIA> valuation exampleModel
```

`[(0,[]),(1,[p]),(2,[q]),(3,[p,q])]`

and similarly for the domain, the list of agents, the relations, and the actual worlds.

As was explained above, public announcements can be viewed as actions that change a model by removing the worlds that do not satisfy the contents of the announcement. Each announcement ϕ comes with a function $M \mapsto M \mid \phi$. In case we add a set of actual worlds U to the model, the effect of $M \mid \phi$ on U is given by:

$$U \mapsto \{w \in U \mid M \models_w \phi\}.$$

The advantage of adding a set of actual worlds is that the effect of a public announcement with falsehood can now simply be encoded, as follows: ϕ is a falsehood in pointed model $M = (W, V, R, U)$ if

$$(W, V, R) \not\models_u \phi$$

for all $u \in U$. The result of updating with a falsehood is an *inconsistent* pointed model, i.e. a pointed model of the form $(W', V', R', \emptyset)$.

As we did earlier (on page 109), we define relations as lists of pairs:

```
type Rel a = [(a,a)]
```

We also define list inclusion and the converse of a relation:

```
containedIn :: Eq a => [a] -> [a] -> Bool
containedIn xs ys = all (\ x -> elem x ys) xs

cnv :: Rel a -> Rel a
cnv r = [ (y,x) | (x,y) <- r ]
```

Next, we repeat the definition of an infix operator for relational composition (cf. page 110):

```
infixr 5 @@

(@@) :: Eq a => Rel a -> Rel a -> Rel a
r @@ s = nub [ (x,z) | (x,y) <- r, (w,z) <- s, y == w ]
```

Here are the three checks on accessibility relations that we need:

```
reflR :: Eq a => [a] -> Rel a -> Bool
reflR xs r = [(x,x) | x <- xs] 'containedIn' r


symmR :: Eq a => Rel a -> Bool
symmR r = cnv r 'containedIn' r


transR :: Eq a => Rel a -> Bool
transR r = (r @@ r) 'containedIn' r
```

Together these allow us to express that a certain relation is an equivalence relation. In modal logic, such a relation is called an S5 relation:

```
isS5 :: Eq a => [a] -> Rel a -> Bool
isS5 xs r = reflR xs r && transR r && symmR r
```

The epistemic model instance `exampleModel` that was given above is in fact an
example of a multi S5 model: each of its three accessibility relations is S5, i.e.
an equivalence relation. Here is an auxiliary function for extracting each of the
relations from an epistemic model:

```
rel :: Agent -> EpistM a -> Rel a
rel a model = [ (x,y) | (b,x,y) <- rels model, a == b ]
```

This gives:

```
CAIA> rel a exampleModel
[(0,0),(1,1),(2,2),(3,3)]
CAIA> rel b exampleModel
[(0,0),(1,1),(2,2),(3,3)]
CAIA> rel c exampleModel
[(0,0),(0,1),(0,2),(0,3),(1,0),(1,1),(1,2),(1,3),
 (2,0),(2,1),(2,2),(2,3),(3,0),(3,1),(3,2),(3,3)]
CAIA>  isS5 (dom exampleModel) (rel a exampleModel)
True
```

Every equivalence relation R on A corresponds to a partition on A, namely
the set $\{[a]_R \mid a \in A\}$, where $[a]_R = \{b \in A \mid (a,b) \in R\}$. Here is an
implementation:

```
rel2partition :: Ord a => [a] -> Rel a -> [[a]]
rel2partition []      r = []
rel2partition (x:xs) r = xclass : rel2partition (xs\\xclass) r
           where xclass = x : [ y | y <- xs, (x,y) 'elem' r ]
```

The function `rel2partition` can be used to write a display function for S5 models that shows each accessibility relation as a partition:

```
showS5 :: (Ord a,Show a) => EpistM a -> [String]
showS5 m = show (dom m)
         : show (valuation m)
         : map show [ (a,(rel2partition (dom m)) (rel a m))
                                   | a <- (agents m)]
        ++ [show (actual m)]
```

Here @ is used to introduce a shorthand or name for a data structure. The following is a function for example display:

```
displayS5 ::  (Ord a,Show a) => EpistM a -> IO()
displayS5 = putStrLn . unlines . showS5
```

It works as follows:

```
CAIA> displayS5 exampleModel
[0,1,2,3]
[(0,[]),(1,[p]),(2,[q]),(3,[p,q])]
(a,[[0],[1],[2],[3]])
(b,[[0],[1],[2],[3]])
(c,[[0,1,2,3]])
[1]
```

Blissful ignorance is the state where you don't know anything, but you know also that there is no reason to worry, for you know that nobody knows anything.

A Kripke model where every agent from agent set A is in blissful ignorance about a (finite) set of propositions P, with $|P| = k$, is a triple (W, V, R) with components that look as follows:

$$W = \{0, \ldots, 2^k - 1\},$$
$$V = \text{any surjection in } W \to \mathcal{P}(P),$$
$$R = \{x \xrightarrow{a} y \mid (x, y) \in W, a \in A\}.$$

A surjection is a function which in onto (cf. page 156). Note that V is in fact a bijection, for $|\mathcal{P}(P)| = 2^k = |W|$. Generating models for blissful ignorance is done with:

```
initM :: [Agent] -> [Prop] -> EpistM Integer
initM ags props = (Mo worlds ags val accs points)
   where worlds = [0..(2^k-1)]
         k      = length props
         val    = zip worlds (sortL (powerList props))
         accs   = [ (ag,st1,st2) | ag  <- ags,
                                   st1 <- worlds,
                                   st2 <- worlds ]
         points = worlds
```

Here `powerList` is the list counterpart of power set:

```
powerList  :: [a] -> [[a]]
powerList  []     = [[]]
powerList  (x:xs) = (powerList xs) ++ (map (x:) (powerList xs))
```

The following function sorts lists by their length:

```
sortL :: Ord a => [[a]] -> [[a]]
sortL = sortBy (\ xs ys -> if   length xs < length ys
                           then LT
                           else if   length xs > length ys
                           then GT
                           else compare xs ys)
```

This gives:

```
CAIA> zip [0..2^3-1] (sortL (powerList [P 1,P 2,P 3]))
[(0,[]),(1,[p1]),(2,[p2]),(3,[p3]),(4,[p1,p2]),
 (5,[p1,p3]),(6,[p2,p3]),(7,[p1,p2,p3])]
```

The general knowledge accessibility relation of a set of agents C is given by

$$\bigcup_{c \in C} R_c.$$

Exercise 13.8 Assume that R_a, the knowledge relation for agent a, and R_b, the knowledge relation for agent b, are equivalence relations. Does it follow that the general knowledge relation for a and b is also an equivalence? Give a proof or a counterexample.

Computing the reflexive transitive closure works as follows. If A is finite, any binary relation R on A is finite as well. In particular, there will be k with $R^{k+1} \subseteq R^0 \cup \cdots \cup R^k$. Thus, in the finite case reflexive transitive closure can be computed by successively computing $\bigcup_{n \in \{0,..,k\}} R^n$ until $R^{k+1} \subseteq \bigcup_{n \in \{0,...,k\}} R^n$. In other words: the reflexive transitive closure of a relation R can be computed from I by repeated application of the operation

$$\lambda S \mapsto (S \cup (R \circ S)),$$

until the operation reaches a fixpoint. Recall from Chapter 5 that a fixpoint of an operation f is an x for which $f(x) = x$. Least fixpoint calculation was done by means of the following function (cf. page 110):

```
lfp :: Eq a => (a -> a) -> a -> a
lfp f x | x == f x   = x
        | otherwise = lfp f (f x)
```

We used this to compute the reflexive transitive closure as follows:

```
rtc :: Ord a => [a] -> Rel a -> Rel a
rtc xs r = lfp (\ s -> (sort.nub) (s ++ (r@@s))) i
  where i = [ (x,x) | x <- xs ]
```

Here is an example:

```
CAIA> rtc [1,2,3] [(1,2),(2,3)]
[(1,1),(1,2),(1,3),(2,2),(2,3),(3,3)]
```

Now it is easy to also compute common knowledge, for the common knowledge relation for a group of agents C is the relation

$$\left(\bigcup_{c \in C} R_c \right)^*.$$

We represent formulas in the following way:

```
data Form = Top
          | Prop Prop
          | Neg  Form
          | Conj [Form]
          | Disj [Form]
          | K    EE Form
          | PA   Form Form
          | PC   [(Prop,Form)] Form
          deriving (Eq,Ord)
```

Formulas of the form `K e f` express that knowledge `e` ensures truth of `f`, formulas of the form `PA f1 f2` express that public announcement `f1` makes `f2` true, and formulas of the form `PC s f` express that public change `s` makes `f` true.

Here is the data type of epistemic expressions:

```
data EE = Agent Agent
        | Test Form
        | Cmp  EE EE
        | Sum  [EE]
        | Star EE
        deriving (Eq,Ord)
```

Example formulas are p and q:

```
p = Prop (P 0)
q = Prop (Q 0)
```

Note the following type difference:

```
CAIA> :t (P 0)
P 0 :: Prop
CAIA> :t p
p :: Form
```

For better readability we define show functions for `Form` and `EE`:

```
instance Show Form where
  show Top                = "T"
  show (Prop p)           = show p
  show (Neg f)            = '-':(show f)
  show (Conj fs)          = '&': show fs
  show (Disj fs)          = 'v': show fs
  show (K e f)            = '[':show e ++"]"++show f
  show (PA f1 f2)         = '[':'!': show f1  ++"]"++show f2
  show (PC s f)           = show s ++ show f

instance Show EE where
  show (Agent a)    = show a
  show (Test f)     = '?': show f
  show (Cmp e1 e2)  = show e1  ++ ";" ++ show e2
  show (Sum es)     = 'U': show es
  show (Star e)     = '(': show e  ++ ")*"
```

It is also useful to have an abbreviation for common knowledge formulas:

```
ck :: [Agent] -> Form -> Form
ck ags f = K (Star (Sum [Agent a | a <- ags])) f
```

Valuation lookup can be used to look up the valuation for a world in a model:

```
apply :: Eq a => [(a,b)] -> a -> b
apply [] _ = error "argument not in list"
apply ((x,z):xs) y | x == y    = z
                   | otherwise = apply xs y
```

In Chapter 5 we defined aR as being the set

$$\{b \in A \mid Rab\}$$

for R a binary relation on A, and $a \in A$. This was called the right section of a relation. We implement it again:

```
rightS :: Ord a => a -> Rel a -> [a]
rightS x r = (sort.nub) [ z | (y,z) <- r, x == y ]
```

Now we turn to the evaluation of formulas. We start with the Boolean cases:

```
isTrueAt :: Ord state => EpistM state -> state -> Form -> Bool
isTrueAt m w Top       = True
isTrueAt m w (Prop p)  = p 'elem' (concat
                            [ ps | (w',ps) <- valuation m, w'==w])
isTrueAt m w (Neg  f)  = not (isTrueAt m w f)
isTrueAt m w (Conj fs) = and (map (isTrueAt m w) fs)
isTrueAt m w (Disj fs) = or  (map (isTrueAt m w) fs)
```

This is the epistemic case:

```
isTrueAt m w (K e f)   = and (map (flip (isTrueAt m) f)
                                  (rightS w (evalEE m e)))
```

Next we consider the public announcement case:

```
isTrueAt m w (PA f1 f2) = not (isTrueAt m  w f1)
                          ||    isTrueAt m' w f2
             where m' = upd_pa m f1
```

Finally, this is the public change case:

```
isTrueAt m w (PC s f) = isTrueAt (upd_pc m s) w f
```

The evaluation of epistemic expressions is defined as follows:

```
evalEE :: Ord state => EpistM state -> EE -> Rel state
evalEE m (Agent a)   = rel a m
evalEE m (Test f)    = [(w,w) | w <- dom m, isTrueAt m w f]
evalEE m (Cmp e1 e2) = (evalEE m e1) @@ (evalEE m e2)
evalEE m (Sum (es))  = (sort.nub) (concat (map (evalEE m) es))
evalEE m (Star e)    = rtc (dom m) (evalEE m e)
```

The state of bliss is evaluated like this:

```
test1 = isTrueAt (initM [a..c] [P 0]) 0
                 (ck [a..c] (Neg (K (Agent a) p)))
```

Now we can use the function `isTrueAt` to implement a function that checks for truth at all the designated states of an epistemic model:

```
isTrue :: Ord state => EpistM state -> Form -> Bool
isTrue m f = and [ isTrueAt m s f | s <- actual m ]
```

Here is another test of `initM`:

```
test2 = isTrue (initM [a..c] [P 0])
               (ck [a..c] (Neg (K (Agent a) p)))
```

Next we implement public announcement updates:

```
upd_pa :: Ord state => EpistM state -> Form -> EpistM state
upd_pa m@(Mo states  agents val  rels  actual)  f =
        (Mo states' agents val' rels' actual')
   where
     states' = [ s      | s         <- states,
                              isTrueAt m s f     ]
     val'    = [ (s,p)  | (s,p)    <- val,
                              s 'elem' states'   ]
     rels'   = [ (a,x,y) | (a,x,y) <- rels,
                             x 'elem' states',
                             y 'elem' states'   ]
     actual' = [ s      | s         <- actual,
                             s 'elem' states'   ]
```

For substitutions we define a type synonym:

```
type Subst = [(Prop,Form)]
```

Public change updates can then be implemented as follows:

```
upd_pc :: Ord state => EpistM state -> Subst -> EpistM state
upd_pc m@(Mo worlds agents val  acc points) subst =
        (Mo worlds agents val' acc points)
   where
     val' = [ (w,[p | p <- ps, isTrueAt m w (liftS subst p)])
               | w <- worlds ]
     ps   = (sort.nub) (concat (map snd val))
     liftS :: Subst -> Prop -> Form
     liftS []           p          = Prop p
     liftS ((x,z):xs) y | x == y    = z
                        | otherwise = liftS xs y
```

Let us consider an example model with three agents and two proposition letters.

```
m0 = initM [a..c] [P 0,Q 0]
```

This model has four worlds, and none of the agents is able to tell any of these apart. After an update with a public announcement of $p \vee q$ the world where p and q are both false has disappeared.

```
CAIA> displayS5 m0
[0,1,2,3]
[(0,[]),(1,[p]),(2,[q]),(3,[p,q])]
(a,[[0,1,2,3]])
(b,[[0,1,2,3]])
(c,[[0,1,2,3]])
[0,1,2,3]

CAIA> displayS5 (upd_pa m0 (Disj [p,q]))
[1,2,3]
[(1,[p]),(2,[q]),(3,[p,q])]
(a,[[1,2,3]])
(b,[[1,2,3]])
(c,[[1,2,3]])
[1,2,3]
```

Note that in the original model the worlds are numbered starting from 0, and in the update result the worlds are numbered starting from 1. It is useful to be able to convert any type of state list to `[0..]`:

```
convert :: Eq state => EpistM state -> EpistM Integer
convert (Mo states  agents val  rels  actual) =
        Mo states' agents val' rels' actual'
   where
     states' = map f states
     val'    = map (\ (x,y)   -> (f x,y))      val
     rels'   = map (\ (x,y,z) -> (x,f y,f z)) rels
     actual' = map f actual
     f       = apply (zip states [0..])
```

This effects a renumbering, as follows:

```
CAIA> (displayS5.convert) (upd_pa m0 (Disj [p,q]))
[0,1,2]
[(0,[p]),(1,[q]),(2,[p,q])]
(a,[[0,1,2]])
(b,[[0,1,2]])
(c,[[0,1,2]])
[0,1,2]
```

In an epistemic model with a set of designated points, we are only interested in the set of those worlds that are accessible via some path from any of the designated worlds. This is called the *generated submodel*. Here is an implementation:

```
gsm :: Ord state => EpistM state ->  EpistM state
gsm (Mo states  ags val  rel  points) =
    Mo states' ags val' rel' points
   where
     states' = closure rel ags points
     val'    = [(s,ps)   | (s,ps)    <- val,
                             s 'elem' states'  ]
     rel'    = [(ag,s,s') | (ag,s,s') <- rel,
                             s 'elem' states',
                             s' 'elem' states'  ]
```

This uses the closure of a state list, given a relation and a list of agents:

```
closure ::  Ord state => [(Agent,state,state)] ->
                          [Agent] -> [state] -> [state]
closure rel agents xs = lfp f xs where
 f = \ ys -> (nub.sort) (ys ++ (expand rel agents ys))
```

The expansion of a relation R given a state set S and a set of agents B is given by $\{t \mid s \xrightarrow{b} t \in R, s \in S, b \in B\}$. Here is an implementation:

```
expand :: Ord state => [(Agent,state,state)] ->
                       [Agent] -> [state] -> [state]
expand rel agents ys = (nub.sort.concat)
  [ alternatives rel ag state | ag    <- agents,
                                state <- ys       ]
```

The epistemic alternatives for agent a in state s are the states in sR_a (i.e. the states reachable through R_a from s):

```
alternatives :: Eq state => [(Agent,state,state)] ->
                            Agent -> state -> [state]
alternatives rel ag current = [ s' | (a,s,s') <- rel,
                                  a == ag, s == current ]
```

This ends the implementation of the epistemic model checker. To show how this can be used, we demonstrate a check of a muddy children scenario. We model the case where there are four children, Alice, Bob, Carol, and Dave, where Bob, Carol, and Dave are the muddy ones.

We use propositions p_1, p_2, p_3, p_4 to express that the first, second, third, or fourth child is muddy:

```
p1, p2, p3, p4 :: Form
p1 = Prop (P 1); p2 = Prop (P 2)
p3 = Prop (P 3); p4 = Prop (P 4)
```

The initial muddy model has 16 worlds; one for each muddiness possibility. Agent a cannot distinguish worlds that differ only in the value of p_1, for Alice cannot see whether she herself is muddy. Agent b cannot distinguish worlds that differ only in the value of p_2, for Bob cannot see whether he himself is muddy. Agent c cannot distinguish worlds that differ only in the value of p_3, for Carol cannot see whether she herself is muddy. Agent d cannot distinguish worlds that differ only in the value of p_4, for Dave cannot see whether he himself is muddy. This information completely determines the accessibility relation.

```
computeAcc :: Agent -> [Integer] -> [Prop] -> [(Integer,[Prop])]
                  -> [(Agent,Integer,Integer)]
computeAcc ag states props val =
  [ (ag,x,y) | x <- states, y <- states,
             apply val x \\ props == apply val y \\ props ]
```

The actual world is the world where p_1 is false and p_2, p_3, p_4 are true. This yields the following definition for the initial epistemic model.

```
initMuddy :: EpistM Integer
initMuddy = Mo states
               [a..d]
               valuation
               (computeAcc a states [P 1] valuation ++
                computeAcc b states [P 2] valuation ++
                computeAcc c states [P 3] valuation ++
                computeAcc d states [P 4] valuation)
               [7]
  where states    = [0..15]
        valuation = zip states (powerList [P 1,P 2,P 3,P 4])
```

Here is a check that this is correct:

```
CAIA> displayS5 initMuddy
[0,1,2,3,4,5,6,7,8,9,10,11,12,13,14,15]
[(0,[]),(1,[p4]),(2,[p3]),(3,[p3,p4]),(4,[p2]),(5,[p2,p4]),
 (6,[p2,p3]),(7,[p2,p3,p4]),(8,[p1]),(9,[p1,p4]),(10,[p1,p3]),
 (11,[p1,p3,p4]),(12,[p1,p2]),(13,[p1,p2,p4]),(14,[p1,p2,p3]),
 (15,[p1,p2,p3,p4])]
(a,[[0,8],[1,9],[2,10],[3,11],[4,12],[5,13],[6,14],[7,15]])
(b,[[0,4],[1,5],[2,6],[3,7],[8,12],[9,13],[10,14],[11,15]])
(c,[[0,2],[1,3],[4,6],[5,7],[8,10],[9,11],[12,14],[13,15]])
(d,[[0,1],[2,3],[4,5],[6,7],[8,9],[10,11],[12,13],[14,15]])
[7]
```

The statement of the father that at least one child is muddy should rule out one of these worlds:

```
m1 = convert (upd_pa initMuddy (Disj [p1,p2,p3,p4]))
```

This yields:

```
CAIA> displayS5 m1
[0,1,2,3,4,5,6,7,8,9,10,11,12,13,14]
[(0,[p4]),(1,[p3]),(2,[p3,p4]),(3,[p2]),(4,[p2,p4]),
 (5,[p2,p3]),(6,[p2,p3,p4]),(7,[p1]),(8,[p1,p4]),
 (9,[p1,p3]),(10,[p1,p3,p4]),(11,[p1,p2]),(12,[p1,p2,p4]),
 (13,[p1,p2,p3]),(14,[p1,p2,p3,p4])]
(a,[[0,8],[1,9],[2,10],[3,11],[4,12],[5,13],[6,14],[7]])
(b,[[0,4],[1,5],[2,6],[3],[7,11],[8,12],[9,13],[10,14]])
(c,[[0,2],[1],[3,5],[4,6],[7,9],[8,10],[11,13],[12,14]])
(d,[[0],[1,2],[3,4],[5,6],[7,8],[9,10],[11,12],[13,14]])
[6]
```

The following formulas express that the children know their states:

```
aK =  Disj [K (Agent a) p1, K (Agent a) (Neg p1)]
bK =  Disj [K (Agent b) p2, K (Agent b) (Neg p2)]
cK =  Disj [K (Agent c) p3, K (Agent c) (Neg p3)]
dK =  Disj [K (Agent d) p4, K (Agent d) (Neg p4)]
```

In the first round, they all say that they do not know their state:

```
m2 = convert (upd_pa m1 (Conj [Neg aK,Neg bK,Neg cK,Neg dK]))
```

Here is the result:

```
CAIA> displayS5 m2
[0,1,2,3,4,5,6,7,8,9,10]
[(0,[p3,p4]),(1,[p2,p4]),(2,[p2,p3]),(3,[p2,p3,p4]),
 (4,[p1,p4]),(5,[p1,p3]),(6,[p1,p3,p4]),(7,[p1,p2]),
 (8,[p1,p2,p4]),(9,[p1,p2,p3]),(10,[p1,p2,p3,p4])]
(a,[[0,6],[1,8],[2,9],[3,10],[4],[5],[7]])
(b,[[0,3],[1],[2],[4,8],[5,9],[6,10],[7]])
(c,[[0],[1,3],[2],[4,6],[5],[7,9],[8,10]])
(d,[[0],[1],[2,3],[4],[5,6],[7,8],[9,10]])
```

[3]

In the second round, again they all say that they do not know their state:

```
m3 = convert (upd_pa m2 (Conj [Neg aK,Neg bK,Neg cK,Neg dK]))
```

The result is:

```
GAIA> displayS5 m3
[0,1,2,3,4]
[(0,[p2,p3,p4]),(1,[p1,p3,p4]),(2,[p1,p2,p4]),
 (3,[p1,p2,p3]),(4,[p1,p2,p3,p4])]
(a,[[0,4],[1],[2],[3]])
(b,[[0],[1,4],[2],[3]])
(c,[[0],[1],[2,4],[3]])
(d,[[0],[1],[2],[3,4]])
[0]
```

In the third round, *a* still does not know, but *b, c, d* know their state.

```
m4 = convert (upd_pa m3 (Conj [Neg aK, bK, cK, dK]))
```

After this round, everything is known:

```
CAIA> displayS5 m4
[0]
[(0,[p2,p3,p4])]
(a,[[0]])
(b,[[0]])
(c,[[0]])
(d,[[0]])
[0]
```

Exercise 13.9 Carry out the model checking process for the wise men puzzle.

Exercise 13.10 Carry out the model checking process for the presuppositions of the update with *Jan is a bachelor* update. Check out what happens if this is preceded with a public announcement of *Jan is male*.

Exercise 13.11 Carry out the model checking process for yes/no questions. Try to find as many different appropriate answers to a question as you can. Implement a check for what constitutes an appropriate answer to a particular question.

Exercise 13.12 Implement translations that remove public announcement operators from the language. The types are `tr1 :: Form -> Form` and `tr2 :: EE -> EE`. Next, perform a number of checks to test whether the translations respect the semantics.

Exercise 13.13 Implement translations that remove public change operators from the language. The types are `tr3 :: Form -> Form` and `tr4 :: EE -> EE`. Next, perform a number of checks to test whether the translations respect the semantics.

13.8 Further Reading

Textbooks on epistemic logic are [FHMV95] and the more recent [DvdHK07]. Dynamic epistemic logic not only analyses knowledge but also the epistemic effects of communication. A key paper is [BMS98]. An elegant version of a very rich dynamic epistemic logic can be found in [BvEK06]. Dynamic epistemic modelling is the art of computing the effects of epistemic updates. A tool for this, implemented in Haskell, is DEMO; see [Eij07a] for documentation.

An illuminating analysis of the role of social rituals in the creation of common knowledge is Chwe's *Rational Ritual* [Chw01]. *Discourses on Social Software* [EV09] gives many examples of the role of (common) knowledge in social interaction.

The analysis of presupposition in terms of common knowledge is based on [EU07], and the analysis of questions and appropriateness of answers was inspired by [UG08].

Afterword

And now, Dear Reader who got this far, let us take a minute to address you, before we take our leave. You have come a long way indeed. You started out wanting to know a thing or two about natural language semantics, and look where you are now. At the end of this book you find yourself well on your way towards mastery of functional programming. Also, you have gained quite a bit of experience in the application of formal tools in semantic and pragmatic analysis of natural language. For sure, there is a lot more to be learned, but now it is time to relax and be proud of what you have achieved. At least treat yourself to a beer. We think you have earned it.

Bibliography

[Als92] H. Alshawi, editor. *The Core Language Engine*. MIT Press, Cambridge, Mass., and London, England, 1992.

[AS96] H. Abelson and G.J. Sussman. *Structure and Interpretation of Computer Programs* (Second edition). MIT Press, 1996.

[AU72] A.V. Aho and J.D. Ullman. *Theory of Parsing, Translation and Compiling*, volume Volume I: Parsing. Englewood Cliffs, NJ, 1972.

[Bar84] H. Barendregt. *The Lambda Calculus: Its Syntax and Semantics* (Second edition). North-Holland, Amsterdam, 1984.

[Bar02] Chris Barker. Continuations and the nature of quantification. *Natural Language Semantics*, 10:211–242, 2002.

[Bar04] Chris Barker. Continuations in natural language. In H. Thielecke, editor, *CW'04: Proceedings of the 4th ACM SIGPLAN continuations workshop*, Tech. Rep. CSR-04-1, pages 1–11. School of Computer Science, University of Birmingham, 2004.

[BAW07] Gilad Ben-Avi and Yoad Winter. The semantics of intensionalization. In Reinhard Muskens, editor, *Workshop on New Directions in Type-Theoretic Grammars*, pages 98–112, 2007.

[BB00] H. Barendregt and E. Barendsen. Introduction to the lambda calculus, revised edition. Technical report, University of Nijmegen, March 2000. Available from `ftp://ftp.cs.kun.nl/pub/CompMath.Found/lambda.pdf`.

[BB05] P. Blackburn and J. Bos. *Representation and Inference for Natural Language: A First Course in Computational Semantics*. CSLI Lecture Notes, 2005.

[BC81] J. Barwise and R. Cooper. Generalized quantifiers and natural language. *Linguistics and Philosophy*, 4:159–219, 1981.

[BCM+02] F. Baader, D. Calvanese, D.L. McGuinness, D. Nardi, and P.F. Patel-Schneider, editors. *The Description Logic Handbook*. Cambridge University Press, 2002.

[BE82] J. van Benthem and J. van Eijck. The dynamics of interpretation. *Journal of Semantics*, 1(1):3–20, 1982.

[Ben86] J. van Benthem. *Essays in Logical Semantics*. Reidel, 1986.

[Ben88] Johan van Benthem. Strategies of intensionalization. In I. Bodnaár, A. Máté, and L. Pólos, editors, *Intensional Logic, History of Philosophy, and Methodology: To Imre Ruzsa on the occasion of his 65th birthday*, pages 41–59. Department of Symbolic Logic, Eötvös University, 1988.

[BGMV93] Patrick Blackburn, Claire Gardent, and Wilfried Meyer-Viol. Talking about trees. In *Proceedings of the 6th Confeence of the European Chapter of the Association for Computational Linguistics*, pages 21–29, 1993.

389

[Bir98] R. Bird. *Introduction to Functional Programming Using Haskell*. Prentice Hall, 1998.

[BJ07] Chris Barker and Pauline I. Jacobson, editors. *Direct Compositionality*. Oxford University Press, 2007.

[BLSW04] David I. Beaver, Beth Levin, Peter Sells, and Maria Wolters. The optimization of discourse anaphora. *Linguistics and Philosophy*, 27:3–56, 2004.

[BMS98] A. Baltag, L.S. Moss, and S. Solecki. The logic of public announcements, common knowledge, and private suspicions. In I. Bilboa, editor, *Proceedings of TARK'98*, pages 43–56, 1998.

[BN02] F. Baader and W. Nutt. Basic description logics. In F. Baader, D. Calvanese, D.L. McGuinness, D. Nardi, and P.F. Patel-Schneider, editors, *The Description Logic Handbook*, pages 47–100. Cambridge University Press, 2002.

[BRVs95] Rolf Backofen, James Rogers, and K. Vijay-shanker. A first-order axiomatization of the theory of finite trees. *Journal of Logic, Language and Information*, 4:5–39, 1995.

[BS94] Dorit Ben-Shalom. A tree characterization of generalized quantifier reducibility. In M. Kanazawa and C.J. Pinón, editors, *Dynamics, Polarity and Quantification*, number 48 in CSLI Lecture Notes, pages 147–171. CSLI, 1994.

[BS06] Chris Barker and Chung-chieh Shan. Explaining crossover and superiority as left-to-right evaluation. *Linguistics and Philosophy*, 29(1):91–134, 2006.

[BS08] Chris Barker and Chung-chieh Shan. Donkey anaphora is in-scope binding. *Semantics and Pragmatics*, 1(1):1–46, 2008.

[BtM97] J. van Benthem and A. ter Meulen, editors. *Handbook of Logic and Language*. Elsevier, Amsterdam, 1997.

[Bur98] Stanley N. Burris. *Logic for Mathematics and Computer Science*. Prentice Hall, 1998.

[Bür05] D. Büring. *Binding Theory*. Cambridge Textbooks in Linguistics. Cambridge University Press, 2005.

[BvEK06] J. van Benthem, J. van Eijck, and B. Kooi. Logics of communication and change. *Information and Computation*, 204(11):1620–1662, 2006.

[Cam08] Aifric Campbell. *The Semantics of Murder*. Serpent's Tail, 2008.

[Cho57] N. Chomsky. *Syntactic Structures*. Mouton, The Hague/Paris, 1957.

[Cho59] N. Chomsky. On certain formal properties of grammars. *Information and Control*, 2(2):137–167, 1959.

[Cho81] N. Chomsky. *Lectures on Government and Binding*. Foris, Dordrecht, 1981.

[Cho92] N. Chomsky. *A Minimalist Program for Linguistic Theory*. MIT Press, 1992.

[Chu36] A. Church. An unsolvable problem of elementary number theory. *American Journal of Mathematics*, 58:345–363, 1936.

[Chw01] Michael Suk-Young Chwe. *Rational Ritual*. Princeton University Press, Princeton and Oxford, 2001.

[CK97] J. Cole and C. Kisseberth. Restricting multi-level constraint evaluation: Opaque rule interaction in Yawelmani vowel harmony. In K. Suzuki and D. Elzinga, editors, *Proceedings of the Arizona Phonology Conference*, pages 18–38, 1997.

[Coo75] R. Cooper. *Montague's Semantic Theory and Transformational Syntax*. PhD thesis, University of Massachusetts at Amherst, 1975.

[Coo83] R. Cooper. *Quantification and Syntactic Theory*. Reidel, Dordrecht, 1983.

[CR02] M. Crochemore and W. Rytter. *Jewels of Stringology*. World Scientific Press, 2002.

[Dal83] D. van Dalen. *Logic and Structure* (Second edition). Springer, Berlin, 1983.

[DE04] Kees Doets and Jan van Eijck. *The Haskell Road to Logic, Maths and Programming*, volume 4 of *Texts in Computing*. College Publications, London, 2004.

[Dek03] P. Dekker. Meanwhile, within the Frege boundary. *Linguistics and Philosophy*, 26:547–556, 2003.

[dG04] Philippe de Groote. Towards a Montegovian account of dynamics. In *Proceedings of Semantics and Linguistic Theory XVI*, CLC Publications, 2004.

[DI07] Hal Daume III. *Yet another Haskell tutorial*, wikibooks.org edition, 2007.

[Dow89] D. R. Dowty. On the semantic content of the notion of 'thematic role'. In B. Partee, G. Chierchia, and R. Turner, editors, *Properties, Type, and Meanings*, volume 2, pages 69–130. Kluwer, Dordrecht, 1989.

[DP90] B.A. Davey and H.A. Priestley. *Introduction to Lattices and Order* (Second edition). Cambridge University Press, 2002 (First edition, 1990).

[DP96] Kees van Deemter and Stanley Peters, editors. *Semantic Ambiguity and Underspecification*. CSLI Press, 1996.

[DvdHK07] H.P. van Ditmarsch, W. van der Hoek, and B.P. Kooi. *Dynamic Epistemic Logic*, volume 337 of *Synthese Library*. Springer, 2007.

[DWP81] D.R. Dowty, R.E. Wall, and S. Peters. *Introduction to Montague Semantics*. Reidel, Dordrecht, 1981.

[Eij00] Jan van Eijck. The proper treatment of context in NL. In Paola Monachesi, editor, *Computational Linguistics in the Netherlands 1999: Selected Papers from the Tenth CLIN Meeting*, pages 41–51. Utrecht Institute of Linguistics OTS, 2000.

[Eij01] Jan van Eijck. Incremental dynamics. *Journal of Logic, Language and Information*, 10:319–351, 2001.

[Eij03] Jan van Eijck. Parser combinators for extraction. In Paul Dekker and Robert van Rooy, editors, *Proceedings of the Fourteenth Amsterdam Colloquium*, pages 99–104. ILLC, University of Amsterdam, 2003.

[Eij05] Jan van Eijck. Normal forms for characteristic functions on n-ary relations. *Journal of Logic and Computation*, 15:85–98, 2005.

[Eij07a] Jan van Eijck. DEMO – a demo of epistemic modelling. In Johan van Benthem, Dov Gabbay, and Benedikt Löwe, editors, *Interactive Logic – Proceedings of the 7th Augustus de Morgan Workshop*, number 1 in Texts in Logic and Games, pages 305–363. Amsterdam University Press, 2007.

[Eij07b] Jan van Eijck. Sequentially indexed grammars. *Journal of Logic and Computation*, 2007. Advance Access published on 30 May 2007.

[EK97] Jan van Eijck and Hans Kamp. Representing discourse in context. In J. van Benthem and A. ter Meulen, editors, *Handbook of Logic and Language*, pages 179–237. Elsevier, Amsterdam, 1997.

[End72] H.B. Enderton. *A Mathematical Introduction to Logic*. Academic Press, New York, 1972.

[EU07] Jan van Eijck and Christina Unger. The epistemics of presupposition projection. In Maria Aloni, Paul Dekker, and Floris Roelofsen, editors, *Proceedings of the Sixteenth Amsterdam Colloquium, December 17–19, 2007*, pages 235–240, Amsterdam, December 2007. ILLC.

[EV09] Jan van Eijck and Rineke Verbrugge, editors. *Discourses on Social Software*, volume 5 of *Texts in Logic and Games*. Amsterdam University Press, Amsterdam, 2009.

[FHMV95] R. Fagin, J.Y. Halpern, Y. Moses, and M.Y. Vardi. *Reasoning about Knowledge*. MIT Press, 1995.

[FL89] R. Frost and J. Launchbury. Constructing natural language interpreters in a lazy functional language. *The Computer Journal*, 32(2):108–121, 1989.

[FL05] Chris Fox and Shalom Lappin. *Foundations of Intensional Semantics*. Wiley-Blackwell, 2005.

[For07] M. Forsberg. *Three Tools for Language Processing: BNF Converter, Functional*

Morphology, and Extract. PhD thesis, Chalmers University of Technology and Göteborg University, 2007.

[Fre92] Gottlob Frege. Über Sinn und Bedeutung. *Zeitschrift für Philosophie und philosophische Kritik*, pages 25–50, 1892. Translated as: *On Sense and Reference*.

[Fro06] Richard A. Frost. Realization of natural language interfaces using lazy functional programming. *ACM Comput. Surv.*, 38(4), 2006.

[Gam91a] L.T.F. Gamut. *Language, Logic and Meaning, Part 1.* Chicago University Press, 1991.

[Gam91b] L.T.F. Gamut. *Language, Logic and Meaning, Part 2.* Chicago University Press, 1991.

[Gaz88] G. Gazdar. Applicability of indexed grammars to natural languages. In U. Reyle and C. Rohrer, editors, *Natural Language Parsing and Linguistic Theories*, pages 69–94. Reidel, Dordrecht, 1988.

[Gea80] P.T. Geach. *Reference and Generality: An Examination of Some Medieval and Modern Theories.* Cornell University Press, Ithaca, 1962 (Third revised edition, 1980).

[GJW95] B. Grosz, A. Joshi, and S. Weinstein. Centering: A framework for modeling the local coherence of discourse. *Computational Linguistics*, 21:203–226, 1995.

[GKPS85] G. Gazdar, E. Klein, G. Pullum, and I. Sag. *Generalized Phrase Structure Grammar.* Basil Blackwell, Oxford, 1985.

[Gra93] P. Graham. *On Lisp.* Prentice Hall, 1993.

[Gri75] H.P. Grice. Logic and conversation. In P. Cole, editor, *Speech Acts, Syntax and Semantics, Vol. III: Speech Acts.* Academic Press, New York, NY, 1975.

[Gru65] J.S. Gruber. *Studies in Lexical Relations.* PhD thesis, MIT, 1965. Published in revised form in 1976.

[GS84] J. Groenendijk and M. Stokhof. *Studies on the Semantics of Questions and the Pragmatics of Answers.* PhD thesis, University of Amsterdam, 1984.

[GS86] B.J. Grosz and C.L. Sidner. Attention, intentions, and the structure of discourse. *Computational Linguistics*, 12:175–204, 1986.

[GS91] J. Groenendijk and M. Stokhof. Dynamic predicate logic. *Linguistics and Philosophy*, 14:39–100, 1991.

[Hal63] P. Halmos. *Lectures on Boolean Algebras.* Van Nostrand, 1963.

[Han04] Chris Hankin. *An Introduction to Lambda Calculi for Computer Scientists.* College Publications, London, 2004.

[Hei82] I. Heim. *The Semantics of Definite and Indefinite Noun Phrases.* PhD thesis, University of Massachusetts, Amherst, 1982.

[Hei92] I. Heim. Presupposition projection and the semantics of the attitude verbs. *Journal of Semantics*, 9(3):183–221, 1992. Special Issue: Presupposition, Part 1.

[Hel78] S. Hellberg. *The Morphology of Present-Day Swedish.* Almqvist & Wiskell International, Stockholm, Sweden, 1978.

[Hen93] H. Hendriks. *Studied Flexibility: Categories and Types in Syntax and Semantics.* PhD thesis, ILLC, Amsterdam, 1993.

[HFP96] P. Hudak, J. Fasel, and J. Peterson. A gentle introduction to Haskell. Technical report, Yale University, 1996. Online version: `http://www.haskell.org/tutorial/`.

[HR04] M. Huth and M. Ryan. *Logic in Computer Science: Modelling and Reasoning about Systems* (Second edition). Cambridge University Press, 2004.

[Hut92] G. Hutton. Higher-order functions for parsing. *Journal of Functional Programming*, 2(3):323–343, 1992.

[Hut07] G. Hutton. *Programming in Haskell.* Cambridge University Press, 2007.

[Jac72] R. Jackendoff. *Semantic Interpretation in Generative Grammar*. MIT Press, 1972.

[Jan97] Theo M.V. Janssen. Compositionality. In Johan van Benthem and Alice ter Meulen, editors, *Handbook of Logic and Language*, pages 417–473. Elsevier, Amsterdam, 1997.

[JS01] J. Jeuring and D. Swierstra. Grammars and parsing. Lecture Notes, Utrecht University, 2001.

[Kam81] H. Kamp. A theory of truth and semantic representation. In J. Groenendijk, T. Janssen, and M. Stokhof, editors, *Formal Methods in the Study of Language*, pages 277–322. Mathematisch Centrum, Amsterdam, 1981.

[Kan09] Makoto Kanazawa. A note on intensionalization. Unpublished note, National Institute of Informatics, Tokio, available from `http://research.nii.ac.jp/~kanazawa/publications/`, December 2009.

[Kee87] E. Keenan. Unreducible n-ary quantification in natural language. In P. Gärdenfors, editor, *Generalized Quantifiers, Linguistic and Logical Approaches*, pages 109–150. Reidel, Dordrecht, 1987.

[Kee92] E. Keenan. Beyond the Frege boundary. *Linguistics and Philosophy*, 15(2):199–221, 1992.

[Kel02] H. Keller. *The Story of my Life*. Dell Publishers, 1978 (1902).

[KF85] Edward L. Keenan and Leonard M. Faltz. *Boolean Semantics for Natural Language*. Reidel, 1985.

[Koh00] M. Kohlhase. Model generation for Discoure Representation Theory. In Werner Horn, editor, *Proceedings of the 14th European Conference on Artifical Intelligence*. Wiley, Chichester, UK, 2000.

[KR93] H. Kamp and U. Reyle. *From Discourse to Logic*. Kluwer, Dordrecht, 1993.

[Kri72] S.A. Kripke. Naming and necessity. In D. Davidson and G. Harman, editors, *Semantics of Natural Language*, pages 253–355. Reidel, Dordrecht, 1972.

[Lan69] Ronald Langacker. Pronominalization and the chain of command. In David Reibel and Sanford Schane, editors, *Modern Studies in English: Readings in Transformational Grammar*, pages 160–200. Prentice Hall, 1969.

[Lap97] Shalom Lappin, editor. *The Handbook of Contemporary Semantic Theory*. Wiley-Blackwell, 1997.

[Lev83] S.C. Levinson. *Pragmatics*. Cambridge University Press, 1983.

[Lew60] C.S. Lewis. *Studies in Words*. Cambridge University Press, 1960.

[Lew70] D. Lewis. General semantics. *Synthese*, 22:18–67, 1970.

[Łuk51] Jan Łukasiewicz. *Aristotle's Syllogistic from the Standpoint of Modern Formal Logic*. Clarendon Press, Oxford, 1951.

[Mon73] R. Montague. The proper treatment of quantification in ordinary English. In J. Hintikka, editor, *Approaches to Natural Language*, pages 221–242. Reidel, 1973.

[Mon74a] R. Montague. English as a formal language. In R.H. Thomason, editor, *Formal Philosophy: Selected Papers of Richard Montague*, pages 188–221. Yale University Press, New Haven and London, 1974.

[Mon74b] R. Montague. Universal grammar. In R.H. Thomason, editor, *Formal Philosophy: Selected Papers of Richard Montague*, pages 222–246. Yale University Press, New Haven and London, 1974.

[Mos57] A. Mostowski. On a generalization of quantifiers. *Fundamenta Mathematica*, 44:12–36, 1957.

[Mos08] Lawrence S. Moss. Completeness theorems for syllogistic fragments. In Fritz Hamm and Stephan Kepser, editors, *Logics for Linguistic Structures*, pages 143–174. Mouton de Gruyter, Berlin, New York, 2008.

[Mus89a] Reinhard Muskens. *Meaning and Partiality*. PhD thesis, University of Amsterdam, 1989.

[Mus89b] Reinhard Muskens. A relational formulation of the theory of types. *Linguistics and Philosophy*, 12:325–346, 1989.

[Mus94] Reinhard Muskens. A compositional discourse representation theory. In P. Dekker and M. Stokhof, editors, *Proceedings 9th Amsterdam Colloquium*, pages 467–486. ILLC, Amsterdam, 1994.

[Mus96] Reinhard Muskens. Combining Montague Semantics and Discourse Representation. *Linguistics and Philosophy*, 19:143–186, 1996.

[Mus07] Reinhard Muskens. Intensional models for the theory of types. *The Journal of Symbolic Logic*, 72(1):98–118, 2007.

[NB02] D. Nardi and R. J. Brachman. An introduction to description logics. In F. Baader, D. Calvanese, D.L. McGuinness, D. Nardi, and P.F. Patel-Schneider, editors, *The Description Logic Handbook*, pages 5–44. Cambridge University Press, 2002.

[OSG08] Bryan O'Sullivan, Don Stewart, and John Goerzen. *Real World Haskell*. O'Reilly, 2008.

[Per83] W. Percy. *Lost in the Cosmos: The Last Self-Help Book*. Simon and Schuster, 1983.

[PH04] I. Pratt-Hartmann. Fragments of language. *Journal of Logic, Language and Information*, 13(2):207–223, 2004.

[PJ03] S. Peyton Jones, editor. *Haskell 98 Language and Libraries: The Revised Report*. Cambridge University Press, 2003.

[Pla] Plato. *Theaetetus*. Many editions.

[PP02] Paul Portner and Barbara H. Partee, editors. *Formal Semantics: The Essential Readings*. Wiley-Blackwell, 2002.

[PR83] B. H. Partee and M. Rooth. Generalized conjunction and type ambiguity. In R. Bauerle, C. Schwarze, and A. von Stechow, editors, *Meaning, Use and Interpretation of Language*. Walter de Gruyter, Berlin, 1983.

[PS87] F.C.N. Pereira and S.M. Shieber. *Prolog and Natural Language Analysis*, volume 10 of *CSLI Lecture Notes*. CSLI, Stanford, 1987. Distributed by University of Chicago Press.

[PS94] C. Pollard and I. Sag. *Head-Driven Phrase Structure Grammar*. CSLI Lecture Notes. CSLI, Stanford, 1994. Distributed by University of Chicago Press.

[PW83] F.C.N. Pereira and H.D. Warren. Parsing as deduction. In *Proceedings of the 21st Annual Meeting of the ACL*, pages 137–111. MIT, Cambridge, Mass., 1983.

[PW06] Stanley Peters and Dag Westerståhl. *Quantifiers in Language and Logic*. Oxford University Press, 2006.

[Ran09] Aarne Ranta. Grammars as software libraries. In Gerard Huet, Jean-Jacques Lévi, and Gordon Plotkin, editors, *From Semantics to Computer Science: Essays in Honour of Gilles Kahn*. Cambridge University Press, 2009.

[Rei47] H. Reichenbach. *Elements of Symbolic Logic*. Macmillan, London, 1947.

[Rei76] T. Reinhart. *The Syntactic Domain of Anaphora*. PhD thesis, MIT, 1976.

[Rei83] T. Reinhart. *Anaphora and Semantic Interpretation*. Croom Helm, London, 1983.

[Rei00] T. Reinhart. The theta system: Syntactic realization of verbal concepts. Technical report, OTS Working Papers, 2000.

[Révon] G.E. Révész. *Introduction to Formal Languages*. Dover Publications, 1991 (revised version of the 1983 McGraw-Hill edition).

[Rey93] J.C. Reynolds. The discoveries of continuations. *Lisp and Symbolic Computation*, 6(3–4):233–247, 1993.

[RH99] C.O. Ringen and O. Heinämäki. Variation in finnish vowel harmony: An OT account. *Natural Language and Linguistic Theory*, 17:303–337, 1999.

[RL99] F. Rabhi and G. Lapalme. *Algorithms: A Functional Programming Approach.*

Addison-Wesley, 1999.

[Rog98] J. Rogers. *A Descriptive Approach to Language-Theoretic Complexity*. Studies in Logic, Language and Information. CSLI & FoLLI, 1998.

[Ros67] J.R. Ross. *Constraints on Variables in Syntax*. PhD thesis, MIT, 1967.

[Rus05] B. Russell. On denoting. *Mind*, 14:479–493, 1905.

[Sha05] Chung-chieh Shan. *Linguistic Side Effects*. PhD thesis, Harvard University, 2005.

[Sha07] Chung-chieh Shan. Linguistic side effects. In Chris Barker and Pauline Jacobson, editors, *Direct Compositionality*, pages 132–163. Oxford University Press, 2007.

[SS99] J. M. Spivey and S. Seres. Embedding Prolog in Haskell. In E. Meijer, editor, *Proceedings of Haskell '99*, Technical Report UU-CS-1999-28, Department of Computer Science, University of Utrecht, 1999.

[Tho99] S. Thompson. *Haskell: The Craft of Functional Programming* (Second edition). Addison Wesley, 1999.

[Tur36] A.M. Turing. On computable real numbers, with an application to the Entscheidungsproblem. *Proceedings of the London Mathematical Society*, 2(42):230–265, 1936.

[UG08] Christina Unger and Gianluca Giorgolo. Interrogation in dynamic epistemic logic. In Kata Balogh, editor, *Proceedings of the 13th ESSLLI Student Session*, pages 195–202, 2008. Available from http://staff.science.uva.nl/~kbalogh/StuS13/StuS13_Proceedings.pdf.

[Ver93] C.F.M. Vermeulen. Sequence semantics for dynamic predicate logic. *Journal of Logic, Language, and Information*, 2:217–254, 1993.

[VV96] A. Visser and C. Vermeulen. Dynamic bracketing and discourse representation. *Notre Dame Journal of Formal Logic*, 37:321–365, 1996.

[WA86] H. Wada and N. Asher. BUILDRS: An implementation of DR theory and LFG. In *11th International Conference on Computational Linguistics. Proceedings of Coling '86*, pages 540–545, University of Bonn, 1986.

[Wad85] P. Wadler. How to replace failure by a list of successes. In Jean-Pierre Jouannaud, editor, *FPCA*, volume 201, pages 113–128, 1985.

[Wij66] Adriaan van Wijngaarden. Recursive definition of syntax and semantics. In T.B. Steel Jr, editor, *Formal Language Description Languages for Computer Programming*, pages 13–24. North-Holland, 1966.

[WJP98] M. Walker, A. Joshi, and E. Prince, editors. *Centering Theory in Discourse*. Clarendon Press, 1998.

[Zee89] H. Zeevat. A compositional approach to Discourse Representation Theory. *Linguistics and Philosophy*, 12:95–131, 1989.

Index